DEATH:

A Bibliographical Guide

by

Albert Jay Miller

and

Michael James Acri

The Scarecrow Press, Inc.
Metuchen, N.J. & London
1977

Library of Congress Cataloging in Publication Data

Miller, Albert Jay.
   Death : a bibliographical guide.

   Includes indexes.
   1. Death--Bibliography. I. Acri, Michael James,
1932-   joint author. II. Title.
Z5725.M54 [BD444]   016.128'5   77-1205
ISBN 0-8108-1025-5

CONTENTS

iii

PREFACE

The primary intention of this guide to the literature of death is to provide a research tool for scholars, professional people and laymen. Hopefully, it will provide teachers and students data for lectures, discussions, seminar reports, and special projects, as well as augment the numerous courses about death now being offered in many colleges and universities throughout the country. At the same time, it will save professional persons time and afford them the necessary information to carry on their special projects. The layman will be able to become involved with the literature of death and the numerous subjects intimately related to it.

There are two salient reasons for the definite need to expand public awareness of death: first, contemporary society has been characterized by many scholars and investigators as manifesting numerous death-denying attitudes, which result in numerous mental disturbances. Secondly, the changing perceptions and concepts about death force upon contemporary man a need to come to grips with this universal phenomenon that always poses questions to human consciousness, cultures, and civilizations. The place of death has certainly contributed to the public's view and responses to it. Contemporary man no longer dies at home; his death has become institutionalized. Communication at the various levels of social life, a dialogue with death, could bring about adequate comprehension and openness about death and the various problems related to it.

The complexity about the theme of death and the tremendous amount of literature written and spoken on the subject throughout the centuries is the scope of this investigation. The authors used the historical phrase "ancient beginnings," meaning earliest writings on the subject, as the starting point and concluded with studies in 1974, although some significant studies have been included beyond the 1974 date for current interest.

The entries consist of articles, books, letters, editorials, pamphlets, and media information. These sources are listed under specific headings; the heading "education," for example will list books, articles, and so forth. The journals in which the entries appear reinforce our criteria of selection and have aided us greatly because of the difficulty of classifying entries which should be placed into several classes. An outstanding example would be euthanasia, which could easily be viewed from the psychological, sociological, legal, or moral perspective. Thus, euthanasia is indexed under euthanasia, and ethical and legal issues. The class divisions, the subject matter index, and the index will facilitate the use of the guide for persons having particular needs, as well as access to general information.

The authors greatly acknowledge the help of libraries and librarians in the United States, Mexico, Germany, France, and England, for providing valuable information necessary in the compilation of this work. Special thanks are due to the many students, secretaries, and colleagues who have contributed and encouraged the development of this bibliographical guide.

Michael James Acri
Albert Jay Miller

Erie and New Kensington,
   Pennsylvania
1976

Part I

GENERAL WORKS

1 Alexander, M. , et al. "Fear of death in parachute jumpers,"
   Perceptual and Motor Skills, 34 (Feb. 1972), 338.

2 American Council for Nationalities Services. Where to write
   for birth and death records. N. Y. : ACNS, 1971.
   Interpreter releases v. 48, no. 41 (20 W 40th St.
   N. Y. 10018).

3 American Friends Service Committee. Who shall live? Man's
   control over birth and death. N. Y. : Hill and Wang, 1970.

4 Anders, G. "Reflections on the H bomb," in Man Alone: Alienation in Modern Society, edited by Eric and Mary Josephson.
   N. Y. : Dell, 1962. pp. 288-300.

5 Anthony, J. E. , and C. Koupernik. The Child in his family:
   the impact of disease and death. N. Y. : Wiley, 1973.
   (The Yearbook of the International Association for Child Psychiatry and Allied Professions.)
       An anthology which brings together international author-
   ities representing various disciplines and cultures. Deals
   with the "reactions that children and their parents have to
   the impact of disease, dying and death. "

6 "Australian way of death is unfairly attacked by leading Sydney
   newspaper, " The American Funeral Director (Jan. 1968),
   39-41.
       Australian funeral directors have adopted American
   methods. States that funeral costs have risen 181% since
   1942.

7 Barker, J. C. Scared to death: an examination of fear; its
   causes and effects. London: F. Muller, 1968.

8 Barton, B. A. As love is deep. N. Y. : Duell, 1957.
       A journal account which reflects the many and diverse
   dimensions of suffering.

9 Basevi, W. H. F. The Burial of the dead. London: Routledge,
   1920.

1

A cross-cultural study of burial and cremation from prehistoric times to the present.

10 Bayly, J. The View from a hearse; a Christian view of death.
   Elgin, Ill.: David C. Cook, 1969.
      In the words of the author, "after losing three sons, we
   found no simple adequate book on death ... and each time I
   saw the same vacuum in the literature of our death-denying
   culture...."

11 Beauvoir, S. A Very easy death. Translated by P. O'Brien.
   N.Y.: Putnam, 1966.
      Story about a mother who is medically kept alive and
   never told of her impending death.

12 Bell, T. In the midst of life. N.Y.: Atheneum, 1961.
      Author chronicles the last months of his life. Describes
   his love and appreciation of life and beauty.

13 Bendann, E. Death customs; an analytical study of burial rites.
   N.J.: Humanities Press, 1969. (Reprint of the 1930 edition.)
      Brings together the conception of death among four geo-
   graphic areas--Australia, Melanesia, Northern Siberia, and
   India.

14 Bender, L. Psychopathology of children with organic brain
   disorders. Springfield, Ill.: C. C. Thomas, 1956.

15 Bernard, H. Y. The Law of death and disposal of the dead.
   N.Y.: Oceana, 1966.
      Explains laws and principles of the death of a person.
   Discusses the right and duty of burial of the deceased, legal
   problems of funerals, and complications of debts.

16 Bernardo, F. M. Death, bereavement and widowhood: a selected bibliography. Gainesville, Fla.: University of Florida, Department of Sociology. (Mimeographed, n.d.)

17 Better Business Bureau. Alerting bereaved families: a special
   bulletin. N.Y.: BBB, 1961.

18 _____. Facts every family should know about funerals and
   interments. N.Y.: BBB, 1961.

19 _____. The Pre-arrangement and pre-financing of funerals.
   N.Y.: BBB, 1960.

20 Bill, A. C. The Conquest of death; an imminent step in evolution. Boston: A. A. Beauchamp, 1935.

21 Birrell, F., and F. L. Lucas, eds. The Art of dying: an

anthology of last words. London: L. and V. Woolf, 1930.

22 Bjorksten, J. Dialogue on death. Madison: Bjorksten Research Foundation, 1960.

23 Blackmar, M. K. "Funeral feasting," Ladies Home Journal, 5 (1963), 9.

24 Blackwood, A. W. The Funeral: a source book for ministers. Philadelphia: Westminster, 1942.

24a Bon, H. La Mort et ses problèmes. Paris: Presses Universitaires de France, 1947.

25 Bosworth, P. "Face life without fear," Good Housekeeping, 178 (March 1974), 58.
    The article is based on the last interview Laurence Harvey gave before his death. He talks frankly about his impending death.

26 Bourdeau, L. Le Problème de la mort, ses solutions imaginaires et la science positive, 2d ed., rev. and enl. Paris: F. Alcan, 1896.
    Early historical account of the attempts at the definition of death.

27 Bowers, M. K.; E. N. Jackson; J. A. Knight; and L. LeShan. Counseling the dying. N.Y.: Nelson, 1964.
    A clinical psychologist, psychoanalyst, and a minister discuss their experiences with the dying.

28 Bowman, L. The American funeral: a study in guilt, extravagance, and sublimity. Washington, D.C.: Public Affairs Press, 1959.
    A critique of the funeral in mass urban society. The author supports cremation and the economic aspects of it.

29 Brecher, E. M., and the Editors of Consumer Reports. Licit and illicit drugs.... Boston: Little, Brown, 1972.
    "Traces the history and sociology of psychoactive drugs in our society--and on our social and legal response to these drugs and their users." Pub. Cat.

30 Brittain, R. P.; D. J. Polson; and T. K. Marshall. The Disposal of the dead. N.Y.: Philosophical Library, 1953.

31 Bullough, V. L. "The Banal and costly funeral," The Humanist, 4 (1960), 213-8.

32 "The Business of dying," Time, 82 (Sept. 20, 1963), 28.
    Deals with the high cost of funerals and changing moral values among people.

33 Butler, R. N. "Attitudes toward death, an interview," <u>Geri-</u>
    <u>atrics</u>, 19 (Feb. 1964), 58a.

34 California. University of Southern California. Ethel Percy
    Andrus Gerontology Center. <u>Dealing with death</u>. The
    Center (n. d.).
       "... [C]ontains discussions of death presented at con-
    ferences at the Andrus Center for those concerned with
    delivery of care service for the elderly...." Pub. Cat.

35 Caras, R. <u>Death as a way of life</u>. Boston: Little, Brown,
    1971.

36 Carr, A. C. "A Grave matter," <u>Homiletic and Pastoral Review</u>,
    64 (Dec. 1963), 280.
       Discusses the expense and extravagance of American
    funerals.

37 Carrington, H. , and J. R. Meader. <u>Death, its causes and</u>
    <u>phenomena</u>. N. Y.: Dodd, 1921.

38 Carter, J. R. , and D. L. Martin. "A Pathology assistant
    program: the role of licensed morticians," <u>American</u>
    <u>Journal of Clinical Pathology</u>, 53 (Jan. 1970), 26-31.

39 Carter, N. <u>Death strain</u>. Lincoln, Neb.: University Pub.
    Co. , 1970.

40 "Changing way of death," <u>Time</u>, 93 (April 11, 1969), 60.
       Discussion on how we are getting away from the
    elaborate funerals and back to the simple, of which
    President Eisenhower's funeral is an example.

41 Choron, J. <u>Modern man and mortality</u>. N. Y.: Macmillan,
    1964.

42 Christopher News Notes. "Let's talk about death." <u>Christopher</u>
    <u>News Notes</u> (New York), no. 206 (1974).
       A dialogue about the stages of dying, preparing to die,
    and how death brings meaning to life.

43 Clarke, R. "War without death," in <u>The Silent Weapons</u>.
    N. Y.: David McKay, 1968. pp. <u>12-33</u>.
       Traces the history of chemical and biological warfare
    and the harmful effects of toxic substances.

44 Clayton, P. J. "A Study of normal bereavement," <u>American</u>
    <u>Journal of Psychiatry</u>, 125 (Aug. 1968), 168-78.

45 _____ ; J. A. Hailkes; and W. L. Maurice. "The Bereave-
    ment of the widowed," <u>Diseases of the Nervous System</u>,
    32 (1971), 597-604.

45a Closs, A. "Death, primitive concepts of," in New Catholic
    Encyclopedia. N.Y.: McGraw-Hill, 1967. pp. 686-7.

46 Cobb, A. G. Earth burial and cremation. N.Y.: Knicker-
    bocker Press, 1892.

47 Cobb, J. S. A Quarter-century of cremation in North America.
    Boston: Knight and Millet, 1901.
    Surveys the early beginnings of cremation societies and
    has relevance historically to some modern day practices.

48 Conklin, R. "Conference examines aging, dying, and death,"
    National Catholic Reporter, 9 (Nov. 3, 1972), 3.

48a Cook, D. T. "Funeral home study makes consumer warnings,
    suggestions," Christian Science Monitor, (Sept. 11, 1975),
    17.

49 Cook, S. S. Children and dying; an exploration and a selective
    bibliography, with additional essays by Domeena C. Ren-
    shaw and Edgar N. Jackson. N.Y.: Health Science Pub.
    Corp., 1973.
    Conceptualizations about the various aspects of death
    and dying, and implications regarding children.

50 Cooper, G. I searched the world for death. London: J. Long
    Ltd., 1940.

51 Cort, D. "Another visit to the undertaker," Nation, 200 (April
    19, 1965), 420-1.
    Discusses the books of LeRoy Bowman and Jessica
    Mitford regarding the funeral industry.

52 Cremation Society of London. Eighty years of cremation in
    Great Britain, 1874-1954. London: Cremation Society,
    1954.
    Chronicles the development of cremation to the modern
    period.

53 _____. Facts about cremation. London: Cremation Society,
    1965.
    A pro-cremation tract describing procedures for ar-
    ranging cremation.

54 Cutter, F. Coming to terms with death: how to face the in-
    evitable with wisdom and dignity. Chicago: Nelson-Hall,
    1974.
    The author's premise is that "long-term preparation
    for death is essential to the survivors of another's death,
    as well as to the potential victim. In essence, life should
    become a rehearsal for death with the individual getting a
    chance to shape the kind of death he will encounter."

55 "Dead, death, and death rates," in Encyclopaedia Britannica. 14th ed. Vol. 7. Chicago: William Benton, 1961. pp. 96-8.

56 "Death customs," in Encyclopedia of the Social Sciences. N.Y.: Macmillan, 1931. pp. 21-7.

57 "The Death industry," Time, 76 (Nov. 14, 1960), 63.
Discusses how undertakers are taking over from the clergy and controlling the funeral service.

57a Denenberg, H. "American way of death--a final rip-off," The Sunday Bulletin, (July 27, 1975), 3.

58 Deslandes, A. F. Réflexions sur les grande hommes qui sont mortes en plaisantant. Amsterdam: Frères Westeing, 1741.

59 Dijik, M. Gies prekkenmet de dood. Kampen: Koh, 1956.

60 Dollen, C. Abortion in context: a select bibliography. N.J.: Scarecrow Press, 1970.

60a Douglas, A. "Heaven our home: consolation literature in the northern United States, 1830-1880," in Death In America, edited by D. E. Stannard. Philadelphia: University of Pennsylvania Press, 1975. pp. 49-68.

61 Douglass, W. A. Death in Murélaga; funerary ritual in a Spanish Basque Village. Seattle: University of Washington Press, 1969.
The author contends that "in a Basque society, the individual and collective responses to the crisis occasioned by a death in the membership, are of such a complex nature and occupy such a prominent place in the world view of the actors, that we can distinguish a death theme in the value systems...."

62 Dowd, Q. L. Funeral management and costs. Chicago: University of Chicago Press, 1921.
One of the very earliest of the social scientific studies regarding the funeral and the development and observations of cremation.

63 Downing, A. B., ed. Euthanasia and the right to death: the case for voluntary euthanasia. N.Y.: Humanities Press, 1970.
Essays by various professionals discussing their attitudes toward voluntary euthanasia.

64 Earley, H. W. "A Funeral is for the living," The Lutheran, (Jan. 4, 1967), 15-17.

65 Eddy, D. C. Angel whispers; or, The echo of spirit voices

designed to comfort those who mourn. 2nd ed. Boston:
Dayton and Wentworth, 1854.
　　Based on "addresses made on funeral occasions."
Pref.

66 Edwards, P., ed. "Death," in Encyclopedia of Philosophy,
vol. 2. N. Y.: Macmillan, 1967. pp. 307-09.

67 Encyclopaedia of superstitions, folklore, and the occult sciences
of the world; a comprehensive library of human belief and
practice in the mysteries of life.... Detroit: Gale Research Company, 1971. 3 Vols.
　　"This is a facsimile reprint of the 1903 edition published in Chicago and Milwaukee by J. H. Yewdale and
Sons Co." Chapter three of vol. 1 deals with apparitions,
crape, death chamber, exhumation, graves, and graveyards.

68 Erichsen, H. The Cremation of the dead. Detroit: D. O.
Haynes and Co., 1887.
　　Another of the early volumes describing the history of
cremation by the founder of the Cremation Society of
America.

69 Erikson, E. H. "Identity and the life cycle," Psychological
Issues, 1 (1959), 1-71.

70 Feifel, H. "Death," in Encyclopedia of Mental Health, edited
by A. Deutsch. N. Y.: Franklin Watts, 1963. pp. 422-
50.

71 _____. "Discussion of a symposium on attitudes toward
death in older persons," Journal of Gerontology, 16 (1961),
44-66.
　　Offers two possible leads for future study as well as
methodological considerations.

72 _____, ed. The Meaning of death. N. Y.: McGraw-Hill,
1959.
　　A collection of articles covering various topics of
death including music, art, literature, and medicine.

73 Fodor, N. Encyclopaedia of psychic science. N. Y.: University Books, 1966.
　　Detailed (800 entries) articles and case-histories explain the "most amazing and baffling phenomena known to
mankind ... it covers the entire field of psychical phenomena and spiritualism, including mediumship, extra-
sensory perception and what is now termed parapsychology."
Foreword is by Leslie Shepard.

74 Fordahl, E. K. Planning and paying for funerals. St. Paul:

Agriculture Extension Service, University of Minnesota, 1967.

75 Forest, J. D. "The Major emphasis of the funeral," Pastoral Psychology, 14 (1963), 19-24.
The author contends that "the funeral must be a witness of the Christian community before God."

76 Fraser, J. W. Cremation: is it Christian? Neptune, N. J.: Loizeaux, 1965.
Repeats and reinforces many of the arguments used against cremation by evangelical theology.

77 Frazer, J. G. "On certain burial customs as illustrative of the primitive theory of the soul," in Garnered Sheaves; essays, addresses, reviews. N. Y.: Macmillan, 1931. pp. 3-50.

78 French, S. "Cemetery as cultural institution: the establishment of Mount Auburn and the rural cemetery government," American Quarterly, 26 (March 1974), 37-59.

79 Fulton, R. L., ed. Death and identity. N. Y.: Wiley, 1965.
An anthology of readings on death and bereavement with editorial comments by a sociologist.

80 _____, and G. Geis. "Social change and social conflict: the Rabbi and the funeral director." Sociological Symposium, 1 (fall, 1968), 1-9.
A sociological symposium held at Western Kentucky University. Discusses how the movement from the city to the suburb in recent years has resulted in a loss of religious practices.

81 _____, et al. "Symposium on death and attitudes toward death," Geriatrics, 27 (Aug. 1972), 52-60.

82 Funeral Directors Institute. The Great controversy; relating to funerals. Chicago: FDI, (n.d.).
The "Great Controversy" concerns the high cost of dying ... or living."

83 Gebhart, J. C. Funeral costs. N. Y.: Putnam, 1928.
An insurance company study of the costs of funerals. Looks at the 1928 origins of funeral customs and then examines costs and management of funerals in the U. S. and in Europe.

84 Giersdorf, P. "Observations on cremation," Zeitschrift für die Gesamte Hygiene und ihre Grenzgebiete, 10 (1964), 17-27.

84a "Giving undertakers something to cry about: FTC investigation," Business Week, (Oct. 6, 1975), 98.

85 Glidden, T. "The American funeral," Pastoral Psychology,
      14 (1963), 9-18.
         Points out the necessity of cooperation between the
      clergy and funeral directors. With cooperation, the funeral
      can be a spiritual experience of value.

86 Gollwitzer, H.; K. Kuhn; and R. Schneider, eds. Dying we
      live. N. Y.: Pantheon, 1956.
         A collection of letters written by men and women of
      the German resistance during World War II. The letters
      clearly indicate the presence of life in the face of death.

87 Goody, J. Death, property and the ancestors: a study of the
      mortuary customs of the Lo Dagaa of West Africa. Stan-
      ford, Calif.: Stanford University Press, 1962.

88 Granquist, H. Muslem death and burial; Arab customs and
      traditions studies in a village in Jordan. Copenhagen:
      Munksgaard, 1965.

89 Grollman, E. A. Talking about death. Boston: Beacon, 1970.

90 Gunther, J. Death be not proud. N. Y.: Harper and Row, 1949.
         Story of a 17-year-old boy and the bravery he showed
      through agonizing months of hope and disappointment until
      he finally died of a brain tumor.

91 Guthrie, G. P. "The Meaning of death," Omega, 2 (Nov.
      1971), 299-302.

92 Habenstein, R. W. "Conflicting organizational patterns in
      funeral directing," Human Organization, 22 (summer 1963),
      126-32.

92a _____, and W. M. Lamers. Funeral customs the world
      over. Milwaukee, Wisc.: Bulfin Printers, Inc., 1963.
         An in-depth profile of the history of the American
      funeral. Focuses on primitive, folk, rural, and urban
      burial customs of peoples and cultures the world over.
      Illustrations enhance the text, and an analytic index facili-
      tates usage. Appended is a line-up of "Funeral Proce-
      dures of Religious Groups and Fraternal Organizations."

93 _____. The History of American funeral directing. Mil-
      waukee, Wisconsin: Bulfin Printers, Inc., 1955.
         Deals with the folkways and business practices of dis-
      posing of the dead. Traces the history of the mortuary
      from pagan times to the present. The final section is an
      inquiry into American funeral directing.

94 Haberlandt, W. F. "Le Questionnaire génétique: suicide

familial et conseil génétique," Journal de Génétique Humaine, 17 (1969), 179-83.

95 Hacker, D. W. "Mobile death traps," The National Observer, 13 (Jan. 26, 1974).
    Discusses the fire hazards involved in living in a mobile home.

96 Harbison, J. "New patterns for American funerals," Presbyterian Life, (Aug. 1, 1964).

97 Harmer, R. M. The High cost of dying. N. Y.: Macmillan, 1963.

98 _____. "The Place of what kind of funeral?" Omega, 2 (Aug. 1970), 150-4. (A response and a rebuttal.)
    "The question is not whether funerals are important. It is where the emphasis shall be placed...."

99 Harmetz, A. "How to beat the funeral industry," Pageant, (May 1964), 68-74.

100 Hartmann, F. Lebendig Begraben. Leipzig: Friedrich, 1896.

101 Hearn, L. "Note on a Hebrew funeral," in Occidental Gleanings: sketches and essays collected by A. Mordell. Vol. 2. N. Y.: Dodd, 1925. pp. 179-83.

102 Hedin, A. "Funerals without flowers," The Forum and the Century, 43 (1935), 306-7.
    Discusses the extravagance of funerals and the huge sums of money spent.

103 Hendin, D. Death as a fact of life. N. Y.: Norton, 1973.

104 Herter, F. "The Right to die in dignity," Archives of the Foundation of Thanatology, 1 (Oct. 1969), 93-7.
    A view that takes the position that the dying should be informed about their death.

104a Hinton, J. M. Dying. N. Y.: Penguin Books, 1967.
    Examines factors relevant to dying and considers the ways people die, how they are to be cared for, and grief and bereavement.

105 Hoedt, W., and K. Pfeifer. "The Causes of death in children who suddenly and unexpectedly expired, 1950-1965," Deutsche Gesundheitswesen, 21 (1966), 1441-48.

106 Hoffman, H. Religion and mental health. N. Y.: Harper, 1962.

107 "Home to the heartland," Time, 93 (April 11, 1969), 26-7.

Describes the funeral of Dwight Eisenhower and the
elaborate ceremonies held in the Capital rotunda to the
long train ride to Abilene where he was born.

107a Howard, T. "The Last enemy," Christianity Today, 18
(March 29, 1974), 31.
Mr. Howard reviews six current books and brings the
reader up-to-date on the current thinking regarding the
subject.

108 International Order of the Golden Rule. "Knowledge regarding
funerals and funeral arrangements never before put in
print." Published as a public service, by the International
Order. (n. d.).
A pamphlet designed to acquaint one with the modern
aspects of funeral service and the role of the funeral
director.

109 Irion, P. E. Cremation. Philadelphia: Fortress Press,
1968.
Deals with the economics of cremation and relates
this to psychological, theological, legal, and pastoral
considerations.

110 _____. The Funeral: an experience of value. Lancaster,
Pa.: Theological Seminary, 1956.

111 _____. "The Funeral and the integrity of the Church,"
Pastoral Psychology, 14 (1963), 25-32.
Author states that "we need to restore the meaning
of the funeral as a religious service, and that we recog-
nize that both minister and funeral director share a common concern for meeting the needs of those who mourn."

112 _____. The Funeral and the mourners. Nashville: Abingdon, 1954.
Discusses the funeral as a significant part of mourning based on studies done on grief.

113 _____. The Funeral: vestige or value? Nashville:
Abingdon, 1966.
Focuses on the functions and significance of the
funeral. Contemporary practices are evaluated and new
designs are proposed to conserve values in terms of
practices in religion, culture, psychological, and social
trends.

114 _____. A Manual and guide for those who conduct a humanist funeral service. Baltimore: Waverly Press, 1971.
"... [I]n order to provide an alternative for the humanist or for the family uncommitted to any religious
institution, this guide or manual offers to funeral directors and those who will lead such a service a pattern

and a collection of resources for a funeral...."

115 _____. "To cremate or not," in A Practical Guide for the
      Living, edited by Earl A. Grollman, Boston: Beacon,
      1974. pp. 241-52.

116 Jacobs, P. "The Most cheerful graveyard in the world," in
      The Borzoi College Reader, edited by Charles Musca-
      tisse and Marlene Griffith. Shorter edition. N.Y.:
      Knopf, 1968. pp. 108-15.
         Description of the famed "Forest Lawn Memorial
      Park" in Los Angeles.

117 The John Crerar Library. A List of books, pamphlets, and
      articles on cremation including the Cremation Association
      of America collection. Chicago: John Crerar Library,
      1918.
         Includes sources in German, French, and English.

118 Jones, P. H., ed. Cremation in Great Britain. London:
      Pharos Press, 1945.
         Contains the history and development of crematoriums
      in Great Britain.

119 Jouhandeau, M. Réflexions sur la vieillesse et la mort.
      Paris: B. Grasset, 1956.

120 Kahana, B., and E. Kahana. "Attitudes of young men and
      women toward awareness of death," Omega, 3 (Feb.
      1972), 37-44.

121 Kalisch, P. "Death down below: coal mine disasters in
      three Illinois counties, 1904-1962," Journal of the
      Illinois State Historical Society, 65 (1972), 5-21.

122 Kalish, R. A. "Death and bereavement: a bibliography,"
      Journal of Human Relations, 13 (1968), 118-41.

123 Kastenbaum, R., and C. E. Goldsmith. "The Funeral di-
      rector and the meaning of death," American Funeral Di-
      rector, 86 (April 1963), 35-7.
         Focuses on the role of the funeral director and the
      various criticisms leveled at the funeral industry.

123a Kelly, P. J. "Death, preparation for," in New Catholic
      Encyclopedia. N.Y.: McGraw-Hill, 1967. pp. 695-6.

124 Klein, S. The Final mystery. N.Y.: Doubleday, 1974.
         "... [T]he author contrasts burial customs of other
      cultures and other times, gives various religious views
      on death, and dips into some philosophical questions
      raised by new medical practices prolonging body func-
      tions." A children's book for grades 4-6.

124a Köster, H. "Death, in the Bible," in New Catholic Encyclopedia. N. Y.: McGraw-Hill, 1967. Vol. 4. pp. 685-6.
Contents: Physiologically considered; Theologically
considered; In metaphorical sense; Bibliography.

125 Kraus, F. Über Tod und Sterben. Berlin: Urban und
Schwarzenberg, 1916.

126 Kreis, B., and A. Pattie. Up from grief; patterns of recovery. N. Y.: Seabury Press, 1968.
"... [E]xplores what happens to all of us when a
close friend or relative dies ... the authors describe
the three stages of grief--shock, suffering, and recovery
--and fills a void not only for the bereaved but also for
counselors and ministers who comfort those who suffer
losses...."

127 Kübler-Ross, E. "Death," in New Encyclopaedia Britannica,
15th ed. Chicago: Encyclopaedia Britannica, Inc., 1973.
Vol. 5. pp. 526-9.
Contents: Concept of death; Biomedical aspects of
death; The prospect of dying; The determination of death;
Bibliography.

127a _____. Death: the final stage of growth. N. Y.: Spectrum Books, 1974. (Human Development Books.)

128 _____. "Facing up to death," Today's Education, 61 (Jan-
1972), 30-2.
Believes that death should be accepted as part of life
and examines the many ways of helping dying patients and
their families face reality. The feelings of children are
considered in terms of the survivors of death.

129 _____. "Lessons for the living on death and dying," National Catholic Reporter, 9 (April 20, 1973), 9-12.

130 _____. On death and dying. N. Y.: Macmillan, 1969.
Outlines the stages of death and studies each.

131 _____. Questions and answers on death and dying. N. Y.:
Macmillan, 1974.
A compilation of typical answers to questions asked
of the author in some 700 conducted workshops.

132 Kutscher, A. H. A Bibliography of books on death, bereavement, loss and grief: 1935-1968. N. Y.: Health Sciences
Pub. Co., 1969.

133 Lamberto, V. "Le ultime parole die moribondi," Minerva
Medica, 49 (Oct. 20, 1950), 256-67.

134 Lamers, W. M., Jr. "Funerals are good for people--M. D.'s

included, " Medical Economics, (June 23, 1969).

135   Lamm, M., and N. Eskreis.   "Viewing the remains: a new
      American custom, " Journal of Religion and Health, 5
      (1964), 137-43.
          States that this custom is of recent American origin
      favoring the economy of the funeral industry.

136   Lamont, C.   A Humanist funeral service.   N. Y.:   Horizon
      Press, 1954.

137   _____.   "Mistaken attitudes towards death, " in Voice in the
      Wilderness, edited by J. Ressich.   N. Y.:   Prometheus,
      1974.   pp. 69-76.

138   Landman, I., ed.   "Death, " in Universal Jewish Encyclopedia,
      Vol. 3.   Universal Jewish Encyclopedia Co., 1941.   pp.
      503-4.

139   Lange, E. R.   Volksglaube/Weichsel/Memel-Gebiet-Sterben und
      Begrabnis.   Wurzbrug: Hulzner, 1955.

140   Langer, M.   Learning to live as a widow.   N. Y.:   Messner,
      1957.

141   Langone, J.   Vital signs.   Boston: Little, Brown, 1974.
          Discusses the thoughts and feelings of ministers and
      doctors who must face death constantly.

142   LeComte, E., ed.   Dictionary of last words.   N. Y.:   Philo-
      sophical Library, 1955.

143   Lee, R. P.   Burial customs, ancient and modern.   Minne-
      apolis: Ayra Co., 1929.

144   Lenz, H.   "Zur Bedeutung des Todesangsterlebnisses, " Acta
      Neurovegetativa (Wein), 4 (1952), 534-42.
          Deals with the experience of the fear of death and
      why it is so significant.

145   McCarthy, R. D.   The Ultimate folly.   N. Y.:   Knopf, 1969.
          Congressman McCarthy is concerned about the
      chemical and biological warfare program and the "poten-
      tial for far more deadly accidents in the immediate fu-
      ture.... "

146   McElwain, A.   "We'll bury you, " Atlas, 17 (Jan. 6, 1969),
      45.
          A lively discussion of the free funerals for all given
      by the city of Milan.   They have attempted to break the
      death ritual practiced by the local undertakers.

147   Maisel, A. Q.   "Facts you should know about funerals, "

Reader's Digest, 89 (Sept. 1966), 81-6.
Acquaints the reader with practical information that
will be useful when a funeral is necessary.

148 "Making a circus out of death," Information, 73 (Nov. 1959),
     60-1.

149 Manning, J. "Soviet funeral service," American Funeral Di-
     rector, 89 (1966), 30.

150 Manya, J. B. La Vida que pasa. Barcelona: Editorial
     Atlántida, 1955.

151 May, W. F. "The Sacral power of death in contemporary ex-
     perience," in Death in American Experience, edited by
     Arien Mack. N. Y.: Schocken Books, 1973. pp. 97-122.
     Contents: Religious categories and the contemporary
     response to death; Philosophical reflections on flight and
     preoccupation with death; The twofold crisis of death and
     the care of the dying; Crisis of the flesh (and) Crisis of
     community.

152 Mayer, M. "On death," in The Great Ideas Today, edited by
     R. Hutchins. Chicago: Encyclopaedia Britannica, 1965.
     pp. 107-64.

153 Merbs, C. F. "Cremated human remains from Point of Pines,
     Arizona: a new approach," American Antiquity, 32 (Oct.
     1967), 498-506.

154 Millar, R. Death of an army--the siege of Kut, 1915-16.
     Boston: Houghton, 1970.
     The story of the doomed Anglo-Indian troops holding
     Kut/Amara for five months against assaults by the Turks
     during World War I.

155 Mills, L. O., ed. Perspectives on death. Nashville: Abing-
     don, 1974.

156 Morgan, A. "The Bier Barons," Sociological Symposium, 1
     (fall 1968), 28-35.
     A study of "the development of the mortuary business
     as a major industry in California. Describes the competi-
     tion for the 'death-luck.'"

157 Morgolins, S. Funeral costs. N. Y.: Public Affairs Commit-
     tee, 1967.

158 Myers, J. Manual of funeral procedure. Casper, Wyo.:
     Prairie Pub. Co., 1956.
     An outline of funeral procedures of religious groups
     and fraternal organizations.

159 National Funeral Directors Association of the U.S., Inc. But
     I never made funeral arrangements before. Milwaukee:
     NFDA (n.d.).
          A brochure which has some thoughts and suggestions
     about funerals when one is confronted unexpectedly with
     the death of a loved one.

160   . Considerations concerning cremation. Milwaukee:
     NFDA, 1974.
          Statistics indicate that less than 5% of American
     families favor cremation. The pamphlet explores all the
     alternatives in the form of questions and answers.

161   . The Funeral facing death as an experience of life:
     an historical review ... a contemporary overview ...
     changes in the future. Milwaukee: NFDA (n.d.).
          The first chapter of this illustrated pamphlet is an
     updating of the one in the original edition of this book
     published in 1960 by Howard Raether and Robert C.
     Slater.

162   . Funeral service; meeting needs ... serving peo-
     ple, edited by Robert C. Slater with acknowledgments to
     Howard C. Raether. Milwaukee: NFDA, 1974.
          Deals with retrospective, contemporary, motivation
     and care-giving duties and responsibilities of the funeral
     service. Included in the pamphlet is a section on oppor-
     tunities for women both on a licensed and non-licensed
     status. Accredited schools and funeral service literature
     are appended.

163   . How would you tell your son his grandpa died?
     Milwaukee: NFDA (n.d.).
          Questions and answers about children and death.

163a   . The Pre-arranging and pre-financing of funerals.
     Milwaukee: NFDA (n.d.).
          Includes the basic data concerning the legal aspects
     of funerals by the various states.

164   . Too personal to be private: a funeral director
     talks about a death in a family. Milwaukee: NFDA,
     1971.
          An illustrated pamphlet reproduced from the 16mm-
     motion picture with the same title.

165   . What do you really know about funeral costs?
     Milwaukee: NFDA, 1974.
          Outlines and describes four categories of charges
     which make up the cost of a funeral as of September 15,
     1974. Also includes a section on "Family-Funeral Di-
     rector Counselling" after death occurs.

166 _____. Why do we have funerals anyway? Milwaukee:
NFDA (n. d.).
A brochure which presents some practical suggestions
when arranging a funeral.

167 Nevin, D. "Home to Abilene," Life, 66 (April 11, 1969), 24-
35.
A news account of the burial and ceremonies surrounding the burial of ex-President Eisenhower.

167a New York Times. Hiroshima plus 20. Introduction by John
W. Finney. N. Y.: Delarcorte, 1965.
"... [C]ompendium of tragedy and hope--a definitive
dialogue that brings us face-to-face at last with the harsh
realities of the atomic age." Includes the famous Albert
Einstein letter to F. D. Roosevelt.

168 Oken, D. "What to tell cancer patients: a study of medical
attitudes," Journal of the American Medical Association,
175 (April 1961), 1120-28.

168a Osbourn, R. A. "Death," in New Catholic Encyclopedia.
N. Y.: McGraw-Hill, 1967. Vol. 4. pp. 684-5.
Contents: Time of death; Signs of death; Legal
death; Ethical considerations of dying; Bibliography.

169 Pearson, L., ed. Death and dying: current issues in the
treatment of the dying person. Cleveland: Press of
Case Western Reserve University, 1969.
Five clinicians examine the psychological, sociological,
and physical aspects of death. The contributors focus on
the interaction between the dying individual and the personnel responsible for his care. A subject bibliography
is appended.

170 Peterson, J. "Jump or burn, you're dead either way," The
National Observer (Aug. 10, 1974), 10.

171 Petri, H. "Schmerz und Leid im Sterben," Hippokrates, 24
(July 15, 1953), 394-7.

172 Purci-Jones, J., et al. "Temporal stability and change in
attitude toward the Kennedy assassination," Psychological
reports, 23 (1969), 907-13.

173 Purpura, G. "Civilizations practicing interment and cremation," Annali della Sanità Publica, 27 (Jan.-Feb. 1966),
188-97.

173a Rabinowicz, H. "Death," in Encyclopaedia Judaica. N. Y.:
Macmillan, 1971. Vol. 5. pp. 1419-26.

174 Raether, H. C. "The Place of the funeral: the role of the
     funeral director in contemporary America," Omega, 2
     (1971), 136-49.
       "The place and meaning of the funeral in contemporary
     America is as it has been defined--a response to death
     which is organized, purposeful, time-limited, flexible and
     group-centered."

175 _____. Successful funeral service practice. Englewood
     Cliffs, N.J.: Prentice-Hall, 1971.

176 _____. "Today determines the 'tomorrow of funeral ser-
     vice'," American Funeral Director, 91 (Feb. 1968), 37-8.

177 Reed, E. Helping children with the mystery of death. Nash-
     ville: Abingdon, 1970.
       Provides information and guidance for teachers,
     parents, ministers, or anyone who must explain death to
     children and to get them to accept an honest approach.

178 Reilly, C. T. "The Diagnosis of life and death," Journal of
     the Medical Society of New Jersey, 66 (Nov. 1969), 601-4.

179 Russell, B. "Your child and the fear of death," The Forum,
     81 (March 1929), 174-8.
       Examines the role of parents and of education in
     dealing with children about attitudes toward death.

180 Sabatier, R. Dictionnaire de la mort. Paris: Albin Michel,
     1967.
       Descriptions and definitions of death by a very large
     segment of important literary scholars.

181 Salls, B. R. Death is no dead end. Chicago: Moody Press,
     1972.
       Discusses the struggle of a young widow to begin a
     new life. Reflects on the temptation to commit suicide
     and the responsibility of raising a family.

182 Sansoni, G. C., ed. "Morte," in Encyclopedia Filosófica.
     Vol. 4. Firenza: Encyclopedia Filosófica, 1967. pp.
     882-5.

183 Schrank, J. "Death: guide to books and audio-visual aids,"
     Media and Methods, 7 (Feb. 1974), 32-5.

184 Shaler, N. S. The Individual: a study of life and death.
     N.Y.: Appleton, 1901.
       The nature of the individual (whether as an atom or
     heavenly body) is defined.

185 Shibles, W. Death: an interdisciplinary analysis. White-
     water, Wisconsin: Language Press, 1974.

Based upon a seminar on death taught by the author in the spring of 1972. Includes a comprehensive bibliography, definitions, and etymologies.

186 Singer, I. "Death," in The Jewish Encyclopedia. Vol. 4. N. Y.: Funk and Wagnalls, 1903. pp. 480-86.

187 Slater, P. E. "Prolegomena to a psychoanalytic theory of aging and death," in New Thoughts on Old Age, edited by R. Kastenbaum. N. Y.: Springer, 1964. pp. 38-55.

188 Smith, A. J. K. Brain death; a bibliography with key-word and author indexes. Bethesda: Applied Neurologic Research Branch, National Institute of Neurological Diseases and Stroke, 1972. (NINDS bibliography series, no. 1.)

189 Strugnell, C., and P. R. Silverman. "The Funeral director's wife as care giver," Omega, 2 (Aug. 1971), 174-8.

190 Thomas, J. W., and R. Dixon. "Cemetery ecology," Natural History, 82 (March 1973), 6-7.

191 Townsend, J. D. "Review of P. E. Irion's Funeral: Vestige or Value?" Christian Century, 83 (March 1966), 369.
Favorable review of a book on funerals which criticizes funerals on the basis of American materialism rather than on economics.

192 Toy, T. W. "Search, recovery and return of the Vietnam War dead," American Funeral Director, (Dec. 1966), 27-8.
Discusses the problems of establishing procedures, trained personnel, equipment, and facilities to meet the need for mortuary service in South East Asia.

193 U. S. Senate. Committee on the Judiciary. Antitrust aspects of the funeral industry--hearings before the subcommittee on antitrust and monopoly. Washington, D. C.: G. P. O., 1964.

194 Van Coevering, V. Developmental tasks of widowhood for the aging woman. A paper presented at the American Psychological Association convention. Washington, D. C.: Sept. 3-7, 1971.
This paper examines the phenomenon of widowhood. It indicates new patterns of health care with "widow-to-widow" programs and widow consultation services provided by private and governmental agencies.

195 Vernick, J. J. Selected bibliography on death and dying. (Prepared by information office, National Institute of child health and human development. Bethesda, Md.) U. S. National Institutes of Health; for sale by the Supt.

of Docs., G. P. O., Washington, D. C.: 1969.

196 "Vital bouyancy of optimism: study by D. Phillips, " Time,
     94 (Sept. 5, 1969), 55.
     States that dying people tend to hold on to life until
     after a birthday, election, or holiday.

197 Wagner, W. "What a funeral can do when death strikes sud-
     denly, " The Director, 6 (1970), 40.

198 Walshe, W. G. "Death and disposal of the dead: Chinese, "
     in Encyclopedia of Religion and Ethics. Vol. 4. N. Y.:
     Scribner's, 1911. pp. 450-54.

199 Weidenmann, J. Furchte dich nicht: der Mensch und der Tod.
     Zurich: Artemis, 1944.

200 White, H. D. With wings as eagles; introduction by Ralph W.
     Sockman. N. Y.: Rinehart, 1953.
     "The wife of the president of Emory University
     describes her journey from despair to hope after the
     death of her oldest son in World War II. "

201 Williams, M. "Changing attitudes to death: a survey of con-
     tributions in Psychological Abstracts over a thirty-year
     period, " Human Relations, 19 (1966), 405-23.

201a Wright, J. H. "Death, theology of, " in New Catholic Encyclo-
     pedia. N. Y.: McGraw-Hill, 1967. pp. 687-95.
     Contents: Problem of death; Mystery of death; The-
     ological understanding of the mystery of death; Bibli-
     ography.

202 Wyschogrod, E. The Phenomenon of death: faces of mor-
     tality. N. Y.: Harper and Row, 1973.
     A selection of essays that include mass death as a
     general heading. The emphasis is cultural and not
     clinical. Texts permeate the humanities and the social
     sciences in its overview.

203 Zim, H. Life and death. N. Y.: Morrow, 1970.
     Presentation of death for young readers including a
     survey of the chief function of living things. Explains
     the difference between death and sleep.

Part II

EDUCATION

204 Ames, L. B. "Death: ways to help children get perspective,"
     Instructor, 78 (Jan. 1969), 59.
           Suggests ways of getting children to understand death.
     States that avoidance of this topic can lead a child into
     difficulty.

205 Arnstein, F. J. "I met death one clumsy day," English
     Journal, 61 (Sept. 1972), 853-8.
           An English teacher expresses concern in her creative
     writing class about the recurrent theme of death in the
     students' poetry. What is brought out in the examples
     given reflects attitudes, fear, irony, and alienation.

206 Ayers, R. H. "The New theology and educational theory,"
     Educational Theory, 18 (spring 1968), 169-77.
           Discusses the "new theology" and its relevance for
     education. Presents principles of it, the major theolo-
     gians of the death of God, and their contributions.

207 Barton, D. "The Need for including instruction on death and
     dying in the medical curriculum," Journal of Medical
     Education, 47 (March 1972), 169-75.
           Because of changing concepts in today's changing so-
     cial structure, the author presents convincing points for
     the inclusion of death instruction in medical schools.

208 _____. "Teaching psychiatry in the context of dying and
     death," American Journal of Psychiatry, 130 (1973),
     1290-1.
           Argues that the subject of death, and instruction in
     death should be included in the psychiatry curriculum.
     It is suggested that the subject could improve psycho-
     social care of patients.

209 Benoleil, J. Q. "Comment: some thoughts about the com-
     plexities of education for humanistic care in the face of
     death," Omega, 2 (Aug. 1971), 215-6.

210 Berg, D. W., and G. G. Daugherty. "On death and dying,"
     Journal of Medical Education, 47 (July 1972), 587.

The authors, both medical educators, are concerned
with death education "affecting persons in all fields."
Their contention is that death is a universal phenomenon
and has social, cultural, aesthetic, emotional, and psychological dimensions, as well as the purely biological.

211   _____. "Teach about death," Today's Education, 62 (March
       1973), 46-7.

212 Blue, R. "Mentioning the unmentionable," Teacher, 92 (Feb.
     1975), 54.
        Suggestions are given for stories to use with children
     about happy endings as well as sad ones. The sub-title
     of the article has the caption, "some ideas that help when
     real life comes into your classroom."

212a Bluestone, G. "Life, death, and 'Nature' in children's TV,"
      in TV As Art: some essays in criticism, edited by P. D.
      Hazard. Illinois: National Council of Teachers of English,
      1966. pp. 157-76.

213 Blumberg, M. S. Trends and projections of physicians in the
     United States: 1967-2002. Report sponsored by the Car-
     negie Commission on Higher Education, 1971.

213a Brown, M. The Dead bird. Reading, Mass.: Addison-Wesley,
      1938.
        An approach to death through the eyes of a group of
      children. A dead bird is found and the children make a
      decision to give it a proper burial. A story for ele-
      mentary school children.

214 Carnegie Commission on Higher Education. Higher education
     and the nation's health policies for medical and dental
     education. N. Y.: McGraw-Hill, 1970.

214a Charpentier, C. "Death education: a search for life," Living
      Light, 8 (winter 1971), 46-52.
        Stresses the need for death education and the role of
      the teacher in dealing with the various attitudes about
      life and death.

215 Colarusso, C. "Johnny, did your mother die?" Teacher, 92
     (Feb. 1975), 57.
        A child psychiatrist discusses some practical things
     a teacher can do when confronted by a child who has lost
     a parent because of death, and how to approach the child
     when he returns to school.

216 Crase, D. R., and D. Crase. "Live issues surrounding
     death education," Journal of School Health, 44 (Feb.
     1974), 70-3.
        Discusses questions for school personnel who teach

in the area of death education: Why death education?
When should it occur? How should it be accomplished
in schools? What are the legal aspects of death?

217 De Muth Berg, C. "Cognizance of the death taboo in counseling children, " School Counselor, 21 (Sept. 1973), 28-33.
Presents a case study in addition to the counselor's
role when they have come to terms with their own feelings related to death. "Art counseling is proposed as a
vehicle for effective expression for many children...."

218 Dittmer, A. E. "The Country mouse and the city mouse--
nowhere to hide, " Media and Methods, 11 (Oct. 1974), 39.
Based upon Michael Lesy's Wisconsin Death Trip, the
author describes "a multimedia approach to investigating
ideas through emerging patterns. " The method is con-
figurational and is adaptable to classroom use.

219 Donnellan, M. "Death education in biblical perspective, "
The Bible Today, 62 (Nov. 1972), 900-05.
Article states that the theology of death was involved
after life, and contemporary theology investigates death
in the context of the meaning of life and freedom.

220 Drummond, E., and J. Blumberg. "Death and the curriculum, " Journal of Nursing Education, (May-June, 1962),
21-8.
Discusses the need of a death-course in adult education programs for nurses.

220a Ebert, R. H. "The Medical school, " in Life and Death and
Medicine. San Francisco: W. H. Freeman, 1973. pp.
103-09. (A Scientific American Reprint book from Sept.
1973.)
"The training of physicians is in the midst of a period of rapid evolutionary change. The probable outcome
will be the production of fewer specialists and more
physicians capable of primary care. "

221 Eron, L. "The Effect of medical education on attitudes: a
follow-up study, " Journal of Medical Education, 33 (Oct.
1958), 25-33.

222 Farmer, J. A., Jr. "Death education: adult education in the
face of a taboo, " Omega, 1 (May 1970), 109-14.

223 Folck, M. M., and P. J. Nie. "Nursing students learn to
face death, " Nursing Outlook, 7 (1959), 510-13.
States the need of incorporating the various concepts
of death from the various disciplines in the early curriculum of nurses.

224 Fontenot, C. "The Subject nobody teaches, " English Journal,

63 (Feb. 1974), 62-3.
   Explores alternative approaches to values in literature.   The author describes how some 94 high schools
   reacted to a unit of study regarding death and dying.   A
   record of the materials used is appended.

225 Formanek, R.   "When children ask about death, " Elementary
     School Journal, 75 (Nov. 1974), 92-7.

226 Galen, M.   "A Matter of 'life and death', " Young Children,
     27 (Aug. 1972), 351-6.
        Evidence is presented for the justification of the topic
     of death in the school curriculum.   Guidelines are pre-
     sented for teachers who work with pre-school children.

227 Green, B. R., and D. P. Irish, eds.   Death education:
     preparation for living.   Massachusetts: Schenkman Pub.
     Co. (dist. by General Learning Press, Morristown,
     N. J., 1971.).
        "Proceedings of the symposium sponsored by Hamiline
     University, St. Paul, Minnesota. "

228 Hair, J. M.   "What shall we teach about death in science
     classes?"   Elementary School Journal, 65 (May 1965),
     414-8.

229 Kastenbaum, R., and R. Koenig.   "Dying, death, and lethal
     behavior: an experience in community education, " Omega,
     1 (Feb. 1970), 29-36.

230 Krahn, J. H.   "Pervasive death: an avoided concept, " Educa-
     tional Leadership, 31 (Oct. 1973), 18-20.
        The author creatively suggests ways in which the con-
     cept of death could be included in the elementary school.

231 Laws, E. H., et al.   "Views on euthanasia, " Journal of
     Medical Education, 46 (June 1971), 540-2.

232 Le Du, J.   Cette impossible pedagogie; l'educateur Chrétien
     confronte à sa propre mort par l'action pedagogique.
     Paris: Tayard; Tours: Mame, 1971.

233 Leviton, D.   "A Course on death education and suicide pre-
     vention: implications for health education, " Journal of
     the American College Health Association, 49 (April 1971),
     217-20.
        The author suggests that concerns about death cause
     anxieties which may cause additional personality prob-
     lems.   The course outline suggests ways in which death
     education can be integrated into classes.

234 _____.   "Education for death, " Journal of Health, Physical
     Education, and Recreation, 40 (Sept. 1969), 46-51.

235 _____. "The Need for education on death and suicide,"
Journal of School Health, 39 (April 1969), 270.
Points out the need for education about the fear of
death and discusses various methods that have had good
results.

236 Lichtenwalner, M. E. "Children ask about death," International Journal of Religious Education, 40 (June 1964), 14-16.

237 Lofland, J. Doomsday cult. Englewood Cliffs: Prentice-
Hall, 1960.

238 Lohman, K. D. "The Student mortician: a study of occupational socialization," Colorado Journal of Educational Research, 9 (summer 1970), 45-50.

239 McCurdy, J. "Death studies should begin with very young,"
Times Educational Supplement, London, 3074 (April 26,
1974), 12.

240 McDonald, M. "Helping children to understand death: an experience with death in a nursery school," Journal of Nursery Education, 19 (March 1963), 19-25.

241 McLure, J. W. "Death education," Phi Delta Kappan, 55
(March 1974), 483-5.
Asserts the need and rationale for including educa-
tion of death and dying in the public school curriculum.

242 McMahon, J. "Death education: an independent study unit,"
Journal of School Health, 43 (Oct. 1973), 526-7.
Contains a list of units compiled for high school and
college students designed to improve their knowledge of
death. Various sub units offered are: The taboo for
death; The crisis of man; and Views on death and dying.

243 Marshall, J., and V. Marshall. "The Treatment of death in
children's books," Omega, 2 (Feb. 1971), 36-45.

244 Miller, P. G., and J. Ozga. "Mommy, what happens when
I die?" Mental Health, 57 (spring 1973), 20.
A chronological description of the child's conceptual
boundaries of death. Excellent do's and don't's for
parents. Death should not be concealed from the child.

245 Moller, H. "Death: handling the subject and affected students in schools," in Explaining Death To Children, edited
by E. A. Grollman. Boston: Beacon, 1967. pp. 145-67.

246 Morgan, E. A Manual of death education and simple burial.
7th ed. North Carolina: Celo Press, 1973.
Contents: Death education; Simple burial and cremation; Memorial Societies; How the dead can help the living.

247 Morris, B. "Young children and books on death," Elementary
     English, 51 (March 1974), 395-8.
          "... [U]ntil we know more about the young human be-
     ing, perhaps 'reality' concerning death should, for in-
     stance, be presented in a cognitive fashion through such
     factual books as Zim's Life And Death and then only to
     children who show an interest."

248 Moss, J. P. "Death in children's literature," Elementary
     English, 49 (April 1972), 530-2.

249 "Out of darkness: preparing the dying for the inevitable,"
     Time, 94 (Oct. 10, 1969), 60.
          Deals with Elizabeth Kübler-Ross' seminars on death
     taught by patients to students, nurses, and social workers.

250 Ozmon, H. "Education and the 'Death of God' theology,"
     Educational Theory, 17 (Oct. 1967), 317-24.

251 Patricia, M. R. "Birthday in heaven," Catholic School
     Journal, 64 (Feb. 1964), 65.

252 Pellegrino, E. R. "The Communication crisis in nursing and
     medical education," Nursing Forum, 5 (1966), 45-53.

253 Peniston, D. H. "The Importance of death education in family
     life," Family Life Coordinator, 11 (1962), 15-8.
          The relevance of death as subject matter, and as a
     taboo topic is discussed as a learning experience. The
     author feels that death should be approached with an open
     mind by both children and adults.

254 Quint, J. C. "Hidden hazards for nurse teachers," Nursing
     Outlook, 15 (April 1967), 34-5.

255 _____. "Preparing nurses to care for the fatally ill,"
     International Journal of Nursing Studies, 5 (March 1968),
     53-61.

256 _____, and A. L. Strauss. "Nursing students, assignments,
     and dying patients," Nursing Outlook, 12 (Jan. 1964), 24-
     7.
          "A sociological approach concerning the problems of
     nursing faculty and students with dying patients and
     death."

257 Robinson, L. "We have no dying patients; some vicissitudes
     encountered in teaching nursing students about death,"
     Nursing Outlook, 22 (Oct. 1974), 651-3.

258 Schoenberg, B. B. "The Nurse's education for death," in
     Death And Bereavement, edited by A. Kutscher. Spring-
     field, Ill.: C. C. Thomas, 1969. pp. 55-74.

How does the nurse cope with the dying patient? The
article discusses her reactions to death.

259 Shapiro, S. I. "Instructional resources for teaching the
    psychology of death and dying," Catalog of Selected Docu-
    ments in Psychology, 3 (fall 1973), 113.

260 Shestov, L. Les Révélations de la mort. Paris: Dostoyev-
    sky-Tolstoy, 1923.

261 Smith, H. C. Care of the dying patient: a comparison of in-
    structional plans. Bloomington: Indiana University Press,
    1965.

262 Somerville, R. M. Death education as part of family life edu-
    cation: using imaginative literature for insights with
    family crisis. Minneapolis: National Council On Family
    Relations, 1971.
        A variety of literary works which could be used as
    examples for conditions of death and bereavement is pre-
    sented. Examples taken from literary themes include:
    Terminal illness; Death of a child; and Suicide. Adapta-
    ble for high school and college teachers for death educa-
    tion courses.

263 Spadafora, J. "Causes of school age deaths in the U.S.,
    1962," Safety Education, 44 (Nov. 1964), 26.

264 Stanford, G. "Miniguide: a mini-course on death," Scholastic
    Teacher, 103 (Sept. 1973), 40-4.

265 Sudwith, J. A. "Interdisciplinary approach to death education,"
    Journal of School Health, 44 (Oct. 1974), 455-8.

266 Swenson, E. J. "The Treatment of death in children's litera-
    ture," Elementary English, 49 (March 1972), 401-4.
        The author states that death must not be hidden from
    children. A healthy and honest attitude must be taken in-
    to consideration in literature.

267 Thorson, J. A. "Continuing education in death and dying,"
    Adult Leadership, 23 (Nov. 1974), 141-4.

268 Wagner, B. M. "Teaching students to work with the dying,"
    American Journal of Nursing, 64 (Nov. 1964), 128-31.

269 Warren, W. E. "Physical education and death," Physical
    Education, 28 (Oct. 1971), 127-8.

270 White, D. K. "An Undergraduate course in death," Omega,
    1 (Aug. 1970), 167-74.

271 Wiener, D. N., and W. Simon. "Personality characteristics

of embalmer trainees, " Journal of Social Issues, 17
(1961), 43-9.

272 Wolf, A. W. M. Helping your child to understand death, rev.
ed. N. Y.: Child Study Association of America, 1973.
Approaches the questions children ask parents regarding aspects of death. Honesty and understanding a
must if children are to develop mature and healthy attitudes toward death.

273 Zazzato, J. "Death be not distorted, " Nation's Schools, 91
(May 1973), 39-42.
Identifies and examines the need for the teaching of
death to young people in grades K-12. Suggests course
objectives and parent participation.

274 Zoepfl, H. Bildung und Erziehung angesichts der Endlichkeit
des Menschen. Donauworth: Ludwig Auer, 1967.

Part III

HUMANITIES

275 Abel, A. "Aspects de la mort dans le théâtre de Camus, Tardieu, Ionesco, Genet, Beckett." Ph. D. dissertation, Louisiana State University, 1966.
". . . [T]he object of this research is to study the multiple aspects of death in a choice of plays from French contemporary theatre to determine whether there is not in this preoccupation with death, a longing for life, a desire to rejoice and a search for light.... "

276 Abel, D. "This troublesome mortality: Hawthorne's marbles and bubbles, " Studies in Romanticism, 81 (summer 1969), 193-7.

277 Abel, R. H. "Gide and Henry James: suffering death and responsibility, " Midwest Quarterly, 9 (July 1968), 403-16.

278 Adams, J. Q. "Shakespeare as a writer of epitaphs, " in Manly Anniversary Studies in Language and Literature, by various contributors. Chicago: University of Chicago Press, 1923. pp. 78-89. (o. p.).

279 Adams, R. P. "The Archetypal pattern of death and rebirth in Milton's Lycidas, " in Myth And Literature: contemporary theory and practice, edited by John B. Vickery. Lincoln: University of Nebraska Press, 1966. pp. 187-91.

280 Addams, J. "Early reactions to death, " in Excellent Becomes the Permanent. N. Y.: Macmillan, 1932. pp. 145-62.

281 Agee, J. A Death in the family. N. Y.: McDowell, Obolensky, 1957.
Story about the impact of tragedy on a closely-knit family demonstrating the concepts of love, bereavement, and grief.

282 Aggeler, W. F. "Seven beasts in Baudelaire's 'Au Lecteur', " Philological Quarterly, 40 (Oct. 1961), 596-602.

283 Albee, E. The Death of Bessie Smith. N.Y.: Coward-
McCann, 1960.
A play that tells of the ugly and shameful circum-
stances of the tragic death of a great blues singer.

284 Alden, H. M. A Study of death. N.Y.: Harper, 1895.

285 Allen, J. L., Jr. "Symbol and meaning in Strindberg's
'Crime and Crime'," Modern Drama, 9 (May 1966), 62-
73.
Complete Title: There Are Crimes and Crimes
(1899).

286 Alley, A. "The Centaur: transcendental imagination and
metaphoric death," English Journal, 56 (Oct. 1967), 982-
3.

287 Allingham, W. "Death deposed," in One Thousand Years of
Irish Poetry, edited by Kathleen Hoagland. N.Y.: Devin-
Adair, 1947. pp. 515-6.

288 Amelineau, E. Histoire de la sépulture et des funérailles
dans l'ancienne Egypte. Paris: Annales du Musée
Guimel, 1896. Vols. 28-30.

289 Anderson, S. "Death in the woods," in Times Four, edited
by Donald Hermes. Englewood Cliffs: Prentice-
Hall, 1968. pp. 368-79.

290 Apostol, P. "96 Sätze über Tod und Freiheit in Hegel's
Philosophie und in unserer Zeit," Praxis (1971), 191-202.

291 Ariès, P. The Reversal of death: changes in attitudes toward death in western societies," American Quarterly,
26 (Dec. 1974), 536.
"Translation of Philippe Ariès, 'La Mort inversée.
Le changement des attitudes devant la mort dans les so-
ciétés occidentale,' Archives Europeennes de Sociologie,
8 (1967), 169-95."

292 _____. Western attitudes toward death: from the Middle
Ages to the present. Translated by Patricia M. Ranum.
Baltimore: Johns Hopkins University Press, 1974.
A collection of lectures (illustrated) concerning the
history of changing attitudes toward death in Western
societies since the Middle Ages, delivered at Johns Hopkins in April 1973.

293 Arnold, E. "Death--and afterwards": reprinted from the
Fortnightly Review with a supplement. London: Kegan
Paul, Trench, Trubner and Co., 1907.

294 Arnold, J. Untersuchungen über Staubinhalation und Staub-

metastase. Leipzig: F. C. W. Vogel, 1885.

295 Aronson, A. Psyche and symbol in Shakespeare. Bloomington: Indiana University Press, 1972.
Includes death as fulfillment and as disguise, as well
as a section on "The Mask. "

296 Assell, R. "An existential approach to death, " Nursing
Forum, 8 (1969), 200-11.

297 Augburn, G. R. The Function of death in the novels of
Charles Dickens. Ph. D. dissertation, Columbia
University, 1968.

298 Austin, M. Experience facing death. Indianapolis: Bobbs-
Merrill, 1931.
Author shares her experiences with death and her beliefs of mankind relative to death and survival, expressed
in religion, magic, folklore, and philosophy.

299 Ayuso Rivera, J. El Concepto de la muerte en la poesía
romantica. Madrid: Fundación Universitaria Española,
1959.

300 Bacon, F. "History of life and death, " in The Works of
Francis Bacon, edited by J. Speeding, and R. Ellis.
London: F. Frommann, 1963. pp. 213-335.

301 _____. "Of death, " in Bacon's Essays, edited by S. H.
Reynolds. Vol. 2. London: Oxford University Press,
1890. pp. 12-8.

302 Badawi, A. Le Problème de la mort dans la philosophie
existentielle. Introduction historique à une ontologie.
Le Caire: Impr. de l'Institut François d'Archéologie
orientale, 1964.

303 Baeizner, E. Der Tod und was dann? Regen: Ulrich-Verlag,
1953.

304 Balthasar, H. U. Hans Urs: der Tod im Houtigen. Denken,
Otten: Anima, 1956.

305 Barash, M. Death in the works of Michelangelo. Jerusalem:
Bialik Institute, 1961.

306 Barnes, H. E. "Death and the cooling sun, " in An Existentialist Ethics. N. Y.: Knopf, 1967. pp. 427-53.
Analyzes and presents an existentialist viewpoint
concerning "individual mortality of the final question of
the destiny of humanity ... the chapter heading is taken
from Sartres' Les Mots '... even yet today and disil-
lusioned, I am unable to think without fear of the cooling of the sun.' "

307 Barnhart, J. E. "Freud's pleasure principle and the death urge." Southwestern Journal of Philosophy, 3 (spring 1972), 113-20.

308 Basdekis, D. "Death in the sonnets of Shakespeare and Camões," Hispania, 46 (March 1963), 102-5.

309 Bauml, F. H. "Der Ackermann aus Bohman and the destiny of man," German Review, 33 (Oct. 1958), 223-32.

310 Beaty, N. L., ed. The Craft of dying: a study in the literary tradition of the Ars moriendi in England. New Haven: Yale University Press, 1970.
  Intensive study of J. Taylor's Holy Dying. Takes into account the devotional tradition which nurtured it. Written clearly with documentation and bibliography.

311 Becker, H. "Some forms of sympathy: a phenomenological analysis," Journal of Abnormal and Social Psychology, 26 (April 1951), 56-8.

312 Bedau, H. A. "The Death penalty as a deterrent: argument and evidence," Ethics, 80 (April 1970), 205-17.

313 _____. "A Social philosopher looks at the death penalty," American Psychiatry, 123 (1967), 1361-70.
  The right to life is discussed within the context of the death penalty. Presents the doctrine of life and the right of life.

314 Bellarmine, R. De Arte bene moriendi libri duo. Antwerp, 1620.

315 Belloc, H. "Talking of epitaphs," in Short Talks with the Dead. N.Y.: Harper, 1926. pp. 202-8.

316 Berdiaev, N. A. Le Suicide. Paris: LeCeo, 1954.

317 Berlinger, R. Das Nichts und der Tod. Frankfurt: Klostermann, 1954.

318 Bertola, E. "Il Problema dell'immortalità dell'anima umana nelle opere di Tommaso d'Aquino," Revista di Folosofia Neo-Scolastica, 65 (April-June, 1973), 248-302.
  Discusses St. Thomas Aquinas' arguments for the immortality of the soul.

319 Beseant, A. Death and after. Wheaton, Ill.: Theosophical House, 1966.

320 Bialik, H. H. "The Death of David," in A Treasury of Jewish Poetry, edited by N. Ausubel and M. A. Ausubel. N.Y.: Crown, 1951. pp. 390.

321 Bierce, A. "An Occurrence at Owl Creek Bridge, " in In the
     Midst of Life and Other Stories. N. Y.: Signet, 1961.
     Persuasive and moving story of the denial of death.

322 Bishop, R. "The Theme of death in French Literature from
     Villon's 'Grand Testament' to the middle of the 16th cen-
     tury. " Ph. D. dissertation, Princeton University, 1943.

323 Bjerre, P. C. Death and renewal; translated from the Swedish
     by I. Von Terl. N. Y.: Macmillan, 1930.
     Shows how "life and death presuppose each other and
     how existence with all its varieties of form can only be
     understood as manifestations of this rhythm. "

324 Blair, R. "The Grave, " in Eighteenth Century Poetry and
     Prose, edited by L. Bredvold, Alan McKellop, and Lori
     Whitney. N. Y.: Ronald Press, 1973. pp. 621-35.

325 Blake, R. "Quest for understanding in the Seventh Seal, "
     Drama Critique, 10 (winter 1967), 16-24.
     Discusses Bergman's statement on man's mortality
     and how it is the beginning of self-understanding. "Be-
     yong death, man is certain of nothing. "

326 Block, W. Der Arzt und der Tod in Bildern aus Sechs Jahr-
     hunderten (Mit. 173). ABB, Stuttgart: Erke, 1966.

327 Bloem, J. C. De Dichter en de dood. Haarlem, Nether-
     lands: Gottmer, 1958.

328 Bloom, H. "Death and the native strain in American poetry, "
     in Death in American Experience, edited by Arien Mack.
     N. Y.: Schocken, 1973. pp. 83-96.
     Also available in Social Research, 39 (autumn 1972),
     449-62. Contrasts the visions of death in British and
     American poetry.

329 Bluefarb, S. "Life and death in Garcia Lorca's 'House of
     Bernarda Alba, ' " Drama Survey, 4 (summer 1965), 109-
     20.

330 Bodenheim, M. "Death, " in A Treasury of Jewish Poetry,
     edited by N. Ausubel and M. A. Ausubel. N. Y.: Crown,
     1951. pp. 387.

331 Boehm, R. Wesen und Funktion der Sterbe Mede in Elisa-
     bethanischen Drama. Hamburg: Cram, de Gruyter, 1964.

332 Bok, S. "Ethical problems of abortion, " Hastings Center
     Studies, 2 (Jan. 1974), 33-52.

333 Borges, J. L. "Remorse for any death, " in Selected Poems,
     1923-1967. N. Y.: Delacorte, 1972.

334 Bornstein, P. Die Dichter des Todes in der modernen Literatur. Berlin: E. Ebering, 1899.

335 Boros, L. The Mystery of death. N.Y.: Herder and Herder, 1965.
Describes death as a metaphysical process and the starting point for philosophical analysis of death.

336 Bosis, L. D. The Story of my death. N.Y.: Oxford University Press, 1933.

337 Botturi, F. "Filosofia della morte e socialità nel Giovane Feuerbach," Revista di Filosofia Neo-Scolastica, 65 (July-Sept., 1973), 551-81.

338 Bouinais, A. M. A., and A. Paulus. Le Culte des mortes dans le Celeste Empire et l'annam Comparé au culte des ancêtres dans l'antiquité occidentale. Vol. 6. Paris: Annals du Musee Guimel, Bibliotheque de Vulgarsation, 1893.

339 Boyd, M. Free to live, free to die. N.Y.: New American Library, 1970.

340 Bradley, A. C. Shakespearean tragedy. London: Macmillan, 1904.

341 Bradley, K. L., and D. J. Bradley, eds. Adventure eternal; an anthology; with a preface by Abbe Ernest Dimnet. Harrisburg: Stackpole, 1937.
An anthology of prose and poetry dealing with themes of death and immortality.

342 Brady, P. "Manifestations of eros and thanatos in L'Etranger," Twentieth Century Literature, 20 (July 1974), 183-8.

343 Brandon, S. G. F. "Time and the destiny of man," in The Voices of Time; a Cooperative Survey of Man's Views of Time as Expressed by the Sciences and by the Humanities, edited by Julius T. Fraser. N.Y.: Braziler, 1966. pp. 140-57.

344 Brandt, R. B. "The Morality of abortion," The Monist, 56 (Oct. 1972), 503-26.

345 Breitinger, E. Der Tod im enalischen Roman von 1800. Untersuchungen zum Englischen Schauerroman. Gottingen: A. Kummerle, 1971.

346/8 Brody, B. A. "Abortion and the law," Journal of Philosophy, 68 (Jan. 17, 1970), 357-68.
Paper discusses questions about abortion, and the author states that there is no reason to legalize abortion.

349 _____. "Abortion and the sanctity of human life," American Philosophical Quarterly, 10 (April 1973), 133-40. Author asks, "Are there any cases in which abortion is morally permissible?"

350 Brown, J. "John Brown bids farewell to his family the night before he is executed," in A Treasury of the World's Great Letters, by M. Lincoln Schuster. N.Y.: Simon and Schuster, 1940. pp. 335. The author's postscript to this letter states that John Brown was "faithful unto death." He was captured near Harper's Ferry and sentenced to death. His letter is dated Charlestown Prison Jefferson Co., Va. 30th. Nov. 1859.

351 Browne, T. "The Shame of death," in The Great English Essayists, edited by W. Dawson, and Coningsby. N.Y.: Harper, 1909. pp. 35-9.

352 Browning, R. "A Death in the desert," in Poetry of the Victorian Period, edited by G. B. Woods, and J. H. Buckley. Glenview, Ill.: Scott, Foresman, 1955. pp. 282.

353 _____. The First born of Egypt; the dance of death. N.Y.: Macmillan, 1913.

354 Brun, J. "Adorateurs de Dionysos et grands prêtres de la mort de l'homme," Revue Internationale de Philosophie, 22 (1968), 338-55.

355 Bryson, K. A. "Being and human death," Journal of the American Catholic Philosophical Association, XLVIII (summer 1974), 343-50.

356 Budge, E. A. W. Egyptian ideas of future life. N.Y.: University Books, 1959.

357 Bugenthal, J. F. "A Critique of Peter Koestenbaum's 'The Vitality of Death,'" Journal of Existentialism, 5 (summer 1965), 433-9.

358 Buonaiuti, E. Amore e morte nei tragici Greci, 3d ed. Florence: La Nuova Italia, 1944.

359 Bürgel, B. H. Saat und Ernte; Betrachtungen über Leben und Tod. (Mit 28 Abbildungen in text und 8 Tafeln.) Berlin: Deutscher Verlag, 1942.

360 Burghardt, W. "The Life and death question," America, 128 (April 21, 1973), 366-7.

361 Burnand, R. "L'Homme devant la mort," Concours Médical, 81 (Oct. 1959), 4113-8.

362 Burroughs, J. "Marcus Aurelius on death," in Under the
     Maples. Boston: Houghton, 1921. pp. 185-6.

363 Cabodevilla, J. Veinte y dos de diciembre; la muerte y
     despué́s de la muerte. Madrid: Editorial Cató́lica, 1969.

364 Calanes, A. Les Mortes mysté́rieuses de l'historie, new ed.,
     rev., corr., with preface by Professeur Lacassaque.
     Paris: A. Michael, 1910.

365 Callahan, D. Abortion, law, choice and mortality. N. Y.:
     Macmillan, 1970.
          "... [T]o Callahan, abortion is ... the killing of po-
     tential, important and valuable human life and not simply
     the emptying of the contents of the uterus."

366 Campbell, M. "The Meaning of immortality in the Phaedo,"
     Kineris, 1 (fall 1968), 29-35.

367 Camus, A. "Absurdity and suicide," in The Myth of Sisyphus,
     translated by Justin O'Brien. N. Y.: Vintage, 1955. pp.
     3-8.

368 _____. A Happy death. N. Y.: Knopf, 1972.
          Camus's first novel is a work that demonstrates his
     philosophical and literary consciousness. His main con-
     cern is about how one should live in order to have a hap-
     py death.

369 _____. The Just assassins. N. Y.: Vintage, 1958.

370 _____. Myth of Sisyphus. N. Y.: Knopf, 1955.
          "The fundamental subject of 'The Myth of Sisyphus'
     is this: it is legitimate and necessary to wonder whether
     life has a meaning; therefore it is legitimate to meet the
     problem of suicide face to face...." Pref.

371 _____. The Plague. N. Y.: Knopf, 1948.
          In the story death plays no favorites in the town of
     Oran in Algeria, when an epidemic of bubonic plague im-
     plicates the people and their ways. Meaning is found in
     loving and healing.

372 _____. The Stranger. N. Y.: Knopf, 1946.
          An Algerian clerk lives quietly until he becomes im-
     plicated over shooting an Arab. He is condemned to die
     and he contemplates his fate with deep insight.

373 _____. "The Wind at Djemila," in Lyrical and Critical
     Essays, edited and with notes by Philip Thody. N. Y.:
     Knopf, 1968. pp. 73-9.

374 _____. "The Wrong side and the right side," in Lyrical

and Critical Essays, edited by Philip Thody. N. Y.:
Vintage, 1970. pp. 58-9.
"... [T]ale of a woman who died young, was buried
late and worshipped death in between. "

375 Canetti, E. "Aphorisms, " Literary Review, 17 (summer
1974), 482-5.

376 Caponigri, A. R. "Reason and death, the idea of wisdom in
Seneca, " Proceedings of the American Catholic Philosophical Association, 42 (1968), 144-51.

377 Capote, T. In cold blood. N. Y.: Random, 1966.
The true account of the Kansas multiple murder by
Perry Smith and Richard Hickock and the aftermath lead-
ing to their eventual capture, treatment, and execution.

378 Caracciolli, L. A. Le Tableau de la mort, new ed., enl.
and corr. Paris: Lyon, 1767.

379 Carlisle, E. F. "The Self, death, and spirit, " in The Uncer-
tain Self: Whitman's Drama of Identity. East Lansing,
Mich.: Michigan State University Press, 1973. pp. 142-
75.
"Because death is a mystery and spirit is seldom
available to Whitman, his poetry about death and spirit
is predominantly a poetry about human existence.... "

380 Carp, E. A. D. De dubbelganger: beschouwingen Over de Dood
en Leven. Utrecht: Het Spectrum, 1964.

381 Carpenter, E. The Drama of love and death. N. Y.: W. E.
Rudge, 1912.
A poetic insight into the phenomena of life and death.

382 Carrier, C. E. "The Comedy of death in the early plays of
Dürrenmatt. " Ph. D. dissertation, Indiana University,
1962.
Investigates early plays from the viewpoint of their
preoccupation with the matter of death. Covers his first
five dramas from 1947-1953.

383 Caruso, I. A. Die Trennung der Liebenden. Eine Phä-
nomenologie des Todes. Bern: Huber, 1968.

384 Casal Muñoz, J. Ser y muerte; ensayo de filosofía integral.
Montevideo: Tip. Atlántida, 1959.

385 Cather, W. Death comes for the Archbishop. N. Y.: Knopf,
1927.
Historical novel, follows somewhat the life of one
bishop of Sante Fe by transposing the life of another.

386 Cavander, K. "Love and death in ancient Greece," Horizon,
     XVI (spring 1974), 103-6.
          "Catching him in the act, an obscure citizen of
     Athens slew his wife's lover. But was it a crime of
     passion--or premeditated murder?"

387 Cavitch, D. "Solipsism and death in D. H. Lawrence's late
     works," Massachusetts Review, 7 (summer 1966), 495-
     508.

388 Cawein, M. "Death," in An American Anthology, 1789-1900,
     edited by Edmund C. Stedman. Boston: Houghton, 1900.
     pp. 709.

389 Celan, P. "Death fugue," in A Treasury of Jewish Poetry,
     edited by N. Ausubel and M. A. Ausubel. N.Y.: Crown,
     1957. pp. 161.

390 Charlot, J. Dance of death; fifty drawings and captions.
     N.Y.: Sheed and Ward, 1951.
          Consists of a series of drawings and captions in
     which the theme of death appears to various people: the
     child, businessman, optimist, pessimist, etc.

391 Chatterton, T. "Bristowe Tragedie," in Eighteenth Century
     Poetry and Prose, edited by Louis Bredvold, Alan McKel-
     lop, and Lois Whitney. N.Y.: Ronald, 1973. pp. 1386-
     90.

392 Chauchard, P. "L'Avortement," Revue Thomiste, 73 (Jan.-
     March, 1973), 33-46.
          States that abortion is unacceptable because a human
     being exists from the moment of conception.

393 _____. La Mort. Paris: Presses Universitaires de
     France, 1956.

394 Chene-Williams, A. "Philosopher, c'est apprendre a
     mourir," Dialogue (Canada), 11 (1972), 337-47.

395 Choron, J. Death and Western Thought. N.Y.: Macmillan,
     1963.

396 _____. "Death as a motive of philosophic thought," in
     Essays in Self-Destruction, edited by Edwin Shneidman.
     N.Y.: Science House, 1967. pp. 59-77.
          Contemporary philosophical thought in many instances
     ignores the subject of death. "The purpose of this pres-
     ent essay [is] to elucidate, as far as possible, the rea-
     sons for this state of philosophic affairs and to show that
     the disregard of death is not necessarily the last word in
     philosophic wisdom...."

397 _____. Suicide: a look at self-destruction. N. Y.:
         Scribner's, 1972.
         "Discussion of human self-destruction by a philosopher
         and recent fellow of the Suicide Prevention Center at Los
         Angeles. "

398 Christensen, C. C. "The Significance of the epitaph monu-
         ment in early Lutheran ecclesiastical art (ca. 1540-1600):
         some social and iconographical considerations, " in The
         Social History of the Reformation, edited by Lawrence P.
         Buck, and Jonathan W. Zophy. Columbus: Ohio State
         University Press, 1972. pp. 297-314.

399 Chudzinski, A. Tod und Totenkultus beiden alten Griechen.
         Gutersloh: Bertelsmann, 1907.

400 Clark, E. "Death cannot surprise us who are driven, " in A
         New Anthology of Modern Poetry, edited by Selden Rod-
         man. N. Y.: Random, 1938. pp. 288.

401 Clarke, J. J. "Mysticism and the paradox of survival, "
         International Philosophical Quarterly, 6 (June 1971), 165-
         79.

402 Cleaveland, F. P. "The Dance of death, " Journal of the
         American Medical Association, 176 (1961), 142-3.
         Interprets and describes the dance of death which was
         a favored expression in art during the middle ages and
         throughout the Renaissance.

403 Coffey, P. J. "Toward a sound moral policy on abortion, "
         The New Scholasticism, 47 (winter 1973), 105-12.

404 Cohen, K. Metamorphosis of a death symbol; the transitomb
         in 15th and 16th century Europe. Berkeley: University
         of California Press, 1974. (California studies in the his-
         tory of art, 15.)
         An illustrated volume which focuses on tomb litera-
         ture and tomb imagery in general.

405 Colin, P. "Will death have the last word?" Lumen Vitae,
         26 (Sept. 1971), 431-46.
         Article points out that "the seed of eternity within
         man rebels against death and perpetual extinction.

406 Comper, F. M. , ed. Ars moriendi: the book of the craft
         of dying and other early English tracts concerning death.
         London: Longmans, Green and Co. , 1917.

407 Conrad, B. Famous last words. N. Y.: Doubleday, 1961.

408 Cooke, M. G. Hallucination and death as motifs of escape in
         the novels of Julien Green. Washington: C. V. Press,
         1960.

409 Cooperman, S. "Death and cojones: Hemingway's 'A Farewell to Arms,'" South Atlantic Quarterly, 63 (winter
1964), 85-92.

410 Corbin, A. "Death has come to visit us today on the Acequia
Madre," in The New Poetry, edited by Harriet Monroe
and Alice Corbin Henderson. N.Y.: Macmillan, 1932.
pp. 95.

411 Cosacchi, S. Makaber tanz: der Totentanz in Kunst, Poesie
und Brauchtum des Mittelaters. Meisenheim am Gilon:
Hain, 1965.

412 Crain, H. "Basic concepts of death in children's literature,"
Elementary English, 40 (Jan. 1972), 111-15.
The author cleverly shows how literature can help in
formulating mature attitudes in children.

413 Crapsey, A. "The Lonely death," in Anthology of American
Poetry, compiled by Conrad Aiken. N.Y.: Random
House, 1944. pp. 236.

414 Crocker, L. G. "Discussion of suicide in the eighteenth
century," Journal of the History of Ideas, 13 (1952),
47-72.
Focuses on the renewed discussion of the ethics of
suicide and its historical importance.

415 Croly, G. "Death and resurrection," in The World's Greatest
Religious Poetry, edited by Caroline Miles Hills. N.Y.:
Macmillan, 1934. pp. 737.

416 Cromp, G. "La Communion a sois-même chez Gabriel Marcel," Laval Théologique et Philosophique, 28 (June 1972),
171-84.

417 Crosson, F. J. "Psyche and persona: the problem of personal immortality," International Philosophical Quarterly,
8 (June 1968), 161-79.
Author discusses "personal immortality as continuity
of self awareness of who I am." He claims that the
formulation of the question of "personal immortality needs
a prior clarification of what it is to be a person."

418 Cumont, F. V. M. ... Recherches sur le symbolisme
funéraire des Romains.... Paris: P. Geuthner, 1966.
(Reprint of the 1942 edition.)

419 Cunningham, M. F. "To live and to die humanly," Religious
Humanism, 3 (summer 1969), 97-100.
Discusses the medical criteria for death and points
out that "each person has the right to select death when
there is loss of control of one's body and mind."

420 Curtin, S. R. Nobody ever died of old age. Boston: Little,
     1972.
       "... [F]irst person narrative dramatizes situations
     typical among our old people.... We dote on youth. We
     shelve the old, and what does this say about how we view
     the whole of life?"

421 Dallas, H. A. Death, the gate of life. N. Y.: Dutton, 1919.
       "... [T]he author confines himself to a consideration
     of that part of the evidence which relates to the question
     of the survival of the personality of Frederic Myers....
     [T]he conclusions arrived at in the book are not only that
     Myers has survived bodily death, but that he has retained
     his former characteristics and interests."

422 Daniel, H. Devils, monsters, and nightmares; an introduction
     to the grotesque and fantastic in art. N. Y.: Abelard-
     Schuman, 1964.

423 Dante. "Death, always cruel," translated from the Italian by
     Dante Gabriel in A Little Treasury of World Poetry,
     edited by Hubert Creekmore. N. Y.: Scribner, 1952.
     pp. 533.

424 Davis, D. R. "The Death of the artist's father: Henrik Ib-
     sen," British Journal of Medical Psychology, 46 (June
     1973), 135-41.
       Examples of the works of Ibsen are discussed after
     his father's death. The death of his father and the effect
     of it on productions are considered in detail. Also exam-
     ples from the lives and works of Freud, Shakespeare, and
     D. H. Lawrence are compared.

425 Day, W. G. "Forbidden embraces: Jeremy Taylor's Holy
     dying," Notes and Queries, 18 (Aug. 1971), 292-3.

425a "Death and Dying"; an Arno Press collection. New York:
     Arno Press, 1976.
       This fine collection contains some forty titles many
     of which are original Arno Press anthologies. Items in-
     clude: Death and the visual arts; Death as a speculative
     theme in religious, scientific and social thought; and vari-
     ous related items on immortality, resurrection, euthanasia,
     and eschatology.

426 "Deed of friendship: M. Happer shot by friend," Newsweek,
     65 (April 26, 1965), 30.
       Reports an incident of mercy killing in Philadelphia,
     where one woman shot and killed her best friend, then
     herself.

427 De Franco, R. "La idea della morte e il suicidio," Giornale
     Critico della Filosofia Italiana, 1 (Oct.-Dec. 1970), 566-
     79.

428 _____. "Morte e alienazione," Giornale Critico della
Filosofia Italiana, 51 (April-June 1972), 263-72.

429 Demske, J. M. Being, man and death. Lexington: University Press of Kentucky, 1970.
"Attempts to document and analyze the connection in
Heidegger's thought between the problem of death and the
problem of being and man."

430 Dennis, L. R. "Mark Twain and the Dark Angel," Midwest
Quarterly, 8 (Jan. 1967), 181-97.

431 De Tollenaere, M. "Immortality: a reflective exploration,"
International Philosophical Quarterly, 10 (Dec. 1970),
556-9.

432 DeVleeshouwer, R. "La Doctrine du suicide dans l'éthique
de Kant," Kant-Studien, 57 (1966), 251-65.

433 Dewart, L. "Fact of death," Commonweal, 91 (Nov. 14,
1969), 206-8.
Discusses certain philosophical objections to the traditional interpretations of death. Rejects the doctrine of
the immortality of the soul that defines man as body and
soul.

434 Dewey, E. "Living value and immortality," Pacific Philosophy
Forum, 3 (Sept. 1964), 57-69.

435 Díaz-Plaja, F. La Muerte en la poesía española. Madrid:
A. Aguado, 1952.

436 Dickinson, E. "Because I could not stop for death," in Interpreting Literature, edited by K. Knickerbocker, and H.
Reninger. N. Y.: Holt, Rinehart and Winston, 1974. pp.
319.

437 _____. "Death," in 1000 Quotable Poems, edited by Thomas
C. Clark. N. Y.: Willett Clark and Co., 1937. pp. 318.

438 _____. "Dying," in Anthology of American Poetry, compiled by Conrad Aiken. N. Y.: Random, 1944. pp. 181.

439 _____. "My life closed twice before its close," in Interpreting Literature, edited by K. Knickerbocker and H.
Reninger. N. Y.: Holt, Rinehart and Winston, 1974. pp.
352.

440 Dietuch, B. C. Death, fate and the Gods: the development
of a religious idea in Greek popular belief and in Homer.
N. Y.: Oxford University Press, 1965.

441 "Doctors who chose death for patients," Newsweek, 50 (July 8,

1957), 50.
Presents Dr. Stuart Scott's views on mercy killing
and describes several cases where the patient was allowed to die.

442 Doebler, B. A. Y. The Quickening seed, death in the sermons of John Donne. Salzburg: Institut für Englische
Sprache und Literatur, Universität Salzburg, 1974.
(Elizabethan and Renaissance studies No. 30--Salzburg
studies in English Literature.)
Originally the author's thesis, University of Wisconsin, 1961.

443 Dommeger, F. C. "Body, mind, and death," Pacific Philosophy Forum, 3 (Feb. 1965), 3-73.

444 Donceel, J. "A Liberal Catholic's view," in Abortion in a
Changing World, edited by W. R. Hall. N.Y.: Columbia
University Press, 1970. pp. 39-45.

445 Donne, J. "At the round earth's imagined corners," in Interpreting Literature, edited by K. Knickerbocker and H.
Reninger. N.Y.: Holt, Rinehart and Winston, 1974.
pp. 320.

446 _____. Biathanatos. N.Y.: Facsimile Text Society,
1930.
A reprint of the first edition of 1644.

447 _____. Death's duel. Menston (Yorks): Scolar Press,
1969.
A facsimile reprint of the first edition published in
London in 1632.

448 _____. "Devotions upon emergent occasions; excerpt," in
Prose and the Essay, edited by C. T. Wells. Boston:
Houghton, 1962. pp. 51-3.

449 _____. "Equality in death," in Treasure Chest, edited by
J. D. Adams. N.Y.: Dutton, 1946. pp. 46.

450 Dostoevsky, F. "Dostoevsky describes his sensations when
he had but one minute to live," in A Treasury of the
World's Great Letters, by M. Lincoln Schuster. N.Y.:
Simon and Schuster, 1940. pp. 299-305.
The letter was written on December 20, 1849, to his
brother Mihail and ... the sentence of death was read ...
"after four years in prison Dostoevsky's sentence was
commuted and throughout his greatest work he alludes
again and again to the shattering experiences of 1849--
as indicated by the actual phrasing of the titles of three
of his famous novels...."

451 Downing, A. B., ed. Euthanasia and the right to death: the
     case for voluntary euthanasia. N.J.: Humanities Press,
     1970.

452 Dubnuck, E. The Theme of death in French poetry of the
     Middle Ages and the Renaissance. The Hague: Mouton
     and Co., 1964.
         Includes chapters on the danse macabre and the
     imagery of death.

453 Ducasse, C. J. The Belief in a life after death. Springfield,
     Ill.: C. C. Thomas, 1961.

454 _____. A Critical examination of the belief in a life after
     death. Springfield, Ill.: C. C. Thomas, 1962.

455 _____. Nature, mind, and death. LaSalle, Ill.: Open
     Court, 1951.

456 Duckett, E. Death and life in the tenth century. Ann Arbor:
     University of Michigan Press, 1967.

457 Dufrenne, M. "L'Anti-humanisme et le thème de la mort,"
     Revue Internationale de Philosophie, 22 (1968), 296-307.

458 Dunne, J. S. Time and myth. Notre Dame, Ind.: University
     of Notre Dame Press, 1973.

459 Durant, W. J. "On life and death," in Pleasures of Philoso-
     phy: a survey of human life and destiny. N.Y.: Simon
     and Schuster, 1953. pp. 397-408.

460 Earle, W. "Some notes on death, existentially considered,"
     in The Autobiographical Consciousness. N.Y.: Quad-
     rangle, 1972. pp. 213-26.

461 Eaton, W. K. "Contrasts in the representation of death by
     Sophocles, Webster, and Strindberg." Ph.D. disserta-
     tion, Syracuse University, 1965.
         "... [P]rimary comparison is made between each
     writer's focus on death as part of the dramatic and
     philosophic meaning in his plays...."

462 Eger, J. C. Le Sommeil et la mort dans la Grèce antique.
     Paris: Sicard, 1966.

463 Egger, V. "Le Moi des mourants, nouveaux faits," Revue
     Philosophique, 42 (1896), 337-68.
         Distinguishes between simple consciousness and the
     ego vis-à-vis death. Consciousness may not be aware
     of impending death, while the ego is aware.

464 Eliot, T. S. Four quartets. N.Y.: Harcourt Brace Jo-

vanovich, 1968.
    Four poems all dealing with time and eternity, and
    named for places. The recurrent themes consist of
    imagery and symbols of earth, water, air, and fire.

465 Ellis, H. R. The Road to hell; a study of the conception of
     the dead in old Norse literature. Westport, Conn.:
     Greenwood Press, 1968.

466 Ellis, S. M. "Lost poet: Herbert Kennedy and the poetical
     attitude to death," in Mainly Victorian. N. Y.: Hutchin-
     son, 1925. pp. 387-96.

467 Elsen, A. E. "Art as a matter of life and death," in Pur-
     poses of Art: An introduction to the history and apprecia-
     tion of art, 3d ed. N. Y.: Holt, Rinehart and Winston,
     1972. pp. 20-36.

468 Emerson, A. E., and R. W. Burhoe. "Evolutionary aspects
     of freedom, death, and dignity," Zygon, 9 (June 1974),
     156-82.

469 Emerson, R. W. "Brahma," in Interpreting Literature, edited
     by K. Knickerbocker, and H. Reninger. N. Y.: Holt,
     Rinehart and Winston, 1974. pp. 321.

470/1 "Euthanasia at 80? Proposal by British health official,"
     Newsweek, 73 (May 12, 1969), 77.
         Gives Dr. Kenneth Vicker's views on euthanasia and
     his contention that it should be enacted after the age of
     80.

472 "Euthanasia: old lady slept," Newsweek, 53 (May 18, 1969),
     44.
         Reports on an incident of mercy killing in Leicester,
     England, where a doctor allows an aged cancer patient
     to die at her request.

473 Eversole, R. "Wooden frail memorial in 'Gray's Elegy,'"
     Notes and Queries, 21 (Feb. 1974) 56-7.

474 Eyck, P. N. V. Over Leven en dood in de Poezie. The
     Hague: Stols, 1947.

475 Farber, L. H. "Despair and the life of suicide," in The
     Ways of the Will; essays toward a psychology and psycho-
     pathology of will. N. Y.: Basic Books, 1966. pp. 76-98.

476 Farnell, L. R. Greek hero cults and ideas of immortality.
     N. Y.: Clarendon Press, 1921.

477 Faulkner, W. As I lay dying. N. Y.: Random, 1964.
         Develops the interrelated mental and emotional life of

a family.   The story is told by different members of the
family and their acquaintances.

478 _____. "Death drag, " in The Portable Faulkner. N. Y.:
          Viking, 1946.

479 Fawerch, F. E.   Het Tehen van Dood en Herleving en het
          Read sel van het Angelsahische Ruhenkist Je.   Hilversum:
          Vitg. Thule, 1953.

480 Fehrman, C. A. D.   Diktaren och doden; dodsbild och For-
          gangelsetanke i literaturen fran Antiken til 1700-Talet.
          Stockholm: Bonner, 1952.

481 Ferrante, J. M.   "Malebolge (Inf. XVIII-XXX) as the key to
          the structure of Dante's Inferno, " Romance Philology, 20
          (May 1967), 456-66.

482 Ferrater-Mora, J.   Being and death (an outline of integration-
          ist philosophy).   Berkeley: University of California
          Press, 1965.
               An investigation of the problem of death that can lead
          to a philosophical system.   Basic branches of a system
          include: an ontology; metaphysics; organic reality; and a
          philosophy of the human person.

483 _____. El sentido de la morte.   Buenos Aires: Editorial
          Sudamericana, 1947.

484 Feuerbach, L.   Tod und Unsterblichkeit.   Stuttgart: Werke,
          1903.

485 Fiedler, L.   Love and death in the American novel.   N. Y.:
          Stein and Day, 1968.
               Looks at American fiction in the light of Freud's
          teachings.   Examines the fantasy presentation of adult
          love and death and how American fiction is generally an
          escape with little reality.

486 Fink, E.   Metaphysik und tod.   Stuttgart: W. Kohlhammer,
          1969.

487 Finnis, J.   "The Rights and wrongs of abortion: a reply to
          Judith Thomson, " Philosophy and Public Affairs, 2 (win-
          ter 1973), 117-45.

488 Fischer, J. A.   Studien zum Todesgedanken in der alten
          Kirche, Baal; Die Beurteilung des natürlichen todes in der
          Kirchlichen Literatur der Ersten drei Jahrhunderte.
          Munich: Huber, 1954.

489 Fisher, B.   "Self-exploration experience in death encounter. "
          Ph. D. dissertation, University of Florida, 1968.

490 Flammarion, C. Death and its mystery. Translated by E. S.
Brooks. N. Y.: Century Company, 1921.
The book is the result of more than 50 years of observation, investigation, and classification of facts concerning immortality. The author presents evidence of a
subconscious life not explained yet by materialistic means.

491 Fletcher, J. "The Control of death," Intellectual Digest, 4
(Oct. 1973), 82-3.
Discusses active and positive euthanasia.

492 _____. "Human experimentation ethics in the consent situation," Law and Contemporary Problems, 32 (1967), 620-
49.

493 _____. "The Patient's right to die," Harper's, 221 (Oct.
1960), 139-43.
Fletcher discusses the question of mercy killing. He
does not give any answers, as there are no universally
accepted solutions to the problem. He is speaking of patients who are being kept alive by artificial means and
who are no more than "vegetables."

493a _____. "The Right to live and the right to die," The Humanist, (July-Aug. 1974), 12-15.
Discusses the legalism of the ethics of right. Major
concern is with "human need--both of life and death."

494 _____, et al. "When should patients be allowed to die?
Some questions of ethics," Postgraduate Medicine, 43
(April 1968), 197-200.

495 Flew, A., ed. Body, mind, and death. N. Y.: Macmillan,
1964.

496 Florit, E. "Death in the sun," in Twelve Spanish-American
Poets, edited by H. R. Hayes. New Haven: Yale University Press, 1943. pp. 115.

497 Foelber, P. F. Bach's treatment of the subject of death in
his choral music. Washington, D. C.: Catholic University
of America Press, 1961. (Thesis--Catholic University of
America.)

498 Forbes, T. R. "Life and death in Shakespeare's London,"
American Scientist, 58 (1970), 511-20.

499 Ford, T. Heaven beguiles the tired: death in the poetry of
Emily Dickinson. University: University of Alabama
Press, 1966.

500 Fosdick, H. The Assurance of immortality. N. Y.: Association Press, 1940.

Discusses the importance of immortality both pro and con.

501 Foss, M. Death, sacrifice, and tragedy. Lincoln: University of Nebraska Press, 1966.

502 Fournier, d'Albe, E. E. New light on immortality. N. Y.: Longmans Green, 1908.

503 Fox, R. C. "Allegory of sin and death in 'Paradise Lost.'" Modern Language Quarterly, 24 (Dec. 1963), 354-64.

504 Frazier, C. A., ed. Is it moral to modify man? Forewords by J. Fletcher, C. A. Hoffman, and Cecil E. Sherman. Springfield, Ill.: C. C. Thomas, 1973.

505 Freeman, H. "The Case for immortality," Pacific Philosophy Forum, 3 (Dec. 1964), 4-46.

506 Freneau, P. "Death in this tomb his weary limbs hath laid [and] Death's epitaph," in American Anthology, 1787-1900, edited by E. C. Stedman. Boston: Houghton, 1900. pp. 4.

507 Frey, J. R. "Schiller's concept and poetic treatment of death," Journal of English and German Philosophy, 58 (Oct. 1959), 557-88.
States that Schiller's poetry shows that death provided the truest test for man's resources; his moral resources and autonomy of will.

508 Friebert, S. "Conrad Ferdinand Meyers 'Die Versuchung des Pescara'," German Quarterly, 35 (Nov. 1962), 475-81.

509 Friedman, M. "Death and the dialogue with the absurd," in The Phenomenon of Death; Faces of Mortality, edited by Edith Wyschogrod. N. Y.: Harper and Row, 1973. pp. 149-65.
This essay is to be a chapter in Mr. Friedman's forthcoming book The Hidden Human Image.

510 Froscher, W. "Death in the family," in Best American Short Stories, edited by Martha Foley. Boston: Houghton, 1953. pp. 137-44.

511 Frost, R. "Home burial," in Anthology of American Poetry, edited and compiled by Conrad Aiken. N. Y.: Random, 1944. pp. 273.

512 Furlow, T. W., Jr. "Tyranny of technology," The Humanist (July-Aug. 1974), 6-9.

513 Gadamer, H. G. "La Morte come problema," Giornale

Critico Della Filosofia Italiana, 52 (April-June 1973), 221-32.

514 Gajdusek, R. E. "Death, incest, and the triple bond in the later plays of Shakespeare," American Imago, 31 (summer 1974), 109-58.

515 Gallagher, K. T. "Gabriel Marcel: death as mystery," Humanitas, 10 (Feb. 1974), 75-86.
Discussion of Marcel's philosophy of death. "Death is both the supreme test for communion and the supreme challenge for the thought which searches for its ontological secret."

516 Gallahue, J. "Tragedy at Liege: Vandeput's thalidomide baby," Look, 27 (March 12, 1963), 72-4.

517 Gardiner, A. H. The Attitude of ancient Egyptians to death and the dead. N.Y.: Cambridge University Press, 1935.

518 Garin, E. "Leon Battista Alberti a il monde dei morti," Giornale Critico della Filosofia Italiana, 52 (April-June, 1973), 178-89.

519 Gaucher, G. Le Thème de la mort dans les romans de Georges Bernanos. Paris: Lettres Modernes, 1967.
For Bernanos, the mystery of death gives its meaning to human life.

520 Gaulupeau, S. André Malraux et la mort. Paris: Lettres Modernes, 1969.

521 Gelinas, E. "Life and death," Pacific Philosophy Forum, 3 (May 1965), 68-83.

522 Genova, A. C. "Death as a terminus ad quemo," Philosophy and Phenomenological Research (Dec. 1973), 270-77.
Interpretation of death from the analytical philosopher's point of view.

523 Gerber, D. "Abortion: the uptake argument," Ethics, 83 (Oct. 1972), 80-3.

524 Gerlach, L. F. "Death of a teacher," in Ports of the Pacific, edited by Yvor Wintors. Second Series. Stanford, Calif.: Stanford University Press, 1949.

525 Gibbons, J. P. "Brightman's philosophy of immortality," The Personalist, 54 (spring 1973), 176-87.

526 Gies, C. La Hermana muerte: Florilegiol de macabrerías a traves del humorisme español. Castellón de la Plana, Spain: Sociedad Castellonense de Culture, 1953.

527 Gillon, E. V., Jr. Victorian cemetery art. With 260
     photos by the author. N. Y.: Dover, 1972.

528 Gleaves, E. S., Jr. "The Spanish influence on Ernest Hem-
     ingway's concepts of death, Nada, and immortality."
     Ph. D. dissertation, Emory University, 1964.
        "... [T]he Spanish influence on Hemingway is seen
     in this study as a long and gradual movement toward an
     affirmation of life despite his constant obsession with
     death...."

529 Goewey, H. A. "The Apology for death and the rejection of
     extended life in nineteenth- and twentieth-century British
     visionary fiction. Ph. D. dissertation, Wayne State Uni-
     versity, 1969.

530 Gold, H. "Death on the east side," in Best American Short
     Stories. Boston: Houghton, 1972. pp. 48-74.

531 Gold, M. S., and R. H. V. Ollendorff. "The Unencounter
     with death," Humanitas, 10 (Feb. 1974), 59.
        The authors explain why we go to a great deal of
     trouble to avoid confrontation with nothingness and uncer-
     tainty. "We must discard our formulas and reflexes with
     respect to the unknown if we are ever to escape unen-
     counter with death."

532 Goldhamer, A. D. "Everyman: a dramatization of death,"
     Quarterly Journal of Speech, 59 (Feb. 1973), 87-98.
        "'Everyman' is regarded as one of the best Medieval
     morality plays. Death occupies a large part of the final
     act. The hero of the drama acts out the stages of death."

533 Goldstein, S. "The Death of Per Hansa," English Journal, 56
     (March 1967), 464-66.

534 Gomez, L. M. "Unamuno, testigo de Dios," Pensamiento,
     25 (Oct.-Dec. 1969), 403-27.
        Discusses the problem of immortality and its rela-
     tion to the existence of God.

535 Gordon, A. G. The Witness to immortality in literature,
     philosophy and life. Boston: Houghton, 1893.

536 Gore, W. Death and reawakening: poems and sketches in
     prose, with occasional rhymes. N. Y.: Exposition
     Press, 1962.

537 Gorer, G. "The Pornography of death; excerpt from 'Modern
     Writing,'" in Identity and Anxiety, edited by M. R.
     Stein, A. J. Vidich, and D. M. White. N. Y.: Free
     Press, 1960. pp. 402-7.

538 _____. "The Pornography of death," in Modern Writing, edited by W. Phillips, and P. Rahv. N.Y.: McGraw-Hill, 1959. pp. 157-88.

539 _____. "The Pornography of death," in Modern Writing, edited by W. Phillips, and P. Rahv. Berkeley Press, 1956. pp. 56-62.
The problem of death is said to have taken over the pornographic theme from sex in the 20th century.

540 Gorostiza, J. Death without end. Austin: University of Texas Press, 1969.
A Spanish and English bilingual version of a long poem concerning existence, the interconnection of form and matter, and intelligence.

541 Gotesky, R. "Disembodied life," Pacific Philosophy Forum, 3 (Dec. 1964), 61-78.

542 Gottlieb, C. "Modern art and death," in The Meaning of Death, edited by H. Feifel. N.Y.: McGraw-Hill, 1959.
Description of images of death portrayed in art. Some contemporary art forms are given.

543 Gould, D. "Better way to die," New Statesman, 77 (April 4, 1969), 474-5.
Believes that legalized euthanasia would be too often employed as an easy option.

544 _____. "Right to die," New Statesman, 77 (March 21, 1969), 402.
A philosophical argument which states that everyone has the "right" to die when he wants to.

545 Graham, J. B. "Acceptance of death--beginning of life," North Carolina Medical Journal, 24 (1963), 317-9.

546 Grassi, E. "La muerta de Dios, una tesis de Mallarmé," Dialogos, 7 (Oct.-Dec. 1971), 75-94.

547 Gray, J. G. "The Problem of death in modern philosophy," in The Modern Vision of Death, edited by Nathan A. Scott, Jr. Atlanta: John Knox Press, 1967. pp. 45-67.
"We can grant the existentialists that awareness of personal death brings greater intensity and clarification to life, but at the same time we need not remove our conviction that death as an occurrence holds, also, the promise of a greater fullness of being."

548 Gray, T. "Elegy written in a country churchyard," in [for example] Interpreting Literature, edited by K. Knickerbocker and H. Reninger. N.Y.: Holt, Rinehart and Winston, 1974. pp. 330.

549 Gregg, R. A. "Two Adams and Eve in the Crystal Palace:
     Dostoevsky, the Bible and We," Slavic Review, 24 (Dec.
     1965), 680-7.

550 Grieve, L. C. G. Death and burial in attic tragedy. Ph. D.
     dissertation, Columbia University Press, 1898.

551 Griffin, D. "Johnson's funeral writings," Journal of English
     Literary History, 41 (summer 1974), 192-211.

552 Griffith, C. "Sex and death: the significance of Whitman's
     Calamus themes," Philological Quarterly, 39 (Jan. 1960),
     18-38.

553 Grimshaw, J. "Amphibology in Shakespeare's sonnet 64,"
     Shakespeare Quarterly, 25 (winter 1974), 127-9.

554 Grohmann, A. "Das Problem von Leben und Tod in der Zeit-
     genossischen Literatur," Zeitschrift fur Deutschkunde, 44
     (1930), 449-60.

555 Grotjahn, M. "About the representation of death in the art of
     antiquity and in the unconscious of modern men," in
     Psychoanalysis and Culture, edited by G. B. Wilbur, and
     W. Muensterberger. N. Y.: International Universities
     Press, 1951. pp. 410-24.

556 Gruber, O. When I die. N. Y.: Vantage Press, 1965.

557 Guardini, R. Death of Socrates; an interpretation of the
     Platonic dialogues, Euthyphce, Apology, Crito and
     Phaedo; translated from the German by Basil Wrighton.
     N. Y.: Meridian Press, 1948.
          Examines the Platonic four dialogues from Plato's
     works. "They describe Socrates, the philosopher in the
     situation of death.... [T]hese texts will tell us how
     Socrates sees death, how his life appears to him in the
     face of death, and how he meets his end."

558 Gueomar, M. Principes d'une esthétique, de la mort, les
     modes de présences, les présences immediates, le sevd
     de l'au-delà. Paris: J. Corti, 1967.

559 Guerry, L. La Thème du "triomphe de la mort" dans la
     pienture italienne. Paris: G. P. Maisonneuve, 1950.

560 Gutmann, D. "Mayan aging: a comparative TAT study,"
     Psychiatry, 29 (1966), 246-59.

561 Hacker, P. M. S. Insight and illusion: Wittgenstein on
     philosophy and the metaphysics of experience. N. Y.:
     Oxford University Press, 1972.

562 Hageboeck, H. "Tragic silence," New York Times Magazine, CXI (Aug. 5, 1962), 4.

563 Hamburger, M. "Death of an old man," in New Poets of England and America, edited by D. Hall, R. Pack and L. Simpson. N. Y.: Meridian Books, 1957. pp. 102.

564 Hardy, T. "The Man he killed," in Interpreting Literature, edited by K. Knickerbocker and H. Reninger. N. Y.: Holt, Rinehart and Winston, 1974. pp. 353.

565 Harnden, R. The High pasture. Boston: Houghton, 1964. A child is sent to his aunt in Colorado while his mother is ill. His personal relationships help him to prepare for his mother's death and a more mature relationship with his father.

566 Haroutunian, J. "Life and death among fellowmen," in The Modern Vision of Death, edited by Nathan A. Scott, Jr. Atlanta: John Knox Press, 1967. pp. 79-96. "It is cowardly and wrong that we should fear death, if we do so without love, for then it is dread that poisons our lives. For the human meaning of death is bound up with the questions of love.... "

567 Harrington, A. Immortalist: an approach to the engineering of man's divinity. N. Y.: Random, 1969. The thesis is that we should finally realize that we are old enough to put away our gods and go after what we want: divinity. The first step is the abolition of death.

568 Harris, E. E. "Spinoza's theory of human immortality," The Monist, 55 (Oct. 1971), 668-85.

569 Harrison, S. M. "The Unwilling dead," Proceedings of the American Catholic Philosophical Association, 46 (1972), 199-208.

570 Hattam, E. "Hemingway's 'An Alpine Idyll'," Modern Fiction Studies, 12 (summer 1966), 261-5.

571 Hay, W. H. "On the immortality of man," in The Renaissance Philosophy of Man. Chicago: University of Chicago Press, 1946.

572 Hazlitt, W. "On the fear of death," in Great English Essayists, edited by W. J. Dawson, and C. W. Dawson. N. Y.: H. W. Wilson Company. pp. 55-64. (Reprint of orig., pub. by Harper in 1909.)

573 _____. "On the feeling of immortality in youth," in Complete Works, edited by P. P. Howe. London: J. M.

Dent and Sons, 1934.

574 Hearn L. "Some poems on death," in Life and Literature;
     selected and edited by J. Erskine. N. Y.: Dodd, 1917.
     pp. 308-23.

575 Heath-Stubbs, J. F. "Death of Digenes Akrikas," in New
     Poets of England and America, edited by D. Hall, R.
     Pack, and L. Simpson. N. Y.: World, 1957. pp. 110-12.

576 Hedenius, I. "A Defense of mercy killing," Atlas, 7 (April
     1964), 229-31.
         Discusses a mercy killing carried out by a district-
     doctor in Sweden and provides the pros and cons about
     euthanasia.

577 Hedwig, K. "Escepticismo en el contexto de la muerte en
     Montaigne," Revista de Filosofia, 6 (May-August 1973),
     221-33.

578 Heidegger, M. Being and time. N. Y.: Harper and Row,
     1962.
         The second part of the text is devoted to temporality
     and death.   Discusses the relationship between anxiety
     and death.

579 Hemingway, E. Death in the afternoon. N. Y.: Scribner's,
     1969.

580 Hershey, N. "Questions of life and death," American Journal
     of Nursing, 68 (Sept. 1968), 1910-12.
         Describes nurses' ethical and legal problems concern-
     ing the prolonging of life.

581 Hesse, H. Steppenwolf. N. Y.: Modern Library, 1963.
         An existential novel with symbolic overtones in a
     penetrating search for self with deep insight into human
     problems.

582 Heuscher, J. E. "Death in the fairy tale," Diseases of the
     Nervous System, 28 (1967), 462-67.
         "... [H]ere the meaning of death consists in the por-
     trayal of crucial steps of development.   It is mainly be-
     cause of this that both the proper existential-philosophic
     attitudes and the offering, at the right age [of] suitable
     fairy-tales, are of paramount importance in the raising of
     children...."

583 _____. "Existential crisis, death and changing 'world de-
     signs' in myths and fairy tales," Journal of Existentialism,
     6 (fall 1966), 45-62.
         Article states that myths and fairy tales are means of
     denying the possibility of one's death.

584 Hiers, J. T.   "Traditional death customs in modern southern
     fiction. "   Ph. D. dissertation, Emory University, 1974.
     "... [T]hus death and funeral customs in modern
     southern fiction often become cultural tableaux for de-
     lineating healthful family and community relationships.... "

585 Higgins, A.   "Dealing with death, " National Catholic Reporter,
     8 (June 23, 1972), 13.

586 Hind, A.   The Dance of death--a complete facsimile of the
     original 1538 edition of "Les Simulachres et historiées
     faces de la mort. "   N. Y. :   Dover, 1971.

587 Hocking, W. E.   The Meaning of immortality in the human ex-
     perience.   N. Y. :   Harper, 1957.

588 _____.   Thoughts on death and life.   N. Y. :   Harper, 1937.

589 Hoffman, F. J.   "Grace, violence and self, " Virginia Quar-
     terly Review, 34 (1958), 139-54.
          Discussion of how the terms grace, violence, and
     self relate to the ways in which death is involved with
     image and metaphor.

590 _____.   The Mortal no: death and the modern imagination.
     Princeton, N. J. :   Princeton University Press, 1964.
          Study of the way death and self are treated in modern
     literature. Metaphors of death and theories of living are
     examined in writers such as Stendhal, Zola, James,
     Mann, Dostoevski, Joyce, Camus, Sartre, Mailer, and
     Kafka.

591 _____.   "Mortality and modern literature, " in The Meaning
     of Death, edited by Herman Feifel.   N. Y. :   McGraw-Hill,
     1959.   pp. 133-56.
          Lively discussion of the subject of death and the im-
     portance given it in contemporary literature.

592 _____.   "No beginning and no end: Hemingway and death, "
     in Interpretations of American Literature, edited by C.
     Feidelson, and P. Brodtkorb.   N. Y. :   Oxford University
     Press, 1959.   pp. 320-31.

593 Hofmannsthal, H.   "Death and the fool, " in Masters of Modern
     Drama, edited by H. M. Block.   N. Y. :   Random, 1962.
     pp. 167-74.

594 Holbrook, D.   Human hope and the death instinct: an explora-
     tion of psychoanalytical theories of human nature and their
     implications for culture and education.   N. Y. :   Pergamon,
     1971.
          Examines the struggle to resolve what strategies
     teachers of English and literature should employ to dis-

cover values (identity) and personal growth within children.
Examples from literature are cited exploring the theme of
death and continuity.

595 Holmes, J. H. , and L. Browne-Olf. The Grail of life: an
anthology of heroic death and immortal life. N.Y.:
Dodd Mead, 1919.

596 Horne, A. Death of a generation: from Neuve Chapelle to
Verdun and the Somme. N.Y.: American Heritage, 1970.

597 Horowitz, L. "The Morality of suicide, " Journal of Critical
Analysis, 3 (Jan. 1972), 161-5.

598 Hotson, L. Death of Christopher Marlowe. N.Y.: Russell
and Russell, 1967.
Attempts to solve the mystery of exactly how and why
and when and where the dramatist, Christopher Marlowe,
was slain, by examining the long lost documents of eye
witnesses given within two days of the tragedy.

599 Howells, W. D. "Practical immortality on earth, " in Imaginary Interviews. N.Y.: Harper, 1910. pp. 194-203.

600 Howes, E. , ed. And a time to die. London: Routledge and
Kegan Paul, 1961.

601 Huber, J. R. "Chaucer's concept of death in 'The Canterbury
Tales', " Ph. D. dissertation, University of Pittsburgh,
1967.

602 Hume, D. "Of suicide, " in Hume's Ethical Writings, edited
by Alasdair MacIntyre. N.Y.: Collier Books, 1965.
pp. 305.

603 Hunsinger, G. Kierkegaard, Heidegger and the concept of
death. Stanford: Leland Stanford Junior University,
1968. (Stanford Honors Essays in Humanities Program,
no. 12.)

604 Hunt, L. "Deaths of little children, " in The English Familiar
Essay, edited by W. F. Bryan, and R. S. Crane. Boston: Ginn, 1916. pp. 290-94.

605 Huntz, B. The Pursuit of death: a study of Shelley's poetry.
N.Y.: Octogan, 1970.
Comprehensive study of Shelley's thought. The
chapters "Playing with Ghosts, " and "Necessity and
Death, " are insightful of the meaning of death.

606 Hurley, E. T. "Death and immortality: George Eliot's solution, " 19th Century Fiction, 24 (Sept. 1969), 222-7.

607 Hutman, N. L. "Inside the circle: on rereading 'Blood
       Wedding,'" Modern Drama, 16 (Dec. 1973), 329-36.

608 Huxley, A. L. "Variations on a Baroque Tomb: excerpt
       from 'Themes and Variations'," in Collected Essays.
       N. Y.: Harper, 1958. pp. 197-206.

609 Hynes, J. "Varieties of death wish: Evelyn Waugh's central
       theme," Criticism, 14 (winter 1972), 65-77.

610 Ingen, F. Vanitas und Momento Mori in der Deutschen
       Barocklyrik, door terdinandus Jacobus Van Ingen.
       Groningen: Wolters, 1966.

611 Ingham, M. B. "Some fifteenth-century images of death and
       their background." (Ph. D. dissertation. University of
       California, Riverside, 1967.)
             "... [A]nalyzes the macabre spirit in early memento
       mori literature of the 12th and 13th centuries and demon-
       strates Chaucer's use of commonplace themes and repre-
       sentations of death in his major poems...."

612 Jacobi, J. "A Phenomenological study of suicide notes,"
       Social Problems, 15 (1967), 60-72.
             Attempts to categorize suicide notes according to
       their formal aspects and interpret causes from them.

613 James, W. Human immortality. Boston: Houghton, 1900.

614 Jankelevitch, S. "La Mort et l'immortalité d'après les
       données de la biologie," Revue Philosophiques, 69 (1910),
       358-80.
             Explains immortality as arising out of the paradox of
       life/death which man attempts to resolve through belief
       in immortality.

615 Jankélévitch, V. La Mort. Paris: Flammarion, 1966.

616 Jankofsky, K. "A View into the grave: 'a disputacion
       betwyx the body and wormes' in British Museum MS Add.
       37049," TAIUS--Journal of Texas A and I University,
       7 (Oct. 1974), 137-59.
             Examines this poem's "dramatic confrontation of beauty
       and decay, and [links] the poem to specific visual repre-
       sentations of this conflict in 15th Century sepulchral
       monuments."

617 Jaspers, K. "Death," in Philosophy, translated by E. B.
       Ashton. Chicago: University of Chicago Press, 1970.
       pp. 193-201.

618 _____. "Death," in Philosophy for Everyman. N. Y.:
       Harcourt Brace and World, 1967. pp. 106-15.

619 Jerphagnon, L. "Le Thème de l'[Ipseitas Moritura] dans
     l'oeuvre de Vladimir Jankelevitch," Revue Philosophique
     de la France et de l'Etranger, 95 (July-Sept., 1970),
     287-99.

620 Johann, H. T. Trauer and Trost; eine quellen und struk-
     turanalytische Untersuchung der philosophischen Trost-
     shriften über den Tod. Munich: W. Fink, 1968.

621 Johnson, A. "The Right to live or the right to die," Nursing
     Times (London), 68 (1971), 575-77.
     Discusses the sophisticated apparatus for maintaining
     vital functions, and legalized euthanasia.

622 Johnson, W. G. "To die as a man: disease, truth and
     Christian ethics," Journal of the Iowa Medical Society,
     56 (Aug. 1966), 813-16.
     Discusses the Christian approach to the telling of
     patients about their impending death.

623 Jolivet, R. Le problème de la mort chez M. Heidegger et
     J. P. Sartre. Paris: Editions Fontenelle, 1950.

624 Jonas, H. "Immortality and the modern temper," Harvard
     Theological Review, 55 (Jan. 1962).
     Presents "the undeniable fact--namely--that the
     modern temper is uncongenial to the idea of immortality."

625 _____. Philosophical essays; from ancient creed to tech-
     nological man. N.J.: Prentice-Hall, 1974.

626 Jones, L. "Preface to a twenty volume suicide note," in
     Interpreting Literature, edited by K. Knickerbocker and
     H. Reninger. N.Y.: Holt, Rinehart and Winston, 1974.
     pp. 413.

627 Jones, W. T. Metaphysics of life and death. N.Y.: George
     H. Doran, 1924.

628 Joseph, G. "Idea of mortality in Tennyson's classical and
     Arthurian poems: honor comes with mystery," Modern
     Philology, 66 (Nov. 1968), 136-45.

629 Kaines, J. Last words of eminent persons. London and New
     York: George Routledge and Sons, 1966.

630 Kallen, H. M. "Philosophy aging and the aged," The Journal
     of Value Inquiry, 6 (winter 1972), 1-21.

631 Kammerer, P. Tod und Unsterblichkeit. Stuttgart: Moritz,
     1923.

632 Kaplan, A. Love ... and death: talks on contemporary and

perennial themes. Ann Arbor: University of Michigan Press, 1973.
Originally presented in eleven parts as the television series "The Worlds of Abraham Kaplan." In these themes he discovers the most important questions of traditional and contemporary human experience. His views reflect a deep concern for human dignity.

633 Kattsoff, L. "Immortality and religious discourse," Pacific Philosophy Forum, 3 (Dec. 1964), 79-84.

634 Kaufman, W. "Existentialism and death," in The Meaning of Death, edited by H. Feifel. N. Y.: McGraw-Hill, 1959. pp. 39-63.

635 Keener, F. M. Shades of Lucian: British dialogues of the dead in the eighteenth century. Ph. D. dissertation, Columbia University, 1965.

636 Keleman, S. Living your dying. N. Y.: Random, 1974. (Bookworks.)

637 Kelly, G. "The Duty of using artificial means to preserve life," Theological Studies, 11 (1950), 203-20.

638 Kenyon, J. B. "Death and night," in American Anthology, 1787-1900, edited by E. C. Stedman. Boston: Houghton, 1900. pp. 630.

639 Kepler, T., and D. Russel. And peace at last: a study of death the unreconciled subject of our times. Philadelphia: Westminster Press, 1953.

640 Kerenyi, K., et al. Mensch, Schiksal und Tod. Berlin: Ulrike Studer-Solzman; Munich: H. Huber, 1963.

641 Kierkegaard, S. "The Sickness unto death," in Fear and Trembling and the Sickness unto Death. N. Y.: Doubleday, 1959.
An analysis of despair as "the disconsolateness of not being able to die."

642 Kincaid, J. R. "Alice's invasion of wonderland," Publications of the Modern Language Association, 88 (Jan. 1973), 88-92.

643 Kinder, M. "Life and death in the cinema of outrage, or, the Bouffe and the Barf," Film Quarterly, 28 (winter 1974), 4-10.
Essentially the article presents reviews of "Sweet Movie" and "The Grande Bouffe." Both films were presented and well received at Berkeley and Venice in California.

644 Kirkmann, E. N. Death and the plowman. Chapel Hill: University of North Carolina Press, 1958.

645 Klein, P. "Are Straucon's persons immortal? A Reply," Philosophical Studies, 20 (Oct. 1969), 65-70.

646 Koch, F. Goethe's Stellung zu Tod und Unsterblichkeit. Weimar: Verlag der Goethe Gesellschaft, 1932.

647 Koenigsberg, R. A. "F. Scott Fitzgerald: literature and the work of mourning," American Imago, 24 (1967), 248-70.

648 Koestenbaum, P. The Vitality of death. N.Y.: Greenwood Pub. Co., 1971.
Perceptive insights into real and symbolic death. The existential view of death is greatly stressed and applied to various problems and situations.

649 Kohl, M. "Abortion and the argument from innocence," Inquiry, 14 (summer 1971), 147-51.
Author "feels that the question of whether a human fetus is a human being is to be answered in the negative."

650 Koller, K. "Art, rhetoric, and holy dying in the 'Faerie Queene' with special reference to the Despair Canto," Studies In Philology, 61 (April 1964), 128-39.

651 Kontoleōn, N. M. Aspects de la Grece preclassique. Paris: College de France, 1970.
Lectures given at the College de France in May 1967.

652 Kovacs, G. "Man and death: an existential phenomenological approach," Proceedings of the American Philosophical Association, 47 (1973), 183-90.

653 Kreyche, G. "The Soul-body problem in St. Thomas," The New Scholasticism, 46 (autumn 1972), 466-84.
Discussion of Aquinas' view of form in respect to immortality and resurrection.

654 Kroeber, T. "Shropshire revisited," Kroeber Anthropological Society Papers, 25 (1961), 1017.
Analysis of A. E. Housman's, "A Shropshire Lad," which is concerned with suicide and hanging as the favored deaths in Shropshire.

655 Kron, S. D. "Euthanasia: a physician's view," Journal of Religion and Health, 7 (1968), 333-41.
A physician discusses active and passive euthanasia. The author points out the difficulty of defining death and states that presently there is no legal definition of it in the U.S.

656 Kuhns, R. "Modernity and death," in Structures of Experi-
    ence: essays on the affinity between Philosophy and
    Literature. N. Y.: Basic Books, 1970. pp. 177-214.
    "... [B]ack in our time coerced lives, where the fu-
    ture threatens, we lose the value of death because we
    fear it. ... "

657 Kunshe, K. Die Legende der drei Lebenden und der drei
    Toten. Freiburg: Herder, 1908.

658 Kupfer, J. "What's so bad about death: Epicurus' catch, "
    A paper presented at a symposium, Philosophical Aspects
    of Thanatology. N. Y.: Columbia University, College of
    Physicians and Surgeons, May 1973.

659 Kurtz, B. P. Gifer the worm; an essay toward the history of
    an idea. Berkeley: University of California Press, 1929.

660 _____. The Pursuit of death: a study of Shelley's poetry.
    N. Y.: Oxford University Press, 1933.

661 Kurtz, D. C. , and J. Boardman. Greek burial customs.
    N. Y.: Cornell, 1971.
    Includes annotations and illustrations on how Greeks
    viewed death, and an account of burial rites and cere-
    monies.

662 Kurtz, L. P. The Dance of death and the macabre spirit in
    European literature. N. Y.: Columbia University, 1934.
    (Publications of the Institute of French Studies, Inc.).

663 Labarriere, P. J. "Le Concept de l'identité hégélien de la
    mort et de la vie, " Archives de Philosophie, 33 (July-
    Sept. , 1970), 579-604.

664 Labby, D. Life or death: ethics and options. Seattle: Uni-
    versity of Washington Press, 1968.

665 Laborit, H. , and P. Morand. Les Destins de la vie et de
    l'homme. Paris: Masson and Cie, 1959.

666 Lake, K. Immortality and the modern mind. Cambridge,
    Mass.: Harvard University Press, 1922.

667 Lamont, C. "The Affirmation of life," in Voice in the Wilder-
    ness; collected essays of fifty years. N. Y.: Prometheus,
    1974. pp. 99-100.

668 _____. "The Crisis called death, " in Coming of Age in
    Philosophy. San Francisco: Cawfield Press, 1973. pp.
    578-80.

669 _____. The Illusion of immortality, 2d ed. N. Y.: Philo-

sophical Library, 1950.

670 _____. Man answers death; an anthology of poetry with an introduction by Louis Untermeyer, 2d and enl. ed. N.Y.: Philosophical Library, 1952.

671 _____. "Mistaken attitudes toward death," Journal of Philosophy, 62 (Jan. 21, 1963), 29-36.

672 Lamont, R. "The Double apprenticeship: life and the process of dying," in The Phenomenon of Death; faces of immortality, edited by E. Wyschogrod. N.Y.: Harper and Row, 1973. pp. 198-224.
Essentially a description of Ionesco's works regarding the 'Double Apprenticeship'.... [M]ost of his metaphysical farces are based on the awareness of death in life.

673 Landor, W. S. "Death of Artemidora," in English Romantic Poetry and Prose, edited by R. Noyes. N.Y.: Oxford University Press, 1956. pp. 485.

674 _____. "Dying speech of an old philosopher," in Interpreting Literature, edited by K. Knickerbocker and H. Reninger. N.Y.: Holt, Rinehart and Winston, 1974. pp. 324.

675 Landsberg, P. L. Essai sur l'experiénce de la mort; Suivi du problème moral du suicide. Paris: Ed. Du Seuil, 1960.

676 _____. The Experience of death: the moral problem of suicide. N.Y.: Philosophical Library, 1953.

677 Larre, C. "La Vie et la mort dans Tchouang Tseu," Ethno Psychologie Revue de Psychologie des Peuples, 27 (March 1972), 59-78.
Tseu sees life as springing from death, and death written in life in a circular linking and a reflection of the one in the other.

678 Laurents, A. A Clearing in the woods. N.Y.: Dramatists Play Service, Inc., 1957.
A play which demonstrates deep insight into the psychotherapeutic program with emphasis on a search for self and meaning in life.

679 Le Clair, T. "Case of death: the fiction of J. P. Donleavy," Contemporary Literature, 12 (summer 1971), 329-44.

680 _____. "Onion eaters and the rhetoric of Donleavy's comedy," 20th Century Literature, 18 (July 1972), 167-74.

681 Ledantec, F. "Le Problème de la mort," Revue Philosophique, 81 (1916), 105-34.

682 _____. Le Problème de la mort et la conscience universelle. Paris: Ernest Flammarion, 1917.

683 Lee, J. Y. Death and beyond in the Eastern perspective; a study based on the Bardo Thodol and the I Ching, new ed. N. Y.: Gordon and Breach Science Pubs., 1974.

684 _____. "Death is birth and birth is death," Systematics, 9 (March 1972), 188-200.

685 Leeds, M. "Poems [on death]," Omega, 3 (Aug. 1972), 175-9.

686 Le Grand, M. "Annoyance of death," in Life's an Art. N. Y.: Holt, 1930. pp. 49-64.

687 Lehmann, C. Der Tod bei Heidegger und Jaspers. Heidelberg: Evangelischer Verlag, 1917.

688 Lehmann, J. "A Death in a hospital," in The Atlantic Book of British and American Poetry, edited by Edith Sitwell. Boston: Little, 1958. pp. 863.

689 LeJeune, J. "On the nature of man," American Journal of Human Genetics, 22 (March 1970), 121-8.

690 Leonardo da Vinci. "Of life and death," in From Confucius to Mencken, edited by F. H. Pritchard. Boston: Little, 1924. pp. 455-6.

691 Lepp, I. Death and its mysteries. N. Y.: Macmillan, 1968. A psychologist, psychotherapist, and a Catholic priest discuss perspectives on death.

692 Lessing, G. E. "How the ancients represented death," in Selected Prose Works, edited by E. Bell. London: 1879. pp. 175-226.

693 _____. Laokoon and how the ancients represented death. London: G. Bell and Sons, 1914. "This edition also includes the essay on how the ancients represented death; translated by H. Zimmern."

694 Lessing, J. De Mortis apud Veteres Figura. Bonnae: Typie F. Kruegeri, 1866.

695 Lesy, M. Wisconsin death trip. N. Y.: Pantheon, 1973. Portrays life in rural Wisconsin in the 1890's, of people fleeing to the cities to escape the forces crushing their lives. The author blends newspaper articles and photographs.

696 Leveton, A. "Time, death and the ego-chill, " Journal of
     Existentialism, 6 (1965), 69-80.
     Describes what can happen when an individual suddenly
     discovers his finiteness and that non-existence is possible.

697 Levin, D. N. "Horace's preoccupation with death, " Classical
     Journal, 63 (April 1968), 315-20.
     Reminds us that from death there are no exemptions.

698 Lewis, S. "Coptic representation of Thetis at the forge of
     Hephaistos, " American Journal of Archaeology, 77 (July
     1973), 309-18.

699 Light, J. "The Religion of death in 'A Farewell to Arms, '"
     Modern Fiction Studies, 7 (1961), 169-73.

700 Little, J. Home from far. Boston: Little, 1963.
     A family scarred by the death of a twin adopts two
     children. The remaining twin must adjust and accept the
     new family. Problems encountered are sensitively
     handled.

701 Loi, M. "La Vie et la mort en Chine contemporaine, " Ethno
     Psychologie, Revue de Psychologie des Peuples, 27 (Mars
     1972), 79-101.
     Analysis of Chinese philosophical and poetic attitudes
     toward death.

702 Long, C. C. "Cocteau's Orphée: from myth to drama and
     film, " Quarterly Journal of Speech, 51 (Oct. 1965), 311-
     25.

703 Long, T. A. "Capital punishment--cruel and unusual?"
     Ethics, 83 (April 1973), 214-23.

704 Lowell, R. "The Dead in Europe, " in Interpreting Literature,
     edited by K. Knickerbocker and H. Reninger. N.Y.:
     Holt, Rinehart and Winston, 1974. pp. 409.

705 Lucas, D. "The More you live the more you die, " Tablet,
     213 (Oct. 10, 1959), 362.

706 Lucas, E. V. "On epitaphs, " in Adventures and Enthusiasms.
     N.Y.: Doran, 1920. pp. 255-59.

707 Lukic, M. "Socrates and indifference toward death, " Southern
     Journal of Philosophy, 9 (winter 1971), 393-8.

708 McClanahan, J. H. "The Patient's right to die; moral and
     spiritual aspects of euthanasia, " Memphis Medical Journal,
     38 (Aug. 1963), 303-16.

709 McCullin, D. Is anyone taking any notice? A book of photo-

graphs and comments; with phrases drawn from the 1970
Novel lecture by Alexander Solzhenitsyn. Cambridge,
Mass.: MIT Press, 1973.
Essentially a journalistic, photographic, pictorial
work of death. The pictures show violence at a time
when man's inhumanity to man is at a cruel stage.

710 McCulloch, F. "Art of persuasion in Helmant's 'Vers de la
mort'," Studies in Philology, 69 (Jan. 1972), 38-54.

711 MacDougall, A. R. "Death of Christ," in Christ in Poetry,
edited by T. C. Clark, and H. D. Clark. N.Y.: Association Press, 1952.

712 McGehee, E., and W. Heider-Brand. Death penalty; a literary
and historical approach. Indianapolis: D. C. Heath, 1964.

713 McGreal, I. "The Impossibility of proving immortality,"
Pacific Philosophy Forum, 3 (Dec. 1964), 47-60.

714 McKay, C. "If we must die," in Interpreting Literature,
edited by K. Knickerbocker and H. Reninger. N.Y.:
Holt, Rinehart and Winston, 1974. pp. 380.

715 McKay, L. R. "The Problem of death in the Viennese school
as represented by Schnitzler, Rilke, and Hofmannsthal."
Ph.D. dissertation, Stanford University, 1939.
"The purpose of this thesis is an attempt to give an
interpretation of the attitudes toward death, and conse-
quently, of life, as expressed in the writings of Schnitzler, Hoffmannsthal, and Rilke, and as exemplified in the
characters of Vienna which they portray...."

716 MacKenna, R. W. Adventure of death. N.Y.: Putnam, 1917.
Contents: The fear of death; The painlessness of
death; Euthanasia: What life gains from death; Does
death end all?

717 McMahon, J. H. "Waiting for death," in Human Being; the
world of Jean-Paul Sartre. Chicago: University of Chicago Press, 1971. pp. 147-67.

718 MacMullen, K. V. "Death imagery in 'Antony and Cleopatra',"
Shakespeare Quarterly, 14 (autumn 1963), 399-410.

719 Macquarrie, J. "Death," in Existentialism. N.Y.: Penguin
Books, 1973. pp. 150-55.
Presents the relationship of death and finitude. Offers insights about Heidegger and Camus concerning death
as a possibility.

720 Madden, J. "An Analysis of the euphemisms of death and
dying," The Director, (Jan. 1966), 8.

721 Maeterlinck, M. Before the great silence. London: Allen
     and Unwin, 1935.
          The great playwright and naturalist looks back on his
     life and forward to death.

722 _____. Death, translated by Alexander Teizera de Mattos.
     N. Y.: Dodd, Mead, 1912.
          A serious attempt to destroy the fear of death. The
     author examines euthanasia, mercy killing, religious fears,
     and discusses aspects of survival.

723 _____. La Grande Porte. Paris: Fasquale, 1939.
          A work made up of aphorisms and dialogues illumi-
     nating some of the author's concerns such as the relation
     of man's soul to infinity, imagination, and memory.

724 _____. The Great beyond. N. Y.: Philosophical Library,
     1947.
          The volume includes fragments, paragraphs, and
     sketches with death, birth, and life as the main focus.
     Appended is a twenty page drama entitled "The Old Man
     Who Does Not Want to Die."

725 _____. Light beyond. N. Y.: Dodd, 1917.
          "A collection of essays by the translator taken from
     the author's three volumes entitled, Our Eternity, The
     Unknown Guest, and The Wrack of the Storm."

726 _____. Our eternity. London: Methuen, 1913.

727 Maeztu, R. La Brevedad de la vida en nuestra poesía,
     lírica. Madrid: Grafia Universal, 1935.

728 Maguire, D. "The Freedom to die," Commonweal, 96 (Aug.
     11, 1972), 423-7.
          Comments on the various dilemmas that medical
     ethics must solve.

729 Mahoney, E. P. "Agostino Nifo's early views on immortality,"
     Journal of the History of Philosophy, 8 (Oct. 1970), 451-
     9.

730 Male, E. Religious art from the twelfth to the eighteenth
     century. N. Y.: Farrar, Straus and Giroux, 1958.
          Work attempts to find sources in Medieval life for
     Medieval art. It was thought that through art, the un-
     educated could learn about the gospel and promise of im-
     mortality.

731 Malraux, A. La Condition humaine. Paris: Gallimard, 1933.
          A story set in China with the struggle between govern-
     ment troops and the communists. The author portrays the
     identical cruelty, cynicism, and even heroism on both

sides as they try to exterminate one another. Far more concerned with seeking their own deaths, the heroes know that ideas, not acts, must survive, and death will make people live.

732 Mangoldt, U. Der Tod als Antwort auf das Leben. Munich: O. W. Barth, 1957.

733 Manheim, L. F. "Thanatos: the death instinct in Dickens' later novels," in Hidden Patterns, edited by L. F. Manheim and E. B. Manheim. N.Y.: Macmillan, 1966. pp. 113-31.

734 Mann, T. Death in Venice. N.Y.: Knopf, 1960.

735 Marcuse, H. "The Ideology of death," in The Meaning of Death, edited by H. Feifel. N.Y.: McGraw-Hill, 1959. pp. 64-76.
    Author states that the "meaning of death is couched in philosophical systems as a natural phenomenon, or in religious language as the beginning of life."

736 Margolis, J. "Abortion," Ethics, 84 (Oct. 1973), 91-61.

737 _____. "Punishment," Social Theory and Practice, 2 (spring 1973), 347-63.

738 Marias, J. "The Horizon of last things: birth and death," in Reason and Life. London: Hollis and Carter, 1956. pp. 370-92.

739 Marino, R. M. "Death in the works of Ramón J. Sender." Ph.D. dissertation, St. Louis University, 1968.

740 Maritain, J. "The Immortality of man," in Man's Destiny in Eternity. Boston: Beacon, 1949.

741 Marks, E. Simone de Beauvoir--encounters with death. New Brunswick, N.J.: Rutgers University Press, 1973.
    Discusses the various kinds of death found in the writings of Simone de Beauvoir.

742 Marminia, A. L'Idée de la mort et de l'éternité. Paris: E. Maillet, 1865.
    Early volume dealing with the historical concepts of death focusing on philosophical aspects.

743 Marriott-Watson, H. B. "Some thoughts on pain and death," North American Review, 173 (1961), 540.

744 Marvin, F. R. "Death and afterwards," in Companionship of Books, and Other Papers. N.Y.: Putnam, 1905. pp. 207-15. (o.p.).

745 _____. The Last words of distinguished men and women. Troy, N.Y.: C. A. Brewster and Co., 1900. Elaborates on the dying quotations of famous men and women from ancient and modern times.

746 Marx, P. The Death peddlers; war on the unknown. Collegeville, Minn.: St. John's University Press, 1971.

747 Marzials, F. T. "Death as the fool," in A Victorian Anthology, 1837-1895. Boston: Houghton, 1895. pp. 493.

748 _____. "Death as the teacher of love-lore," in A Victorian Anthology, 1837-1895, by E. C. Stedman. Boston: Houghton, 1923. pp. 493.

749 Masalio, A. "A Living-dying life," Pacific Philosophy Forum, 3 (May 1965), 96-102.

750 Mathieu, V. "Rilke contro il concetto umanistico di salvezza della morte," Giornale Critico della Filosofia Italiana, 52 (April-June 1973), 204-12.

751 Mattieson, E. Das Personliche Uberleben des Todes; eine Darstellung der Erjahrungsbeweise. Berlin: de Gruyter, 1936.

752 Maurer, A. "On Bugenthal's critique of Koestenbaum's 'The Vitality of Death'," Journal of Existentialism, 6 (winter 1965-66), 223-4. Koestenbaum's idea is that man should become aware of death for its therapeutic effect.

753 Mead, M. "The Right to die," Nursing Outlook, 16 (1968), 20-1. Discusses the problem of being 'kept alive' beyond any hope of ever again being humanly related to the family, and the right to die.

754 Medearis, M. "Death of a country doctor," in Best American Short Stories. Boston: Houghton, 1942. pp. 174-200.

755 Mendelssohn, M. Phadon. Leipzig: P. Reclam jun., 1871.

756 "Mercy and Mr. Blanshard," Commonweal, 72 (Oct. 30, 1959), 1444. A Roman Catholic's negative response to an article by Mr. Blanshard favoring euthanasia.

757 Merleau-Ponty, M. Humanism and terror. Boston: Beacon, 1969.

758 Metzger, A. Freedom and death, translated by R. Manheim. London: Chaucer Pub. Co., 1972. (Human Context

Books.)
Contents: Introductory considerations of death;
Answer to death: The Counter Movement: On the history
of the concept of being, or of the permanent; Freedom
and death.

759 Meyer-Baer, K. Music of the spheres and the dance of death.
Princeton, N.J.: Princeton University Press, 1970.
Creatively traces music as being symbolic of death,
sin, and resurrection.

760 Michaux, H. "Death chant," in Mid-Century French Poets,
edited by W. Fowlie. Boston: Twayne, 1955. pp.
239.

761 Michel, P. "Last stanza of Emily Dickinson's 'One Dignity
Delays for All'," English Studies, 50 (Feb. 1969),
98-100.

762 Millard, C. K. "A Plea for the legalization of euthanasia," Public Health, 45 (Nov. 1931), 39-
47.

763 Millay, E. "Death devours all lovely things," in The Oxford
Book of American Verse, edited by F. O. Matthiessen.
N.Y.: Oxford University Press, 1950. pp. 886.

764 _____. "Elegy before death," in Anthology of American
Poetry, edited by C. Aiken. N.Y.: Random, 1944. pp.
394.

765 _____. "The Shroud," in The New Poetry, edited by H.
Monroe and A. C. Henderson. N.Y.: Macmillan, 1947.
pp. 387.

766 Miller, A. Death of a salesman ... text and criticism,
edited by G. Weales. N.Y.: Viking, 1967.

767 Miller, J. "At the grave of Walker," in Anthology of American Poetry, edited by C. Aiken. N.Y.: Random, 1944.
pp. 199.

768 Miller, P. "Provenience of the death symbolism in Van
Gogh's cornscapes," Psychoanalytic Review, 52 (1965),
60-6.

769 Milton, J. "On time," in Interpreting Literature, edited by
K. Knickerbocker and H. Reninger. N.Y.: Holt, Rinehart and Winston, 1974. pp. 328.

770 Miro, M. G. "Merciful or sinful?" Americas, 10 (April
1958), 37-8.

771 "Modified euthanasia," Time, 76 (July 4, 1960), 38.
     A Bishop's views on euthanasia are given. He sees
     no reason for prolonging life through extraordinary means.

772 Molina, E. Tragedia y realización del espíritu; del sentido de
     la muerte y del sentido de la vida, 2d ed. Santiago, Chile:
     Nascimento, 1953.

773 Mollo, S. "La Thème de la mort dans la littérature scholaire
     français contemporaine," Ethno Psychologie, Revue de
     Psychologie des Peuples, 27 (Mars 1972), 45-58.
     Study of the influence of literature upon the reactions
     of French children concerning death.

774 Montague, W. P. The Chances of surviving death. Cam-
     bridge, Mass.: Harvard University Press, 1934. (Inger-
     sall Lecture presented in 1932.)
     A philosophical discussion of the argument for sur-
     vival after death.

775 Montaigne, M. E. "Of judging of the death of others," in
     Complete Works. Stanford: Stanford University Press,
     1957.

776 _____. "That men are not to judge of our happiness till
     after death," in Century Readings in the English Essay,
     edited by L. Wann. N.Y.: Appleton-Century, 1926.
     pp. 62-4.

777 _____. "That to philosophize is to learn to die," in
     Complete Works. Stanford, Calif.: Stanford University
     Press, 1957. pp. 56-8.

778 Montandon, R. La Morte, cette inconnue. Paris: Victor
     Ahinger, 1948.

779 Montgomery, R. Here and hereafter. N.Y.: Fawcett, 1968.
     Reincarnation is discussed through the psychic experi-
     ences of noted Americans.

780 Mooney, S. "Assassination at Memphis," in Interpreting
     Literature, edited by K. Knickerbocker and R. Reninger.
     N.Y.: Holt, Rinehart and Winston, 1974. pp. 407.

781 Mooney, W. E. "Gustav Mahler: a note on life and death in
     music," Psychoanalytic Quarterly, 37 (1968), 80-102.

782 Moorand, P. L'Art de mourir, suivi du le suicide en littera-
     ture. Paris: Editions des Cahiers Libres, 1932.

783 Moore, C. H. Ancients' beliefs in immortality. N.Y.:
     Cooper Square Publ., 1963.
     Summary of Grecian and Roman beliefs in immortality.

Beginning with Homer, the author traces man's ever increasing interest with what follows death.

784   _____. Pagan ideas of immortality during the early Roman
       empire. Cambridge, Mass.: Harvard University Press,
       1918.
       A lecture concerning the beliefs in immortality by
       peoples of the Mediterranean world from the Greeks to
       the emergence of Christianity as a major religion.

785 Moore, E. C., et al. "Abortion: the new ruling, " Hastings
       Center Report, 3 (April 1973), 4-7.
       Describes the significant interpretation of personhood.
       Comments on the lack of consensus about the person in
       medicine and philosophy.

786 Moore, J. R.   Masks of love and death: Yeats as dramatist.
       N. Y.: Cornell, 1966.
       Significant in reviving Yeats' plays in performance.

787 Moore, M. "Death came to him so quickly, " in An Anthology
       of American Poetry, edited by A. Kreymborg. N. Y.:
       Tudor Publ. Co., 1941. pp. 531.

788   _____. "Death is the strongest of all living things, " in
       The New Poetry, edited by H. Monroe and A. C. Men-
       derson. N. Y.: Macmillan, 1947. pp. 416.

789 Moran, M. E.   The Consolations of death in ancient Greek
       literature. Washington, D. C.: National Capital Press,
       Inc., 1917.

790 More, S. T. "Four last things: death, " in Wisdom of
       Catholicism, edited by A. C. Pegis. N. Y.: Random,
       1955. pp. 496-518.

791 Morin, E. L'homme et la mort dans l'histoire.   Paris:
       Correa, 1951.

792 Morley, J.   Death, Heaven, and the Victorians.   London:
       Studio Vista, 1971.
       Deals with "how death was looked upon (and re-
       sponded to, and celebrated, and written about) during
       the 19th century. " A series of photographs on Victorian
       mourning supplement the text.

793 Morrison, K. D.   Death and dying in modern British drama.
       Cambridge, Mass.: Harvard University Press, 1966.

794 Moses, R. J. "The Theme of death in the plays of Edward
       Albee. " Ph. D. dissertation, University of Huston, 1974.
       "This study demonstrates that death permeates his
       plays, that Albee uses death as both fact and metaphor

and that death is the unifying theme in the thirteen
plays...."

795 Muggeridge, M. "Christmas diary." New Statesman, 78 (Dec.
     1969), 920.
         Discussion of death as a forbidden topic. The au-
     thor's attitude is that death makes life bearable.

796 "Murder or mercy?" Newsweek, 51 (Feb. 3, 1958), 56.
         Elaborates on the views of Dr. Charles F. Potter,
     founder of the Euthanasia Society of America.

797 Murphy, B. W. "Creation and destruction: notes on Dylan
     Thomas," British Journal of Medical Psychology, 41
     (1968), 150-67.

798 Murray, H. A. "Dead to the world: the passions of Herman
     Melville," in Essays in Self-Destruction, edited by E. S.
     Shneidman. N.Y.: Science House, 1967.

799 "My little girl is happy: case of Suzanne Vandeput," News-
     week, 69 (Nov. 19, 1962), 62.
         Discusses a euthanasia trial which took place in
     Liège, Belgium, where a mother killed her deformed
     baby.

800 Myers, F. W. H. Human personality and its survival of
     bodily death. N.Y.: Longmans Green, 1903.
         Attacks the problem of survival and the existence of
     a soul after physical death.

801 Myers, J. A., Jr. "Death in the suburbs," English Journal,
     52 (May 1963), 377-9.
         Description of the use made of Richard Wilbur's poem
     with junior and senior high school students.

802 Nagel, T. "Death," Nous, 4 (Feb. 1970), 73-80.

803 Natanson, M. "Death and situation," American Imago, 4
     (1959), 447-57.
         Discussion of Sartres' view of death.

804 _____. "The Dialectic of death and immortality," Pacific
     Philosophy Forum, 3 (Sept. 1964), 70-9.

805 _____. "Humanism and death," in Moral Problems in Con-
     temporary Society. New Jersey: Paul Kurtz, 1969. pp.
     285-89.

806 Nathan, H., et al. "Death and the physician in art,"
     Medizinsche Welt, 52 (Dec. 28, 1968), 2845-52.

807 Needleman, J. "Imagining absence non-existence and death:

a sketch, " Review of Existential Psychology and Psychiatry, 6 (1966), 230-36.
   Author states that "our view of the mortality of
another person depends on the way we understand life,
man, and the self. "

808/9 Nelson, B. "The Games of life and the dances of death, "
      in The Phenomenon of Death; faces of mortality, edited
      by E. Wyschogrod. N. Y.: Harper and Row, 1973.   pp.
      113-31.
         Describes in essay form countless illustrations of the
      relationships between the games of life and the dances of
      death found in novels, films, art, and plays. The games
      of life turn out to be dances of death. "Appended to the
      article are some forty-three references which illustrate
      'games of life, and dances of death'. "

810 Nes, C. Over Dood en Leven. The Hague: Van Stockum,
    1958.

811 Newman, J. "The Motivation of Martyrs: a philosophical
    perspective. " The Thomist, 35 (Oct. 1971), 581-600.

812 Nilsen, A. P. "Death and dying: facts, fiction, folklore, "
    English Journal, 62 (Nov. 1973), 1187-9.

813 Nohl, J. The Black death. N. Y.: Ballantine Books, 1961.
    The plague, its precursors and the limited means of
    combating it.

814 Noyes, R. , Jr. "Montaigne on death, " Omega, 1 (Nov. 1970),
    311-23.

815 Nussbaum, M. C. "Psyche in Heraclitus, II, " Phronesis, 17
    (1972), 1-16.
       Discussion of the fragments of Heraclitus that are
    about human life and death.

816 Oates, J. C. "Love and death, " in Archetypal Themes in the
    Modern Story, edited by Jack Matthews. N. Y.: St. Mar-
    tins Press, 1973. pp. 35-50.

817 Ochs, P. "Crucification, " in Interpreting Literature, edited
    by K. Knickerbocker and H. Reninger. N. Y.: Holt,
    Rinehart and Winston, 1974. pp. 266.

818 O'Connor, M. C. The Art of dying well. N. Y.: Columbia
    University Press, 1942.
       A discussion of the many versions of the Ars moriendi.
    In the Middle Ages this was a document which told how
    one might die well. Also considered in the book are
    many literary questions.

819 Olds, C. C. "Ars moriendi: a study of the form and content of fifteenth century illustrations of the art of dying." Ph. D. dissertation, University of Pennsylvania, 1966.
Attempts to "interpret the often enigmatic imagery of these illustrations, to determine the date and provenance of the original series, and to trace the development of the theme in the various illustrated editions ... published between 1425 and 1525...."

820 Ollesch, H., ed. Der letzte Weg. Witten: Verlag, 1955.

821 Olney, J. "Experience, metaphor and meaning: the death of Ivan Ilych," Journal of Aesthetics and Art Criticism, 31 (fall 1972), 101-13.
Discusses "Tolstoy's unique experience of feeling himself always in death...."

822 O'Mahony, B. E. "Martin Heidegger's existential of death," Philosophical Studies, 18 (1969), 58-75.

823 Oppenheim, J. "Death," in The World's Greatest Religious Poetry, edited by C. M. Hill. N.Y.: Macmillan, 1934. pp. 685.

824 Ormea, F. "Marxisten Angesichts des Todes," Internationale Dialog Zeitschrift, 3 (1970), 98-114.

825 Orwell, G. "How the poor die," in Shooting an Elephant. London: Secker and Warburg, 1950. pp. 18-32.

826 O'Sheel, P. "Hippocrates perplexed," Humanitas, 4 (Dec. 1974), 3-8.
Relates the work-in-progress in medical schools where support is provided by the National Endowment for the Humanities. The article includes a list of Humanities seminars for physicians and other members of the health care professions.

827 Pachmuss, T. "Themes of love and death in Tolstoy's 'The Death of Ivan Ilvich'," American Slavic and East European Review, 20 (Feb. 1961), 72-83.

828 Paget, S. "Wonder of death," in I Wonder. N.Y.: Macmillan, 1911. pp. 70-84.

829 Pain, P. Daily meditations; reproduced from the original edition of 1668 in the Huntington Library; with an introduction by Leon Howard. San Marino, Calif.: Henry E. Huntington Library and Art Gallery, 1936.

830 Parrinder, G. The Indestructible soul. The nature of man and life after death in Indian thought. N.Y.: Harper and Row, 1973.

831 Parvillez, A. Joy in the face of death. N. Y.: Desclee,
     1963.

832 Paskow, A. "The Meaning of my own death, " International
     Philosophical Quarterly, XIV (March 1974), 51-69.

833 Paton, L. B. Spiritism and the cult of the dead in antiquity.
     N. Y.: Macmillan, 1921.

834 Paz, O. "The Day of the death, " in Labyrinth of Solitude:
     life and thought in Mexico, translated by S. Kemp. N. Y.:
     Grove Press, 1961. pp. 47-64.
     A Mexican poet writes nine essays on his country's
     character, culture, and the meaning of death.

835 _____. The Labyrinth of solitude. N. Y.: Grove Press,
     1962.
     "... [T]ell me how you die and I will tell you who
     you are. "

836 Pecheux, M. C. "Aspects of the treatment of death in Middle
     English poetry. " Ph. D. dissertation, Catholic University
     of America, 1951.
     "The present study was undertaken in order to demon-
     strate that, contrary to the opinions of many scholars,
     there was in Middle English poetry a pronounced trend to-
     ward an emphasis on peace and hope in the face of
     death.... "

837 Pellew, G. "Death, " in An American Anthology, 1787-1900,
     edited by E. C. Stedman. Boston: Houghton, 1900. pp.
     649.

838 Perloff, M. "Death by water: the Winslow elegies of Robert
     Lowell, " ELH, 34 (March 1967), 116-40.

839 Perry, R. B. The Hope for immortality. N. Y.: Vanguard,
     1945.
     Man's desire for future life is discussed along with
     the importance of hope in relation to death.

840 Peterson, J. Das Todes problem bei Rilke. Wurzburg:
     Triltson, 1935.

841 Pfannmüller, D. G. Tod, Jenseits und unsterbdichkeit in der
     Religion, Literatur und Philosophie der Griechen und
     Römer. Basel: Ernst Reinhardt, 1953.

842 Phillips, C. "Death in art, " in Emotion in Art. Boston:
     Houghton, 1925. pp. 165-74.

843 Phillips, D. Z. Death and immortality. London: St. Mar-
     tin's, 1970.

844   Phipps, J. Death's single privacy, grieving and personal
      growth. N.Y.: Seabury, 1974.
            A personal narrative concerning grief and bereave-
      ment.

845   Pieper, J. "Death and immortality," Philosophy Today, 6
      (1962), 34-43.

846   Pirlot, J. "La Mort et la liberté," Revue Philosophique de
      Louvain, 56 (Nov. 1958), 573-85.

847   Plath, S. "Suicide off egg rock," in Interpreting Literature,
      edited by K. Knickerbocker and H. Reninger. N.Y.:
      Holt, Rinehart and Winston, 1974. pp. 412.

848   Plato. "Last days of Socrates," in Points of Departure,
      edited by Arthur J. Carr, and William R. Steinhoff.
      N.Y.: Harper, 1960. pp. 548-67.

849   "Playing God," America, 107 (Nov. 24, 1962), 1118.
            Discussion of the acquittal of five persons involved
      in the "mercy killing" of a deformed baby girl.

850   Plessner, H. "On the relation of time to death," in Man and
      Time. (Papers from the Eranos Yearbooks, Bollingen
      Series) XXX-3. N.Y.: Pantheon, 1957. pp. 233-63.

851   Pohl, F. "Intimations of immortality," Playboy, (June 1964),
      79-80.

852   Pole, N. "To respect human life," Philosophy in Context, 2
      (1973), 16-22.

853   Pomeroy, R. "Contingency and the intended self," Pacific
      Philosophy Forum, 3 (Sept. 1964), 46-56.

854   Pool, P., comp. ... [P]oems of death; verses chosen by P.
      Pool, with original lithographs by M. Ayrton. London:
      F. Muller Ltd., 1945.

855   Pound, L. "American euphemisms for dying, death and
      burial," American Speech, 11 (1936), 195-202.
            Sources include newspapers, books, pamphlets, and
      monographs.

856   Prichard, H. If they don't come back: some thoughts on im-
      mortality. N.Y.: Macmillan, 1943.
            An essay on immortality originally designed to com-
      fort a friend whose daughter had been killed while on war
      service.

857   Pristin, T. "Auschwitz symposium to communicate the tale,"
      Village Voice, (June 20, 1974), 5-6.

A lively discussion about Elie Weisel's reminder of
the world's indifference to the plight of the Jews. Describes Auschwitz and modern anti-semitism.

858 Pritcher, J. L. A History of capital punishment. N. J.:
     Citadel, 1960.

859 Pruitt, V. D. Yeats, old age and death: the dynamic of the
     mask. Ph. D. dissertation, University of Virginia, 1974.
     "... [T]o justify the hope that death shall not be
     master, and that the imagination and the spirit shall ul-
     timately prevail" (Abstract).

860 Purtill, R. L. "Disembodied survival," Sophia, 12 (July
     1973), 1-10.

861 "Quality of mercy: mongoloid son," Time, 76 (July 11, 1960),
     64.
     Significant article which discusses the mercy killing
     of an infant mongoloid son by the father and the legal im-
     plications which resulted.

862 Quell, G. Die Affassung des Todes in Israel. Leipzig: R.
     Diechert, 1925.

863 Raisor, P. "Matthew Arnold's Balder dead; an exercise in
     objectivity," Studies in English Literature, 13 (autumn
     1973), 653-69.

864 Raleigh, W. "Sir Walter Raleigh bids farewell to his wife a
     few hours before he expects to be executed," in A
     Treasury of the World's Great Letters, by M. Lincoln
     Schuster. N. Y.: Simon and Schuster, 1940. pp. 81-5.
     Raleigh was sent to the Tower of London in 1603
     under James I. The introduction to this letter contains
     his famous apostrophe to death as well as his History of
     the World.

865 Ramfos, S. "Heraclite: Le Circle de la Mort," Philosophia,
     1 (1971), 176-94.

866 Ramsey, P. "Abortion: a review article," The Thomist,
     372 (Jan. 1973), 174-226.
     A review of Robert Morison's article Death: Process
     or Event in which Ramsey attempts to refute his pro abor-
     tion views and brings together arguments in favor of life
     over death.

867 Randall, D. "To the mercy killers," in Interpreting Litera-
     ture, edited by K. Knickerbocker and H. Reninger. N. Y.:
     Holt, Rinehart and Winston, 1974. pp. 402.

868 Rankin, H. D. "Socrates' approach to thanatos," American

Imago, 21 (fall 1964), 111-26.

869   Rehm, W. Orpheus, der Dichter und die Toten: Selbstdeutung
      und Totenkult bei Novalis-Hölderlin-Rilke. Düsseldorf:
      L. Schwann Verlag, 1950.

870   Reisner, G. A. The Egyptian conception of immortality.
      Boston: Houghton, 1912.
          A lecture which includes various mutations in the
      Egyptian's idea of his soul as indicated by burial rites
      and types of furniture.

871   Reno, R. H. "Hamlet's quintessence of dust, " Shakespeare
      Quarterly, 12 (spring 1961), 107-13.

872   Rewak, W. J. "James Agee's 'The Morning Watch': Through
      Darkness to Light, " Texas Quarterly, 16 (autumn 1973),
      21-37.

873   Rice, H. S. Life is forever. Old Tappan, N. J.: Revell,
      1974.
          A volume of American Christian poetry dealing with
      various points of view.

874   Richards, A. B. Death and the Magdalen. The memory of
      sale, the idle scholar's lament, and other poems. Lon-
      don: W. Pickering, 1846.

875   Richards, S. "Marlowe's Tamburlaine II: a drama of death, "
      Modern Language Quarterly, 26 (Sept. 1965), 375-87.

876   Richmond, V. Laments for the dead in Medieval narrative.
      Pittsburgh: Duquesne University Press, 1966.
          Offers insights about human nature and behavior re-
      garding death. Points out how death was used to develop
      emotions of individuals.

877   Riva, R. T. "Death and immortality in the works of Marcel
      Proust, " French Review, 35 (April 1962), 463-71.

878   Rivers, E. L. "Fenix's sonnet in Calderone's 'Principe
      Constante', " Hispanic Review, 37 (Oct. 1969), 452-8.

879   Roberts, L. E. "Conrad's tragic vision: a study of four rep-
      resentative novels. " Ph. D. dissertation, University of
      Massachusetts, 1968.
          "The purpose of this study is to illustrate the origins,
      nature, and complexity of the tragic sense of life which
      permeates the writing of Joseph Conrad.... "

880   Roberts, W. A Bibliography of D. H. Lawrence. London:
      Rupert Hart-Davis, 1962.
          See appropriate sections, especially: Dead Mother;

Dead Pictures on the Wall; Death of Our Era; Death Is Not Evil.

881 Robinson, E. A. "For a dead lady," in Anthology of American Poetry, edited by C. Aiken, N. Y.: Random, 1944. pp. 248.

882 Robinson, T. M. "Soul and immortality in 'Republic', X." Phronesis, 12 (1967), 147-51.

883 Robison, R. "Time death and the river in Dickens' novels," English Studies, 53 (Oct. 1972), 436-54.

884 Rodrígues, U. T. O tema da morte. Lisbon: Gronos, 1966.

885 Rodríguez, L. A. Las grandes muertes de la historia. México: Editorial Polis, 1938.

886 Roesler, M. C. "The Sea and death in Walt Whitman's Leaves of Grass." Ph. D. dissertation, Catholic University of America, 1963.
"Although the sea is only one of the many symbols Whitman employs in Leaves of Grass to present death, it is a major one, used frequently in poems, where death references occur...."

887 Rohde, E. Psique; la idea del alma y alma y la immortalidad entre los Griegos. México: Fondo de Cultura Economica, 1948.

888 Rollins, A., and A. Wellington. "Death of Azron," in An American Anthology, 1787-1900, edited by E. C. Stedman. Boston: Houghton, 1900. pp. 499.

889 Rosenfeld, A. The Second genesis: the coming control of life. N. J.: Prentice-Hall, 1969.
"... [E]xamines the philosophical, moral, and ethical questions.... [T]he term death takes on new meaning when parts of a dead person function perfectly in another living being" (Library Journal).

890 Rostand, J. Deux Angoisses: la mort, l'amour. Paris: Charpentier, 1924.

891 Routh, H. V. "This world's ideas of the next," in English Association, London. Essays and studies by members of the association. N. Y.: Oxford, 1933. v. 11. pp. 117-44.

892 Saint John-Stevas, N. The Right to life. N. Y.: Holt, Rinehart and Winston, 1964.
The principle of the sanctity of life is applied to the problems of abortion, euthanasia, capital punishment, sui-

cide, and killing in wartime.

893 Salinas, P. "Lorca and the poetry of death," in Tulane
Drama Review. Theatre in the twentieth century; edited
by Robert Willoughby Corrigan. N.Y.: Grove, 1963.
pp. 273-81.

894 Sánchez-Camargo, M. La Muerte y la Pintura Española.
Madrid: Editora Nacional, 1954.

895 Sanders, T. E., and W. W. Peek. Literature of the Ameri-
can Indian. New York: Glencoe Press, 1973.
See especially Chapter 3, "The Soul of the Indian:
Pre-Columbian Poetry."

896 Santayana, G. "Death bed manners," in Soliloquies in England,
and later soliloquies. N.Y.: Scribner's, 1922. pp. 90-
2.

897 _____. "Long way round to Nirvana; excerpt from 'Some
Turns of Thought in Modern Philosophy'," in Philosophy
of Santayana. N.Y.: Scribner's, 1953. pp. 563-71.

898 Sardello, R. J. "Death and the imagination," Humanitas, 10
(Feb. 1974), 61-73.
Each person should form his image regarding the
major point of life and death thereby giving meaning to his
life. The function of vulnerability and hope explained and
related to the concept of the meaning of death in life.

899 Sartre, J. P. El Ser y la nada. Buenos Aires: Ibere-
Americana, 1948.

900 Saugnicux, J., comp. Les danses macabres de France et
d'Espagne et leurs prolongements littéraires. Lyon: E.
Vitte, 1972.

901 Schaerer, R. "La Philosophie moderne devant la mort," in
L'Homme face à la mort. Neuchâtel: Delachaux and
Nestle, 1952.

902 Schalk, A. "The Power of positive dying," U. S. Catholic,
38 (Sept. 1973), 32-6.

903 Schaub, K. Albert Camus und der Tod. Zürich: EVZ-Verlag,
Abt: Editio Academica, 1968.

904 Scheler, M. F. Mort et survie, suivi de le phénomène du
tragique. Paris: Aubier, 1952. (Philosophie de
l'esprit.)

905 Scherer, G. Der Tod als Frage an die Freiheit. Essen:

Fredebeul und Koenen, 1971.

906 Schiff, A. F. "Euthanasia yes, but kind," Medical Economics, 47 (May 25, 1970), 259.
Points out the changing attitudes about euthanasia, and states that man will reverse his present ethical code in keeping people alive at all costs.

907 Schlueter, W. Warum denn Sterben? Leipzig: Excelsior Verlag, 1911.

908 Schlunk, R. R. "Note on Horace 2.14: eheu fugaces postume," Classical Journal, 68 (Feb. 1973), 274-5.

909 Schmalenberg, E. Das Todesverständnis bei Simone de Beauvoir; eine theologische Untersuchung. Berlin: De Gruyter, 1972.

910 Schnaufer, A. Frühgriechischer Totenglaube; Untersuchungen zum Totenglauben der mykenischen und homerischen Zeit. Hildesheim: Olms, 1970.

911 Schneider, C. I. Das Todesproblem bei Hermann Hesse. Marburg: N. G. Elwert, 1973.
Based on the author's thesis, University of California, 1968.

912 Schopenhauer, A. "On death and its relation to the indestructability of our true nature," in Philosophy of Schopenhauer, by B. Bay and B. Saunders. N. Y.: Tudor, 1936. pp. 304-17.
Deals with the interrelation between nature and death.

913 _____. "On the doctrine of the indestructibility of our true nature by death," in The Wisdom of Life, and Other Essays, by A. Schopenhauer, translated by B. Saunders and E. B. Bax. Washington, D. C.: M. W. Dunne, 1901.

914 _____. "On suicide," in Philosophy of Schopenhauer, by B. Bay and B. Saunders. N. Y.: Tudor, 1936. pp. 318-22.

915 Schwebel, O. Der Tod in Deutscher Sage und Dichtung. Berlin: Weile, 1876.

916 Sciacca, M. F. Morte ed immortalita. Milan: Marzorati, 1959.

917 Scott, N. A., Jr. Modern vision of death. Atlanta: John Knox, 1967.

918 Scott, R. F. "Captain Robert Falcon Scott tells the British public that 'These Rough Notes and Our Dead Bodies

Must Tell the Tale'," in A Treasury of the World's Great
Letters, by M. L. Schuster. N.Y.: Simon and Schuster,
1940. pp. 456-60.
"... I do not regret this journey, which has shown
that Englishmen can endure hardships, help one another,
and meet death with as great a fortitude as ever in the
past...."

919 Scullard, H. H., ed. Death and burial in the Roman world.
N.Y.: Cornell University Press, 1971.

920 Segerberg, O., Jr. The Immortality factor. N.Y.: Dutton,
1974.
Traces the way man has looked at death and immortality throughout history. The author deals with the
science of senescence and the ecology of immortality.

921 Seth, P., and A. Pattison. The Idea of immortality. N.Y.:
Oxford University Press, 1922.

922 Shapiro, A. K. "A Contribution to a history of the placebo
effect," Behavioral Science, 5 (1960), 109-35.

923 Shaw, W. D. "Tennyson's Tithonus and the problem of
mortality," Philological Quarterly, 52 (April 1973), 274-
85.

924 Shearing, J. The Angel of the assassination. London: William Heinemann, 1935.
True story of Charlotte de Corday, the daughter of
executed Royalists, who assassinated the French revolutionary and head of the Paris mob.

925 Shenkin, A. "Attitude of old people to death," Achievements
in Geriatrics, edited by W. Anderson and B. Isaacs.
London: Cassell, 1964.

926 Shepard, N. W. "This I believe--about questioning the right
to die," Nursing Outlook, 16 (Oct. 1968), 22-5.
Suggests that professionals should have a well-defined
personal philosophy regarding death and dying and that
there should be freedom to die.

927 Sherlock, W. A Practical discourse concerning death. London: R. Chisell, 1868.

928 Sherwin, B. L. "Jewish views on euthanasia," The Humanist,
(July-Aug., 1974), 19-21.

928a Shneidman, E. S., ed. "Death as a motive in philosophic
thought," in Essays in Self-Destruction. N.Y.: Science
House, 1967. pp. 59-77.

929 Shute, N. On the beach. N.Y.: Morrow, 1957.
Novel that describes the last moments of the survivors of the atomic blast. It points out the reactions
of the various characters approaching their impending
deaths.

930 Simmel, G. Zur Metaphysik des Todes. Tübingen: Logos,
1910.

931 Sjogren, C. O. "Isolation and death in Stifter's Nachsommer, "
Publications of the Modern Language Association, 80
(June 1965), 254-8.

932 Slochower, H. "Eros and the trauma of death, " American
Imago, 21 (fall 1964), 11-22.
Concepts of death are discussed in contemporary
philosophy, literature, art, and psychology.

933 Smith, S. M. "This great solemnity: a study of the presentation of death in 'Antony and Cleopatra', " English Studies,
45 (April 1964), 163-76.

934 Smith, W. D. "Romeo's final dream, " Modern Language Review, 62 (Oct. 1967), 579-83.

935 Snell, D. "How it feels to die, " Life, (May 26, 1967), 38.
Description of how the author came very close to
death from an allergic reaction.

936 Sobosan, J. G. "Passion and faith; a study of Unamuno, "
Religious Studies, 10 (June 1974), 141-52.

937 Socrates. "On being sentenced to death, " in Classics in
Philosophy and Ethics. N.Y.: Philosophical Library,
1960. pp. 235-40.

938 Soderblom, N. Death and resurrection of Christ: reflections
on the passion. Minneapolis: Augsburg, 1968.

939 Sontag, S. Death kit. N.Y.: New American Library, 1967.

940 Sosnowski, S. "La intuición de la muerte en Las armas
secretas de Julio Cortazar, " Hispania, 52 (Dec. 1969),
846-51.

941 Spanos, W. V. "Charles William's seed of Adam: the
existential flight from death, " Christian Scholar, 40
(summer 1966), 105-18.

942 Spencer, T. Death and the Elizabethan drama. N.Y.:
Pageant Books, 1960.
Attempts to defend and evaluate attitudes toward
death and how they affected Elizabethan drama. The

medieval background, 16th-century conflict, language, ideas, dramatic technique, and the Renaissance mind are all considered in this study.

943 Spengler, O. The Decline of the West. N. Y.: Knopf, 1926.

944 Spirito, U. "La metafisica dell'Io e il problema della morte, " Giornale Critico della Filosofia Italiana, 52 (April-June 1973), 233-40.

945 Spratt, S. E. The English debate on suicide. LaSalle, Ill.: Open Court Press, 1961.

946 Sprigge, T. L. "Ideal immortality, " Southern Journal of Philosophy, 10 (summer 1972), 219-36.
     Time, truth, and eternity are examined in George Santayana's philosophy.

947 Stace, W. T. "Survival after death, " in Man Against Darkness and Other Essays. Pittsburgh: University of Pittsburgh Press, 1967. pp. 53-64.
     Examines "what the different cultures and world religions have to tell us about the nature of the life hereafter and the quality of immortality.... "

948 Stammler, W. Der Totentanz. Munich: Hanser, 1948.

949 Stannard, D. E. "Death and dying in Puritan New England, " American Historical Review, 78 (Dec. 1973), 1305-50.

950 _____. "Death and the Puritan child, " American Quarterly, 26 (Dec. 1974), 456-76.

951 Stark, L. R. "Origin of the Penitente death cart, " Journal of American Folklore, 84 (July 1971), 304-10.

952 Starobinski, J. "Montaigne et la dénonciation du Mensonge, " Dialectics, 22 (1968), 120-31.
     Discusses Montaigne's use of the Stoic tradition regarding death.

953 Starzyk, L. J. "Coming universal wish not to live in Hardy's modern novels, " 19th Century Fiction, 26 (March 1972), 419-35.

954 Steele, R. "Death, the film, and the future, " Motive, 24 (Jan.-Feb. 1964), 40-3.
     The Grapes of Wrath, Camille, and All Quiet on the Western Front are discussed with death as the dominant theme.

955 Steiner, G. "Dying is an art, " in The Art of Sylvia Plath. Bloomington: Indiana University Press, 1970. pp. 211-18.

Sylvia Plath's poetry and its relation to Wallace
Stevens and Emily Dickinson are discussed.

956 Sternberger, D. Der verstandene Tod: Eine Untersuchung
     Zu M. Heideggers Existential Ontologie. Leipzig:
     Hirzel, 1934.

957 Stevens, W. "Peter Quince at the Clavier," in Interpreting
     Literature, edited by K. Knickerbocker, and H. Reninger.
     N.Y.: Holt, Rinehart and Winston, 1974. pp. 372.

958 _____. "Sunday morning," in Interpreting Literature,
     edited by K. Knickerbocker and H. Reninger. N.Y.:
     Holt, Rinehart and Winston, 1974. pp. 370.

959 Stoehr, A. Gedonken über Weltdauer und Unsterblichkeit.
     Vienna: Deuticke, 1894.

960 Strem, G. G. "Death and the will to redeem: the theatre
     of Ugo Betti," Texas Quarterly, 9 (summer 1966), 112-
     21.

961 Stroker, E. "Der Tod im Denken," Man and World, 1 (May
     1968), 191-207.

962 Studer-Salzmann, U., ed. Mensch, Schicksal und Tod. Bern:
     Huber, 1963.

963 Sullivan, M. T. "The Dying person--his plight and his
     right," New England Law Review, 8 (spring 1973),
     197-216.

964 Sulzberger, C. My brother death. N.Y.: Harper, 1961.
     Contains a series of meditations on death assembled
     from materials throughout history creating a running and
     sometimes poetic commentary on dying and facing death.

965 Sumner, F. B. "A Biologist reflects upon old age and
     death," Scientific Monthly, 61 (1945), 14.

966 Szasz, T. S. "Ethics of suicide," Antioch, 74 (spring 1971),
     32-6.
     Discusses the fundamental concepts that are combined
     and confused in most discussions of suicide.

967 Tabachnick, S. E. "Great circle voyage of Conrad Aiken's
     Mr. Arcularis," American Literature, 45 (Jan. 1974),
     590-607.

968 Tate, A. "Ode to the Confederate dead," in Anthology of
     American Poetry, edited by C. Aiken. N.Y.: Random,
     1944. pp. 437.

969 Taylor, J. A. "Death as escape in Fritz von Unguh's 'Ein Geschlecht', " German Review, 44 (March 1969), 110-20.

970 Teichmuller, G. Uber die Unsterblichkeit der Seele. Leipzig: Duncker und Humblat, 1874.

971 Tenenti, A. Il senso della morte e l'amore della vitannel rinascimento. Turin: G. Einaudi, 1957.

972 _____. "Proiezioni di sopravvivenza nell età dell umanesimo (XV-XVI), " Giornale Critico della Filosofia Italiana, 52 (April-June 1973), 190-203.

973 _____. La Vie et la mort à travers l'art du siècle, avant-propos de Félix Lecoy. Paris: Colin, 1952.

974 Tennyson, A. L. "Break, break, break, " in Interpreting Literature, edited by K. Knickerbocker and H. Reninger. N.Y.: Holt, Rinehart and Winston, 1974. pp. 342.

975 "Thalidomide homicide, " Time, 30 (Nov. 16, 1962), 67.
Description of an actual case of mercy killing in Belgium where a mother and sister killed a thalidomide-deformed baby.

976 Theocritus. "The Death of Daphnis, " in The World's Best Poems, edited by Mark Van Doren, and G. M. Lapolla. N.Y.: World, 1946. pp. 108-13.

977 Thomas, D. "Do not go gentle into that good night, " in Interpreting Literature, edited by K. Knickerbocker and H. Reninger. N.Y.: Holt, Rinehart and Winston, 1974. pp. 404.

978 Thompson, E. J. Sutee: a historical and philosophical enquiry into the Hindu rite of widow burning. London: Allen and Unwin, 1928.

979 Thompson, W. H. Life, death and immortality. N.Y.: Funk, 1911.
Life and personality are related. Argues against the sufficiency of evolution to explain either life or personality, and points out the significance of immortality.

980 Thompson, W. M. Der Tod in der Englischen Lyrik des Siebzehnten Jahrhunderts. Breslau: Priebatsch, 1935.

981 Thomson, J. J. "A Defense of abortion, " Philosophy and Public Affairs, 1 (fall 1971), 47-66.

982 _____. "Rights and deaths, " Philosophy and Public Affairs, 2 (winter 1973), 146-51.

983 Tindall, G. Dances of death; short stories on a theme. London: Hodder and Stoughton, 1973.

984 Tindall, W. Y. A Reader's guide to Dylan Thomas. N. Y.: Octagon, 1973.

985 "Today I killed my best friend: Dorothy Butts shoots Mary Happer, " Time, 85 (April 23, 1965), 744.
     Description of the famous mercy killing case and the responses of various religious leaders to it.

986 Tolstoy, L. The Death of Ivan Ilych. London: Oxford University Press, 1960.

987 _____. "Three deaths, " in Interpreting Literature, edited by K. Knickerbocker and H. Reninger. N. Y.: Holt, Rinehart and Winston, 1974. pp. 137.

988 Tooley, M. "Abortion and infanticide, " Philosophy and Public Affairs, 2 (fall 1972), 37-65.

989 Tormey, J. "Teaching about death, " Religion Teacher's Journal, 7 (March 1973), 7-9.

990 Toynbee, A. Death and burial in the Roman world. N. Y.: Cornell University Press, 1970.
     Sets the stage with a look at Etruscan customs, then summarizes the beliefs of the Romans about life after death. Other topics treated include funerary gardens, gravestones, and tomb furniture.

991 _____. "The Relation between life and death, living and dying, " in Man's Concern with Death, edited by A. Toynbee, et al. N. Y.: McGraw-Hill, 1968. pp. 271.

992 Tremain, R. "Black death, " British History Illus. , 1 (Dec. 1974), 2-11.
     Historical analysis of mass death and the impact of the bubonic plague on the population.

993 Truscott, L. "Down the coast highway--tribute to a dying man, " Village Voice, (July 25, 1954), 5-8.
     Reflections about a grandfather, who is dying; discusses how he refused power and did not enter the "rat-race" of human existence as a young man.

994 Turgenev, I. "The Sparrow, " in Death: a book of preparation and consolation, compiled by B. Ulanov. N. Y.: Sheed and Ward, 1959. pp. 107-8.

995 Unamuno y Jugo, M. Del sentimento trágico de la vida en los hombres en los peublos. Buenos Aires: España-Calpe Argentina, 1939. ʼ

996 _____. Tragic sense of life. N. Y.: Dover, 1954.
Concerns the views of the scholar on religions and
his conclusions about them. He looks at Luther, Loyola,
scholasticism, mysticism, and Catholicism. He concludes
that Christianity is the only religion for a modern European.

997 Unger, R. Herder, Novalis und Kleist. Studien über die
Entwicklung des Todesproblems im Denken der Romantik.
Darmstadt: Wissenschaftliche Gesellschaft, 1968.

998 Valdés, M. J. "Death in the literature of Unamuno." Ph. D.
dissertation, University of Illinois, 1962.
Deals with the theme of death as a motivating force
and as an element of Unamuno's literary creation.

999 Valeri, D. "Riflessioni di un letterato sul problems della
Morte," Giornal Critico della Filosofia Italiana, 52
(April-June 1973), 213-20.

1000 Vandenburg, D. "Kneller, Heidegger and death," Educational
Theory, 15 (July 1965), 217-21.

1001 Vanderbilt, K. "Art and nature in 'The Masque of the Red
Death'," 19th Century Fiction, 22 (March 1968), 379-89.

1002 Van Doren, M. "Bereavement," in Collected and New Poems,
1924-1963. N. Y.: Hill and Wang, 1963. pp. 570.

1003 _____. "Death," in Collected and New Poems, 1924-1963.
N. Y.: Hill and Wang, 1963. pp. 76.

1004 _____. "Death bed," in Collected and New Poems, 1924-
1963. N. Y.: Hill and Wang, 1963. pp. 77.

1005 _____. "Death of light," in Collected and New Poems,
1924-1963. N. Y.: Hill and Wang, 1963. pp. 77.

1006 _____. "Death of old men," in Collected and New Poems,
1924-1963. N. Y.: Hill and Wang, 1963. pp. 274.

1007 _____. "Death's hands," in Collected and New Poems,
1924-1963. N. Y.: Hill and Wang, 1963. pp. 529.

1008 _____. "Epitaph," in Collected and New Poems, 1924-
1963. N. Y.: Hill and Wang, 1963. pp. 458.

1009 _____. "In memoriam," in Collected and New Poems,
1924-1963. N. Y.: Hill and Wang, 1963. pp. 413.

1010 _____. "None but death," in Collected and New Poems,
1924-1963. N. Y.: Hill and Wang, 1963. pp. 223.

1011 _____. "Unto death," in Collected and New Poems, 1924-
        1963. N.Y.: Hill and Wang, 1963. pp. 370.

1012 Van Evra, J. W. "On death as a limit," Analysis, 31 (April
        1971), 170-6.
        The significance of phenomenal death depends on
        how we use it in our life styles.

1013 Verbeke, G. "L'Immortalité de l'âme dans le 'DeAnima 'd
        Avicenne: une synthèse de l'Aristotélisme et du Néo-
        platonisme," Pensamiento, 25 (Jan.-Sept., 1969), 271-
        90.

1014 Vichery, W. N. Death of a poet. Bloomington: Indiana
        University Press, 1962.

1015 Viggiani, C. A. "Camus and the Fall from Innocence,"
        Yale French Studies No. 25, (1960), 65-71.

1016 Von Abele, R. Death of the artist--a study of Hawthorne's
        Disintegration. Folcroft, Pa.: Folcroft Press, 1958.

1017 Vos, M. "The Process of dying in the plays of Edward
        Albee," Education Theatre Journal, 252 (March 1973),
        80-5.
        Author states that the "settings, characters and
        actors of Albee's plays are haunted by death." The
        play 'All Over' is concerned with the process of dying.
        See also entry number 794.

1018 Vrasdonk, W. G. "Beyond thanatology: immortality," The
        Journal of Value Inquiry, 6 (winter 1972), 280-5.

1019 Vuillemin, J. Essai sur la signification de la mort. Paris:
        Presses Universitaire de France, 1948.

1020 Waddington, R. B. "Death of Adam; vision and voice in
        Books XI and XII of Paradise Lost," Modern Philology,
        70 (Aug. 1972), 9-21.

1021 Wagner, A. H., ed. What happens when you die? Twenti-
        eth century thought on survival after death. N.Y.:
        Abelard-Schuman, 1968.
        Nearly 100 of the country's philosophers, sci-
        entists, statesmen explore death in the light of modern
        scientific knowledge and thought. The book attempts to
        confront the problem from all points of view, and chal-
        lenge the reader to a new awareness.

1022 Waldson, H. M. "Death by water: or, the childhood of
        William Meister," Modern Language Review, 56 (Jan.
        1961), 44-53.

1023 Wallace, A. F. The Death and rebirth of Seneca. N.Y.: Knopf, 1970.

1024 Walley, K. W. "Suicide in opera: a brief analysis," Omega, 2 (Aug. 1971), 191-4.

1025 Warren, C. C. "Death in the novels of Konstantin Fedin and Leonid Leonov. Ph.D. dissertation, Columbia University, 1973.
"Careful analysis ... reveals an almost always worthwhile, sometimes fascinating, even intimate account of a number of features of the complex question of death as it is dealt with by two writers whose lives and careers are similar in many respects...." (Abstract).

1026 Warren, M. A. "On the moral and legal status of abortion," The Monist, 57 (Jan. 1973), 43-61.

1027 Warthin, A. S. The Physician of the dance of death. N.Y.: Paul B. Hoeber, 1931.
Historical study of the evolution of the death mythus in art. Includes examples as late as those inspired by World War I.

1028 Wasmuth, E. Vom Sinn des Todes. Heidelberg: Lambert Schneider, 1959.

1029 Watson, H. M. "The Theme of death in three plays of Paul Claudel." Ph.D. dissertation. Boulder: University of Colorado, 1965.

1030 Waugh, E. "Death in Hollywood," Life, 23 (Sept. 29, 1947), 73-4.
A nonfictional account of Forest Lawn.

1031 Weber, F. P. Aspects of death and correlated aspects of life in art, epigram and poetry; contributions toward an anthology and an iconography of the subject; illustrated especially by medals, engraved gems, jewels, ivories, antique pottery, etc., 4th ed., rev. and much enl. with 145 illustrations. London: T. F. Unwin, 1922.
"... [I]ntended to be an essay on the mental attitudes towards ideas of death, 'thanatopsis' and immortality, and the various ways in which (from Ancient Greek and Roman to modern times) they have, or may be supposed to have, affected the living individual...."

1032 Weiss, P. "Death and sleep," in Philosophy in Process (Nov. 26, 1964--Sept. 2, 1965). Carbondale: Southern Illinois University Press, 1969. Vol. 4, pp. 316-9.

1033 _____. "Kinds of death," in Philosophy in Process (Nov.

26, 1964-Sept. 2, 1965). Carbondale: Southern Illinois
University Press, 1969. Vol. 4, pp. 323-25.

1034 _____. "Life and death, " in Philosophy in Process (Nov.
26, 1964-Sept. 2, 1965). Carbondale: Southern Illinois
University Press, 1969. Vol. 4, pp. 319-22.

1035 _____. "Primal emotions: death, " in Philosophy in Process (Nov. 26, 1964-Sept. 2, 1965). Carbondale:
Southern Illinois University Press, 1969. Vol. 4, pp.
312-6.

1036 Wellman, P. Death on the prairie. N. Y.: Macmillan,
1934.
Historical account of warfare between Indians and
whites in the West from the 1862-3 Minnesota Massacre
to Wounded Knee.

1037 Wenkart, A. "Death in life, " Journal of Existentialism, 8
(1967), 75-90.
Discusses the question of "how much living is being
effected and how much death is being encountered in
life...." The individual must be helped to achieve a
constructive integration of the concept.

1038 Wentzlaff, E., and W. Friedrich. Das Problem des Todes
in der deutschen Lyrik des 17 Jahrunderts. Leipzig:
Mayer und Muller, 1931.

1039 Wenzel, S. "Dante's rationale for the seven deadly sins
'Purgatorio XVII'. " Modern Language Review, 60 (Oct.
1965), 629-33.

1040 Wertenbaker, L. T. Death of a man. N. Y.: Random,
1957.
Story about how the author's husband met his death
with courage, patience, wit, and decency despite the
agony he suffered from cancer of the liver.

1041 Wertheimer, R. "Understanding the abortion argument, "
Philosophy and Public Affairs, 1 (fall 1971), 67-95.

1042 Wessely, J. E. Die Gestalten des Todes und des Teufels im
der darstellenden Kunst. Leipzig: H. Vogel, 1876.

1043 West, D. "On Goodrich's 'The Mortality of Killing', "
Philosophy, 45 (July 1970), 233-36.

1044 West, M. "Death of Miles in 'The Turn of the Screw', "
Publications of the Modern Language Association, 79
(June 1964), 283-8.

1045 West, R. "Every third thought, " in Ending in Earnest.

N. Y.: Doubleday, 1931. pp. 142-56.

1046 Westheim, P. La Calavera. Traducción de Mariana Frenk
      (Portada de Elvira Gascon). México: Antigua Libreria
      Roliedo, 1953.

1047 White, E. B. Charlotte's web. N. Y.: Harper and Row,
      1952.
           A story for elementary children about a girl, a pig,
      and a spider. Near the end of the story, the girl and
      the pig are overcome with grief.

1048 White, H. With wings of eagles. N. Y.: Rinehart, 1953.
           Story of the author's loss of a son in war and how
      she grieved and refused to accept his death. Finally,
      when she made peace with God she came to terms with
      death, and herself.

1049 White, L. , Jr. "Indic elements in the iconography of
      Petrarch's Trionfo della morte, " Speculum, 49 (Aug.
      1974), 201-21.

1050 White, R. E. , Jr. "Milton's allegory of sin and death: a
      comment on backgrounds, " Modern Philology, 70 (May
      1973), 337-41.

1051 Whitman, W. "When Lilacs last in the doorway bloom'd, "
      in The Poetry and Prose of Walt Whitman. N. Y.:
      Simon and Schuster, 1949. pp. 323.

1052 _____. "Whispers of heavenly death, " in Anthology of
      American Poetry, edited by C. Aiken. N. Y.: Random,
      1944. pp. 170.

1053 Wicker, C. V. Edward Young and the fear of death; a study
      in romantic melancholy. New Mexico: University of
      New Mexico Press, 1952. (University of New Mexico
      publications in language and literature, no. 10.)

1053a Widney, J. P. Whither away. The problem of death and the
      hereafter. Los Angeles: Pacific Publishing Co. , 1934.
           Contents: Whither away; Udraka, the Buddhist;
      Ahasuerus; The Wonder of His coming; Nevermore; Et
      corpus mortale; Et ultra.

1054 Wienpohl, P. "Reflections on life and death, " Pacific
      Philosophy Forum, 3 (May 1965), 6-67.

1055 Wilbur, R. "The Death of a toad, " in American Poetry.
      (American Literary Forms). N. Y.: Crowell, 1960.

1056 Wilden, A. "Death desire and repetition in Svevo's Zeno, "
      Modern Language Notes, 84 (Jan. 1969), 98-119.

1057 Wilder, A. N. "Mortality and contemporary literature," in
      The Modern Vision of Death, edited by Nathan A. Scott,
      Jr. Atlanta: John Knox Press, 1967. pp. 17-43.
      "Death is a catalyst of transcendence [and] there can
      be many variations on this theme."

1058 Wilding, M. "Epitaph to Gray's elegy: two early printings
      and a parody," Notes and Queries, 15 (June 1968), 213-
      14.

1059 Williams, C. J. "On dying," Philosophy, 44 (Sept. 1969),
      217-30.
      Plato's arguments about life and death are discussed.
      The correct analysis of death is still obscure.

1060 Williams, W. C. "Death," in The Oxford Book of American
      Verse, edited by F. O. Matthiessen. N.Y.: Oxford,
      1950. pp. 684.

1061 Wimberly, L. C. "Death and burial lore in the English and
      Scottish popular ballads," University of Nebraska Studies
      in Language, Literature and Criticism, Number 8: 1-138,
      1927.
      Topics covered include: blood revenge, capital
      punishment, death omens, and dreams. This present
      study is based on Child's English and Scottish Popular
      Ballads, a work that may fairly be called definitive.

1062 Winters, Y. "Death goes before me," in The New Poetry,
      edited by H. Monroe, and A. C. Henderson. N.Y.:
      Macmillan, 1947. pp. 656.

1063 Wismer, L. H. "Changing concepts of death in American
      drama, 1883-1960." Ph.D. dissertation, Stanford Uni-
      versity, 1963.

1064 Wolfe, T. From death to mourning. N.Y.: Scribner, 1958.

1065 Wolff, E. "Kant et l'immortalité de l'âme," Archives de
      Philosophie, 34 (July-Sept. 1971), 451-71.
      Discusses Kant's view of the immortality of the
      soul and the relationship between the temporal and the
      eternal.

1066 Wolff, E. D. "Why we mourn in black," in Why We Do It.
      N.Y.: Macaulay, 1939. pp. 137-42.

1067 _____. "Why we send flowers to funerals," in Why We
      Do It. N.Y.: Macaulay, 1929. pp. 52-7.

1068 Wordsworth, W. "Upon epitaphs," in Century of English
      Essays, compiled by E. Rhys, and L. Vaughan. N.Y.:
      Dutton, 1913. pp. 297-311. (Everyman's Library.)

1069 Worthen, T. D.   "Death in Plato."   Ph. D. dissertation,
      University of Washington, 1968.

1070 Wyschogrod, E.   "Sport, death, and the elemental," in The
      Phenomenon of Death; faces of immortality, edited by
      E. Wyschogrod.   N. Y.:   Harper and Row, 1973.   pp.
      166-97.
          The author attempts to show that certain sports
      (long-distance running, auto racing, motorcycling, moun-
      tain climbing, surfing, and those of acute exhilaration
      and degree of risk) "represent a grappling with the ele-
      mental such that the experience sought is that of the
      body's identity with the elemental...."

1071 Young, E.   "The Complaint," in Eighteenth Century Poetry
      and Prose, edited by L. Bredvold, A. McKillop, and L.
      Whitney.   N. Y.:   Ronald, 1973.   pp. 447-56.

1072 _____.   Night thoughts on life, death and immortality.
      London: Printed for R. Dodsley, at Tully's Head in
      Pall-Mall, 1742.
          A poem written in nine books in blank verse.   An
      outstanding example of the melancholy "graveyard
      school" in 18th century English literature.

1073 Young, H. T.   "Two poems on death by Juan Ramón Jiménez,"
      Modern Language Notes, 75 (June 1960), 502-7.

1074 Young, M.   "Death by rarity," in A Little Treasury of Amer-
      ican Poetry, edited by O. Williams.   N. Y.:   Scribner,
      1946.   pp. 843.

1075 Yunck, J. A.   "Natural history of a dead quarrel: Heming-
      way and the humanists," South Atlantic Quarterly, 62
      (winter 1963), 29-42.

1076 Ziegler, P.   The Black death.   N. Y.:   John Day, 1969.
          Outlines the progress of the black death across
      Europe during the mid-14th century and speculates on
      the total lives lost.

Part IV

MEDICAL PROFESSION AND NURSING EXPERIENCES

1077 Ackerknecht, E. "Death in the history of medicine," Bulletin of the History of Medicine, 42 (Jan.-Feb. 1968), 19-23.
      Chronicles the historical significance that death has played in the annals of medicine and implications it has for the future.

1078 Adamek, M. E. "Some observations on death and a family," Nursing Science (Aug. 1965), 258-67.

1079 Adelson, L., and E. R. Kenney. "Sudden and unexpected death in infancy and childhood," Pediatrics, 17 (1956), 663-7.
      "Despite the frequency of its occurrence less is known concerning the cause of sudden and unexpected death in infancy and childhood than any other age group."

1080 Adelson, S. E. "Dying patient: an unspoken dialogue," New Physician, 20 (Nov. 1971), 706.

1081 Adelstein, A. M. "Precision in death certification," Lancet, 1 (1969), 682.
      Draws the attention of doctors to the need for having certain details of diagnosis on death certificates.

1082 Adler, C. S. "The Meaning of death to children," Arizona Medicine, 26 (March 1969), 266.

1083 Aitken, P. Q. "The Right to live and the right to die," Medical Times, 95 (Nov. 1967), 1184-7.

1084 Aitken-Swan, J. "Nursing the late cancer patient at home," Practitioner, 183 (1959), 64-69.

1085 _____, and E. C. Easson. "Reactions of cancer patients on being told of their diagnosis," British Medical Journal, 1 (March 21, 1959), 779-83.

1086 Akaishi, S. "Problems concerning death from the viewpoint of legal medicine," Naika, 23 (May 1969), 861-9.

95

1087 Alby, N. , and J. M. Alby. "The Doctor and the dying
       child, " in The Child in his Family, edited by E. James
       Anthony, and C. Koupernik. Vol. 2. N.Y.: Wiley,
       1973. pp. 145-57.
       Describes the role of the PSY person in relation-
       ship to the medical model and the team-patient relation-
       ship.

1088 Aldrich, C. K. , and M. Knight. "The Dying patient's grief, "
       Journal of the American Medical Association, 184 (May
       4, 1963), 329-31.

1089 _____. "Personality factors and mortality in the reloca-
       tion of the aged, " Gerontologist, 4 (1964), 92-4.
       Studies the relationship between relocation of
       chronically-ill elderly residents in nursing homes, to
       the mortality rate as a result of that move.

1090 Alexander, G. H. "An Unexplained death coexistent with
       death wishes, " Psychosomatic Medicine, 5 (1943), 188-
       94.
       Discusses the question as to whether an abnormal
       fear of death or desire to die, can, without the inter-
       vention of non-psychological forces, actually terminate
       life in man.

1091 Allen, G. "Individual differences in survival and reproduc-
       tion among old colony Mennonites in Mexico, " Eugenics
       Quarterly, 14 (Oct. 1966), 103-11.
       Describes the social, familial, and religious cus-
       toms of the old colony Mennonites of Mexico and how
       these customs affect the birth and death rates.

1092 Alsop, S. "Stay of execution, " Saturday Review World,
       (Dec. 18, 1973), 20-3.
       A noted columnists account of his battle with leu-
       kemia--and his reflections on death.

1093 Alvarez, W. C. "Care of the dying, " Journal of the Ameri-
       can Medical Association, 150 (Sept. 1952), 86-91.
       States that the philosophic physician will try always
       to give comfort to the dying, not only by relieving
       physical pain but by lessening mental distress.

1094 _____. "Death is often not so difficult or painful, "
       Geriatrics, 18 (March 1963), 165-6.

1095 _____. "Help for the dying patient, " Geriatrics, 18 (Feb.
       1964), 69-71.

1096 _____. "Some aspects of death, " Geriatrics, 19 (July
       1964), 465-6.

1097 American Journal of Nursing Co. Educational Services Div.
     The Dying patient: a nursing perspective. N. Y.:
     AJNC, 1973.
     Viewpoints from many areas combine to offer ma-
     terial for thought, discussion, and stimuli for further
     study and research.

1098 "American Medical Association passes 'death with dignity'
     resolution," Science News, 104 (Dec. 15, 1973), 375.

1099 American Veterinary Medicine Assoc. "Report of the
     American Veterinary Medicine Association panel on
     euthanasia." Journal of the American Veterinary Medi-
     cine Association, 42 (1963), 162-70.

1100 "American ways of death," Scientific American, 231 (Aug.
     1974), 46-7.
     Describes and interprets statistical findings "of a
     study by the National Center for Health Statistics of
     mortality trends from 1950 to 1969 for the 15 leading
     causes of death, which in 1969 accounted for 89% of
     the country's deaths."

1101 Anderson, F. "Death and the doctors: who will decide who
     is to live?" New Republic, 160 (April 19, 1969), 9-10.
     The purpose of this article is to summarize the re-
     port of the "Ad Hoc Committee of the Harvard Medical
     School to examine the definition of brain death."

1102 Anderson, J. "Changes in emotional responses with age,"
     in Feelings and Emotions, edited by M. Reymert. N. Y.:
     McGraw-Hill, 1950. pp. 418-27.

1103 Anderson, R. "Notes of a survivor." A paper presented at
     the University of Rochester School of Medicine on April
     29, 1971. The conference was titled, "The Patient,
     Death, and the Family."

1104 Anderson, W. "Suicide: its causes and prevention," Pacific
     Medical Journal, 51 (1908), 539-51.

1105 Angrist, A. A. "A Pathologist's experience with attitudes
     toward death," Rhode Island Medical Journal, 43 (1960),
     693-7.
     Relates experiences of thirty years dealing with dy-
     ing persons, their families, and their attitudes towards
     death.

1106 Annas, G. J. "Rights of the terminally ill patient," Journal
     of Nursing Administration, 4 (March-April 1974), 40-4.

1107 Annis, J. W. "The Dying patient," Psychosomatics, (Sept.-
     Oct., 1969), 289-92.

1108   Ansohn, E. "The Physician and the end of life," Wiener
       Medizinische Wochenschrift, 118 (Nov. 30, 1968), 1025-
       9.

1109   "Any man's death diminishes me," New England Journal of
       Medicine, 278 (June 27, 1968), 1455.
            Article discusses the potential conflicts between the
       medical and legal definitions of death.

1110   Aring, C. D. "Intimations of mortality," Annals of Internal
       Medicine, 69 (1968), 137-51.
            What is the role of the physician in caring for the
       dying? This article is concerned about the small
       amount of instruction given to medical school students.

1111   Armiger, B. "About questioning the right to die: reprise
       and dialogue," Nursing Outlook, 16 (Oct., 1968), 26-8.
            Who makes the decision about the end of a life?

1112   Arnold, J., et al. "Public attitudes and the diagnosis of
       death," Journal of the American Medical Association,
       206 (Nov. 25, 1968), 1949-54.
            Studies public attitudes toward the diagnosis of death
       as it relates to single-organ transplants.

1113   Arnstein, R. L. "The Threat of death as a factor in psy-
       chological reaction to illness," Journal of the American
       College Health Association, 23 (Dec. 1974), 154-6.
            The author discusses two questions regarding how
       the individual copes emotionally with impending death and
       how health care personnel help in their interaction with
       the patient.

1114   Aronson, G. J. "Treatment of the dying person," in The
       Meaning of Death, edited by H. Feifel. N. Y.: McGraw-
       Hill, 1959. pp. 251-8.
            Advice to physicians on how to treat a dying person.

1115   Aronson, M. J. "Emotional aspects of nursing the cancer
       patient," Mental Hygiene, 2 (April 1958), 267-73.
            Deals with the role of the nurse, the cancer patient,
       and the various emotional problems that confront nurses
       daily.

1116   Asch, S. S. "Sudden unexpected death may be infanticides,"
       Pediatric Herald (March 1968), 7.

1117   Autton, N. "... To Comfort All That Mourn," Nursing
       Times, 58 (1962), 1516-7.
            States that a better understanding of the basic ele-
       ments of grief will help medical personnel with the be-
       reaved. Discusses grief responses and outlines various
       aspects of it.

1118   Avorn, J.   "Beyond dying; experiments using psychedelic
       drugs to ease the transition from life," Harpers, 246
       (March 1973), 56-64.
          "What accounts for the ability of the psychedelic ex-
       perience to ease the psychological pain of dying? Dr.
       Grof offers an answer: 'Death appears ... suddenly as
       a transition into a different type of existence for those
       who undergo the destruction--rebirth--cosmic unity ex-
       perience'."

1119   Ayd, F. J.   "When is a person dead?"   Medical Science, 18
       (1967), 33-6.

1120   Baer, R.   "The Sick child knows," in Should the Patient
       Know the Truth, edited by S. Standard, and H. Nathan.
       N.Y.: Springer, 1955. pp. 100-6.

1121   Bahrmann, E., et al.   "Problems of determination of death,"
       Deutsche Gesundheitswesen, 23 (Dec. 19, 1968), 2403-7.

1122   Baker, J. M., and K. C. Sorensen.   "A Patient's concern
       with death," American Journal of Nursing, 63 (1963),
       90-2.
          Article points out the need of having a philosophy of
       death.

1123   Bakke, J. L.   "Managing the fatal illness," Northwest Medi-
       cine, 59 (1960), 901-4.
          Discusses patient reactions to death, the role of the
       physician, grief, and the family's reaction.

1124   Bakker, C. B., et al.   "Physicians and family planning: a
       persistent ambivalence," Obstetrics and Gynecology, 25
       (1965), 279-84.

1125   Balduzzi, P. C., and R. M. Greendyke.   "Sudden unexpected
       death in infancy and viral infection," Pediatrics, 38
       (1966), 201-6.

1126   Baler, L. A., and P. J. Golde.   "Conjugal bereavement: a
       strategic area of research in preventive psychiatry," in
       Working Papers in Community Mental Health, published
       by Harvard School of Public Health, 2 (spring 1964).

1127   Barber, T. X.   "Death by suggestion: a critical note,"
       Psychosomatic Medicine, 23 (1961), 153-5.

1128   Barckley, V.   "Enough time for good nursing," Nursing Out-
       look, 12 (April 1964), 44-8.
          How nurses live with impending death which occurs
       daily.

1129   _____.   "What can I say to the cancer patient?" Nursing

Outlook, 6 (June 1958), 316-8.

1130   Barnard, M.   "Sudden infant death syndrome," Medico-Legal
       Bulletin, 224 (Dec. 1971), 1-12.

1131   Barnett, C.   "A Defense of sweetness," American Journal of
       Nursing, 61 (Feb. 1961), 99-101.
       A nurse describes her experiences with a cancer
       patient and the complex problems involved.

1132   Barnsteiner, J. H.   "Death and dying: anxieties, needs and
       responsibilities of the nurse," Journal of Practical
       Nursing, 24 (June 1974), 28-30.

1133   Barr, A.   "Still births and infant mortality in twins,"
       Annals of Human Genetics, 25 (1961), 131-40.

1134   Barry, H.   "Significance of material bereavement before age
       of eight in psychiatric patients," Archives of Neurology
       and Psychiatry, 62 (1949), 630-7.
       States that the incidence of maternal death is three
       times as great among psychotic persons and lists ways
       that their deaths effect children before the eighth year.

1135   _____, and E. Lindemann.   "Critical ages for maternal
       bereavement in psychoneurosis," Psychosomatic Medicine,
       22 (1960), 166-81.

1136   Barry, H., Jr., H. Barry, III, and E. Lindemann.   "A Study
       of bereavement: an approach to problems in mental
       disease," American Journal of Orthopsychiatry, 9 (1939),
       355-9.

1137   Barton, E. A.   "Old age and death," Practitioner, 123 (Aug.
       1929), 111-19.
       States that the condition of the vessels rather than
       blood pressure determines the physical and mental con-
       dition of elderly patients and is the determinant factor
       in the length of years.

1138   Bassett, S. D.   "Death, dying, and grief: a personal view,"
       Texas Reports on Biology and Medicine, 32 (spring
       1974), 347-50.

1139   Baxter, C.   "Three days with Mrs. M.," American Journal
       of Nursing, 67 (April 1967), 774-8.
       A nurse describes her experiences, the patient's
       increasing anxiety, and the role of the doctor with the
       family of the stricken patient.

1140   Beahan, L. T.   "Emergency mental health services in a
       general hospital," Hospital and Community Psychiatry,
       21 (March 1970), 81.

Emphasizes the need for emerging mental health
service in general hospitals due to the number of attempts at suicide.

1141 Beatty, D. "Shall we talk about death?" Pastoral Psychology,
6 (1955), 11-4.

1142 Beau, W. B. "On death," Archives of Internal Medicine, 12
(Feb. 1958), 199-202.

1143 Becker, D., and F. Margolin. "How surviving parents
handled their young children's adaptations to the crisis
of loss," American Journal of Orthopsychiatry, 37 (July
1967), 753-7.
Describes how surviving parents help their children
adapt to the loss of a parent and how parents deal with
the child's questions and theories about death.

1144 Beckwith, J. B., and A. B. Bergman. "The Sudden death
syndrome of infancy," Hospital Practice, 2 (Nov. 1967),
44-52.

1145 Beecher, H. K. "After the definition of irreversible coma,"
New England Journal of Medicine, 281 (Nov. 6, 1969),
1070-1.
Description of a Harvard Medical School Committee
assignment about defining death. It evaded the assignment because of the complexity concerning the many aspects of death.

1146 _____. "Definitions of life and death for medical science
and practice," Annals of the New York Academy of Science, 169 (Jan. 21, 1970), 471-4.
Focuses on the reasons why a new medical definition of death is needed, contrasted against medical education, practice and technology.

1147 _____. A Study of the deaths associated with anesthesia
and surgery, based on a study of 599,548 anesthesias
in 10 institutions, 1948-1952 inclusive. Springfield,
Ill.: C. C. Thomas, 1954.
A monograph in the American Lecture Series in
Anesthesiology.

1148 Beigler, J. S. "Anxiety as an aid in the prognostication of
impending death," Archives of Neurological Psychiatry,
77 (Feb. 1957), 171-7.
Keen observations suggest that dying patients have
an unconscious awareness of impending death which acts
as a repressor of anxiety.

1149 Bennholdt-Thomsen, C. "Sterben und Tod des Kindes,"
Deutsche Medizinische Wochenschrift, 84 (Aug. 14,

1959), 1437-42.

1150 Benoleil, J. Q. "Death and bereavement: the nurses role," Alberta Association of Registered Nurses, 26 (Sept.-Oct. 1970), 4-6.

1151 _____. "The Dying patient: a nursing dilemma," Washington State Journal of Nursing, 43 (Jan.-Feb., 1971), 3-4.

1152 _____. "Talking to patients about death," Nursing Forum, 9 (1970), 254-68.

1153 Benson, G. "Death and dying: a psychoanalytic perspective," Hospital Progress, 53 (March 1972), 52-9.

1154 Beraeksen, B. S., ed. Distance and the dying patient. St. Louis: Mosby, 1967.

1155 Berardi, R. S. "Deaths in a small community hospital," Journal of the Kentucky Medical Association, 67 (Oct. 1969), 749-51.
        Details a study of all deaths in a four-and-one-half-year period in a small hospital.

1156 Berger, M. "A Clinical study of dying patients in the hospital," Psychologie Medicale, 5 (1973), 369-85.
        Psychological reactions of dying patients are described. Personal observations and examination of case histories were made and utilized.

1157 Bergman, A. B. "Crib deaths exact needless toll of grief in infants' families," Hospital Topics, 17 (Feb. 1969), 69-73.

1158 _____. "A Shared experience," International Nursing Review, 14 (Oct. 1967), 39-42.
        Explains in a sensible way the significance of viewing death as a shared experience and the need for dialogue for mutual benefit.

1159 _____. "What you can do after crib death," Consultant, 14 (Aug. 1974), 85-7.

1160 _____, et al. Sudden infant death syndrome. Seattle: University of Washington Press, 1970.

1161 _____, and C. Schulte, eds. "Care of the child with cancer," Pediatrics, 4 (Sept. 1967), 492-546.
        Article discusses some of the principles of management of children with fatal illnesses. It also points out how the child responds to imminent death.

1162 Bermann, E. "Death, bereavement, and transplanting hearts and lungs: some psycho-social observations and some clinical comments," in Is It Moral to Modify Man? Edited by C. A. Frazier. Springfield, Ill.: C. C. Thomas, 1973.
Concerned with the preoperative behavior of six subjects who were candidates for transplants. The author examines death-related themes in their verbal conversations and notes the absence or presence of these.

1163 Bibring, G. L. "The Death of an infant: a psychiatric study," New England Journal of Medicine, 283 (1970), 370-1.
Attempts to discover whether taking care of the baby, or just touching him before death, has any special effect on the mourning mother.

1164 "Bill of rights for patients," Nursing Outlook, 21 (Feb. 1973), 82.
Twelve rights of hospitalized patients are summarized which have been adopted by the American Hospital Association.

1165 Binet, L. R. Nouveaux Aspects de la lutte contre la mort. Paris: Presses Universitaires de France, 1945.

1166 Binger, C. M., et al. "Childhood leukemia: emotional impact on patient and family," New England Journal of Medicine, 230 (1969), 414-18.
A professional team interviewed 20 families who had lost a child from leukemia and the findings are summarized with implications for ongoing programs.

1167 Biorck, G. "On the definitions of death," World Medical Journal, 14 (Sept.-Oct., 1967), 137-9.

1168 Black, W. An arithmetical and medical analysis of the diseases and mortality of the human species. London, 1789. With an introduction by D. V. Glass. Farnborough: Gregg International, 1973.
A reprint of the 2d rev. ed. printed for the author by J. Crowder with new introduction.

1169 Bloomfield, K. J. "Johnny is my most difficult ... and dearest patient," Nursing, 14 (Oct. 1964), 68-70.
A nurse recounts her feelings and emotions in caring for her two-year-old son who is suffering from acute lymphoblastic leukemia.

1170 Bluestone, E. M. "On the significance of death in hospital practice," Modern Hospital, 3 (March 1952), 86-8.
Reviews the attitude towards the subject of death in hospitals. Author states that in a New York Hospital

one-eighth of all deaths were friendless and this is a strong argument for a social service department.

1171 Boba, A. Death in the operating room. Springfield, Ill.: C. C. Thomas, 1965.
A Monograph in the American Lecture Series in anesthesiology.

1172 Booth, H. "The Christian nurse: a nurse's special problems, 2, care for the dying, " Nursing Times, 60 (Dec. 4, 1964), 1615.

1173 Borel, C. M. "Defining death, " General Practitioner, 39 (Jan. 1969), 171-8.

1174 Bouchard, R. Nursing care of the cancer patient. St. Louis: Mosby, 1967.

1175 Bourguignon, A. "La Mort et la médecin, " Semaine des Hôpitaux de Paris, 22 (May 14, 1963), 2-3.

1176 Bozeman, M. F.; C. E. Orbach; and A. M. Sutherland. "Psychological impact of cancer and its treatment: III. The adaptation of mothers to the threatened loss of the children through leukemia: Part 1, " Cancer, 8 (1955), 1-19.

1177 Brackenbury, H. B. Patient and doctor. London: Hodder and Stoughton, 1935.

1178 Brainard, F. "Rather than scream: what's it like to have a terminal disease?" Today's Health, 49 (June 1971), 32-7.

1179 Branch, C. H. H. "Psychiatric approach to patients with malignant disease, " Rocky Mountain Medical Journal, 49 (1953), 749-53.
Lists ways a physician can tell a patient of a malignant illness by considering the physical and psychiatric condition of the patient.

1180 Brandstatter, J., and F. Kisser. "Ein Beitrag zur Frage des Selbstmordes, " Deutsche Zeitschrift für die Gesamte Gerichtliche Medizin, 4 (1924), 237-47.

1181 Branson, H. K. "The Terminal patient and his family, " Bedside Nurse, 3 (June 1970), 21-3.

1182 Brauer, P. "Should the patient know the truth, " Nursing Outlook, 8 (Dec. 1960), 672-6.
Patient and family reactions about terminal illness are observed. Poses questions concerning the concept of truth and death.

1183   Braun, A.   "Das Problem des Todes," Medizinische Welt,
       10 (Sept. 26, 1936), 1422-23.

1184   Breed, J. E.   "Management of the patient with terminal ill-
       ness," Illinois Medical Journal, 139 (May 1971), 503.

1185   _____. "New questions in medical morality," Illinois
       Medical Journal, 135 (1969), 504.
       Lecture presents some new questions in medical
       morality which the AMA code does not cover and which
       are of interest to both doctors and clergyman.

1186   Breen, P.   "Who is to say?" American Journal of Nursing,
       8 (Aug. 1967), 1689-90.
       Reflections of a family concerning the impending
       death of an old man. What is revealed are numerous
       attitudes about death.

1187   Brenner, M.   "Fetal, infant, and maternal mortality during
       periods of economic instability," International Journal of
       Health Services, 3 (spring 1973), 145-59.
       That infant mortality rate is an indicator of the
       socioeconomic level of a nation has long been known.
       Research has now indicated that major economic reces-
       sions have played a role in maternal mortality.

1188   Brewster, H. H.   "Separation reaction in psychosomatic
       disease and neurosis," Psychosomatic Medicine, 14
       (1952), 154-60.
       An important study that observes the effects of
       separation and the need to compare it with bereavement.

1189   Bright, F., and M. L. France.   "The Nurse and the termi-
       nally ill child," Nursing Outlook, 15 (Sept. 1967), 39-42.
       Deals with family-oriented philosophy. The article
       uses a number of clinical examples and reports research
       to illustrate how the nurse cares for patients and their
       families.

1190   Brim, O. H., et al. Dying patient. N.Y.: Russell Sage
       Foundation, 1970.
       In two parts: the first considers all the profession-
       al analyses and decisions along with personal feelings
       involved in determining when and how a person dies.
       The second part involves what the actual process of dying
       is like and what can be done to make it easier for both
       the dying person and those who love him.

1191   Brooks, S. M. Our murdered presidents: the medical story.
       N.Y.: Frederick Fell, 1966.

1192   Brown, F.   "Childhood bereavement and subsequent crime,"
       British Journal of Psychiatry, 112 (1966), 1035-41.

1193   Brown, J. P. "Terminal nursing care," Nursing Times, 61
       (Nov. 1965), 1562.

1194   Brown, N. D., et al. "How do nurses feel about euthanasia
       and abortion," American Journal of Nursing, 711 (July
       1971), 1413-6.

1195   Brown, N. K., et al. "The Preservation of life," Journal of the
       American Medical Association, 211 (Jan. 1970), 76-82.
         Study of physicians who are changing their attitudes
       toward terminal illness and terminal patients.

1196   Bruce, S. J. "Reactions of nurses and mothers to still-
       births," Nursing Outlook, 10 (Feb. 1962), 88-91.
         Describes the emotions of nurses and mothers to
       stillbirths, and the symptoms of guilt and grief in ac-
       cepting this reality.

1197   Bucove, A. D. "Death and confidentiality," American Journal
       of Psychiatry, 127 (Dec. 1970), 845.
         In a letter written to the editor, the doctor ques-
       tions indecent exposure of confidential information after
       a patient's death. He states that "ethical abuses offer
       yet another impediment in a patient's trusting his
       psychiatrist."

1198   Bulger, R. "Dying patient and his doctor," Harvard Medical
       Alumni Bulletin, 34 (1960), 23.

1199   Burnett, W. M. Sudden death in infants: proceedings of the
       conference on causes of sudden death in infants, Seattle,
       Wash., 1963. Washington, D.C.: U.S. Gov. Printing
       Office, 1966.

1200   Buxbaum, R. E. "Grief begins not with death, but with
       knowing it is near," Texas Medicine, 62 (1966), 44-5.
         Discusses how grief frequently begins before death
       and includes information about the dying patient, his
       friends and family.

1201   Cain, A. C. "Children's disturbed reactions to their
       mother's miscarriage," Psychosomatic Medicine, 24
       (1964), 58-66.

1202   _____, and C. J. Fast. "Children's disturbed reactions
       to parent suicide," American Journal of Orthopsychiatry,
       36 (1966), 873-80.

1203   Caldwell, D., and B. L. Mishara. "Research on attitudes
       of medical doctors toward the dying patient: a method-
       ological problem," Omega, 3 (Nov. 1972), 341-6.
         Seventy-three medical doctors were interviewed re-
       garding their attitudes toward the dying patient. Their

responses indicate that the topic may be more of a problem to the doctor than one may believe.

1204 Caldwell, J. R. "One hundred deaths in practice: a study of terminal care, " Journal of the Royal College of General Practice, 21 (Aug. 1971), 460-3.

1205 Callaway, E. "The Psychological care of the cancer patient, " Journal of the Medical Association of Georgia, 41 (Nov. 1952), 503-4.

1206 Cameron, C. "Professional attitudes and terminal care, " Public Health Reports, 67 (Oct. 1952), 955-9.
      Points out that the problem of terminal care for patients with cancer presents increasing responsibility for physicians because of the various situations presented by it.

1207 Camps, F. E. "When infant death occurs, " Nursing Mirror, 133 (Nov. 12, 1971), 14-15.

1208 Cannon, W. B. "Voodoo death, " Psychosomatic Medicine, 19 (1957), 182-90.
      Interesting account of testimony of voodoo death from Brazil, Australia, Africa, and New Zealand.

1209 Cantor, P. "Adolescent suicide, " Time (April 26, 1971), 48.

1210 "Care for the dying, " Canadian Medical Association Journal, 91 (Oct. 24, 1964), 926.
      Article is concerned with the relationship the physician has to death and how he prepares others for facing the inevitable.

1211 "Care of the dying, " Lancet, 1 (Feb. 20, 1965), 424-5.
      Suggests ways to care for the dying patient effectively, based on a study by Russell and Miller in England.

1212 Carlova, J. "New support for doctor-aided deaths, " Medical Economics, (1970), 254-7.
      Author describes the way General Eisenhower died and called it a disgrace. What is advocated is a doctor-aided death.

1213 Carlozzi, C. G. Death and contemporary man: the crisis of terminal illness. Grand Rapids, Mich.: Eerdmans, 1974.
      Written for those who must make ethical decisions when death threatens one's self or a loved one.

1214 Carpenter, R. G., and C. W. Skaddick. "Role of infection, suffocation and bottle feeding in cot death: an analysis of some factors in the histories of 110 cases and their controls," British Journal of Preventive and Social Medicine, 19 (1965), 1-7.

1215 _____, et al. "Identification and follow-up of infants at risk of sudden death in infancy," Nature, 250 (Aug. 1974), 729.

1216 Carr, J. "Suicide," International Record of Medicine, 170 (1957), 615.

1217 Carr, J. L. "The Coroner and the common law, III. Death and its medical imputations," California Medicine, 93 (1960), 32-4.
      Discusses the role of the family physician regarding the signing of the death certificate and the recording of legal details of personal identity of the patient.

1218 Carruthers, M. The Western way of death: stress, tension and heart attacks. N.Y.: Pantheon, 1974.

1219 Carson, J. "Learning from a dying patient," American Journal of Nursing, 71 (Feb. 1971), 333-4.

1220 Cassell, E. J. "Being and becoming dead," in Death in American Experience, edited by Arien Mack. N.Y.: Schocken Press, 1973. pp. 162-76.
      Contains taped interviews of lay people who were asked the question "How would you define a dying patient?"

1221 _____. "Death and the physician," Commentary, 47 (June 1969), 73-4.

1222 Cavanagh, J. R. "The Reaction of student nurses to their first professional experience with death," Guild of Catholic Psychologists, 14 (April 1967), 101-7.

1223 _____. "The Right of the patient to die with dignity," The Catholic Nurse, 11 (Dec. 1963), 24-33.

1224 Chandra, R. K. "A Child dies," Indian Journal of Pediatrics, 35 (July 1968), 363-4.

1225 Chapman, R. F. "Suicide during psychiatric hospitalization," Bulletin of the Menninger Clinic, 29 (1965), 35-44.
      Study of 18 psychiatric patients who committed suicide while hospitalized at Topeka Veterans hospital between 1946 and 1962.

1226 Chase, P., and I. Beck. "Making a graceful exit," Rhode

Island Medical Journal, 39 (Sept. 1956), 497-9.
Author makes a strong plea for helping to make
an elderly dying patient's death more graceful and
dignified.

1226a Child, C. G., III. "Surgical intervention, " in Life and Death
and Medicine. San Francisco: W. H. Freeman, 1973.
pp. 59-66. (A Scientific American reprint book of
Sept. 1973.)

1227 Chodoff, P. "The Dying patient, " Medical Annals of Washington, D. C., 29 (Aug. 1960), 447-50.

1228 Christenson, L. "The Physicians role in terminal illness
and death, " Minnesota Medicine, 46 (1963), 881-3.
"States that the most controversial aspect of
terminal illness, however, is probably whether or not
to tell a patient that he has a fatal illness with a
sharply limited life expectancy. "

1229 Clansen, C. R., et al. "Studies of the sudden infant death
syndrome in King County, Washington: IV. Immunologic
studies, " Pediatrics, 52 (July 1973), 45-51.
The medical profession is presented with special
health challenges regarding sudden infant death and
attendant problems connected with them.

1230 Clarke, K. S. "Calculated risk of sports fatalities, " Journal
of the American Medical Association, 197 (Sept. 1966),
894-6.
Expresses a need for a new design in sports programs so that the undue risk question can be put on an
individual basis.

1231 Cleaveland, F. P. "Masquerades, homicide, suicide, accident or natural death, " Journal of the Indiana Medical
Association, 53 (1960), 2181-4.
Discusses how death can appear as natural and yet
may have been produced by violence.

1232 Clouse, G. D. "Introductions to widowhood: the role of the
family physician, " Ohio Medical Journal, 62 (Dec. 1966),
1281-4.
Suggestions as to how doctors can tactfully introduce
a woman to widowhood.

1233 Cockerill, E. E. "The Cancer patient as a person, " Public
Health Nursing, 40 (1948), 78-83.
Actual case studies are described, and states that
individuals usually handle a threat to their lives in the
same manner as they have met other crises.

1234   Cohen, S.   "LSD and the anguish of dying," Harpers, 231
       (Sept. 1965), 69-78.
          States that LSD is useful for helping dying patients
       face death more honestly and relieving the fear of death.

1235   _____; C. V. Leonard; N. L. Farberow; and E. S.
       Shneidman.   "Tranquilizers and suicide in the schizo-
       phrenic," Archives in General Psychiatry, 1 (1964),
       312-21.

1236   Colby, M.   "The Significance, evolution, and implementation
       of standard certificates," American Journal of Public
       Health, 55 (1965), 596-99.

1237   Collins, S. D., et al.   Major causes of illness of various
       severities and major causes of death in six age periods
       of life.   Washington, D.C.: U.S. Gov. Printing Office,
       1955.   (Public Health service publication no. 440 and
       monograph no. 30.)

1238   Collins, V. J.   "Consideration in defining death," Linacre
       Quarterly, 38 (May 1971), 49-101.
          Discusses the primary determinants regarding the
       physician's decision.

1239   _____.   "Limits of medical responsibility in prolonging
       life.   Guide to decisions," Journal of the American
       Medical Association, 20 (Oct. 7, 1968), 389-92.

1240   Committee of the Harvard Medical School, ad hoc.   "A
       Definition of irreversible coma," Journal of the American
       Medical Association, 250 (1968), 337-40.
          Attempts to define irreversible coma as a new cri-
       terion for death by determining the characteristics of a
       permanently non-functioning brain.

1241   Conley, S. R.   "The Will to live," Tomorrow's Nurse, 4
       (Oct. 1963), 20.
          Article discusses a nurse's experience with a 77-
       year-old man with terminal carcinoma of the prostate
       gland.

1242   Cooke, R. T., and R. G. Welch.   "A Study in cot death,"
       British Medical Journal, 2 (1964), 1549-54.

1243   Corder, M. P., et al.   "Death and dying--oncology discus-
       sion group--department of nursing and oncology service,
       department of medicine, Letterman Army Medical Cen-
       ter, Presidio of San Francisco," Journal of Psychiatric
       Nursing and Mental Health Services, 12 (July-Aug.,
       1974), 10-14.

1244   "Cot deaths," British Medical Journal (Oct. 30, 1971), 250-1.

1245 Cotter, M. M. "Sudden death in the work situation, " Occupational Health, 22 (Feb. 1970), 39.
      Suggests methods for the occupational health nurse to help in cases of fatal accidents and heart attacks.

1246 Cotter, Z. M. "Institutional care of the terminally ill, " Hospital Progress, 52 (June 1971), 42-8.

1247 Cox, P. R., and J. R. Ford. "The Mortality of widows shortly after widowhood, " Lancet, 1 (Jan. 18, 1964), 163-4.

1248 Crafoord, C. C. "Cerebral death and the transplantation era, " Diseases of the Chest, 55 (Feb. 1969), 141-5.
      Discusses the ability of modern medical technology to keep parts of the body functioning even with brain damage and the problem of determining when death occurs.

1249 Cramond, W. A. "Medical, moral and legal aspects of organ transplantation and long-term resuscitative measures: psychological, social and community aspects, " Medical Journal of Australia, 2 (1968), 522-7.

1250 Crane, D. "Dying and its dilemmas as a field of research, " in The Dying Patient, edited by Orville C. Brim, Jr., et al. N.Y.: Russell Sage Foundation, 1970.

1251 Crile, G. W. "An Experimental investigation of the physical nature of death, " American Philosophical Society, (1929), 69-81.
      An early study which describes circulation and respiratory problems in determing the nature and cause of death.

1252 Cumpston, J. H. L. "Life and death, " Medical Journal of Australia, 1 (June 1, 1929), 728-40.
      The life-cycle is traced expanding on such concepts as vitality and growth.

1253 Curran, W. J. "Legal and medical death: Kansas takes the first step, " New England Journal of Medicine, 284 (Feb. 4, 1971), 260-1.

1254 Cutter, D. R., ed. Updating life and death: essays in ethics and medicine. Boston: Beacon, 1969.
      Discusses the various modes and levels of inquiry into organ transplantation. Focuses on abortion as well as the value and sanctity of life.

1255 Davidson, H. A. "Emotional precipitants of death, " Journal of the Medical Society of New Jersey, 16 (1949), 350-2.
      How emotional factors alter organic function which

can then result in death.

1256 Davidson, R. P. "To give care in terminal illness, "
      American Journal of Nursing, 1 (Jan. 1966), 74-5.

1257 Davidson, S. "Bereavement in children, " Nursing Times, 62
      (Dec. 16, 1966), 1650-2.

1258 Davis, J. L. "Suicide, with some illustrative cases, "
      Journal of the American Medical Association, 43 (1904),
      121-3.
          Investigates the alarming increase of suicide in the
      U. S. Several case studies are included, and an attempt
      is made at explaining why people commit suicide.

1259 Davis, K. G. "Eros and thanatos: the not-so-benign neglect
      or, sexuality, death and the physician, " Texas Reports
      on Biology and Medicine, 32 (spring 1974), 43-8.
          Discusses "areas of neglect in sexuality and death
      as evidenced in medical literature. "

1260 Davis, R. H. , ed. The Doctor and the dying patient. Los
      Angeles: California School of Medicine, 1971.

1261 Davoli, G. "The Child's request to die at home, " Pediatrics,
      38 (Nov. 1966), 925.
          Article states that a terminally-ill child should have
      the right to die at home under the proper circumstances.

1262 Davost, P. H. , ed. "The Doctor in the face of death: twelfth
      international symposium of medical psychology organized
      by the society of medical psychology of the French lan-
      guage. " Lyon. April 3, 4, and 5. (1970) Psychologie
      Medicale, 2 (1970), 311-452.

1263 Day, S. Proceedings: death and attitudes toward death.
      Minneapolis: Ball Museum of Pathology, University of
      Minnesota Medical School, 1972.

1264 "Death ... a concept to reconsider, " Journal of the Florida
      Medical Association, 56 (1969), 799.
          Determining death is discussed, and states the need
      for a definition of death that is not medical.

1265 "Decline in infant and child mortality, " World Health Organiza-
      tion Chronicle, 19 (1965), 112-15.
          Infant and child mortality in Australia, Belgium,
      Canada, Ceylon, Colombia, Denmark, the U. S. , and
      Venezuela is discussed.

1266 Dedellarossa, G. S. "The Concept of death in your self-
      development, " Revista de Psicoanalysis, 22 (1965), 26-
      44.

The author concludes his research with five concepts dealing with the fear of death.

1267   "Definition of death," Science Digest, 65 (March 1969), 77.

1268   Dempsey, D.   "Learning how to die," New York Times Magazine, (Nov. 14, 1971), 58.

1268a Detre, T. P., and H. G. Jarecki. Modern psychiatric treatment. Philadelphia: Lippincott, 1971.

1269   Deutsch, A.   The Mentally ill in America.   N. Y.:   Columbia University Press, 1949.

1269a "Dialogue on death: physician and patient," Geriatric Focus, 5 (Feb. 1966), 1.

1270   Diaz, E.   "A Death on the ward," Hospital Topics, 47 (May 1969), 83-7.
       Deals with the account of a two-and-a-half-year-old girl on a pediatric ward, her death, and the effects it had on personnel and other patients.

1271   Dickinson, A. R.   "Nurse's perceptions of their care of patients dying with cancer." Unpublished doctoral dissertation, Columbia University, 1966.
       Focuses on the preparation of nurses to meet the religious needs of dying patients.

1272   Dieudonne, D.   "Schulerselbstmorde," Medizinische Welt, 3 (1929), 1210-13.

1273   Dionis, P.   Dissertations sur la mort subite; avec l'historie d'une fille cataleptique.   Paris: L. D. Houry, 1710.

1274   "Do you often lose touch with a dying patient?" Patient Care, 4 (May 31, 1970), 59.

1275   Dodge, J. S.   "How much should the patient be told--and by whom?" Hospitals, 37 (Dec. 16, 1963), 66-70.
       Discusses patient-response regarding the lack of medical information given by doctors and nurses about their impending death.

1276   Doring, C.   "Distress in dying," British Medical Journal, 5 (Aug. 17, 1963), 400-1.
       Points out that a great number of dying patients are depressed because of physical distress and that anxiety was noticeable when distress was not relieved.

1277   Dorn, H. F., et al.   "Uses and significance of multiple cause tabulations for mortality statistics," American Journal of Public Health, 54 (1964), 400-6.

1278 Drake, C. "And to Die Is Different," Tomorrow's Nurse,
      4 (Aug.-Sept. 1963), 14-7.
          Offers a fictional story that relates to a real person
      who is about to die. States that nurses can become in-
      volved with the technical aspects of their patients.

1279 Drewry, P. H., Jr. "Some aspects of suicide," Virginia
      Medical Monthly, 69 (1942), 252-6.

1280 Dripps, R. D., et al. "Medical, social and legal aspects of
      suicide," Journal of the American Medical Association,
      171 (1959), 523.
          Presents suicide as one of the major causes of
      death, and the need for better laws, and care for the
      suicidal patient.

1281 Driver, M. V. "E. E. G. and the declaration of death,"
      Electroencephalography and Clinical Neurophysiology,
      27 (Sept. 1969), 332.
          "This communication is a review of E. E. G. studies
      of coma and their relevance to problems concerning re-
      suscitation following cardiac arrest."

1282 Drummond, E. E. "Communication and comfort for the dy-
      ing patients," Nursing Clinics of North America, 5 (May
      1970), 55.
          Points out that the topics of death--loss, grief, re-
      morse--are difficult to handle personally.

1283 Dusinberre, R. K., et al. "Statutory definition of death,"
      New England Journal of Medicine, 286 (March 1972),
      549-50.

1284 Dynes, J. B. "Sudden death," Diseases of the Nervous Sys-
      tem, 30 (Jan. 1969), 24-8.
          Studies the phenomenon of sudden death on the basis
      of autopsies performed on seventeen schizophrenic pa-
      tients who died in Veterans Administration Hospital in
      Salem, Virginia.

1285 Easson, W. M. "Care of the young patient who is dying,"
      Journal of the American Medical Association, 205 (July
      22, 1968), 203-7.
          Discusses the physician's need to appreciate and
      learn to manage his own normal reactions to death.

1286 _____. Dying child: the management of the child or
      adolescent who is dying. Springfield, Ill.: C. C.
      Thomas, 1970.

1287 _____. "The Living dead," Medical Insight (1972), 20-5.

1288 "Effects of bereavement," Canadian Medical Association Journal, 90 (1964), 668.

1289 Eisenberg, J. A., and P. Bourne. The Right to live and die.
      Toronto: Institute for Studies in Education, 1973.
      (Canadian Critical Issues Series.)

1289a Eisenberg, L. "Preventive psychiatry," Annual Review of
      Medicine, 13 (1962), 343-69.

1290 _____. "Psychiatric intervention," in Life and Death and
      Medicine. San Francisco: W. H. Freeman, 1973. pp.
      80-7. (A Scientific American reprint book from Sept.
      1973.)
      "Although enduring remedies for mental disorders
      are elusive, psychoactive drugs and community treat-
      ment programs have markedly reduced the number of
      people in mental hospitals."

1290a Eisenberg, P. B. "Rest in peace, ruthless Roger," Ameri-
      can Journal of Nursing, 70 (Jan. 1970), 132.
      Reflection of the discovery of a patient's identity
      and the new questions that arose after his death.

1291 Elkinton, J. R. "Life and death and the physician," Annals
      of Internal Medicine, 67 (Sept. 1967), 669.
      Editorial discusses the new relationship between doc-
      tor and patient that has been so complicated in our time.
      The contemporary physician has more power to influence
      the health of the patient and now must make more ethical
      judgments.

1292 Engel, G. L. "Grief and grieving," American Journal of
      Nursing, 64 (Sept. 1964), 38-41.
      Discusses the theoretical and practical problems of
      grief. Suggests that relatives of a dead patient be led
      to private places where they can openly express their
      grief.

1293 _____. "Is grief a disease?" Psychosomatic Medicine,
      23 (1961), 18-22.
      Suggests that grief over loss is a disease because it
      involves suffering and impairment to proper functioning
      for long periods of time.

1294 _____. "Sudden death and the 'medical model' in psy-
      chiatry," Canadian Psychiatric Association Journal, 15
      (Dec. 1970), 527-38.

1295 Englander, O. "Cot deaths," British Medical Journal, 4
      (Dec. 1971), 625-6.

1296 "Ethics in medical progress--a commentary on life and
      death," World Medical Journal, 14 (Sept.-Oct. 1967),
      150-1.

1297 "Euthanasia," Lancet, 2 (Aug. 12, 1961), 351-2.
      A doctor discusses the pros and cons of euthanasia,
      and how, if legalized, the doctor should make the deci-
      sion as to life and death.

1298 Evans, A. E. "If a child must die," New England Journal of
      Medicine, 278 (Jan. 1968), 138-42.
      Primary aim of this paper is to discuss the care of
      a dying child and the necessary support of the family
      through this difficult period.

1299 Evans, P. R. "The Management of fatal illness in child-
      hood," Proceedings of the Royal Society of Medicine,
      62 (June 1969), 549-52.
      Discusses the many responses to the unexpected
      death of a child, the disbelief and anger displayed.

1300 Exton-Smith, A. N. "Terminal illness in the aged," Lancet,
      2 (1961), 305-8.
      Outlines the patients' mental state about impending
      death, and assesses the pain and distress of the elderly,
      and gives attention to the circumstances of death.

1301 Farberow, N. L.; W. McKelligott; and S. Cohen. "Suicides
      among patients with cardio respiratory illnesses,"
      Journal of the American Medical Association, 145 (1966),
      422-8.

1302 Feifel, H. "Older persons look at death," Geriatrics, 11
      (1956), 127-30.

1303 _____ . "Perception of death," in Care of Patients with
      Fatal Illnesses, edited by L. P. White. Annals of the
      New York Academy of Sciences, 1969. Vol. 164. pp.
      669-77.

1304 _____ ; J. Freilich; and L. J. Hermann. "Death fear in
      dying heart and cancer patients," Journal of Psycho-
      somatic Research, 17 (July 1973), 161-66.

1305 _____ ; S. Hanson; and R. Jones. "Physicians consider
      death," Proceedings of the 75th Annual Convention of the
      American Psychological Association, 2 (1967), 201-2.
      "Investigated the hypothesis that one of the major
      reasons certain physicians may enter medicine is to
      master their own above average fears of death...."

1306 Fermaglich, J. L. "Determining cerebral death," American
      Family Physician, 3 (March 1971), 85-7.

1307 Filbey, E. E. "Some overtones of euthanasia," Hospital
      Topics, 43 (Sept. 1965), 55-8.

1308 Fischer, J. A. Die Kriminalpolizeiliche Todesermittlung. Wiesbaden: Bundes Kriminalamt, 1969.

1309 Fishbein, M. "Signs of death, " Medical World News, 12 (Dec. 10, 1971), 80.

1310 _____. "Some international aspects of abortion, " Medical World News, 12 (Sept. 17, 1971), 68.

1311 Fisher, G. "Psychotherapy for the dying: principles and illustrative cases with special references to the use of LSD, " Omega, 1 (Feb. 1970), 3-15.

1312 Fisher, J. R. "The Nursing care of terminally ill patients, " Nursing Research, 15 (1966), 92.
        Concerned with the emotional responses and needs of patients with terminal illness.

1313 Fitts, W. T. "What Philadelphia physicians tell patients with cancer, " Journal of the American Medical Association, 153 (Nov. 7, 1953), 901-4.

1314 Fitzgerald, R. G. "Broken heart: a statistical study of increased mortality among widowers, " British Journal of Medicine, 1 (1967), 740.

1315 Fitzgibbons, J. P., Jr., et al. "Sudden unexpected and unexplained death in infants, " Pediatrics, 43 (1969), 980-88.

1316 Fletcher, J. Morals and medicine, rev. ed. Boston: Beacon, 1960.
        This revision of the 1954 edition examines such controversial issues as truth-telling in medicine, euthanasia, and medical ethics among others.

1317 Flinchum, G. A. "Death registration practices and problems, " North Carolina Medical Journal, 29 (April 1968), 176-7.
        States the death registration practices in North Carolina are not followed according to law, and discusses other problems which need state attention as it relates to the disposition of bodies.

1318 Folta, J. R. "The Perception of death, " Nursing Research, 14 (summer 1963), 233-5.

1319 Fond, K. I. "Dealing with death and dying through family-centered care, " Nursing Clinics of North America, 7 (March 1972), 53-64.

1320 Fowler, M. "Sudden unexpected death in infancy, " Journal of West Australian Nurses, 36 (Jan. 1970), 16.

1321   Fox, J. E.   "Reflections on cancer nursing, " American
          Journal of Nursing, 6 (June 1966), 1317-9.
                States that the primary goal of the nurse is to guide
          the patient with love and understanding to a peaceful
          death.

1322   Fredlund, D.   "A Nurse looks at children's questions about
          death, " ANA Clinical Sessions, (1970), 105-12.

1323   Fredrick, J. F.   "Physiological reactions induced by grief, "
          Omega, 2 (May 1971), 71-5.

1324   Freedman, A. R.   "Interview the parents of a dead child?
          Absolutely, " Clinical Pediatrics, 8 (Oct. 1969), 564-5.

1325   Freeman, W.   "Biometrical studies in psychiatry, " American
          Journal of Psychiatry, 8 (Nov. 1928), 425-41.
                Study of the disease incidence and cause of death as
          determined at necropsy in 1150 psychotic patients during
          the period of 1910 to 1928.

1326   Friedman, H. J.   "Physicians management of dying patients:
          an exploration, " Psychiatry in Medicine, 1 (Oct. 1970),
          295-305.

1327   Froggatt, P.; M. A. Lynas; and T. K. Marshall.   "Sudden
          death in babies: epidemiology, " American Journal of
          Cardiology, 22 (Oct. 1968), 457-68.

1328   Fujimuri, B.   "Standards of determining death: cerebral
          death from the standpoint of neurophysiology, " Surgical
          Therapy, (April 1969), 415-22.

1329   Furman, E.   A Child's parent dies.   Introduction by Anna
          Freud.   New Haven, Conn.:   Yale University Press,
          1973.
                Study of 23 children who suffered the death of a
          parent during childhood; seeks to understand the psy-
          chological impact of bereavement on the young.

1330   Gavey, C.   The Management of the "hopeless" case.   Lon-
          don: H. K. Lewis, 1952.

1331   Gaynor, M.   "On facing death, " Nursing Outlook, 7 (Sept.
          1959), 509.
                Discusses the experiences of nurses who feel unable
          to handle the relatives of the dying patient.

1332   _____.   "What man shall live and not see death?" Nursing
          Outlook, 12 (Jan. 1964), 23.

1333   Geber, M.   "The Physician, the child and death. 2.   The
          anguish of death during psychotherapy of children, "

Revue de Médecine Psychosomatique et de Psychologie
Médicale, 10 (Oct.-Dec. 1968), 419-23.

1334 Geertinger, P. Sudden death in infancy. Springfield, Ill.:
      C. C. Thomas, 1968.

1335 Geill, T. "Old age, diseases and death," Excerpts of Medi-
      cine, 20 (Sept. 1960), 447-50.

1336 Geis, D. P. "Mothers perceptions of care given their dying
      children," American Journal of Nursing, 65 (Jan. 1965),
      105-7.
         Discusses "how 26 mothers who had lost children
      while under hospital care felt about their children's final
      experiences with nurses."

1337 Gerard, E. I. "Der Tod als Erlebnis bei Kindern und Jugend-
      lichen," Internationale Zeitschrift für Individual-psycholo-
      gie, 8 (1930), 551-8.

1338 Germann, D. R. Too young to die. N. Y.: Farnsworth,
      1974.
         Begins with ten simple steps to improve your health
      and extend your life expectancy. "100,000 deaths can be
      avoided every year."

1339 Gester, M. "Morticians are in," Atlas, 12 (July 1966), 40-
      2.

1340 Gifford, S. "Some psychoanalytic theories about death," in
      Care of Patients with Fatal Illness, edited by L. P.
      White. Annals of the New York Academy of Sciences,
      1969. Vol. 164. pp. 638-68.
         Article examines the biological theory of Freud.
      Discusses the concept of unconscious immortality and
      his view of death in various works.

1341 Gilli, R., et al. "On the ascertainment of death and on
      freedom to remove organs for transplantations," Minerva
      Anestesiologica, 34 (Nov. 1968), 1340-51.

1342 Gillison, T. H. "Prolongation of dying," Lancet, 2 (Dec. 22,
      1962), 1327.
         A letter deals with euthanasia, the doctor who is
      looked upon as the preserver of life, and the difficult
      judgments involved.

1343 Ginzberg, R. "Should the elderly cancer patient be told,"
      Geriatrics, 4 (1949), 101-7.
         Details both sides of the issue of truthfulness where
      the elderly cancer patient is involved with impending
      death.

1344 Girwood, R., and M. Ballinger. "The Factors that commonly
      worry the patient in the hospital," Edinburgh Medical
      Journal, 56 (1949), 347-52.
          Discusses the fear of death as well as the fear of
      getting well. Cites the need to abolish the practice of
      referring to a person in a hospital as a "case."

1345 Glaser, B. G. "Disclosure of terminal illness," Journal of
      Health and Human Behavior, 7 (summer 1966), 83-91.
          Describes the physician's dilemma of telling the pa-
      tient that he has a terminal illness.

1346 _____. "Dying on time," Trans-Action, 2 (May-June
      1965), 27-31.

1347 _____, and A. L. Strauss. Awareness of dying. Chicago:
      Aldine, 1965.
          A publication in the observations series, edited by
      Howard S. Becker.

1348 Glass, R. D. "Cot deaths," Medical Journal of Australia, 2
      (July 1971), 10.

1349 Goetz, H. "Needed: a new approach to the care of the dy-
      ing," Registered Nurse, 25 (Oct. 1972), 60-2.

1350 Goff, W. C. "How can a physician prepare his patient for
      death," Journal of the American Medical Association,
      201 (July 21, 1967), 280.
          The preparation of a patient for death varies with
      age, sex, marital status, occupation, country of origin,
      and religious background.

1351 Gold, E., et al. "Viral infection: a possible cause of sud-
      den unexpected death in infants," New England Journal
      of Medicine, 264 (1961), 53-60.

1352 Goldfogel, L. "Working with the parents of a dying child,"
      American Journal of Nursing, 70 (Aug. 1970), 1675-79.
          Discussion of a nurse's experiences with a mother
      of a dying child.

1353 Golding, S. L.; G. E. Atwood; and R. A. Goodman. "An-
      xiety and two cognitive forms of resistance to the idea
      of death," Psychological Reports, 18 (April 1966), 359-
      64.

1354 Goldstein, S. "Jewish mortality and survival patterns:
      Providence, Rhode Island--1962-1964," Eugenics Quar-
      terly, 13 (March 1966), 48-61.
          Explores the patterns of Jewish mortality, survival,
      and attempts to ascertain the way in which these pat-
      terns differ from those of the general population.

1355 Golub, S., and M. Reznikoff. "Attitudes toward death: a comparison of nursing students and graduate nurses," Nursing Research, 20 (Nov.-Dec. 1971), 503-8.

1355a Goodman, L. S., and A. Gilman. The Pharmacological basis of therapeutics. N.Y.: Macmillan, 1970.

1356 Googe, M. C. S. "The Death of a young man," American Journal of Nursing, 64 (Nov. 1964), 133-5.
A nurse describes her experiences about the impending death of a young man and the response of his family to his early death.

1357 Gordon, I. "The Mechanism of death," Journal of Forensic Medicine, 14 (Oct.-Dec. 1967), 125-30.
Discusses the "mechanism of death from the viewpoint of a forensic pathologist. Points out the deaths of medico-legal importance which should be described as due to coma, or syncope, or asphyxia."

1358 Gotz, B. "Sexualität Erkenntnis, Tod," Zeitschrift fur Sexualiwissenschaft, 17 (1931), 486-96.

1359 Graham, J. B. "Acceptance of death--beginning of life," North Carolina Medical Journal, 24 (Aug. 1963), 317-9.

1360 Grant, I. "Care of the dying," British Medical Journal, 5060 (Dec. 28, 1957), 1539-40.
Article contains information about the role of the general practitioner, need for hospital accommodation, telling the patient, and the use of drugs.

1361 Grant, R. N. "The Child with leukemia and his parents," CA Cancer Journal for Clinicians, 14 (March-April, 1964), 73-6.

1362 Gray, V. R. "Dealing with dying," Nursing '73, 3 (June 1973), 26-31.
Deals with the needs both psychological and physiological in the care of dying patients. Explains the changed perceptions of body needs.

1363 Green, M.; S. Friedman; and M. B. Rothenberg. "Something can be done for a child with cancer," Hospital Tribune, 1 (July 1967), 8.

1364 Greenberg, H. R. "Dreams of a dying patient," British Journal of Medical Psychology, 43 (Dec. 1970), 355-62.
Story of a man with caloric carcinoma whose dreams prevented an opportunity to study the unconscious issues of death. Mr. E's dreams revealed an unconscious recognition of death.

1365 Greenberg, I. M. "Attitudes toward death in schizophrenia,"
      Journal of the Hillside Hospital, 13 (1964), 104-13.

1366 _____. "Death and dying: attitudes of patient and doctor,
      4. Studies on attitudes toward death," Group for the Ad-
      vancement of Psychiatry, (Symposium No. 11), 5 (Oct.
      1965), 623-31.

1367 _____, and I. E. Alexander. "Some correlates to thoughts
      and feelings concerning death," New York Hillside Hos-
      pital Journal, 1 (April-July, 1962), 120-6.

1368 Greenberg, S. "The Right to die: to what extent should the
      medical profession prolong life after all medical hope is
      gone? Should people be allowed to choose voluntary
      euthanasia," Progressive, 30 (June 1966), 27-40.

1369 Greene, W. A. "The Physician and his dying patient,"
      Paper presented at the University of Rochester School
      of Medicine, at a conference entitled The Patient, Death,
      and the Family. April 29, 1971.

1370 _____. "Role of a vicarious object in the adaption to ob-
      ject loss, I. Use of a vicarious object...," Psycho-
      somatic Medicine, 20 (1958), 344-50.

1371 Greer, H. S. "Suicidal patients," Nursing Mirror, 130
      (Jan. 16, 1970), 36.
            Attempts to define suicidal behavior. Describes the
      causes, motives, and suggests methods for managing the
      suicidal patient.

1372 Gruman, G. A History of ideas about the prolongation of
      life: the evolution of prolongivity hypothesis to 1800.
      N.Y.: American Philosophical Society, 1966.

1373 Gubrium, J. Living and dying at Murray Manor. N.Y.:
      St. Martin's Press, 1975.
            "... [T]he author explores the social world of care
      within a nursing home for the aged by studying the
      everyday life of staff members, residents, and their
      families."

1373a Gustafson, E. "Dying: the career of the nursing home pa-
      tient," Journal of Health and Social Behavior, 13 (Sept.
      1972), 226-35.
            Contents: The career; The career participants; The
      timetable; Bargaining; Conclusions.

1374 Gutmacher, A. F. "Changing attitudes and practices con-
      cerning abortion: a sociomedical revolution," Maryland
      State Medical Journal, 20 (Dec. 1971), 59-63.

1375 Guttentag, O. E. "The Meaning of death in medical theory,"
      Stanford Medical Bulletin, 17 (1959), 165-70.

1376 Gyomroi, E. L. "The Analysis of a young concentration
      camp victim," The Psychoanalytic Study of the Child,
      18 (1963), 484-510.

1377 Hackett, T. P. "Current approaches to the care and under-
      standing of the dying patient," Archives of the Founda-
      tion of Thanatology, 1 (1969), 109.

1378 _____. "Definitions of death," New England Journal of
      Medicine, 279 (1968), 834-5.

1379 Haller, J. A., ed. The Hospitalized child and his family.
      Baltimore: Johns Hopkins University Press, 1967.

1380 Halley, M. M., and W. F. Harvey. "Medical vs. legal
      definitions of death," Journal of the American Medical
      Association, 204 (May 6, 1968), 423-5.

1381 Halpern, W. I. "Some psychiatric sequelae to crib death,"
      American Journal of Psychiatry, 129 (Oct. 1972), 398-
      402.

1382 Hamburger, J. "Medical ethics and organ transplantation,"
      American Medical Women's Association Journal, 23 (Nov.
      1968), 981-4.

1383 Hammer, M. "Reflections on one's own death as a peak ex-
      perience," Mental Hygiene, 55 (April 1971), 264-5.

1384 Hamner, R. T. "Legal death--can it be defined?" Journal
      of the Medical Association of Alabama, 38 (Jan. 1969),
      610-14.
         Discussion of the way the various states have de-
      fined death, the time of death, and the difficulty in de-
      veloping a common definition.

1385 Harp, J. R. "Criteria for the determination of death,"
      Anesthesiology, 40 (April 1974), 391-7.

1385a Harvey, A. M., et al. The Principles and practice of medi-
      cine. N. Y.: Appleton-Century-Crofts, 1972.

1386 Havinghurst, R., Jr., and B. Neugarten, eds. "Attitudes
      toward death in older persons: a symposium," Journal
      of Gerontology, 16 (1961), 44-66.

1387 Haynes, W. S. "Preservation of the unfit," Medical Journal
      of Australia, 58 (1971), 750-1.
         Discussion of those whose only hope for relief from
      pain is death and whether or not their lives should be
      preserved.

1388 Hays, J. S. "The Night Neil died," Nursing Outlook, 10
      (Dec. 1962), 801-3.
      Report of reactions of nurses to a child's death.

1389 Helson, G. A. "House dust mites and possible connection
      with sudden infant death syndrome," New Zealand Medi-
      cal Journal, 74 (Sept. 1971), 209.

1390 Henderson, D. K. "Suicide," Edinburgh Medical Journal, 45
      (1938), 245-63.
      Author states that "socially and medically we have
      neglected suicide and have been content with rationaliza-
      tions and glib explanations."

1391 Hendrix, R. C. Investigation of violent and sudden death; a
      manual for medical examiners. Springfield, Ill.: C. C.
      Thomas, 1972.

1392 Hershey, N. "On the question of prolonging life," American
      Journal of Nursing, 71 (March 1971), 521-22.

1393 _____. "Questions of life and death," American Journal
      of Nursing, 68 (Sept. 1968), 1910-12.

1394 Heuyer, G. , et al. "Le Sens de la mort chez l'enfant,"
      Revue de Neuropsychiatric Infantile et d'Hygiene Mentale
      de l'Enfance, 3 (May-June, 1955), 219-51.

1395 Hicks, W. , et al. "The Dying patient, his physician and
      the psychiatric consultant," Psychosomatics, 9 (Jan. -
      Feb. 1968), 47-52.

1396 Hilgard, J. R. , and M. F. Newman. "Early parental depriva-
      tion in schizophrenia and alcoholism," American Journal
      of Orthopsychiatry, 33 (1963), 409-20.
      Describes how parental loss at an early age effects
      schizophrenic and alocholic patients.

1397 _____. "Parental loss by death in childhood as an
      etiological factor among schizophrenic and alcoholic
      patients compared with a non-patient community sample,"
      Journal of Nervous and Mental Disease, 137 (1963), 14-
      28.
      States that the death of a parent in childhood may
      make a person more vulnerable than others to mental
      illness. Points out difficulties and limitations of this
      kind of investigation.

1398 Hill, O. W. "Childhood bereavement and adult psychiatric
      disturbance," Journal of Psychosomatic Research, 16
      (Aug. 1972), 357-60.

1399 Hingley, S. "Today I saw death," American Journal of

Nursing, 67 (April 1967), 823.

1400   Hintermann, R.   "Ursachen des Selbstmordes bei Jugend-
       lichen."   Thesis, Zurich, 1953.

1401   Hinton, J. M.   "Facing death," Journal of Psychosomatic
       Research, 10 (1966-67), 22-8.
              Paper contains two parts: "Discusses the opinions
       expressed by people about their wish to be told that
       they have a potential fatal disease.   The second part is
       concerned with reported reactions of patients on being
       told they have a fatal illness."

1402   _____.   "The Physical and mental distress of the dying,"
       Quarterly Journal of Medicine, 32 (1963), 1-21.
              Attempts to assess the amount of mental and physical
       distress experienced in terminal illness and how the pain
       can be relieved.

1403   _____.   "Problems in the care of the dying," Journal of
       Chronic Diseases, 17 (1961), 201-5.
              Article discusses the problem of emotion in caring
       for the dying.   Various articles that have covered this
       topic are also mentioned.

1404   _____.   "Talking with people about to die," British Medi-
       cal Journal, 3 (July 6, 1974), 25-7.

1405   Hodge, J. R.   "Help your patients to mourn better," Medical
       Times, 99 (June 1971), 53-64.

1406   _____.   "How to help your patients approach the inevita-
       ble," Medical Times (Manhasset), 102 (Nov. 1974), 123.

1407   Hoevet, M.   "Dying is also living," Nursing Care, 7 (July
       1974), 12-15.

1408   Hoffman, J. W.   "When a loved one is dying: how to decide
       what to tell him," Today's Health, 134 (Feb. 1972), 41-
       3.

1409   Hollingsworth, J. W.   "Delayed radiation effects in survivors
       of the atomic bombings," New England Journal of Medi-
       cine, 263 (Sept. 8, 1960), 381-7.

1409a The Hour of our death; a record of the conference on the
       care of the dying held in London, 1973.   Papers by
       Cardinal Heenan and others; edited by S. Lack and R.
       Lamerton.   London: G. Chapman, 1974.

1410   Howard, E.   "The Effect of work experience in a nursing
       home on the attitudes toward death held by nurse aides,"
       Gerontologist, 14 (Feb. 1974), 54-6.

The death-avoidance pattern exhibited by some 28
nurses' aides with various amounts of experience make
this a contribution to the literature.

1411 Howell, D. A. "A Child dies," Hospital Topics, 45 (Feb.
      1967), 93-6.

1412 Howie, D. L. "Scared to death," Journal of the Florida
      Medical Association, 55 (Sept. 1968), 861-2.

1413 Huber, B.; R. Sieber; and M. Schmaus. Krankheit und Tod.
      Munich: Zink, 1959.

1414 Hughes, H. L. G. ... [P]eace at the last; a survey of ter-
      minal care in the United Kingdom. A report to the
      Calouste Gulbenkian Foundation. London: United King-
      dom and British Commonwealth Branch, 1960.

1415 Huntington, R. W., Jr., and J. J. Jarzynka. "Sudden and
      unexpected death in infancy, with special reference to
      the so-called crib deaths," American Journal of Clinical
      Pathology, 38 (Dec. 1962), 637-8.

1416 Hussey, H. H. "The Cause of death," Journal of the Ameri-
      can Medical Association, 229 (July 1, 1974), 75.
          Hussey refers to his work he did 40 years ago with
      Yater regarding the death certificate as an important
      document. In an editorial, four case reports are pre-
      sented which "illustrate that there is often something
      behind the death certificate--a life event or a circum-
      stance that never enters vital statistics, yet is the true
      cause of death, undetectable at postmortem examina-
      tion."

1417 Hutschnecker, A. A. The Will to live. N.J.: Prentice-
      Hall, 1951.
          A discussion of emotions in connection with illness
      from a Freudian view of the interplay between destruc-
      tive and constructive impulses. A number of cases are
      presented.

1418 Hwang, J. C. "The Sudden infant death syndrome," Archives
      of Pathology, 94 (Oct. 1972), 370-1.

1419 Inman, W. S. "Emotion, cancer, and time: coincidence or
      determinism?" British Journal of Medical Psychology,
      40 (1967), 235-31.
          Advances the theory that death "may be postponed
      or advanced by the patient to coincide with dates of
      some significance to the patient."

1420 Innes, G., et al. "Mortality among psychiatric patients,"
      Scotland Medical Journal, 15 (April 1970), 143-8.

Concludes that there is an association between high mortality rates and psychiatric illness. Over 2000 patients were used in the study.

1421 Isaacs, B., et al. "The Concept of pre-death," Lancet, 1 (May 29, 1971), 1115-8.

1422 Isler, C. "Let the parents help care for the child with leukemia," Registered Nurse, 25 (June 1962), 44-57.

1423 Jablon, S., et al. "Studies of the mortality of A-bomb survivors," Radiation Research, 25 (1965), 25-52.
Describes the program of studies of the survivors of Nagasake and Hiroshima. Sample consisted of 100,000 persons whose names were drawn from listings. Persons eligible were those located within 2500 meters of the hypocenter at the time of the bombing. Each member was interviewed and gave details of exposure.

1424 Jackson, N. A. "A Child's preoccupation with death," American Nurse's Association Clinical Sessions (1968), 172-9.

1425 Jacques, J. Le Faut mourir, suivi de médecin líberal, qui donne gratis rémedes contre les frayeurs de la mort. Lyons, 1966.

1426 Jaffe, L. "Terminal: love story was just a story--this is real," Pittsburgh Renaissance, 6 (April 1975), 27-40.
"... [I]t made me realize that I had been extremely happy and fulfilled in my life and that I really wanted to continue doing exactly what I had been doing: teaching, doing therapy, being a wife, a mother. I had no desire to hop on a boat to Tahiti. I simply wanted to get into remission and go back to doing what I had enjoyed for so many years...."

1427 Jaisrub, S. "The Fade-out," Archives of Internal Medicine, 121 (June 1968), 511.
Editorial discusses the difficulty of defining death because respirators and cardiac pacemakers have led to a vagueness about the definition.

1428 Jakobovits, I. "The Dying and their treatment in Jewish law," Hebrew Medical Journal, 2 (1961), 242-51.

1428a James, T. N. "Sudden death in babies," American Journal of Cardiology, 22 (1968), 456-506.

1429 Jantz, H. "Schizophrenie und Selbstmord," Nervenarzt, 22 (1951), 126-33.

1430 Jeffers, F. C.; C. R. Nichols; and C. Eisdorfer. "Attitudes

of older persons toward death," Journal of Gerontology,
16 (1961), 53-6.

1431 Jensen, G. D., and J. G. Wallace. "Family mourning process," Family Process, 6 (1967), 56-66.
Includes cases to illustrate "how mourning can be
managed therapeutically as a family process."

1432 Johnson, A. B. "Right to live or the right to die," Nursing
Times, 67 (May 1971), 573-4.

1433 Johnston, E. H., et al. "Investigation of sudden death in
addicts, with emphasis on the toxicological findings in
thirty cases," Medical Annals of the District of Columbia, 38 (July 1969), 375-80.

1434 Jones, J. C. "Premonition of death," British Medical Journal, 2 (1958), 1051.

1435 Jones, K. S. "Death and doctors," Medical Journal of
Australia, 49 (Sept. 1, 1962), 329-34.
Seeks to set up criteria for the determination of
death, and better regulations concerning the death certificate.

1436 Jones, T. T. "Dignity in death. The application and with-
holding of interventive measures," Journal of the Louisiana Medical Society, 13 (1961), 180-3.
"A plea for comfort and relief to the dying patient--
not euthanasia but agathanasia."

1437 Jonkman, E. J. "Cerebral death plus the Isaelectric E.E.G.,"
Electroencephalography and Clinical Neurophysiology,
(Aug. 1969), 215.

1438 Kalish, R. A. "Dealing with the grieving family," Registered
Nurse, 26 (May 1963), 80-4.

1439 _____. "The Practicing physician and death research,"
Medical Times, 97 (Jan. 1968), 211-20.
Suggests a number of behavioral science factors
which medical practitioners can use in their research on
death, dying, and bereavement.

1440 Kalsey, V. "As life ebbs," American Journal of Nursing,
48 (1948), 170-3.
States the duty of making death as beautiful and as
meaningful as the experience can be.

1441 Kanders, O. "Der Todesgedanke in der Nervöse und in der
Psychose," Der Nervenarzt, 6 (1934), 288.

1442 Kane, H. "Nursing--the end," American Mercury, 19 (April

1930), 458-61.
Article describes the experiences of a trained nurse
about what happens several hours before death.

1443 Karon, M., and J. J. Vernick.   "An Approach to the emotional support of fatally ill children, " Clinical Pediatrics,
7 (May 1968), 274-80.
Discusses how many physicians hide the diagnosis of
leukemia from their young patients, and stresses that
these particular patients need emotional support.

1444 Kasper, A. M.   "The Doctor and death, " in The Meaning of
Death, edited by H. Feifel.   N. Y.:   McGraw-Hill, 1959.
pp. 259-70.
Concerned with the absence of courses on death in
medical schools, and stresses the need for death-educa-
tion.

1445 Kass, L. R.   "Problems in the meaning of death, " Science,
170 (Dec. 1970), 1235-6.
In medicine today there is a conflict of values--be-
tween ethics and a practice based on a fundamental respect for human life per se.

1446 Kast, E.   "LSD and the dying patient, " Chicago Medical
School Quarterly, 26 (summer 1966), 82.

1447 Kastenbaum, R.   "Multiple perspectives on a geriatric 'Death
Valley', " Community Mental Health Journal, 3 (spring
1967), 21-9.
"Considers perceptions of 'Death Valley' (Cushing
Hospital, Framingham, Mass.), the intensive treatment
unit of a geriatric hospital.   Information was gathered
from various sources, including patients who had sur-
vived a period of residence in 'Death Valley, ' and hospital personnel. "

1448 _____.   "Viewpoint: helping the patient prepare for
death, " Geriatrics, 22 (1967), 80-9.
Interesting dialogue which discusses those who are
able to approach various aspects of death.   Some patients are willing to discuss their views.

1449 Katz, A. H.   "Who shall survive?"   Medical Opinion and Review, 3 (1967), 52-61.
Presents the question as it relates to those who
need treatment on a dialyzer when there are more patients than machines and methods.

1450 Kaufer, C., et al.   "Time of death determination following
dissociated death of the brain: clinical and electro-
encephalographic criteria, " Deutsche Medizinische
Wochenschrift, 93 (April 5, 1968), 679-84.

Discusses the stoppage of biological aspects of the organism and the cessation of neuracerebral functions.

1451 Kavanaugh, R. "Helping patients who are facing death, " Nursing, (May 1974), 35-42.
Deals with the painful but necessary task of communicating with a terminally ill patient.

1452 Kay, D., et al. "Prognosis in psychiatric disorder of the elderly: an attempt to define indicators of early death and early recovery, " Journal of Mental Science, 102 (1956), 129-40.
"Authors were able to predict death and discharge from care of 75% of a group of patients admitted to a mental care unit. "

1453 Kazzaz, D. S., and R. Vickers. "Geriatric staff attitudes toward death, " Proceedings of the 20th Annual Meeting of the Gerontological Society, 1967.
"... [S]taff attitudes and reactions to the issue of death, and other conflict areas related to it, were studied through direct observations, and consultative and psychodrama sessions.... [P]atients seemed better able than staff to face the actual occurrence of death.... "

1454 Keefe, D. J. "The Life and death of the law, " Hospital Progress, 53 (March 1972), 64-74.

1455 Keeley, K. A., et al. "Alcohol and drug abuse: causes of sudden death, " Southern Medical Journal, 67 (Aug. 1974), 970-2.

1456 Kelly, G. S. J. Medico-moral problems. St. Louis: Catholic Hopsital Assoc. of the U. S. and Canada, 1949.

1457 Kemph, J. P. "Renal failure, artificial kidney and kidney transplant, " American Journal of Psychiatry, 122 (May 1966), 1270-74.

1458 Kennedy, I. M. "The Kansas statute on death--an appraisal, " New England Journal of Medicine, 285 (Oct. 1971), 946-50.

1459 Kennell, J. H. "The Mourning response of parents to the death of a newborn infant, " New England Journal of Medicine, 283 (Aug. 1 970), 344-9.
Reports the results of interviews with 20 women after the death of their infants.

1460 Kerenyi, N. A., and I. F. Fekete. "Sudden unexpected death in infancy, " Canadian Journal of Public Health, 60 (Sept. 1969), 357-61.
States that most of the theories that try to explain

sudden unexpected death in infants are not generally accepted.

1461 Kern, R. A. "The Growing problem of suicide," California Medicine, 79 (1953), 6-29.
"Informed as to the epidemiologic aspects of suicide, and as to warning signs, physicians could by appropriate action, prevent self-destruction in many cases."

1462 Kimora, J., et al. "The Isoelectric electroencephalogram: significance in establishing death in patients on mechanical respirators," Archives in Internal Medicine, 121 (June 1968), 511-17.
Points out that an isoelectric EEG indicates a low-voltage record on a total absence of electrical activity of the cortex that suggests cerebral death.

1463 King, J. M. "Denial," American Journal of Nursing, 66 (May 1966), 1010-13.

1464 Kirschner, D. "Some reactions of patients in psychotherapy to the death of the president," Psychoanalytic Review, 51 (1964-65), 665-9.
Discusses the observations on psychotherapy sessions with eight female patients after the death of President Kennedy. "All could be considered 'good' neurotic patients and the emotional reactions were quite uniform."

1465 Kitay, W. "Let's retain the dignity of dying," Today's Health, (May 1966), 62-9.
Discusses ways to take the shame out of dying and making death less tragic.

1466 Klebba, A. J., et al. "Mortality trends for leading causes of death: United States, 1950-69; a study of the trends during 1950-69 for the 15 leading causes of death which accounted for 89% of the 1,921,990 deaths occurring in the United States in 1969." Rockville, Md., National Center for Health Statistics, 1974.
"Data from the national vital statistics system. Series 20, no. 16. DHEW publication, no. (HRA)-74-1853."

1467 Klerman, G. L. "Drugs and the dying patient," Journal of Thanatology, 2 (winter 1972), 574-87.
Discusses the uses of psychopharmacologic drugs to help the patient meet his impending death.

1468 Klintworth, G. K. "Suicide and attempted suicide," South African Medical Journal, 34 (1960), 363.
Study to determine the incidence of suicide and attempted suicide in Johannesburg.

1469 Kluge, Eike-Henner W. The Practice of death. New Haven,
      Conn.: Yale University Press, 1974.
          Presents convincing arguments for and against is-
      sues on suicide, senicide, infanticide, and abortion.

1470 Knapp, V. S., and H. Hansen. "Helping the parents of
      children with leukemia," Social Work, 18 (July 1973),
      70-5.
          Parents begin to anticipate mourning when their child
      is diagnosed as having leukemia. The group meetings
      with other parents with similar problems help them to
      live through the process.

1471 Kneisl, C. R. "Thoughtful care of the dying," American
      Journal of Nursing, 68 (March 1968), 550-3.

1472 Knight, J. A. "Philosophic implications of terminal illness,"
      North Carolina Medical Journal, 22 (1961), 493-5.
          Stresses the importance of the physician's handling
      the hopelessly dying person in a philosophical manner
      when all hope for survival is gone.

1473 Knudson, A. G., and J. M. Natterson. "Participation of
      parents in the hospital care of fatally ill children,"
      Pediatrics, 26 (1960), 482-90.
          Reports on the various experiences of a program
      for the participation of parents of fatally ill children.

1474 Kohlhaas, M. "On the determination of the time of death
      of the deceased," Deutsche Medizinische Wochenschrift,
      93 (March 1968), 412-14.

1475 _____. "Once again: on determination of the time of
      death of the deceased," Deutsche Medizinische Wochen-
      schrift, 93 (Aug. 1968), 1575.

1476 Kohn, L. A. "Thoughts on the care of the hopelessly ill,"
      Medical Times, 89 (1961), 1177-81.
          A doctor offers suggestions and guidelines for caring
      for the hopelessly ill patient.

1477 Koop, C. E. "The Death of a child," Bulletin of the Ameri-
      can College of Surgeons, 52 (July-Aug. 1967), 173-4.

1478 _____. "The Seriously ill or dying child: supporting the
      patient and the family," Pediatric Clinics of North
      America, 16 (Aug. 1969), 555-64.

1479 Kopel, K.; W. E. O'Connell; and J. Paris. "A Didactic
      experimental death and dying lab," Newsletter for Re-
      search in Mental Health and Behavioral Sciences, 15
      (Aug. 1973), 1-2.
          The VA hospital in Houston, Texas, designed a hu-

man relations laboratory on death and dying. The design of the lab is described and the team approach included nurses, nursing students, and social workers.

1480 Korschelt, E. Lebensdauer, Altern und Tod. Jena: G. Fischer, 1924.

1481 Kosambi, D. "Seasonal variation in the Indian death rate," Annals of Human Genetics, 19 (1954), 100-19.
Discusses the accuracy of death statistics in India. "The time lag for [reporting a] death cannot be greater than one day [after the event]."

1482 Kostelnik, A. R. "A Study of the nursing needs of the critically ill dying patients," Thesis, University of Pittsburgh, 1959.

1483 Kram, C., et al. "The Dying patient," Psychosomatics, (Sept.-Oct. 1969), 293-5.
Relates the results of a survey sent to lawyers, psychiatrists, physicians and clergymen. The survey concerned incurable diseases and how one should be told of them.

1484 Krame, M., and C. Young. "Administrator helps determine the quality of dying," Modern Nursing Home, 24 (April 1970), 49.
"States that the hospital administrator can encourage a warm safe atmosphere in which the patient is allowed to die with dignity."

1485 Krant, M. J. Dying and dignity: the meaning and control of a personal death. Springfield, Ill.: C. C. Thomas, 1974.
Written in essay form for families and health care staff. The book is based on experiences in the care of terminal cancer patients. Clarifies the concept of dignity in the death of an individual.

1486 _____. "Helping patients die well," New England Journal of Medicine, 280 (Jan. 23, 1960), 222.

1487 _____. "The Organized care of the dying patient," Hospital Practice, (Jan. 1972), 101-8.
Encourages an organized method in the health care system which will help the terminally ill patient get the care and support needed to die well.

1488 _____, and A. Sheldon. "The Dying patient: medicine's responsibility," Journal of Thanatology, 1 (Jan.-Feb. 1971), 1.

1489 Kraus, A. S., and A. M. Lilienfeld. "Some epidemiologic aspects of the high mortality rate in the young widowed group," Journal of Chronic Diseases, 10 (Sept. 1959), 207-17.

1490 Kraus, F. Über Tod und Sterben. Berlin: Urban and Schwarzenberg, 1911.

1491 Kravitz, H., et al. "Deaths in suburbia," Clinical Pediatrics, 5 (May 1966), 266-7.
      Discusses automobile accidents in driveways in suburbia which claim the lives of hundreds of children and suggests ways to correct the situation.

1492 Kretschmer, H. "Determination of the time of death from the neurosurgical viewpoint," Zeitschrift für Aerztliche Fortbildung, 63 (Aug. 15, 1969), 884-5.

1493 Kretz, J., and O. Potzel. "Die Psyche des Krebshranhen," Krebsarzt (1946), 19-29.

1494 Krupp, G. R. "Notes on identification as a defense against anxiety in coping with loss," International Journal of Psychoanalysis, 46 (1965), 303-14.

1495 Kubie, L. S. "Instincts and homoeostasis," Psychosomatic Medicine, 10 (1948), 15-30.

1496 Kübler-Ross, E. "On the use of psychopharmacologic agents for the dying patient and the bereaved." Paper presented at a seminar of the Thanatology Foundation, Columbia College of Physicians and Surgeons, New York. Nov. 12, 1971.

1497 Kuller, L., et al. "Sudden and unexpected death in young adults. An epidemiological study," Journal of the American Medical Association, 198 (Oct. 1966), 248-52.
      Studies 322 cases of non-traumatic deaths of which 31.4% were sudden and unexpected and concludes that these types of deaths need further research.

1498 Kutscher, A. H., and M. R. Goldberg, eds. Caring for the dying patient and his family; a model for medical education and medical center conferences. N.Y.: Health Science Publishing Corp., 1973.
      Description of the proceedings of a conference presented by Tulane medical school, and the Foundation of Thanatology, held March 12, 1971.

1499 _____; B. B. Schoenberg; and A. C. Carr. "Death, grief and the dental practitioner: thanatology as related to dentistry," Journal of the American Dental Association, 81 (Dec. 1970), 1373-7.

1500   Kyle, M. W.   "The Nurse's approach to the patient attempt-
       ing to adjust to inoperable cancer, " Nursing Research,
       14 (spring 1965), 178-9.

1501   LaDue, J. S.   "The Management of terminal patients with
       inoperable carcinoma, " Journal of the Kansas Medical
       Society, 54 (Jan. 1953), 1-6.

1502   Lamers, W. M. Jr.   "Funerals are good for people--M. D. 's
       included, " Medical Economics (June 23, 1969).   (A re-
       print c1969 by Medical Economics, Inc.)
          "This physician firmly believes that funerals play a
       therapeutic role by helping patients vent their grief after
       a death.   Doctors who understand this, he says, can
       better help the grief-stricken adjust to their loss. "

1503   Lamm, R. D. , and S. Davison.   "Abortion and euthanasia, "
       Rocky Mountain Medical Journal, 68 (fall 1971), 40-2.

1504   Lancaster, H. D.   "The Mortality from violence in Aus-
       tralia, 1863 to 1900, " Medical Journal of Australia, 1
       (1964), 388-93.

1505   Langston, B.   "Essex and the art of dying, " Huntington Li-
       brary Quarterly, 13 (Feb. 1950), 109-29.

1506   Lardé de Venturino, A.   Es la electricidad el origen de la
       vida y de la meurte?   Santiago de Chile: Impre. El
       Imparcial, 1943.

1507   Lasagna, L.   Life, death, and the doctor.   N. Y. :   Knopf,
       1968.
          Discusses the role of the doctor, educational meas-
       ures required to prevent death from accidents, air pol-
       lution, and cigarette smoking.

1508   Lascarl, A. D.   "The Family and the dying child: a com-
       passionate approach, " Medical Times, 97 (May 1969),
       207-15.

1509   Laurie, W.   "Athletes' deaths, " British Medical Journal, 4
       (Jan. 23, 1971), 233-4.

1510   Lazare, A.   "Hidden conceptual models in clinical psychiatry, "
       New England Journal of Medicine, 288 (Feb. 15, 1973),
       345-51.

1511   Lazarus, H. , and J. J. Kosten, Jr.   "Psychogenic hyper-
       ventilation and death anxiety, " Psychosomatics, 10
       (1969), 14-22.
          Offers suggestions for the diagnosis of psychogenic
       hyperventilation as it relates to death anxiety, dizziness,
       chest pain, and fear of impending death.

1512 Leak, W. N. "The Care of the dying, " Practitioner, 161
      (1948), 80-7.
          Article states that "the patient always be considered
      a person and that medical procedure always reflect a hu-
      man approach. "

1513 Lee, S. C. Death of a transplant. Huntsville, Ala.: Strode
      Publ. , 1969.

1514 Leibowitz, S. "The Conduct of the internist toward the patient
      and his family when a diagnosis of malignancy is estab-
      lished, " New York Journal of Medicine, 11 (June 1,
      1951), 1421-4.
          A doctor suggests ways that an internist can help
      when malignancy is diagnosed both before and after sur-
      gery.

1515 LeShan, L. "Mobilizing the life force, " Annals of the New
      York Academy of Sciences, 164 (Dec. 1969), 847-61.
          Paper is concerned with the "problem of increasing
      the will to live in physically ill patients. "

1516 _____, and M. Gassman. "Some observations on psycho-
      therapy with patients suffering from neoplastic disease, "
      American Journal of Psychotherapy, 12 (1958), 723-34.

1517 Lester, D. ; C. Getty; and K. Getty. "Attitudes of nursing
      students and nursing faculty toward death, " Nursing Re-
      search, 23 (Jan. 1974), 50-3.
          Nurses with various degrees of specialization were
      tested for general fear of death and attitudes toward
      death; "... results indicate that fears of death and dy-
      ing decreased with increased education, but differences
      based on area of clinical specialization were not signifi-
      cant" (Abstract.)

1518 Lester, J. "Voluntary euthanasia, " New England Journal of
      Medicine, 280 (1969), 1225.

1519 "Let the hopelessly ill die?" U. S. News, 55 (July 1, 1963),
      18.
          Presents views of the Rev. Fulton J. Sheen and Dr.
      Rynearson concerning keeping people alive by extra-
      ordinary measures.

1520 Letourneau, C. U. "Dying with dignity, " Hospital Manage-
      ment, 109 (1970), 27-30.
          Discusses voluntary euthanasia, the difficult situa-
      tion of the physician, and the certainty of his decision.

1521 Leventhal, B. G. , et al. "Modern treatment of childhood
      leukemia: the patient and his family, " Children Today,
      3 (May-June, 1974), 2-6. (Pictorial Analysis.)

1522 Levine, G. N. "Anxiety about illness: psychological and
     social bases, " Journal of Health and Human Behavior, 3
     (1962), 30-4.

1523 Levinson, B. M. "The Pet and the child's bereavement, "
     Mental Hygiene, 51 (April 1967), 197-200.

1524 Leviton, D. "A Time to die, " Medical Journal of Australia,
     1 (1969), 127-8.
     Author suggests that it is when the possibility of eu-
     thanasia is found that we face the inevitable and the idea
     of a time to die.

1525 Lewin, R. "Truth versus illusion in relation to death, "
     Psychoanalytic Review, 51 (summer 1964), 190-200.

1526 Lewis, M. "The Management of parents of acutely ill chil-
     dren in the hospital, " American Journal of Orthopsychi-
     atry, 32 (1962), 60-6.

1527 Lewis, W. R. "A Time to die, " Nursing Forum, 4 (1965),
     7-26.

1528 Lieberman, M. A. "Relationship of mortality rates to en-
     trance to a home for the aged, " Geriatrics, 16 (1961),
     515-9.

1529 Liebman, S. Stress situations. Philadelphia: Lippincott,
     1955.

1530 "Life in death, " New England Journal of Medicine, 256 (1957),
     760-1.
     Implies that modern medical methods which keep the
     dying person alive for long periods of time may be rob-
     bing death of its dignity.

1531 Lifton, R. J. "On death and death symbolism: the Hiro-
     shima disaster, " Psychiatry, 27 (Aug. 1964), 91-210.
     Discusses the psychological effects of the atomic
     bomb in Hiroshima. Study is over a six-month period,
     from April to September, 1962. Includes interviews with
     two groups of atomic bomb survivors.

1532 _____. "Twentieth annual Karen Horney lecture, the sense
     of immortality: on death and the continuity of life, "
     American Journal of Psychoanalysis, 33 (1973), 3-15.

1533 Lipman, A., and P. Marden. "Preparation for death in old
     age, " Journal of Gerontology, 21 (July 1966), 426-31.

1534 Lirette, W. L. "Management of patients with terminal can-
     cer, " Postgraduate Medicine, 46 (Dec. 1969), 145-9.

1535 Litin, E. M. "Should the cancer patient be told?" Post-
      graduate Medicine, 28 (Nov. 1960), 470-5.
          "The author presents arguments to support the con-
      tention that, with few exceptions, patients should be told
      that they may be dying of cancer."

1536 _____; E. H. Rynearson; and G. A. Hallenbeck. "Sym-
      posium: what shall we tell the cancer patient?" Pro-
      ceedings of the Staff Meetings of the Mayo Clinic, 35
      (May 11, 1960), 239-57.

1537 "The Living donor," in To Live and to Die: When, Why and
      How, by J. R. Elkinton, edited by R. H. Williams.
      N. Y.: Springer-Verlag, 1973. pp. 123-33.

1538 Loesser, L. H., and T. Bry. "The Role of death fears in
      the etiology of phobic anxiety as revealed in group
      therapy," International Journal of Group Psychotherapy,
      10 (1960), 287-97.
          States that preoccupation with death fear was present
      in all phobic patients on both a conscious and uncon-
      scious level.

1539 Lourie, R. S. "The Pediatrician and the handling of terminal
      illness," Pediatrics, 32 (1963), 477-9.
          Concerned with the awareness of the neglected as-
      pect of pediatric responsibility about the impending death
      of patients.

1540 Loux, N. L. "Some clinical aspects of suicide," Rhode Is-
      land Medical Journal, 36 (1953), 248-50.
          States the need for a better understanding of the
      causes of suicide, and gives clinical statistics as a
      means of discovering some of the factors involved.

1541 Love, E. "Do all hands help ease the sting of death by
      tact and kindliness?" Hospitals, 18 (Dec. 1944), 47-8.

1542 Lowrey, J. J. "Changing concepts of death," Hawaii Medical
      Journal, 30 (July-Aug. 1971), 251-7.

1543 Lucente, F. E. "Thanatology: a study of 100 deaths on an
      otolaryngology service," Omega, 3 (Aug. 1972), 211-16.
          The survey covered the period between 1965 and
      1970. The study considered the themes of denial, pain,
      loneliness and fear. Suggestions are made for the caring
      of the dying patient.

1544 Luchi, R. J. "Diagnosis of cerebral death," Journal of the
      Iowa Medical Society, 61 (May 1971), 281-4.

1545 Luchina, I., and S. Aizemberg. "Una aguda amenaza de
      muerte: 'El infarto de miocardio'," Revista de Psico-

ánalisis, 19 (Jan.-June, 1962), 103-6.

1546   Luke, J. L. "Certification of death by coronor," New
       England Journal of Medicine, 280 (June 12, 1969), 1364.
            Points out that drawing inferences from uncritical
       analyses of death certificate data will lead to perhaps
       unwarranted correlations put forth by authors them-
       selves.

1547   _____, et al. "Sudden unexpected death from natural
       causes in young adults; a review of 275 consecutive
       autopsied cases," Archives of Pathology, 85 (Jan. 1968),
       10-17.

1548   Lund, C. "The Doctor, the patient and the truth," Annals of
       Internal Medicine, 24 (June 1946), 955-9.
            Points out the difficulty and the results of informing
       a patient about his impending death.

1549   Lyman, M., and J. Burchenal. "Acute leukemia," American
       Journal of Nursing, 63 (April 1963), 82-6.

1550   Lynch, J. J. "Autopsy: how soon after death?" Linacre
       Quarterly, (Aug. 1960), 98-101.
            Discusses the need for an autopsy in an unexpected
       and sudden death. States the Catholic position regarding
       post-mortem examinations and affirms that real death is
       certain.

1551   Lyons, C. Organ transplants: the moral issues. Phila-
       delphia: Westminister, 1970.

1552   Lyons, K. "Death and the student nurse," Tomorrow's
       Nurse, 4 (Oct.-Nov. 1963), 21-2.
            Reveals the thoughts of a student nurse about death
       and the patient's awareness of it.

1553   MacCarthy, D. "The Repercussions of the death of a child,"
       Proceedings of the Royal Society of Medicine, 62 (June
       1969), 553-4.

1554   McCormick, R. A. "To save or let die," America, 130
       (July 13, 1974), 6-10.
            Daily advances in medical technology mean that more
       and more infants can be saved.

1555   McGrath, M. J. "The Care of the patient in terminal ill-
       ness," Canadian Nurse, 57 (June 1961), 556-71.

1556   McInery, T. K., et al. "Sudden unexpected death," Ameri-
       can Journal of Diseases of Children, 120 (Aug. 1970),
       167.
            Points out that decongestant nose drops may be dan-
       gerous.

1557 McKain, W. C., et al. "Effect of motor accidents and other causes of death on work-like expectancy in Connecticut," Public Health Report, 79 (1964), 85-6.

1558 McKintosh, R. D. "Sudden death: a therapeutic challenge," Indian Heart Journal, 26 (July 1974), Suppl.: 140-4.

1559 McNulty, B. "Discharge of the terminally ill patient," Nursing Times, 65 (Jan. 9, 1969), 50-2.

1560 Maddison, D. "The Consequences of conjugal bereavement," Nursing Times, 65 (Jan. 9, 1969), 50-2.

1561 _____. "The Nurse and the dying patient," Nursing Times, 65 (Feb. 1969), 265-6.
          States that the topic of death is avoided in hospitals because difficulties in dealing with the dying patient spring from the personal anxieties of nurses.

1562 _____, and B. Raphael. "Normal bereavement as an illness requiring care," A paper presented at a seminar of the Thanatology Foundation at Columbia College of Physicians and Surgeons. Nov. 12, 1971.

1563 Maguire, D. C. "Death by chance, death by choice," Atlantic, 233 (Jan. 1974), 57-65.
          Medicine marches on; the law and ethics struggle behind. We have the knowledge to prolong life; a Catholic theologian asks if we have the wisdom to end it.

1564 Maingay, H. C. "Cremation regulation," British Medical Journal, 3 (Sept. 1971), 770-1.

1565 "Man, medicine and mercy," Nursing Times, 59 (1963), 402-3.
          Summary of a residential study in Scotland which discussed the dying patient and the need for compassion, solitude, and understanding.

1566 Mann, S. A. "Symposium on crisis intervention. Coping with a child's fatal illness: a parent's dilemma," Nursing Clinics of North America, 9 (March 1974), 81-7.

1567 Mant, A. "The Medical definition of death," in Man's Concern with Death, by A. Toynbee, et al. N.Y.: McGraw-Hill, 1969. pp. 13-24.
          Focuses on the criteria used for determining medical death.

1568 Marino, E. B. "Vinnie was dying, but he wasn't the problem. I was," Nursing '74, 4 (Feb. 1974), 46-7.

A frustrating experience of one who cared for a
person who never got beyond Kübler-Ross's bargaining
stage. The patient still denied the finality of his condition.

1569 Mark, L. C., and A. H. Kutscher. "Acupuncture: a statement concerning terminal care and anticipatory grief."
Paper presented at a seminar on psychological aspects
of anticipatory grief. Columbia University College of
Physicians and Surgeons. April 14, 1972.

1570 Martí-Ibáñez, F. "Doctors look at death," Reader's Digest,
84 (March 1964), 145-6.
Explains the main fears people have of dying and
how they can minimize them.

1571 Martin, D. S. "The Role of the surgeon in the prospect of
death from cancer," in Care of Patients with Fatal Illness, edited by L. P. White. N. Y.: Annals of the New
York Academy of Sciences. Vol. 164. 1969. pp. 739-
48.
Essentially a way of approaching the patient. Loss
of trust in the physician makes the reality of the illness
and death more difficult.

1572 Martin, G. M. "Brief proposal on immortality: an interim
solution," Perspectives in Biology and Medicine, 14
(winter 1971), 339-40.

1573 Martin, H. L., et al. "The Family of the fatally burned
child," Lancet, 2 (Sept. 14, 1968), 628-9.
Report describes some of the reactions of parents
before and after the death of a child from extensive
burns treated by exposure.

1574 Mason, J. K. "Multiple disinterments in equatorial Africa,"
Aerospace Medicine, 36 (1965), 636-9.
Details an aircraft accident in equatorial Africa and
how the dismembered and broken bodies were burned.

1575 Masserman, J. H. "Emotional reactions to death and suicide," American Practitioner and Digest of Treatment,
5 (Nov. 1954), 41-6.

1576 _____. "A Note on the dynamics of suicide," Diseases of
the Nervous System, 8 (1947), 324-5.

1577 Matsukura, T., et al. "Symposium: discussion on the problems of the determination of death," Japanese Journal
of Legal Medicine, 23 (July 1969), 365-9.

1578 Maxwell, I. "When to turn off the respirator," Nova Scotia
Medical Bulletin, 47 (Dec. 1968), 225-6.

Discusses the problem of when life becomes mean-
ingless for those being kept alive by artificial means.
Discusses the physician's role and medical technology
and "the need of the legal and medical professions to
re-examine their traditional attitudes in the case of the
comatose patient. "

1579 Meerloo, J. Patterns of panic. N. Y.: International Univer-
      sities Press, 1950.

1580 Mehl, R. Le Vieillissement et la Mort. Paris: Presses
      Universitaires de France, 1956.

1581 Meier, C. A. "Sudden infant death syndrome: death without
      apparent cause, " Life-Threatening Behavior, 3 (winter
      1973), 298-304.
           Description of one case. Two parent self-help
      groups have been organized to help eliminate the guilt
      which accompanies the syndrome. The goals of the
      group are to educate the public and to support further
      research into causes.

1582 Melcher, A. "Der Tod als Thema der neueren medizinischen
      Literatur, " Jahrbuch für Psychologie und Psychotherapie,
      3 (1955), 371-83.

1582a Mellinkoff, S. M. "Chemical intervention, " in Life and
      Death and Medicine. San Francisco: W. H. Freeman,
      1973. pp. 69-76.

1583 Melton, J., III, et al. "Sudden and unexpected deaths in in-
      fancy, " Virginia Medical Monthly, 95 (1968), 63-70.

1584 Mengert, W. F. "Terminal care, " Illinois Medical Journal,
      112 (1957), 99-104.
           "There is a tendency, with young practitioners for
      the science of medicine to outweigh the art of medicine
      when a terminal prognosis is given. "

1585 Mervyn, F. "The Plight of dying patients in hospitals, "
      American Journal of Nursing, 71 (Oct. 1971), 1988-90.
           Examines the actions and reactions of hospital per-
      sonnel to dying patients.

1586 Metschnikoff, E. The Prolongation of life. N. Y.: Putnam,
      1908.
           Early history of ideas about the prolongation of life.

1587 Meyerson, A. "Prolonged cases of grief reactions treated
      by electric shock, " New England Journal of Medicine,
      230 (1944), 255-6.
           Describes four cases classified as reactive depres-
      sions. Electric-shock therapy was used with excellent
      results.

1588 Milici, P. S. "The Involutional death reactions," Psychiatric
      Quarterly, 24 (1950), 775-81.
           Defines pre-involutional melancholia psychosis and
      describes it as a reaction to internal dissatisfaction to
      external problems in a pathologically regressive manner.

1589 Miller, A. "The Patient's right to know the truth," Canadian
      Nurse, 58 (1962), 25-9.
           States that the treatment of this subject would vary
      with the individual, his life experience, and educational
      background.

1590 Miller, J. B. "Children's reactions to the death of a parent:
      a review of the psychoanalytic literature," Journal of the
      American Psychoanalytic Association, 19 (Oct. 1971),
      697-719.

1591 Miller, M. B. "Decision-making in the death process of the
      aged," Geriatrics, 26 (May 1971), 105-16.

1592 Miller, R. W. "Childhood cancer and congenital defects. A
      study of U. S. death certificates during the period 1960-
      1966," Pediatric Research, 3 (Sept. 1969), 389-97.
           Study of cancer deaths among 29, 457 children under
      15 years of age. "Lists some new understanding of the
      relation between oncogenesis and teratogenesis."

1593 Mills, D. H. "Medico-legal ramifications of current practices
      and suggested changes in certifying modes of death,"
      Journal of Forensic Science, 13 (Jan. 1968), 70-5.

1594 _____. "Statutory brain death?" Journal of the American
      Medical Association, 229 (Aug. 26, 1974), 1225-6.

1595 Mira y Lopez, E. "Psychopathology of anger and fear re-
      actions in wartime," American Clinician, 5 (1943), 98-9.

1596 Mirsky, I. A. Metabolic responses in acute stress situations.
      Symposium: Army Medical Service Graduate School,
      Washington, D. C. March 1953.

1597 Miya, T. M. "The Child's perception of death," Nursing
      Forum, 11 (1972), 214-20.

1598 Miyamoto, S. F., and S. M. Dornbusch. "A test of the inter-
      actionist hypothesis of self-conception," American Journal
      of Sociology, 61 (1956), 399-403.

1599 Moellenhoff, F. "Ideas of children about death," Bulletin
      of the Menninger Clinic, 3 (1939), 148-56.

1600 Mohandas, A., and S. N. Chou. "Brain death: a clinical
      and pathological study," Journal of Neurosurgery, 35

(Aug. 1971), 211-8.

1601 Moll, A. E. "Suicide," Canadian Medical Association Journal,
      74 (1956), 110-11.

1602 The Moment of death, a symposium, edited by Arthur Winter.
      Springfield, Ill.: C. C. Thomas, 1969.

1603 Moore, F. D. "Medical responsibility for the prolongation of
      life," Journal of the American Medical Association, 206
      (Oct. 7, 1968), 384-6.

1604 "Moratorium day," American Journal of Nursing, 69 (Dec.
      1969), 2645.
          Discusses the nurse's role with the family at the
      very moment of death.

1605 Moriarty, D. M. "Early loss and the fear of mothering,"
      Psychoanalysis and the Psychoanalytic Review, 49 (1962),
      63-9.
          Paper presents "case histories of four patients who
      had in common the fear of mothering and the history of
      the loss of a sibling in childhood."

1605a Morison, R. S. "Dying," in Life and Death and Medicine.
      San Francisco: W. H. Freeman, 1973. pp. 39-45.
      (A Scientific American reprint book from Sept. 1973.)
          "In the industrialized countries nearly two-thirds of
      the deaths are now associated with the infirmities of old
      age. Medicine can fend off death, but in doing so it
      often merely prolongs agony."

1606 Moritz, A. R., and N. Zamcheck. "Sudden and unexpected
      death of young soldiers," Archives of Pathology, 42
      (1946), 459-94.

1607 Moriyama, I. M. "Development of the present concept of
      cause of death," American Journal of Public Health, 46
      (1956), 436-41.

1608 Morris, K., and J. Foerster. "Team work: nurse and
      chaplain," American Journal of Nursing, 72 (Dec. 1972),
      2197-99.
          Description of the successes made when all pro-
      fessionals work together with terminally ill patients.

1609 "Mortality trends in the western world," Geriatrics, 24
      (1969), 64.

1609a Moses, L. E., and F. Mosteller. "Institutional differences
      in post-operative death rates," Journal of the American
      Medical Association, 203 (Feb. 12, 1968), 492-4.

1610 Movat, K. "Murder or mercy?" World Medicine, 6 (1971),
      54-9.

1611 Muensterberger, W. "Vom Ursprung des Todes: a psycho-
      analytic and ethnological study on the fear of death, "
      Psyche, 17 (1963), 169-84.

1612 Muhl, A. M. "America's greatest suicide problem. A study
      of over 500 cases in San Diego, " Psychoanalytic Review,
      14 (1927), 317-25.

1613 Mulvey, P. M. "Cot deaths, " Medical Journal of Australia,
      2 (Aug. 7, 1971), 337-8.

1614 Munk, W. Euthanasia: or medical treatment in aid of an
      easy death. N. Y.: Longmans Green, 1887.

1615 Munnichs, J. M. A. "Discussion of a symposium on atti-
      tudes toward death in older persons, " Journal of Geron-
      tology, 16 (1961), 44-66.

1616 Munro, A. "Bereavement as a psychiatric emergency, "
      Nursing Times, 66 (July 1970), 841-3.
          Attempts to help those who have not experienced be-
      reavement by explaining what constitutes normal behavior.
      Outlines pathological grief, adequate warning, and natural
      manifestations of grief.

1617 Murphey, B. "Psychological management of the patient with
      incurable cancer, " Geriatrics, 9 (1953), 130-4.

1618 Murstein, B. "Personality and intellectual changes in leu-
      kemia: a case study, " Journal of Projective Techniques
      and Personality Assessment, 22 (Dec. 1958), 421-6.

1619 Muslin, H. L.; S. P. Levine; and H. Levine. "Partners in
      dying, " American Journal of Psychiatry, 131 (March
      1974), 308-10.
          Describes the clinical course toward death of two
      60-year-old male patients who, with their physicians be-
      came "partners in dying. " The "management of each
      dying patient requires a careful assessment of the spe-
      cific object relationships that will promote equilibrium. "

1620 Myerowitz, J. H. , and H. B. Kaplan. "Familial responses
      to stress: the case of cystic fibrosis, " Social Science
      and Medicine, 1 (Sept. 1967), 249-66.

1621 Nagera, H. "Children's reactions to the death of important
      objects: a developmental approach, " Psychoanalytic
      Study of the Child, 25 (1970), 360-400.

1622 Nahum, L. H. "Dealing with the last chapter of life, "

Connecticut Medicine, 39 (1964), 170-4.
Discusses the role of the physician in the treatment
of terminal cases and his relationship to the family after
death.

1623 _____. "The Dying patient's grief," Connecticut Medicine,
28 (April 1964), 241-5.
Expresses concern that too much attention may be
given to the patient's fear of death rather than his grief.

1624 _____. "Emotional stress and sudden death," Connecticut
Medicine, 35 (Sept. 1971), 558-60.

1625 Nakagawa, Y. "Standards for determining death: philosophy
of death under present standards of medical practice,"
Surgical Therapy, 20 (April 1969), 405-8.

1626 Nau, S., and E. Pearlman. "Randy--the silent teacher,"
Canadian Nurse, 61 (1965), 903-6.
"A sensitive account of student reaction to the death
of a child. "

1627 Neale, A. V. "The Changing pattern of death in childhood:
then and now," Medical Science Law, 4 (1964), 35-9.

1628 Neilson, C. "The Childhood of schizophrenics," Acta Psychiatrica Scandinavica, 29 (1954), 281-9.

1629 Newcombe, H. B. "Risk of fetal death to mothers of different ABO and Rh blood types," American Journal of
Human Genetics, 15 (1963), 449-64.
States that information about the strengths of the selection force of ABO and Rh blood types pertaining to
fetal death is still limited.

1630 Newman, B. "The Role of paramedical staff with the dying
adult patient," Therapeutic Recreation Journal, 8 (First
Quarter 1974), 29-33.
Outlines a variety of helps for the patient while he
fights death.

1631 Nix, J. T. "Study of the relationship of environmental factors to the type and frequency of cancer causing death
in Nuns, " Hospital Progress, 45 (1964), 71-4.
Attempts to collect and verify the cause of the death
of nuns from data obtained from 262 communities with a
nun population of 116 and 173.

1632 Niyogi, A. K., et al. "Diurnal variations in death," Indian
Journal of Medical Research, 52 (1964), 1092-98.
Discusses the case records of all deaths of indoor
patients in Shri Sayaji General Hospital, Baroda. Deaths
covered a 24 month period during 1962 and 1963.

1633 Norman, M. G. "Sudden infant death syndrome," Canadian Nurse, 70 (July 1974), 22-3.

1634 Norris, C. M. "The Nurse and the dying patient," American Journal of Nursing, 55 (Oct. 1955), 1214-7.
      Stresses the need of nurses to express the ideas and values that people in their community have about dying.

1635 Norton, C. E. "Attitudes toward living and dying in patients on chronic hemodialysis," in Care of Patients with Fatal Illness, edited by L. P. White. N. Y.: Annals of the New York Academy of Sciences, 1969. Vol. 164. pp. 720-32.

1636 Noyes, R., Jr. "The Act of death, the art of treatment," Medical Insight, 3 (March 1971), 22-33.

1637 _____. "The Art of dying," Perspectives in Biology and Medicine, 14 (spring 1971), 432-47.

1638 _____. "The Care and management of the dying," Archives of Internal Medicine, 128 (Aug. 1971), 299-303.

1639 _____, and R. Klette. "The Experience of dying from falls," Omega, 3 (Feb. 1972), 45-72.

1640 Oakden, E. C., and M. Sturt. "The Development of the knowledge of time in children," British Journal of Psychology, 12 (1922), 309-36.

1641 Ogilvie, H. "Journey's end," Practitioner, 179 (Oct. -Dec. 1957), 584-91.
      Suggests ways that man can face death with a sense of completeness.

1642 Olbrycht, J. S. "Contributions on the theory of death by hanging," Deutsche Zeitschrift für die Gesamte Gerichtliche Medizin, 54 (Feb. 1964), 407-23.

1643 Olin, H. S. "Failure and fulfillment: education in the use of psycoactive drugs in the dying patient," Journal of Thanatology, 2 (winter 1972), 567-73.
      Contrasts death as a failure with death as fulfillment. These two viewpoints are discussed in relationship to the use of psycoactive drugs.

1644 Oliven, J. F. "The Suicidal risk: its diagnosis and evaluation," New England Journal of Medicine, 245 (1951), 488-94.
      Paper discusses the physician's problem on deciding the degree of suicidal risk of a particular patient. It

offers several case studies.

1645   Olmstead, R. W. "Care of the child with a fatal illness,"
       Journal of Pediatrics, 76 (May 1970), 814.

1646   Oppenheim, G. "When patients ask tough questions," Medical
       Economics, 38 (1961), 54-8.
              Makes some excellent suggestions to answer patients'
       questions concerning their illness and their chances of sur-
       viving.

1647   Osis, K. Deathbed observations by physicians and nurses.
       N. Y.: Parapsychology Foundations, 1961.

1648   Oughterson, A. W., and S. Warren. Medical effects of the
       atomic bomb in Japan. N. Y.: McGraw-Hill, 1956.

1649   Pacyna, D. A. "Response to a dying child," Nursing Clinics
       of North America, 5 (Sept. 1970), 421-30.
              Relates admirably an interpersonal relationship be-
       tween a nurse and a dying child.

1650   Park, R. "Thanatology," Journal of the American Medical
       Association, 58 (1912), 1243-6.
              Thanatology is defined as a department of science
       for the study of death. Questions when death occurs as
       it relates to transplants and other related problems.

1651   Parkes, C. M. Bereavement. N. Y.: International Univer-
       sities Press, 1972.

1652   _____. "Determination of bereavement," Proceedings of
       the Royal Society of Medicine, 64 (March 1971), 279.

1653   _____. "Effects of bereavement on physical and mental
       health--a study of the medical records of widows,"
       British Medical Journal, 2 (1964), 274.
              Paper is concerned with the high mortality rate of
       widows and widowers. It points out that grief, the
       psychological reaction to the loss of a loved one, has
       had very little attention.

1654   _____. "'Seeking' and 'finding' a lost object: evidence
       from recent studies of the reaction to bereavement,"
       Social Service and Medicine, 4 (Aug. 1970), 187-201.

1655   _____, and J. Birtchnell. "Determination of outcome fol-
       lowing bereavement," Proceedings of the Royal Society
       of Medicine, 64 (March 1971), 279-82.

1656   _____, and R. J. Brown. "Health after bereavement: a
       controlled study of young Boston widows and widowers,"
       Psychosomatic Medicine, 34 (Sept.-Oct. 1972), 449-61.

1657 _____, et al. "Broken heart: a statistical study of increased mortality among widowers," British Journal of Medicine, 1 (March 22, 1969), 740-3.

1658 Parkes, L. C. "Life, death, kidney transplantation and nursing at the Johns Hopkins Hospital," Alumnae Magazine, 70 (March 1971), 2-6.

1659 Parnell, R. W., and I. Skottowe. "Toward preventing suicide," Lancet, 272 (1957), 206-8.
     Various signs of suicide are discussed, and states that suicide can be prevented if the warning signs are recognized.

1660 The Patient, death, and the family, edited by Stanley B. Troup and William A. Greene. N.Y.: Scribner's, 1974.
     Contains essays which grew out of a conference sponsored by Rochester General Hospital, Rochester, N.Y. April 29-30, 1971.

1661 Paton, A. "Life and death: moral and ethical aspects of transplantation," Seminars in Psychiatry, 3 (Feb. 1971), 161-8.

1662 Patterson, K., et al. "Nursing care begins after death when the disease is: sudden infant death syndrome," Nursing '74, 4 (May 1974), 85-8.

1663 Patterson, M. G. "The Care of the patient with cancer," Public Health Nursing, 42 (July 1950), 377-85.

1664 Patterson, R. D. "Grief and depression in old people," Maryland Medical Journal, 18 (Sept. 1969), 75-9.

1665 Pattison, C. P., Jr. "Dealing with the dying patient," Journal of the Kansas Medical Society, 72 (Aug. 1971), 354-60.

1666 Paul, N. L. "The Use of empathy in the resolution of grief," Perspectives in Biology and Medicine, 11 (1967), 153-68.
     Deals with family disequilibrium caused by inability to resolve grief. Empathy is important in the development of identity and the interpersonal relationships with others.

1667 Pearlman, J.; B. A. Stotsky; and J. R. Dominick. "Attitudes toward death among nursing home personnel," Journal of Genetic Psychology, 114 (1969), 63-75.
     Explains that nurses having more experience with death felt more uncomfortable discussing death than those with less experience.

1668 Pearson, L. S. "Medical certification of death," Pennsyl-
      vania Medicine, 72 (March 1969), 17.
           States the Pennsylvania State Law concerning the
      death certificate as it relates to doctors, nurses, and
      funeral directors. Some special problems are discussed.

1669 Pentney, B. H. "Grief," Nursing Times, 60 (Nov. 13, 1964),
      1496-8.
           Reviews some of the problems presented by grief,
      and makes suggestions that nurses may find helpful in
      specific situations.

1670 _____. "Grief reaction," District Nursing, 5 (1963), 226-
      7.

1671 Perelman, R. "Sudden death in infants," Concours Medical
      (Paris), 85 (Jan. 19, 1963), 347-52.

1672 Pericoli, R. F. "The Diagnosis of death," Policlinico
      Sezione Pratica, 76 (July 7, 1969), 865-77.

1673 Perrin, G. M., and I. R. Pierce. "Psychosomatic aspects
      of cancer," Psychosomatic Medicine, 21 (Sept.-Oct.
      1959), 397-421.
           Four categories are used to describe the literature
      of the psychological aspects of cancer.

1674 Peterson, D. R. "Sudden unexpected death in infants,"
      American Journal of Epidemiology, 84 (1966), 478-82.

1675 _____, et al. "A Method for assessing the geographic
      distribution and temporal trends of the sudden infant
      death syndrome in the United States from vital statistics
      data," American Journal of Epidemiology, 100 (Nov.
      1974), 373-9.

1676 Pfeiffer, M., and E. Lemon. "A Pilot study in the home
      care of terminal cancer patients," American Journal of
      Public Health, 43 (1953), 909-14.

1677 Pinner, M., and B. F. Miller, eds. When doctors are pa-
      tients. N.Y.: W. W. Norton, 1952.
           Autobiographical accounts of 33 doctors who suf-
      fered various diseases, some fatal and some disabling.

1678 Plank, E. N. "Death on a children's ward," Medical Times,
      92 (July 1964), 638-44.
           Discusses the role of the physician in preparing
      children for questioning life and death. Points out that
      children find little help in managing their fears and
      anxious fantasies about the loss of a parent or friend.

1679 Platt, R. "Reflections on aging and death," Lancet, 7

(Jan. 5, 1963), 1-6.

1680   Playfair, L.   "Reflections on aging and death," Lancet, 1
       (Jan. 5, 1963), 1-6.

1681   Podolsky, E.   "Soviet studies on death," in Red Miracle:
       story of Soviet medicine, " N. Y.: Beechhurst Press,
       1947. pp. 180-6.

1682   Pomeroy, M. R.   "Sudden death syndrome," American Jour-
       nal of Nursing, 69 (Sept. 1969), 1886.
       A nurse's explanation to parents about the sudden
       infant death syndrome.

1683   Potthoff, C. J.   "First aid: determination of death," Today's
       Health, 47 (Sept. 1969), 74.

1684   Preston, C. E., et al.   "Views of the aged on the timing
       of death," Gerontologist, 11 (winter 1971), 300-4.

1685   Pretty, L. C.   "Ministering to the bereaved and dying, "
       Nebraska State Medical Journal, 44 (May 1959), 243-9.

1686   Pritchard, R.   "Dying--some issues and problems," in Care
       of Patients with Fatal Illness, edited by L. P. White.
       Annals of the New York Academy of Sciences, 1969.
       Vol. 164. pp. 707-19.

1687   "Proposed criteria for the determination of death," Journal
       of Forensic Medicine, 16 (1969), 4-6.

1688   "Protocol for the determination of death endorsed by the
       Allegheny County Ad Hoc committee on tissue transplanta-
       tion," Pennsylvania Medicine, 72 (March 1969), 17-20.
       Results of a committee's investigation about the de-
       termination of death and lists a number of criteria.

1689   Provonsha, J. W.   "Prolongation of life," Bulletin of the
       American Protestant Hospital Association, 35 (spring
       1971), 14-16.

1690   Pruit, A., and P. Rice.   "On death," Tomorrow's Nurse, 4
       (Aug.-Sept. 1963), 17-18.
       Discusses the thoughts of student nurses and the
       need to clarify their own personal philosophy concerning
       death.

1691   Puffer, R. R., et al.   "Cooperative international research
       on mortality," Boletin de la Oficina Sanitaria Panameri-
       cana, 58 (1965), 1-16.

1692   _____.   "International collaborative research on mor-
       tality," World Health Organization, Public Health Pa-

pers, 27 (1975), 113-30.

1693 Putthoff, C. J. "First aid: determination of death,"
      Today's Health, 47 (Sept. 1969), 74.

1694 Quevauviller, A. "The Public health specialist in the face of
      death," Produits et Problemes Pharmaceutiques, 19 (Nov.
      1964), 505-18.

1695 Quint, J. C. "Awareness of death and the nurse's com-
      posure," Nursing Research, 15 (winter 1966), 36-7.
          The author is concerned with the various kinds of
      death which hospital personnel face. Outlines various
      ethical problems involved.

1696 _____. "Communication problems affecting patient care in
      hospitals," Journal of the American Medical Association,
      195 (Jan. 3, 1966), 36-7.

1697 _____. "The Dying patient: a difficult nursing problem,"
      Nursing Clinics of North America, 2 (Dec. 1967), 763-
      73.

1698 _____. The Nurse and the dying patient. N. Y.: Mac-
      millan, 1967.

1699 _____. "Nursing services and the care of dying patients:
      some speculations," Nursing Science, 2 (Dec. 1964),
      432-43.

1700 _____. "Obstacles to helping the dying," American
      Journal of Nursing, 66 (July 1966), 1568-71.

1701 _____. "Search or research?" Nursing Outlook, 13 (1965),
      13.
          Discusses the difficult forms of death and how staffs
      react to and cope with them.

1702 _____. "The Threat of death: some consequences for
      patients and nurses," Nursing Forum, 8 (1969), 286.
          Points out the need of personalizing human death in
      today's complex world and that nurses are in a position
      to help bring about these changes.

1703 _____. "When patients die: some nursing problems,"
      Canadian Nurse, 63 (1967), 1-4.
          Presents interactional difficulties involved between
      the nurse and the dying patient, where medical tech-
      nology has forced emphasis to be placed on recovery
      and comfort.

1704 _____, and B. Glaser. "Improving nursing care of the
      dying," Nursing Forum, 6 (fall 1967), 368-78.

1705 Rahe, R. H. , and E. Lind. "Psychosocial factors and sud-
      den cardiac death: a pilot study, " Journal of Psycho-
      somatic Research, 15 (March 1971), 19-24.

1706 Raimbault, G. "Theme of death in children with chronic
      disease, " Archives Françaises de Pédiatrie, 26 (1969),
      1041-53.
      Presents a series of cases of children who express
      different views of death.

1707 Ramsey, P. The Patient as person: explorations in medical
      ethics. New Haven: Yale University Press, 1970.
      Explores and clarifies ethical procedures regarding
      the patient and his rights.

1708 Raphael, S. S. "Sudden death in infants, " Lancet, 1 (Feb. 5,
      1972), 325.

1709 Ratcliff, J. D. "Let the dead teach the living, " Reader's
      Digest, (Aug. 1961), 87-90.
      Discusses the reasons for the shortage of available
      cadavers for medical schools and the need for more
      bodies for research.

1710 Ravitch, N. M. "Let your patient die with dignity, " Medical
      Times, 93 (June 1965), 594-6.
      Author states that "today we are guilty of assault
      on the dignity of the conscious dying. "

1711 Ray, S. K. , et al. "Exhumation, " Journal of Indian Medical
      Association, 46 (Feb. 1966), 193-7.

1712 Redmond, C. K. , et al. "Longterm mortality study of steel
      workers, " Journal of Occupational Medicine, 11 (Oct.
      1969), 513-21.

1713 Rees, W. D. , and S. G. Lutkins. "Mortality of bereavement, "
      British Medical Journal, 4 (Oct. 7, 1967), 13-16.

1714 Reeves, R. B. , Jr. "A Study of terminal cancer patients, "
      Journal of Pastoral Care, 14 (1960), 218-23.

1715 "Refinements in criteria for the determination of death: an
      appraisal, " Journal of the American Medical Association,
      221 (July 5, 1972), 48-52.

1716 Regan, P. F. "Death and the dying, " Medical Insight (Dec.
      1969), 48.

1717 _____. "The Dying patient and his family, " Journal of the
      American Medical Association, 192 (1965), 666-7.
      Interaction involved with the crisis of death for the
      patient, family, physician, and the physician's role in

giving direction for a satisfactory outcome.

1718 Reid, D. D. "Assessing the comparability of mortality sta-
      tistics, " British Medical Journal, 54 (1964), 1437-9.
      Discusses hematoma of the umbilical cord and
      points out that this condition is quite often associated
      with fetal death.

1719 Reimanis, G., and R. F. Green. "Imminence of death and
      intellectual decrement in the aging, " Developmental Psy-
      chology, 5 (Sept. 1971), 270-2.

1720 Renneker, R. "Counter transference reactions to cancer, "
      Psychosomatic Medicine, 19 (1957), 409-18.
      Paper is concerned with counter transference re-
      actions on the part of the author and six analysts of
      cancer. A section of the paper is devoted to terminal
      patients and the therapists who accompany the patient to
      the brink of death.

1721 Resnik, H. L. P. , ed. Suicidal behaviors: diagnosis and
      management. Boston: Little Brown, 1968.

1722 Rezek, P. R. "Dying and death, " Journal of Forensic Sci-
      ence, 8 (April 1963), 200-8.
      Author points out that "dying is of no interest to
      the clinician and the pathologist. Since agony (dying)
      has an influence on autopsy findings, it may have forensic
      value. "

1723 Rhoads, P. S. "Management of the patient with terminal ill-
      ness, " Journal of the American Medical Association,
      192 (May 24, 1965), 661-5.

1724 Rhudick, P. J. , and A. S. Dibner. "Age, personality, and
      health correlates of death concerns in normal age in-
      dividuals, " Journal of Gerontology, 16 (1961), 44-9.
      Investigates the relationship of death concerns in a
      normal age group with various sociological, psychologi-
      cal, and health variables.

1725 Rice, C. O. "Euthanasia--to set you straight, " Minnesota
      Medicine, 49 (Aug. 1966), 1269.

1726 Rich, T. "The Dying patient, " Mind--Psychiatry in General
      Practice I, 1 (Jan. 1963), 18-19.

1727 _____, and G. M. Kalmanson. "Attitudes of medical
      residents toward the dying patients in a general hos-
      pital, " Postgraduate Medicine, 40 (Oct. 1966), A127-
      130.

1728 Richardson, P. "A Multigravida's use of a living child in

the grief and mourning for a lost child. " Thesis,
nursing, University of Pittsburgh, 1973.

1729 Richter, C. P. "The Phenomenon of unexplained sudden
death in animals and man, " Psychosomatic Medicine, 19
(1957), 191-8.
Attempts to explain sudden and unexplained death
due to voodoo and other fears that induced death in man
and animals.

1730 Ries, H. "An Unwelcome child and her death instinct, " International Journal of Psychoanalysis, 26 (1945), 197-
230.

1731 "The Right to abortion: a psychiatric view, " Group for the
Advancement of Psychology, 7 (Oct. 1969), 197-230.

1732 "Right to die, " Lancet, 8 (Oct. 1970), 926.
A letter expressing the concern among the general
public about being allowed to die.

1733 Ristau, R. "The Loneliness of death, " American Journal of
Nursing, 58 (Sept. 1958), 1283-4.
A nurse discusses the importance of answering per-
sonal questions of a patient who is near death.

1734 Rizzo, R., and J. Yonder. "Definition and criteria of
clinical death, " Linacre Quarterly, 40 (Nov. 1973),
223-33.

1735 Roberts, J. L., et al. "How aged in nursing homes view
dying and death, " Geriatrics, 25 (April 1970), 115-19.

1736 Robinson, A. M. "Loss and grief, " Journal of Practical
Nursing, 21 (May 1971), 18.

1736a Rodman, J. S. History of the American board of surgery.
Philadelphia: Lippincott, 1956.

1737 Rom, P. "Should I bequeath my corpse to a teaching hospital?" Omega, 1 (May 1970), 141-2.

1738 Roose, L. J. "To die alone, " Mental Hygiene, 53 (July
1969), 321-6.
Discusses the relationship between doctor and patient in coping with the emotional response of the patient
during the last phase of life.

1739 Rose, M. S. "Who should choose?" Lancet, 1 (March 1,
1969), 465-6.

1740 Rosecrans, C. J. "Attitudes toward death and bereavement, " Alabama Journal of Medical Science, 8 (April
1971), 242-9.

1741 _____. "Is acceptance of non-being possible?" Alabama
Journal of Medical Sciences, 7 (Jan. 1970), 32-7.

1741a Rosenthal, D. Genetic theory and abnormal behavior. N.Y.:
McGraw-Hill, 1970.

1742 Rosenthal, H. "Psychotherapy for the dying," American
Journal of Psychotherapy, 11 (1957), 626-33.
States that "the therapist's first task is to find out
whether the patient has been informed about the fatality
of his sickness."

1743 Rosenthal, P. "The Death of the leader in group psychotherapy," American Journal of Orthopsychiatry, 17 (1947),
266-277.

1744 Rosner, A. "Mourning before the fact," Journal of the
American Psychoanalytic Association, 10 (1962), 564-70.

1745 Rosoff, S., et al. "The EEG in establishing brain death:
a ten-year report with criteria and legal safeguards in
the 50 states," Electroencepholography and Clinical
Neurophysiology, 24 (March 1968), 283-4.

1746 Ross, K. K. "The Right to die with dignity," Bulletin of the
Menninger Clinic, 36 (May 1972), 302-12.

1747 Roudybush, A. Death of a moral person. N.Y.: Doubleday,
1967.

1748 Ruff, F. "Have we the right to prolong dying," Medical
Economics, 37 (1960), 39-44.

1749 Ruiz, P. "Sudden deaths during phenothiazine treatment,"
Journal of the Bronx State Hospital, 1 (fall 1973), 145-9.
Description of a sudden unexplained death of a 14-
year-old girl during therapy. It was suggested that
phenothiazine is of some therapeutic value when it is
needed.

1750 Russell, J. K., and M. R. Miller. "Care of women with
terminal pelvic cancer," British Medical Journal, 1
(1964), 1214.

1751 Rynearson, E. H. "You are standing at the bedside of a patient dying of untreatable cancer," CA Bulletin of Cancer
Progress, 9 (1959), 85-7.

1752 Sacco, R. N. "Euthanasia by experts," Northwest Medicine,
69 (1970), 83.
A critical reply to an article on illegal abortion in
the U.S.

1753 Safier, G. "A Study in relationships between life-death concepts in children," Journal of Genetic Psychology, 105 (Dec. 1964), 283-94.

1754 Salk, L., et al. "Sudden infant death: impact on family and physician," Clinical Pediatrics, 10 (May 1971), 248-50.

1755 Sand, P.; G. Livingston; and R. G. Wright. "Psychological assessment of candidates for a hemodialysis program," Annals of Internal Medicine, 64 (March 1966), 602-9.

1756 Sarwer-Foner, G. J. "Denial of death and the unconscious longing for indestructibility and immortality in the terminal phase of adolescence," Canadian Psychiatric Association Journal, 17 Supp. 2 (1972), SS51.

1757 Saul, L. J. "Reactions of a man to natural death," Psychoanalytic Quarterly, 28 (1959), 383-6.
Observes the psychological reaction of a man to the gradual approach of death from cancer with a view to alleviating this type of psychic pain.

1758 _____. "Sudden death at impasse," Psychoanalytic Forum, 1 (1966), 88-9.
Paper discusses sudden death from psychogenic causes and offers case-studies where hopelessness was present.

1759 Saul, S. R., and S. Saul. "Old people talk about death," Omega, 4 (spring 1973), 27-35.
Describes a psychotherapy taping session of eight 75- to 88-year-old female residents of a nursing home. Moods of depression and suppression were noticed.

1760 Saunders, C. Care of the dying. N.Y.: Macmillan, 1959.

1761 _____. "And from Sudden Death," Nursing Times, 58 (Aug. 17, 1962), 1045-56.

1762 _____. "The Control of pain in terminal cancer," Nursing Times (Oct. 23, 1959), 1031.
Discusses "controlling terminal pain only by increasing large doses of morphine and heroin." Advocates management of drugs.

1763 _____. "The Last stages of life," American Journal of Nursing, 65 (March 1965), 70-5.
The author describes her lengthy work and experience with patients who have terminal malignancies and stresses the positive approach that brings comfort to the dying.

1764 _____. "Mental distress in the dying," Nursing Times,

(Oct. 30, 1959), 1067-8.
"Fear of death is only one of the attacks on our patients' minds and we often underestimate this side of
their distress. "

1765 _____. "The Moment of truth: care of the dying person, " in Death and Dying, edited by L. Pearson.
Cleveland: Press of Case Western Reserve University,
1969. pp. 49-78.
The moment of truth is concerned with prolonging
life, family considerations, communicating with the dying, euthanasia, and the role of religion.

1766 _____. "The Problem of euthanasia, " Nursing Times
(Oct. 1959), 960-1.
Presents arguments against euthanasia and points
out that the society in Great Britain which is campaign-
ing for change in the law is not able to produce any
statistics of patients who suffer pain and ask for a release from it.

1767 _____. "Should a patient know... ?" Nursing Times
(Oct. 16, 1959), 994-5.
Presents various cases of impending death: the
rage, the hostility, the acceptance and peace that ac-
companies the patient. Describes the responsibility for
the decision and its complexities.

1768 _____. "When a patient is dying, " Nursing Times (Nov.
13, 1959), 1129-30.
Discusses the care of terminal patients and offers
insights about helping the patient come to grips with
death.

1769 Sautler, C. "The Physician, the child and death: the
psychoanalytic approach, " Revue de Médecine Psychosomatique et de Psychologie Médicale, 10 (Oct.-Dec.
1969), 425-9.

1770 Scheinfeld, A. "The Mortality of men and women, " Scientific
American, 198 (1958), 22-3.
Studies of male and female in various countries
show the tendency of women to live longer than men.

1771 Scherlis, L. "Death: the diagnostic dilemma, " Maryland
Medical Journal, 17 (Dec. 1968), 77-8.
States that the diagnosis of death is conditioned by
many factors, since death does not occur simultaneous-
ly to all organs, cells, or enzyme systems.

1772 Schilder, P. Goals and desires of man. N.Y.: Columbia
University Press, 1942.

1773 _____. "Uber die Stellung nähen Todranker, " Medizinische
Welt, 22 (May 27, 1927), 783-6.

1774 Schillito, J., Jr. "The Organ donor's doctor: a new role
for the neuro-surgeon, " New England Journal of Medicine, 281 (1964), 1071-2.
Discusses the problem of when death occurs in relation to the donation of organs and the neuro-surgeon's
role in it.

1775 Schleyer, F. "The Value of the determination of the time of
death, " Beitrage zur Gerichtichen Medizin, 25 (1969),
66-8.

1775a Schlicke, C. P. "American surgery's noblest experiment, "
Archives of Surgery, 106 (April 1973), 379-85.

1776 Schnaper, N. "Care of the dying patient, " Medical Times,
92 (May 1965), 537-43.
Discusses the role of the physician regarding the
process of dying and the complex problems confronting
the family.

1777 _____. "Management of the dying patient, " Modern Treatment, 6 (July 1963), 746-59.

1778 Schneider, H. "Confirmation of brain death, " Deutsche
Medizinisches Wochenschrift, 94 (Nov. 14, 1969), 2404-5.
Deals with cerebral death of patients in intensive
care units.

1779 _____. "Criteria of the beginning of death, " Öffentliche
Gesundheitswesen, 31 (Nov. 1969), 536-41.

1780 Schoenberg, B. B., et al. "Physicians and the bereaved, " ·
General Practitioner, 40 (Oct. 1969), 104-8.

1781 Schonwalter, J. E. "The Experience of death on an adolescent pediatric ward as experienced by the nurse in
dreams and reality, " in The Child and His Family,
edited by E. J. Anthony, and C. Koupernik. Vol. 2.
N.Y.: Wiley, 1973. pp. 211-8.
Collection of dreams by nurses on the Pediatric
Adolescent Ward at the Yale New Haven Hospital. The
usefulness of the manifest dream content is described
by the staff who care for dying patients.

1782 Schulz, R., and D. Alderman. "Clinical research and the
stages of dying, " Omega, 5 (summer 1974), 137-43.
"Kübler-Ross's claim that terminal patients near
death pass through five psychological stages in a predictable order is examined and found not to be supported
by other investigations.... " (Abstract.)

1783 Schwab, M. L. "The Nurse's role in assisting families of
      dying patients to manage grief and guilt," American
      Nurses Association Clinical Sessions (1968), 110-16.

1784 Scoville, A. B., Jr. "The Physician and the terminal pa-
      tient," Journal of the Tennessee Medical Association,
      58 (June 1965), 208.

1785 Scripcara, G., et al. "Attempts of estimating risk factors
      in sudden death of children," Revista Medico-Chirurgicala
      a Societatii di Medici si Naturalisti din Iasi, 16 (July-
      Sept. 1972), 633-9.

1786 Seeling, M. G. "Should the cancer victim be told the
      truth?" Missouri Medicine, 40 (Feb. 1943), 33-5.

1787 Selvini, A. "Tell the truth to the patient," Minerva Medica,
      62 (May 16, 1971), 1985-90.

1788 Senescu, R. "The Problem of establishing communication
      with the seriously ill patient," Annals of the New York
      Academy of Sciences (Dec. 19, 1969), 696-706.

1789 Shah, B. S. "Death without disease?" New York State
      Journal of Medicine, 74 (Oct. 1974), 2053-4.

1790 Shapiro, H. A. "Brain death and organ transplantation,"
      Journal of Forensic Medicine, 15 (July-Sept. 1968),
      89-90.
          States that with the emergence of heart transplants
      a new criteria for the determination of death is needed.

1791 _____. "Criteria for determining that death has occurred:
      the Philadelphia protocol," Journal of Forensic Medicine,
      16 (1969), 1-3.

1792 Sharp, D. "Lessons from a dying patient," American
      Journal of Nursing, 68 (July 1968), 1517-20.
          Points out the various patterns of behavior of dying
      patients that offer insights to nurses.

1793 Shaw, E. B. "Sudden unexpected death in infancy syndrome,"
      American Journal of Diseases of Children, 116 (Aug.
      1968), 115-19.
          Nose obstructions due to mild infections may trigger
      apnea and asphyxia and cause sudden death in infancy.

1794 Shephard, M. W. "This I believe--about questioning the
      right to die," Nursing Outlook (Oct. 1969), 22-5.
          The writer states that nurses should develop "a
      well-defined personal philosophy regarding dying and
      death."

1795 Sheps, J. "Management of fear of death in chronic disease, "
Journal of the American Geriatric Society, 5 (1957),
793-7.
States that the fear of death in the chronically
diseased person should be managed so that the patient
can be encouraged to use all his remaining resources.

1796 Silverman, D. "Cerebral death--the history of the syndrome
and its identification, " Annals of Internal Medicine, 74
(June 1971), 1003-5.

1797 _____, et al. "Cerebral death and the electroencephlo-
gram, " Journal of the American Medical Association,
209 (Sept. 8, 1969), 1505-10.

1798 _____, et al. "Criteria of brain death, " Science, 170
(Nov. 27, 1970), 1000.

1799 Simmons, S., and B. Given. "Nursing care of the terminal
patient, " Omega, 3 (Aug. 1972), 217-25.

1800 Simpson, K. "The Moment of death. A new medico-legal
problem, " Acta Anasthesiologica Scandinavica Supplement,
29 (1968), 361.
Discusses the problem of when death occurs in light
of artificial means of keeping vital organs functioning.

1801 Simpson, M. A. "Teaching about death and dying, " Nursing
Times, 69 (April 1973), 442-3.
Criticizes the frequent avoidance of critically-ill
patients by hospital personnel because of revulsion.
Calls for education on death to alleviate the problem.

1802 Sisler, G. C. "The treatment of suicidal attempts, " Canadian
Medical Association Journal, 74 (Jan. 15, 1956), 112-5.
Author states that a "study of the psychopathology
of suicide involves unconscious psychodynamics as well
as conscious phenomena. "

1803 Skipper, J. K. "What communication means to patients, "
American Journal of Nursing, 64 (April 1964), 101-3.

1804 Skipper, J. K., Jr., and R. C. Leonard, eds. Social interaction and patient care. Philadelphia: Lippincott, 1965.

1805 Smith, A. G., et al. "The Dying child: helping the family
cope with impending death, " Clinical Pediatrics, 8
(March 1969), 131-4.

1806 Smith, C., et al. "Help for the hopeless, " Rhode Island
Medical Journal, 39 (Sept. 1956), 491-9.
How modern medicine and methods offer hope and a
cure to those who would have died from various ailments.

1807   Smith, H. L.   Ethics and the new medicine.   Nashville:
       Abingdon Press, 1970.
              Examines key controversial issues.   The author, a
       minister, contends that "humanity comes with the ca-
       pacity to enter and participate in relationships. "

1808   Smith, S. L.   "Right to die, " Lancet, 2 (Nov. 1970), 1088-9.

1809   Solitare, G. B.   "Sudden unexpected death, " Lancet, 1 (March
       1970), 564.

1810   Solnit, A. J.   "The Dying child, " Developmental Medicine and
       Child Neurology, 7 (1965), 693-704.

1811   _____.   "Emotional management of family stressed in care
       of the dying child, " Pediatric Currents, 17 (Sept. 1968),
       65.

1812   _____, and M. Green.   "Psychological considerations in the
       management of deaths on pediatric hospital services: I.
       The doctor and the child's family, " Pediatrics, 24 (1959),
       106-12.
              Discusses certain guides for aiding the family of the
       fatally-stricken child.

1813   Solow, V. D.   "I died at 10:52 a. m. , " Reader's Digest, 105
       (Oct. 1974), 178-82.
              A man tells his experiences when his heart stopped
       beating for 23 minutes, and he relates his moment of
       death.

1814   Spann, W.   "Definite concepts regarding legislation on the
       actual time of death, " Munchener Medizinische Wochen-
       schrift, 111 (Oct. 31, 1969), 2253-55.

1815   Spiers, P. S. , et al.   "Sudden infant death syndrome in the
       United States: a study of geographic and other vari-
       ables, " American Journal of Epidemiology, 100 (Nov.
       1074), 380-9.

1816   Spitzer, S. P. , and J. R. Folta.   "Death in the hospital: a
       problem for study, " Nursing Forum, 3 (1964), 85-92.
              Responses to an investigation of the effects of death
       upon the communication system of the hospital, and of-
       fers several techniques of overcoming problems.

1817   Squillante, A. M. , et al.   "New dimensions in the diagnosis
       of death--the doctor's liability--a lawyer's advice, "
       Journal of the Iowa Medical Society, 61 (May 1971),
       285-8.

1818   Stamp, L. D.   The Geography of life and death.   N. Y. :
       Cornell, 1965.

"Examines a wide range of diseases ... explains
their importance, and demonstrates the need for adequate statistics and their geographical analysis." Pub.
Cat.

1819 Standard, S., and N. Helmuth, eds. Should the patient know
the truth. N. Y.: Springer, 1955.

1820 Stauder, K. H., et al. "Soll der Arzt dem Kranken die
Wahrheit sagen?" Medizinische Klinik, 48 (1953), 403-5.

1821 Stein, Z., and M. Susser. "Widowhood and mental illness,"
British Journal of Preventive Social Medicine, 23 (May
1969), 106-10.

1822 Steingiesser, H. Was die Artze aller Zeiten vom Sterben
wussten. Griefswald, East Germany: Arbeiten der
Deutschen Nord, Gesellschaft für Geschichte der Medizin,
1936.

1823 Stekhoven, W. "Professor Van den Berg's plea for active
euthanasia," Nederlands Tijdschrift voor Geneeskunde,
113 (Aug. 2, 1969), 1358-60.

1824 Stern, E. Kind, Krankheit und Tod. Basel, Switzerland:
Ernst Reinhardt, Verlag, 1957.

1825 _____. "Kind und Tod," Zeitschrift für Kinderfaschung,
41 (1933), 221-40.

1826 _____. "La Psychologie de la Mort," Folia Psychiatrica,
Neurologica et Neurochirurgica, Neerlandica, 52 (July-
Aug. 1949), 227-46.

1827 _____. Vieillir: Psychologie du vieillissment et de la
Vieillesse. Neuchatel: Baconiere, 1956.

1828 Sternglass, E. J. "Infant mortality and nuclear tests,"
Bulletin of the Atomic Scientists, 25 (April 1969), 18-20.

1829 Stevens, A. C. "Facing death," Nursing Times, 58 (1962),
777-8.
"Helping a patient to die is a task of a nurse."
Offers a brief synopsis of attitudes about life and death
held by Jews and Roman Catholics.

1830 Stevens, L. A. "When is death?" Reader's Digest, 94 (May
1969), 225.
Deals with the reclassifying of death because there
are means of keeping the organs functioning when they
should be stopped.

1831 Stickel, D. L. "Ethical and moral aspects of transplanta-

tion, " Monographs in the Surgical Sciences, 3 (1966),
267-301.

1832 _____. "Medicolegal and ethical aspects of organ transplantation, " Annals of the New York Academy of Sciences,
169 (Jan. 21, 1970), 362-75.

1833 Still, J. W. "The Three levels of human life and death, the
presumed locations of the Soul, and some of the implications for the social problems of abortion, birth control and euthanasia, " Medical Annals of the District of
Columbia, 37 (June 1968), 316-8.

1834 _____. "To be or not to be--alive or dead?" Journal of
the American Geriatrics Society, 17 (May 1969), 522-4.

1835 Stitt, A. "The Dying patient and his family, " Emergency
Medicine, 2 (May 1970), 112.

1836 Stojic, B. "Is a man who is pulseless and has stopped
breathing dead?" Medical Journal of Australia, 2 (1969),
571.
Presents cases in which persons who were thought
to be dead were still alive.

1837 Stolnitz, G. J. "Recent mortality trends in Latin America,
Asia and Africa, " Population Studies, 19 (Nov. 1965),
117-38.

1838 Strauss, A. L. "Family and staff during last weeks and days
of terminal illness, " Annals of the New York Academy
of Sciences (Dec. 19, 1969), 687-95.
Focuses on the emotions of the family and nursing
staff in the dying process.

1839 _____. "Reforms needed in providing terminal care and
understanding of dying patients, " Archives of the Foundation of Thanatology, 1 (1969), 21.

1840 _____, B. Glaser, and J. C. Quint. "The Non-accounta-
bility of terminal care, " Hospitals, 38 (1964), 73-87.
Presents various arrangements of hospital structure
that should bring about certain consequences for terminal
patients.

1841 Strubbe, W., et al. "Children who didn't die: the so-called
'vulnerable child' syndrome, " Nederlands Tijdschrift
voor Geneeskunde, 116 (Sept. 30, 1972), 1782-6.

1842 Suarez, R. M., et al. "Morbidity and mortality in aged
Puerto Ricans, " Journal of the American Geriatrics Society, 13 (1965), 805-14.

1843   "Sudden death in young adults, " Journal of the American
       Medical Association, 203 (Jan. 8, 1968), 138.
           Focuses upon unexpected deaths from natural
       diseases and the very small amount of material published
       on this subject.

1844   "Sudden unexpected death, " Journal of the American Medical
       Association, 209 (Sept. 1, 1969), 1358.
           States that 10% of deaths among the general popula-
       tion are unexpected, and the first step to investigation
       should be a complete autopsy.

1845   Sudnow, D.   "Dead on arrival, " Trans-Action, 5 (1967), 36-
       43.
           Explains the legal, medical and practical definition
       of DOA.

1846   _____. Passing on: the social organization of dying.
       N. J.: Prentice-Hall, 1967.

1847   Sugar, M.   "Adolescent depression related to mourning pro-
       cesses, " Roche Report: Frontiers of Clinical Psychiatry,
       4 (Feb. 15, 1967), 3.

1848   Sutton, R. N. P. , and J. L. Emery.   "Sudden death in in-
       fancy: a microbiological and epidemiological study, "
       Archives of Diseases in Childhood, 41 (1966), 674-77.

1849   Swenson, W. M.   "Attitudes toward death among the aged, "
       Minnesota Medicine, 42 (1959), 399-402.
           "Physician is in a key position to discuss the prob-
       lem of death with his patient and must listen, review
       data and pose questions about death.   Do geriatric in-
       dividuals all have the same ideas about death? How do
       they deal with it?"

1850   _____.   "A Study of death attitudes in the gerontic popula-
       tion and their relationship to certain measurable physical
       and social characteristics. "   Ph. D. dissertation, Uni-
       versity of Minnesota, 1958.

1851   Switzer, D. K.   "Repressed affect and memory reactive to
       grief: a case fragment, " Omega, 3 (May 1962), 121-6.

1852   Symmers, W. S.   "Not allowed to die, " British Medical
       Journal, 1 (Feb. 17, 1968), 442.
           Discusses the case of a doctor who long had
       carcinoma of the stomach and stated that he did not
       want his life prolonged, but his wish was unheeded.

1852a Symposium on Sudden Coronary Death Outside Hospitals,
       Minneapolis, 1974.   Sudden coronary death outside
       hospital.   Proceedings of a symposium..., edited by

R. J. Prineas and H. Blackburn. Dallas, Texas:
American Heart Assoc., 1975. (American Heart Association Monograph, no. 47.)

1853 Tabachnick, N., and D. Klugman. "Suicide research and the
death instinct," Yale Scientific Magazine (March 1967),
12-15.

1854 Tarnower, W. "The Dying patient: psychological needs of
the patient, his family and the physician," Nebraska
Medical Journal, 54 (Jan. 1969), 6-10.

1855 "Task force on death and dying, Institute of Society, ethics
and the life sciences," Refinements in criteria for the
determination of death: an appraisal," Journal of the
American Medical Association, 22 (July 3, 1972), 48-53.

1856 Teicher, J. D. "Combat fatigue, or death anxiety neurosis,"
Journal of Nervous and Mental Disease, 117 (1953), 234-
43.
Attempts to determine the difference between combat
fatigue and death anxiety neurosis, and points out similarities and difficulties in separating the two.

1857 Thaler, O. F. "Grief and depression," Nursing Forum, 5
(1966), 8-22.
Discusses the role of the public health nurse in
helping mothers talk about an impending death and the
drastic change in their lives.

1858 Thomas, B. B., et al. "Learning to live with death and
grieving," UNA Nursing Journal, 69 (April 1971), 9-17.

1859 Thomas, E. "Terminal illness," District Nursing, 4 (Oct.
1961), 156-8.

1860 Thomson, G. P., et al. "Right to die," Lancet, 2 (Nov.
1970), 1037.

1861 "A Time to die," Medical Journal of Australia, 1 (1969),
127-8.

1862 Toole, J. F. "Danger ahead: problems in defining life and
death," North Carolina Medical Journal, 28 (Nov. 1967),
464-6.

1863 _____. "The Neurologist and the concept of brain death,"
Perspectives in Biology and Medicine, 14 (1971), 559-
607.

1864 Touch, R. "Management of the child with a fatal disease,"
Clinical Pediatrics, 3 (July 1964), 418-27.
Suggests ways of discussing a fatal disease to chil-

dren, and cites various cases of terminal illness.

1865 Towbin, A. "Spinal injury related to syndrome of sudden
      death in infants," American Journal of Clinical Pathology,
      19 (1968), 562-7.

1866 Tunbridge, R. E. "Terminal care," Practitioner, 196 (Jan.
      1966), 110-13.
      Discusses the ethical, social, and medical problems
      of terminal care in which a fairly rapid decline can be
      expected in the dying patient.

1867 Turczynowski, R., et al. "Birth and death certificates as a
      source of information on the cause of death in past cen-
      turies," Archives of Historical Medicine, 31 (1968), 213-
      19.

1868 Ujhely, G. B. "Grief and depression: implications for pre-
      ventive and therapeutic nursing care," Nursing Forum,
      5 (1966), 23-35.

1868a U. S. Department of Health, Education, and Welfare. Sudden
       infant death syndrome; selected annotated bibliography,
       1960-1971. Washington, D. C.: G. P. O., 1973.

1869 University of North Carolina. Chapel Hill. Developing a new
      definition of death. Health Law Bulletin Number 35.
      Chapel Hill: University of North Carolina, 1972.
      Discusses pros and cons of cerebral or brain death
      and circulatory and respiratory death.

1870 Vail, D. G. "Suicide and medical responsibility," American
      Journal of Psychiatry, 157 (1959), 1007.
      Studies suicides that occurred in New Hampshire
      during 1955-1956 consisting of 140 cases using data from
      death certificates.

1871 Vakhovskii, A. I. "Our experiences in the treatment of
      terminal cases," Klinicheskaia Khirurgiia (Kiev), 4
      (April 1963), 41-5.

1872 Valdés-Dapena, M. A. "Crib-deaths and focal fibrinoid
      neurosis of the infant larynx," Journal of Forensic Sci-
      ences, 3 (1958), 503.

1873 _____. "Sudden and unexpected death in infancy: a re-
      view of the world literature, 1954-1966," Pediatrics,
      39 (1967), 123-38.

1874 _____. "Sudden and unexpected death in infants: the
      scope of our ignorance," Pediatric Clinics of North
      America, 10 (1963), 693.

VALDES-DAPENA   168   Medicine/Nursing

1875 _____, and R. P. Felipe. "Immunofluorescent studies in
     crib deaths: absence of evidence of hypersensitivity in
     cow's milk," American Journal of Clinical Pathology, 56
     (1971), 412-15.

1876 _____, et al. "Sudden unexpected death in infancy: a sta-
     tistical analysis of certain socio-economic factors,"
     Journal of Pediatrics, 73 (Sept. 1968), 386-94.

1877 Van Deilen, T. R. "Sudden death-premonition of things to
     come," Illinois Medical Journal, 14 (April 1973), 392.

1878 Van den Bergh, R. L. "Let's talk about death to overcome
     inhibiting emotions," American Journal of Nursing, 66
     (Jan. 1966), 71-3.

1879 Van Leeuwen, W. S. "Symposium on the significance of EEG
     for 'statement on death'," Introduction, Electroenceph-
     alography and Clinical Neurophysiology, 27 (Aug. 1969),
     214-5.

1880 Vaughan, D. H. "Families experiencing sudden unexpected
     infant death," Journal of the Royal College of General
     Practitioners, 16 (1968), 359-67.

1881 Vernick, J. J., and M. Karon. "Who's afraid of death on a
     leukemia ward?" American Journal Diseases of Chil-
     dren, 109 (May 1965), 393.

1882 Verwoerdt, A. "Communication with the fatally ill," Southern
     Medical Journal, 57 (July 1964), 787-95.

1883 _____. "Euthanasia: a growing concern for physicians,"
     Geriatrics, 22 (Aug. 1967), 44.
          An interview with the author concerning the current
     opinion in the medical profession on euthanasia, and the
     approaches to it in medical schools.

1884 _____. "Informing the patient with fatal illness," Post-
     graduate Medicine, 40 (Dec. 1966), A95-99.

1885 Vitale, L. D. "Le ultime parole dei moribondi," Minerva
     Medica, 49 (Oct. 20, 1950), 256-67.

1886 Voigt, J. "The Criteria of death particularly in relation to
     transplantation surgery," World Medical Journal, 14
     (Sept.-Oct. 1967), 143-6.

1887 Volkan, V. "The Recognition and prevention of pathological
     grief," Virginia Medical Monthly, 99 (May 1972), 535-40.

1888 Vorreith, M., et al. "Causes of death in the army," Vojen-
     ski Zdravotnicke Listy, 34 (Dec. 1965), 240-3.

1889 Wahl, C. W. "Bolstering the defenses of the dying patients, "
Hospital Physician, 5 (March 1969), 160.

1890 _____. "The Physician's management of the dying patient, "
Current Psychiatric Therapy, 2 (1962), 127-36.
Presents ways that the physician can effectively
handle the dying patient so that his encounter with death
is comfortable.

1891 Walker, A. E. "The Death of a brain, " Johns Hopkins Medical Journal, 124 (1969), 190-201.
Discusses the medical, legal, religious and sociological implications of the problem of brain death as it
relates to organ donors.

1892 Walker, K. M. The Circle of life; a search for an attitude
to pain, disease, old age, and death. College Park,
Md.: McGrath, 1970.
"Reprint of the 1942 ed. "

1893 Wallace, E., and B. D. Townes. "Dual role of comforter
and bereaved: reactions of medical personnel to the dying child and his parents, " Mental Hygiene, 53 (July
1969), 327-32.
Discusses "the triphasic pattern of mourning of the
parents upon the death of children, the reaction of the
parents and medical personnel to the dying child. "

1894 Wallace, H. M., and I. W. Gabrielson. Inter-American investigation of mortality in childhood: California Study.
Final Report. California University, School of Public
Health, 1972.
Focuses on the nature and extent of childhood mortality in geographically, socioeconomically and culturally
disparate populations. Recommendations are for international collaborative studies, and for community-wide
research on childhood mortality.

1895 Wallace, L. "Death and the nurse, " Nursing Monthly, 128
(Feb. 28, 1969), 22.

1896 _____. "The Needs of the dying, " Nursing Times, 68
(Nov. 13, 1969), 1450-1.
States that each individual dying patient must be
studied individually and each of his particular needs
satisfied in the way that's right for him.

1897 Wamsley, F. X. "How to cope with the high cost of dying, "
Rhodesan Nurse, 37 (Aug. 1974), 57-9.

1898 Wangensteen, O. H. "Should patients be told they have cancer?" Surgery, 27 (1950), 944-7.

1899 Warbasse, J. P. "The Ultimate adventure," Geriatrics, 11 (1956), 468-9.
States that "the aged need to know how to die and how to approach the great adventure with poise, if not with satisfaction."

1900 Warshofsky, F. "Death rides on two wheels," Reader's Digest, 156 (Dec. 1967), 39.

1901 Waxenberg, S. G. "The Importance of the communication of feelings of cancer," New York Academy of Sciences, 125 (1966), 1000-5.
Study shows that a large majority of physicians tell their patients they have cancer and that families of the patient wish to be told.

1902 Weber, M. "Dealing with death: thanatology looks at the doctor and the dying patient," Medical World News, 12 (May 21, 1971), 30-6.

1903 Weisberg, L. M. "Casebook with the terminally ill," Social Casework, 55 (June 1974), 337-42.
The author, a caseworker, demonstrates through a casestudy that new approaches to the management of the terminally ill are needed to bring comfort and dignity to the final phase of life.

1904 Weisman, A. D. "Misgivings and misconceptions in the psychiatric care of terminal patients," Psychiatry, 33 (1970), 67-81.
Considers how the private attitudes of doctors, in contrast to their professional pronouncements, determine the kind of care that terminal patients may receive.

1905 _____. "The Patient with a fatal illness--to tell or not to tell," Journal of the American Medical Association, 201 (1967), 646-8.
Discussion about the physician's guidelines for "telling" or "not telling" the patient.

1906 _____, and J. J. Warden. "Social significance of the danger list," Journal of the American Medical Association, 215 (1971), 1963-6.
States that the danger list is not a good indication of impending death and needs revision.

1907 Weiss, M. O. "Attempted suicide; then what?" American Journal of Nursing, 49 (1949), 290-3.
Discusses the obligations of nurses regarding attempted suicide.

1908 West, N. D. "Terminal patients and their families," Journal of Religion and Health, 13 (Jan. 1974), 65-9.

Suggests that physicians who treat patients have been poorly trained. The author also presents the "what" and "when" of revealing the news to a patient and his family.

1909 Westberg, G. "Good grief," Practical Nursing, 12 (March 1962), 14-15.
Article is concerned with "loss relating to the aging process. The loss of vocation, of one's work, of one's friends." We think of grief only in terms of loss through death.

1910 Weston, D., and R. C. Irwin. "Preschool child's response to death of infant sibling," American Journal of Diseases of Childhood, 106 (1963), 564-7.

1911 "What to tell a child?" Time, 93 (March 14, 1969), 67.

1912 "When do we let the patient die?" Annals of Internal Medicine, 68 (March 1968), 695-700.
Editorial discusses the physicians' efforts to preserve life and the obligation to relieve suffering and allow the patient to die with dignity.

1913 Whetmore, R. "The Role of grief in psychoanalysis," International Journal of Psychoanalysis, 44 (1963), 97-103.
Re-emphasizes the importance of psychoanalysis as a process, placing special emphasis on grief work and the peculiar characteristics which differentiate it from all previous experience.

1914 White, R. J. "The Scientific limitation of brain death," Hospital Progress, 53 (March 1972), 48-51.

1915 Wiener, I. H. "Death criteria," Journal of the American Medical Association, 222 (Oct. 2, 1972), 86.

1916 Wilkes, E. "Terminal cancer at home," Lancet, 1 (1965), 799-801.

1917 Wilkes, P. "When do we have the right to die? Three case histories," Life, 72 (Jan. 14, 1972), 48.
Explores briefly the problem of euthanasia and whether modern science keeps man alive too long.

1918 Wilkinson, L. "Death is a family matter," Registered Nurse, 33 (Sept. 1970), 50.

1919 Williams, H. "On a teaching hospital's responsibility to counsel parents concerning their child's death," Medical Journal of Australia, 2 (Oct. 1963), 643-5.

1920 Williams, J. S., Jr. "Infant and child mortality in Burma by ethnic group," Eugenics Quarterly, 13 (June 1966), 128-32.

Study reveals the Chinese and Indian minorities in
Burma have distinctly lower child mortality rates than
the Burmese population grouping.

1921 Williamson, W. P. "Life or death--whose decision?" Journal of the American Medical Association, 197 (Sept. 5,
1966), 793-5.
States that each physician should give examples of
different diseases, situations, and conditions concerning
the preservation of life.

1922 _____, et al. "Prolongation of life or prolonging the act
of dying," Journal of the American Medical Association,
202 (Oct. 9, 1967), 162-3.
Discusses whether the physician is actually prolonging life, or whether by therapeutic treatment he is preventing the patient's death.

1923 Wilson, F. G. "Social isolation and bereavement," Nursing
Times, 67 (1971), 269-70.

1924 Wingate, D. "Definition of death," British Medical Journal,
2 (May 11, 1968), 363.

1925 Wittner, D. "Life or death," Today's Health, 52 (March
1974), 48-53.
Describes a new speciality--bioethics--to give advice and confront the situations where lives are hanging
in the balance. Also describes medical techniques used
to prolong life.

1926 Wodinsky, A. "Psychiatric consultation with nurses on a
leukemia service," Mental Hygiene, 48 (1964), 282-7.
Article is primarily concerned with the nurse's
problems on leukemia service. It discusses how the
nurse can hopefully cope with her own anxieties.

1927 Wolff, K. H. "Helping elderly patients face fear of death,"
Hospital Community Psychiatry, 18 (May 1967), 142-4.
States that the majority of older persons do not accept death as the natural end to life, and suggests ways
to help them face this fact.

1928 _____. Personality type and reaction toward aging and
death. N.Y.: Child Study Association, 1958.
Discusses "attitudes about aging and death in 90 patients in nine psychopathological groups."

1929 _____. "The Problem of death and dying in the geriatric
patient," Journal of the American Geriatrics Society, 18
(Dec. 1970), 954-61.

1930 Wolters, W. H. G. "The Dying child in hospitals," in The

Child in His Family, edited by E. James Anthony, and
C. Koupernick. Vol. 2. N. Y.: Wiley, 1973. pp. 159-
68.
Discussion of the proper care of the dying child and
his parents in the context and organization of a hospital
or children's ward.

1931 Woolnough, J. "A Time to die: further reflections, "
Medical Journal of Australia, 1 (1969), 427.

1932 Worcester, A. The Care of the aged, the dying and the
dead, 2d ed. Springfield, Ill.: C. C. Thomas, 1961.

1933 World Health Organization. Medical certification of cause of
death; instructions for physicians on use of international
form of medical certificate of cause of death. 3rd ed.
Geneva, 1968.

1934 Wrigley, J. E. "Critical questions in medical transplants, "
America, 120 (March 22, 1969), 334-7.
Discusses the moment when a human being is dead
and the equally important question of who will decide
when death has occurred.

1935 Wygant, W. E., Jr. "Dying, but not alone, " American
Journal of Nursing, 67 (March 1967), 574-7.

1936 Yater, W. M., and H. H. Hussey. "The Cause of death, "
Medical Annals of the District of Columbia, 4 (1935),
119-24.
The authors consider the inaccuracy of death certificates and probe into the true causes of death.

1937 Yeaworth, R. C.; F. T. Kapp; and C. Winget. "Attitudes
of nursing students toward the dying patient, " Nursing
Research, 23 (Jan. 1974), 20-4.
A questionnaire measuring attitudes towards death
and the dying person answered by 108 freshmen and 69
seniors. A nursing curriculum is described which explores caring for the dying patients, classes on loss
and grief, and one-to-one counseling for students who
care for dying patients.

1938 Yoeli, M. "Death and compassion in medicine and literature, " American Journal of Medical Science, 263 (June
1972), 432-43.

1939 Young, M.; B. Benjamin; and C. Wallis. "The Mortality
of widowers, " Lancet, 2 (Aug. 31, 1963), 454-6.
Article discusses the high suicide rate among widows and widowers.

1940 Young, P. "Closing in on a killer, " National Observer,

9-A (Feb. 2, 1974).
Informs the reader about certain important facts
concerning emphysema.

1941 _____. "Stalking a baby killer, " National Observer, 1
(April 20, 1974), 20.
Discusses sudden infant death that kills some 10, 000
infants each year, and points out many of the causes.

1942 Yudkin, S. "Children and death, " Lancet, 1 (Jan. 1967),
37-41.
States that children who are dying should be given
the opportunity to show their fear, and talks about what
death means to them.

Part V

RELIGION AND THEOLOGY

1943 Abhedananda, S. The Mystery of death; a study in the
philosophy and religion of the Katha Upanishad. Cal-
cutta: Ramakrishna Vedanta Math, 1967.

1944 Adams, J. R. The Sting of death. N. Y.: Seabury, 1971.

1944a Ahmad Said. What happens after death; Marne ke baad kia
hoga, by Ahmed Saeed Dehlvi; translation, Rahm Ali
al-Hashmi; edited by Safir Ahmed Qadri. Delhi: Dini
Book Department: Agent in foreignland, M. I. Nana,
Johannesburg, 1974.

1945 Albacete, L. "Humanae Mortis, " Triumph, 5 (Nov. 1970),
16-19.

1946 Aldrich, C. K.; M. Knight; and C. Nighswonger. A Pastoral
counseling casebook. Philadelphia: Westminster Press,
1968.

1947 Aldwinckle, R. Death in the secular city. London: George
Allen & Unwin, 1972.
Reminds Christians that hope is not confined to this
world. Presents chapters on resurrection and immortality.

1948 Alexander, I. E., and A. M. Alderstein. "Death and religion, " in The Meaning of Death, edited by H. Feifel.
N. Y.: McGraw-Hill, 1959. pp. 271-83.
Analyzes the new turn to religion as an outbreak of
the fear caused by the new power of man which brings
death through holocaust closer to everyone.

1949 Alexander, W. M. "Death of God or God of death?" in
Radical Theology: phase two, edited by C. W. Christian,
and G. R. Wittig. Philadelphia: Lippincott, 1967. pp.
63-8.

1950 Allen, D. Finding our father. Atlanta: John Knox Press,
1974.

1951 Altizer, T. J. J. "The Death of God and the uniqueness of Christianity, " in The History of Religions; essays on the problem of understanding, by J. Wach, and others. Chicago: University of Chicago Press, 1967. pp. 119-41.

1952 _____, comp. Toward a new Christianity: readings in the death of God theology, edited by T. J. J. Altizer. N.Y.: Harcourt, Brace and World, 1967.

1953 _____, and W. Hamilton. Radical theology and the death of God. Indianapolis: Bobbs, 1966.

1954 Anderson, H. Learning and teaching about death and dying. Princeton, N.J.: Princeton Theological Seminary, 1972.
Divided into two parts, "the first is an attempt to organize the various dimensions of death education in order to clarify educational foci ... " and the second "includes an outline of a course on death for prospective pastoral caretakers, and some reflections on that process" (Author).

1954a Ars moriendi; The Book of the craft of dying and other early English tracts concerning death, taken from manuscripts and printed books in the British Museum and Bodleian Libraries, now-first done into modern spelling and edited by F. M. M. Cowper, with a preface by the Rev. G. Congreve. N.Y.: Longmans Green, and Co., 1917.
Short treatises rescued from the shelves of the British Museum and Bodleian Libraries. "This presentation of death as mediaeval Christianity saw it ... is naively sincere, full of awful anticipation of judgment, and of hope in the Divine mercy. "

1955 Asquith, G. Death is all right. Nashville: Abingdon, 1970.

1956 Assheton, W. A Method of devotion for sick and dying persons: with particular directions from the beginning of sickness to the hour of death, 2d ed. London: 1718.

1957 St. Augustine. Immortality of the Soul. N.Y.: Cima Pub. Co., 1947.

1958 Bachmann, C. C. Ministering to the grief sufferer. Philadelphia: Fortress Press, 1967.
A guide for clergy in aiding victims of grief, looking at clergy's relationship to the victim, what grief consists of, techniques for treating it, and the role of funerals and funeral directors.

1959 Bacon, A. Consolation. Boston: Atlantic Monthly Press, 1922.
A reprint of 35 pages originally published in the Atlantic Monthly, recording a "spiritual experience which

brought the writer an assurance of immortality.... "

1960 Banks, S. A. "Dialogue on death: Freudian and Christian
     views, " Pastoral Psychology, 14 (June 1963), 41-9.

1961 Barnes, E. W. "Is there an after-life?" in The Mysteries
     of Life and Death; great subjects discussed by great au-
     thorities. London: Hutchinson and Co., 1936.
     "I muse over this question of immortality, and find
     myself holding fast to the belief that God preserves what
     is worth keeping.... [T]here is, in man's spirit, that
     which is worth keeping--and it shall never die."

1962 Bartsch, F. Der letzte Feind; Erlebnisse einer Schwester.
     Berlin: Wichern-Verlag, 1939.

1963 Bayly, J. T. The View from a hearse; a Christian view of
     death. Elgin, Ill.: David C. Cook, 1939.

1964 Beatty, D. "Shall we talk about death, " Pastoral Psychology,
     6 (1955), 11-14.
     Discusses the need to encourage the dying to speak
     about their death and not to be condemned to silence by
     hospital personnel.

1965 Beberman, A. "Death and my life, " Review of Metaphysics,
     17 (1963), 18-32.

1966 Becque, M., and L. Becque. Life after death. N.Y.:
     Hawthorn, 1960.
     Discusses the Christian view of death regarding
     man's future life and the resurrection.

1967 Benda, C. E. "Bereavement and grief work, " Journal of
     Pastoral Care, 16 (spring 1962), 1-13.

1968 Bendit, L. J. The Mirror of life and death. Wheaton, Ill.:
     Theosophical Pub. House, 1965.

1969 Berkovits, E. "Death of a God, " Judaism, 20 (1971), 75-86.

1970 Berman, A. L. "Belief in afterlife, religion, religiosity and
     life-threatening experiences, " Omega, 5 (summer 1974),
     127-35.

1971 Best, P. "An Experience in interpreting death to children, "
     Journal of Pastoral Care, 2 (1948), 29-34.

1971a Bishop, J. P., and E. Wilson, Jr. The Undertaker's gar-
     land, decorations by Boris Artzybasheff. N.Y.:
     Haskell House, 1974 [a reprint of 1922 ed.].

1972 Boettner, L. Immortality. Philadelphia: Presbyterian and

Reformed Pub. Co., 1956.
Partial contents: Certainty and reality of death;
Penalty for sin; Three kinds of death: spiritual, physi-
cal, eternal; Christian attitudes toward death; Scripture
teaching regarding immortality; Terms: Sheol--Hades--
Purgatory.

1973 Bok, S. "Euthanasia and the care of the dying," Bioscience,
8 (Aug. 1973), 461-66.

1973a Bonnell, G. C. "The Pastor's role in counselling the bereaved," Pastoral Psychology, 22 (Feb. 1971), 27-
36.

1974 Booth, H. "The Christian nurse: a nurse's special problems, 2. Care for the dying," Nursing Times, 60
(Dec. 4, 1964), 1615.
Discusses the tasks of a Christian nurse and the
need to listen with understanding. The chaplain should
be told of the prognosis as soon as possible because the
patients should be informed when they ask about their
chances of recovery.

1974a Boots, D. D. "Helping the cancer patient: the minister
and the social worker," Pastoral Psychology, 22 (Jan.
1971), 35-40.

1975 Boros, L. The Moment of truth, trans. from the German
by Gregory Bainbridge. London: Burns and Oates,
1965.

1976 _____. Mysterium Mortis; der Mensch in der letzten
Entscheldung. Olten: Walter, 1962.

1977 Bossard, J. Ritual in family living. Philadelphia: University of Pennsylvania, 1950.
See especially pages 14-30.

1978 Bosselman, B. Self-Destruction; a study of the suicidal impulse. Springfield, Ill.: C. C. Thomas, 1958.

1979 Bouquet, A. C. "Palestinian habits: births, marriages and
deaths," in Everyday Life in New Testament Times,
New York: Scribner's, 1953. pp. 148-50.

1980 Brandon, S. G. F. The Judgment of the dead: the idea of
life after death in the major religions. N.Y.: Scribner's Sons, 1969.
An investigation of man's interest in the death process. Some descriptions of burial rites and the connection between belief in afterlife and morality.

1981 _____. "Origin of death in some ancient near eastern

religions, " Religious Studies, 1 (1966), 217-28.

1982 Branson, R. "Is acceptance a denial of death? Another look
      at Kübler-Ross, " Christian Century, XCII (May 7, 1975),
      464-8.

1983 Bremer, P. L. Paul's understanding of the death of Christ
      according to Romans 1-8. Doctoral dissertation, Prince-
      ton Theological Seminary, 1974.

1984 Brooks, D. P. Dealing with death--a Christian perspective.
      Nashville: Broadman Press, 1974.

1985 Brown, R. E. The Virginal conception and bodily resurrec-
      tion of Jesus. N.Y.: Paulist-Newman, 1973.

1986 Brown, R. M. "Immortality, " in A Handbook of Christian
      Theology, edited by M. Halverson, and A. A. Cohen.
      N.Y.: World, 1958. pp. 184-5.

1987 Brown, W. A. "The Christian's fulfillment: or what to be-
      lieve about immortality, " in Beliefs That Matter. N.Y.:
      Scribner's, 1928. pp. 281-303.

1988 Brunner, S. Büchlein gegen die Todesfurcht. Vienna:
      Wendelin, 1856.

1989 Budge, E. A. W. The Book of the dead. N.Y.: Universi-
      ties Books, 1960.
      A translation of the Egyptian Book of the Dead with
      additions of funeral texts coming after the book had been
      written. The book's chapters were considered "as all-
      powerful guides along the road which, passing through
      death and the grave, led into the presence of the divine
      being...."

1990 Bulka, R. P. "Death in life--Talmudic and logotherapeutic
      affirmations, " Humanitas, 10 (Feb. 1974), 33-41.
      Rabbi Bulka recommends two linking traditions to
      help contemporary man accept a philosophy of life. The
      religious tradition is found in Talmudic and Midrashic
      literature of Judaism. The secular tradition is found
      in the logotherapy of Viktor Frankl. Both traditions
      take a positive attitude toward death.

1991 Bush, M. The Adventure called death. New York: Bond
      Wheelright, 1950.
      A discussion of what it means to die in religious
      and philosophical terms. Many scriptural references re-
      inforce the theme that death is a release instead of an
      end.

1992 Busse, E. W. Behavior and adaptation in late life. Boston:

Little Brown, 1970.

1993 _____. Therapeutic implications of basic research with
the aged. Philadelphia: Institute of Pennsylvania Hospital, 1967. (Strecker Monograph Series, no. 4.)

1994 "But this is forever," Liguorian, 52 (March 1964), 19-22.
Article discusses life after death and the Christian
view of it.

1995 Callahan, R. J. "Overcoming religious faith: a case history," Rational Living, 2 (1967), 16-21.
"Refutes the notion that once a person is reared religiously he must hopelessly always remain so--at least
subconsciously--and that the threat of death will make
him return to his early faith."

1996 Callaway, J. A. "Burials in ancient Palestine; from the
stone age to Abraham," The Biblical Archaeologist, 26
(Sept. 1963), 74-91.

1997 "Capital theology," Christian Century, 89 (March 15, 1972),
32.
Advocates the abolishment of capital punishment as
unconstitutional, rather than on the grounds that it's un-
Christian.

1998 Cappon, D. "The Psychology of dying," Pastoral Psychology,
12 (1961), 35-44.

1999 Cargas, H. J., and A. White, eds. Death and hope. Washington, D. C.: Corpus Books, 1970.

2000 _____. "Death is alone: excerpt from Death and Hope,"
Catholic World, 210 (March 1970), 269-72.

2001 Carnell, E. J. "Fear of death," Christian Century, 80
(1963), 136-7.

2002 Carr, W. "Theological reflections on death," North Carolina
Medical Journal, 28 (Nov. 1967), 461-4.
Article attempts to offer some theological insight
about death which represents the doctrinal posture of a
good number of ministers and theologians.

2003 Carrigan, R. L. "The Hospital, chaplain, research and
pastoral care," Pastoral Psychology, 17 (June 1966),
39-48.

2004 Carrington, H. Death: its causes and phenomena; with
special reference to immortality. N. Y.: Dodd, 1921.
An abridged edition of an earlier English work with
J. R. Meader as the joint author.

2005 Carson, R. A. "Amidst children and witnesses: reflections on death," Humanitas, 10 (Feb. 1974), 9-19.
Reflections into a variety of ways, past and present, of meeting death and of the attendant fears which complicate and distort the meaning of death.

2006 Carter, P. A. "Science and the Death of God," American Scholar, 42 (summer 1973), 406-21.
Presents a discussion of the "God Is Dead" movement of the sixties with implications for science and theology. Mr. Carter backs up his arguments with convincing examples taken from history, science, and theology.

2007 "Catholic theologian defends man's right to die," Journal of the American Medical Association, 180 (1962), 23-4.

2008 Cavanagh, J. R. "The Chaplain and the dying patient," Hospital Progress, 52 (Nov. 1971), 34-40.

2009 Charles, R. Eschatology: the doctrine of a future life in Israel, Judaism and Christianity. N. Y.: Schocken Books, 1963.

2010 Chinmoy, S. Death and reincarnation: eternity's voyage. N. Y.: Agni Press, 1974.

2011 Choy, L. "Death is but a part of life," Catholic Charities, 55 (Nov. 1971), 9-13.
Discusses a friend who gave the author a sensitivity to the process of death as being a vital part of life.

2012 Clancey, R. "The Death of God in the American Catholic college," Thought, 43 (spring 1968), 39-52.
Discusses American Catholic education and the criticisms of it. "Unless the criticisms are met with enlightened improvements, God will die on the Catholic College campus."

2013 Clancy, R. Death: what does it mean? Chicago: Claretian Publications, 1969.

2014 _____. Life after death. Chicago: Claretian Publications, 1969.

2015 Coblentz, S. A. Answer of the ages. N. Y.: Cosmopolitan, 1932.
A history of man's beliefs concerning death and immortality from prehistoric times thru the ages, as found in the world's mythologies and religions, the testimony of science and psychical research and the thoughts of poets, priests, mystics and philosophers.

2016 Collins, J. J. "Apocalyptic eschatology as the transcendence of death," Catholic Biblical Quarterly, 36 (Jan. 1974), 21-43.

2017 Congar, Y. Le Mystère de la mort et la célébration. Paris: Editions du Cerf, 1951.

2018 Consultation Clinic. "On fatal illness," Pastoral Psychology, 6 (Feb. 1955), 42-53.
Author states that role of the clergy is to help the parishioner to consider the possibility of death. In the cases of terminal illness, the clergy should allow the person the privilege of being told of it if he wants to be.

2019 Cousins, N. The Celebration of life. N.Y.: Harper and Row, 1974.
Discusses immortality and the meaning of human life in light of human values.

2020 Cox, I. W. Mercy killing is murder. N.Y.: Paulist Press, 1935.

2021 Crane, E. "Why remember dust and ashes?" Liguorian, 51 (March 1963), 42-5.
A discussion about the season of Lent and the significance of the Christian reminder of man's limitations.

2022 Cranfield, C. E. B. "On some of the problems in the interpretation of Romans 5:12," Scot. Journal of Theology, 22 (Sept. 1969), 324-41.

2022a Crosby, T. The Work of a Christian: An important case of practical religion; or, Directions how to make religion one's business. Accompanied with another discourse, about preparation for sudden death. Boston, 1702.

2023 Cullman, O. Immortality of the Soul or resurrection of the dead. N.Y.: Macmillan, 1964.
Discusses similarities and differences between the Greek notion of immortality, and the Christian view of the resurrection of the dead.

2024 Curtis, C. J. "Radical theology: Altizer, Hamilton, and Van Buren," in Contemporary Protestant Thought. N.Y.: Bruce, 1970. pp. 85-96. (Contemporary Theology Series.)

2025 D'arcy, M. C. Death and life. N.Y.: Longmans, 1942.
A Roman Catholic priest deals with a general discussion of immortality and pursues the teachings of the Church on such topics as: the after-life, meanings of hell, heaven and purgatory.

2026 Darcy-Berube, F. "When your child asks about death,"
      New Catholic World, 216 (March-April, 1973), 55-7.
      Description of how the child comes to grips with the
      reality of death. The author outlines specific objectives
      for parents to help the child face death and share in the
      Christian hope.

2027 Davidson, G. W. "Basic images of death in America: an
      historical analysis." Ph. D. dissertation, Claremont
      Graduate School and University Center, 1964.

2028 "Death and presence; documents and commentaries," Lumen
      Vitae, 26 (Sept. 1971), 391-406.
      Comments on: "A letter, an interview and two es-
      says expressing Christian statements on death, the dead,
      and the presence of the dead."

2029 De Liguori, S. A. Preparation for death. N. Y.: Re-
      demptionist Fathers, 1926.

2030 Delooz, P. "Who believes in the hereafter; international
      survey," Lumen Vitae, 26 (Sept. 1971), 369-90.
      Discusses the question about the number of con-
      temporary people who believe that there is life after
      death.

2031 De Wolf, L. H. "Facing death," in The Enduring Message
      of the Bible, rev. ed. Atlanta: John Knox Press,
      1965. pp. 57-60.

2032 Dicks, R. , and T. Kepler. And Peace at the last. Phila-
      delphia: Westminster Press, 1953.
      Attempts to lessen a person's future emotional dif-
      ficulty in dying and meeting death. The first part con-
      cerns how a hospital chaplain has ministered to the dy-
      ing and how they die well. Part II is a collection of
      essays by other writers which gives reassurance about
      death and dying.

2033 Didier, J. C. Death and the Christian. N. Y.: Hawthorn
      Books, Inc. , 1960.

2034 Diggory, J. C. "Death and self-esteem," Paper presented
      at a meeting of the American Psychological Association,
      St. Louis, Mo. , 1962.

2035 Dijik, K. Tussen Sterven en Opstanding. Kampen,
      Netherlands: Koh, 1951.

2036 Dole, C. The Hope of immortality. N. Y.: Crowell, 1906.
      Offers many explanations for life after death. Points
      out that the idea of immortality is related to values.

2037 Donnelly, D. I. "The Requiem for God," Religious Education,
      62 (July 1967), 316-20.
           Author describes the "themes of fundamentalism,
      social justice, suffering and technology that can be found
      in the death of God theologians. "

2038 Dooley, K. "Easter gives the answer to a quest," Ave, 89
      (March 28, 1959), 30.
           Presents the Catholic attitude toward death for the
      physician.

2039 Doss, R. W. The Last enemy; a Christian understanding of
      death. N. Y.: Harper and Row, 1974.

2040 Driver, T. F. "Loss of the histrionic and the modern
      quandary of theology," Soundings, 51 (summer 1968),
      208-23.

2041 Dunne, J. S. The City of the Gods. N. Y.: Macmillan,
      1965.
           The political and social mythologies on man's mor-
      tality from ancient times to the present and the rele-
      vance in each to the Christian framework of the solu-
      tion to death.

2042 Eckardt, A. R. "Death in the Judaic and Christian tradi-
      tions," in Death in American Experience, edited by A.
      Mack. N. Y.: Schocken Press, 1973. pp. 123-48.
           Reflections and an analysis of the Judaic and Chris-
      tian traditions with documented references of immortality
      and resurrection. The same reference may also be
      found in Social Research, 39 (Aug. 1972), 489-515.

2043 Eliade, M. Rites and symbols of initiation; the mysteries
      of birth and rebirth, trans. from the French by W. R.
      Trask. N. Y.: Harper and Row, 1965. (Harper Torch-
      book.)
           Deals with the initiation symbolism of death and
      resurrection in both primitive and higher religions. The
      book consists of the Haskell Lectures which the author
      delivered at the University of Chicago in 1956 under the
      title "Patterns of Initiation. "

2044 Elimann, B. "Christian death," North American Liturgical
      Week, 22 (1961), 83-8.

2045 Ellis, R. S. "The Attitude toward death and the types of
      belief in immortality," Journal of Religions, 7 (1965),
      466-510.

2046 Ernst, C. "The Theology of death," Clergy Review, 44
      (Oct. 1959), 588-603.

2047 "Euthanasia in England: a growing storm," America (May 2, 1970), 463.
      Editorial discusses the euthanasia lobby in England and the opposition to it.

2048 Evans-Wentz, W. Y. The Tibetan book of the dead. N. Y.: Oxford University Press, 1960.

2049 The Experience of dying, edited by Norbert Greinacher and Alois Müller. N. Y.: Herder and Herder, 1974. Concillium; new series, v. 4, no. 10 (94), Pastoral Theology.

2050 Fairbanks, R. J. "Ministering to the dying," Journal of Pastoral Care, 2 (1948), 6-14.
      Article discusses reactions to dying, behavior patterns, the truth of terminal illness, and pastoral opportunities.

2051 Falque, F. C. "Comfort of the afflicted," Homiletic and Pastoral Review, 59 (July 1959), 944-5.
      Article points out that the teaching of Christ is a way to overcome mourning and fear.

2052 Fannon, P. "And after death..."? Clergy Review, 58 (July 1973), 500-17.
      Author states that "death, judgment, hell and heaven continue to be dressed up in primitive thought forms as to offend both reason and sensitivity." We have to review the whole structure of Christian teaching on eschatology.

2053 Fargues, M. Child and the mystery of death. N. J.: Paulist Press, 1966.

2054 Fechner, G. T. The Little book of life after death. Boston: Little Brown, 1904.

2055 Fitch, R. E. "Death comes to an atheist," Christian Center, 76 (Dec. 1959), 1431-33.

2056 Flammarion, C. Death and its mystery; after death. N. Y.: Century, 1923.
      The last in the trilogy in which "the author attempts to prove that scientific observation has succeeded in establishing beyond a doubt, that the soul is independent of the material organism and continues to live after death.... [H]he also holds that the theory of transmigration is probable and may some day submit to scientific proof."

2057 _____. Death and its mystery; before death; proofs of the existence of the soul, trans. by E. S. Brooks.

N. Y. :   Century, 1921.
The first volume of a trilogy which examines facts
concerning immortality. Part of the book reports psychic
research and communication.

2058   Forest, J. D.   "The Major emphasis of the funeral, " Pastoral
Psychology, 14 (1963), 19-24.

2059   Forestier, M. D.   "Dieu même a craint la mort; la méditalia
de l'Agonie de Jesus de Péguy," Vie Spirit, 106 (April
1962), 424-44.

2060   Fosdick, H. E.   "Deathless hope that man cannot escape, "
in Great Time to Be Alive; sermons on Christianity in
wartime.   N. Y. :   Harper, 1944.   pp. 226-35.

2061   Foster, A. D. , Jr.   "Resurrection of God, " Religion In Life,
38 (spring 1969), 131-47.

2062   Frankl, V. E.   "Psychiatry and man's quest for meaning, "
Journal of Religion and Health, 1 (1962), 93-103.

2063   Frazer, J. G.   Fear of the dead in primitive religions; lectures delivered on the William Wyse Foundation at
Trinity College, Cambridge, 1932-1933.   N. Y. :   Macmillan, 1933.
Six lectures deal with the attitudes "of primitive
man to the souls of the departed, his fear of the dead,
the benefits and the evils which in his belief the spirits
of the dead can bring to worshippers, and the means
which he uses to send the spirits away or keep them at
a distance. "

2064   Fulton, R. L.   "The Clergyman and the funeral director: a
study in role conflict, " Social Forces, 39 (May 1961), 32.
Views of white Protestant and Catholic clergy concerning the role funeral directors are playing in the
funeral.

2065   Gaboriau, F.   Interview sur la mort avec Karl Rahner.
Paris: P. Lethielleux, 1967.

2066   Gallup Poll, 1966.   "What Americans think of heaven and
hell, " Catholic Digest (Jan. 1967), 113-4.
Survey in which 75% of the people interviewed believed that their souls would live after death.

2067   Gatch, M. M.   Death; meaning and mortality in Christian
thought and contemporary culture.   N. Y. :   Seabury,
1969.
History of the beliefs and concepts of death from
Greek and Old Testament times to the Reformation and
concludes with contemporary interpretations.

2068   Gaus, H. Tod, Jenseits, Auferstehung. Munich: Kosel,
       1973.

2069   Gealt, F. D. "The Biblical understanding of death, " Pastoral
       Psychology, 14 (June 1963), 30-40.

2070   Gerord, H. I. The Relationship between religious belief and
       death affect. Princeton, N. J.: Princeton University
       Press, 1958.

2071   Gijsen, W. Over Dood en Heirnamaals. Dialogen met
       Vertegenwoordigers van de Anthroposofie, het Boedd-
       hisme, het Hindoeïsme, het Humanistisch Verbond, de
       Islam, de Jehova's Getuigen, de Jesus Beweging, het
       Jodendom, een Protestants Christelijke kerk, de Rooms-
       Katholieke Kerk, de Rozekruisers, de Soefi-Beweging en
       het Theosofisch Genootschap. Deventer, Netherlands:
       Ankh-Hermes, 1974.

2072   Gleason, R. "Death: man's greatest act--interview by K.
       Peter, " Ave Maria, 103 (Nov. 30, 1965), 13-15.

2073   Gleason, R. W. The World to come. N. Y.: Sheed and
       Ward, 1958.
       A Jesuit priest gives a discussion of the teachings
       of his church on the topics of sin, death, judgment,
       suffering, hell, resurrection, and heaven.

2074   Godin, A. Death and presence: studies in the psychology
       of religion. Brussels: Lumen Vitae Press, 1972.
       Teaches that parents should share honestly with the
       child. Used successfully with children, and belongs to
       the "Come to the Father Program. " Useful for children
       from ages six to nine. Includes charts, graphs, and a
       fair amount of references.

2075   _____. "Has death changed?" Lumen Vitae, 26 (Sept.
       1971), 407-30.
       Discusses and interprets the vast amount of psycho-
       logical research on death.

2076   Goes, H. Der Tod des Menschen in theologis-gesichlichtlicher
       Sicht. Erich Roth. Wie Bereiten wir zum Sterben?
       Berlin-Brandenburg: Evangelisches Konsistorium, 1968.

2077   Gray, C. "Meaning of pain, consciousness and death, " The
       Downside Review, 79 (summer 1961), 189-200.

2078   Greeley, A. "Youth in the age of renewal, part 3: Life is
       forever, " Ave, 98 (Oct. 5, 1963), 13-15.
       Article discusses the need for the re-evaluation of
       faith and points out that "the most oppressive thing about
       the world is the phenomenon of death. Faith must an-

swer the questions of life and death. "

2079 Grelot, P. De la morte à la vie éternelle; études de
      théologie biblique. Paris: Editions du Cerf, 1971.

2080 Grollman, E. A. Explaining death to children. Boston:
      Beacon, 1967.
          An anthology drawn from many different disciplines
      intended to aid parents and ministers in explaining death
      to children. Written in an inter-denominational manner,
      the book explains what children view as death, how
      death should be explained, and what will aid them in ac-
      cepting it.

2081 _____. "Way of dialogue on death between parents and
      children, " Religious Education, 69 (March 1974), 198-
      206.
          Comments on fairy tales and death, death as a long
      journey, death as sleep, the funeral, and grief reactions.

2082 Guardini, R. The Last things concerning death, purification
      after death, resurrection. N.Y.: Pantheon Books, 1954.

2083 Guinness, H. W. The Last enemy: living with terminal ill-
      ness. London: Church Pastoral Aid Society, 1974.

2084 Haldane, J. B. S. "What is death?" in The Mysteries of
      Life and Death; great subjects discussed by great au-
      thorities. London: Hutchinson, 1936.
          The author sees death "as the end of a particular
      pattern of material and mental happenings which are
      bound up with one another. "

2085 Hartland, E. S. "Death and the disposal of the dead, " En-
      cyclopedia of Religion and Ethics. N.Y.: Scribner's,
      1928. Vol. 4. pp. 411-444.

2086 Hatt, H. E. "Mystery of death and the problem of trans-
      plants, " Christian Century, 86 (April 2, 1969), 441-44.
          Discusses the theological implications of organ
      transplants, and states that doctors performing such
      operations should keep the total person in mind.

2087 Heaney, J. J. "Beyond death, " Thought, 50 (March 1975),
      35-55.
          Deals with parapsychology and personal survival.
      Offers suggestions about the use of parapsychology by
      the Christian theologian.

2088 Heller, J. J. "The Resurrection of man, " Theology Today,
      XV (July 1958), 222.

2089 Hight, J. "Life after death: a study in contrasts, " Motive,

(Jan.-Feb. 1964), 30-1.
Presents the results from eight interviews as a
part of a research project in Christian beliefs. The
questions asked: "What do you believe happens to a person after death?" and "What do you think of when you
hear the phrase, 'the resurrection of the dead'?"

2090 Holck, F. H. Death and Eastern thought; understanding
death in Eastern religions and philosophies, ed. by
Frederick H. Holck. Nashville: Abingdon, 1974.

2091 Howard, T. "Human experience of death," Christianity Today, 14 (Nov. 21, 1969), 6-8.
Discusses the Christian understanding of human experiences regarding death, and the process of salvation.

2092 Huber, M. J. "Learning how to die," Liguorian, 46 (Nov.
1958), 15-19.

2093 Hunt, G. The Christian way of death. Grand Rapids, Mich.:
Zondervan, 1971.
The author explains that death, though never
pleasant, can be a triumphant experience for the Christian. Your reaction to death will be conditioned by your
reaction to God. Those who are afraid of God are most
fearful of death."

2094 Hunter, E. F. The Questioning child and religion. Boston:
Beacon, 1956.
Concerned with the problems which face children
with regard to religion. Such things as death and immortality are examined with a view to explaining the religious connection to children.

2095 "I want out--teens who threaten suicide," Today's Health,
(Jan. 1971), 32-34.

2096 "Is God dead?" Time, 93 (May 2, 1969), 44.
The "God is dead" controversy.

2097 Jackson, E. N. The Christian funeral--its meaning, its
purpose, and its practice. N.Y.: Channel Press, 1966.

2098 _____. "Grief and guilt," Pastoral Counselor, 1 (spring
1963), 34-38.

2099 Jacobs, H. L. "Spiritual resources for the aged in facing
the problem of death," Bulletin of the Institute of
Gerontoloty--Supplement 3, 6 (1950), 3-8.

2100 James, E. O. Prehistoric religion. London: Thames and
Hudson, 1957.

2101 Jones, M. A. "Life, death, and life eternal, " in The
        Christian Faith Speaks to Children. Nashville: Abing-
        don, 1965. pp. 152-71.
            ". . . [I]n its ministry to children, the Church is
        called to involve them within the Christian fellowship in
        consideration of all issues of life and death and life
        eternal in the light of God's revelation of his nature and
        his purpose for his children. "

2102 Kakoure, K. I. Death and resurrection; concerning drama-
        tized ceremonies of the Greek popular worship. Athens:
        G. C. Elefteroudakis, 1965. (A translation of Thanatos
        --Anastase.)

2103 Kapleau, P. The Wheel of death; a collection of writings
        from Zen Buddhist and other sources on death--rebirth--
        dying. Assisted by P. Simons. N. Y.: Harper and
        Row, 1971.

2104 Kavanaugh, R. Facing death. N. Y.: Nash, 1973.
            A priest voices his view of the religious position
        concerning death. "Arguing for the value and accepta-
        bility of human emotions in crisis, he pleads the rights
        of the terminally ill, including children, to be told when
        death is medically certain. "

2105 "Keeping the dying alive: moral problem of mercy killing, "
        America, 6 (Jan. 1, 1966), 114.

2106 Kidd, J. L. "An Ecumenical funeral service for the 'New'
        church, " The Director, 3 (1969), 39.

2107 Kidorf, I. W. "Jewish tradition and the Freudian theory of
        mourning, " Journal of Religion and Health, 2 (1963),
        248-252.
            Discusses the relationship between Jewish mourning
        rituals and the Freudian notion of mourning.

2108 _____ . "The Shiva: a form of group psychotherapy, "
        Journal of Religion and Health, 1 (Jan. 1966), 43-6.
            Discusses the dynamics of a particular rite of
        Jewish mourning custom, the Shiva.

2109 Kirk, R. "Politics of death, " National Review, 23 (March
        1971), 315.
            Discusses the anti-life movement in America. The
        author feels that the declining birth rate in the U. S. is
        a sign of decadence.

2110 Kliener, L. D. "Mapping the radical theologies, " Religion
        in Life, 36 (spring 1967), 8-27.

2111 Knight, J. A. "The Care of the dying, " in A Psychiatrist

Looks at Religion and Health. Nashville: Abingdon,
1964. pp. 180-8.
Description of the roles of the pastor and physician
and how they together re-direct the patient and his
family to complete and honest understanding.

2112 Knowles, J. "The Role of the Chaplain in patient relationships: care of the critically ill, " Journal of Pastoral
Care, 7 (summer 1953), 112-6.

2113 Köllerström, O. The Actual and the real. London: Turn-
stone Books, 1974.

2114 Kort, W. A. "The Fixer and the death of God, " in Shriven
Selves: religious problems in recent American fiction.
Philadelphia: Fortress Press, 1972. pp. 90-115.

2115 Kosnik, A. "Theological reflections on criteria for the
moment of death, " Hospital Progress, 54 (Dec. 1973),
64-9.

2116 Kübler-Ross, E. "The Dying patient as teacher: an experiment and an experience, " Chicago Theological Seminary
Register, 57 (Dec. 1966), 1-14.

2117 Lackemann, M. "Death and resurrection, " Listening, 3 (winter 1968), 5-12.

2118 Lambert, R. "Man alive: Christians and death, " Today, 17
(Nov. 1961), 13-5.

2119 Lamm, M. The Jewish way in death and mourning. N.Y.:
Jonathan David, 1969.

2120 Lampl-De Grott. "Symptom formation and character formation, " International Journal of Psychoanalysis, 44 (1963),
1-11.

2121 Lancisi, G. De Subitaneis Mortibus. N.Y.: St. John's
University Press, 1971.

2122 Landorf, J. Mourning song. Old Tappan, N.J.: F. H.
Revell Co., 1974.

2123 Lawler, P. "The Personal character of Christian death, "
Liturgy, 33 (Oct. 1964), 87-90.

2124 Le Blond, J. "Living faith in Christ, " Way, 4 (Jan. 1964),
33-41.

2125 Lester, D. "Religious behavior and the fear of death, "
Omega, 1 (Aug. 1970), 189-200.

2126 "Life and death, a discursive dialogue," Fortune, 98 (1912),
      698-708.

2127 Linser, H. Tod und Unsterblichkeit. Paris: Universitas,
      1951.

2128 Litvak, S. "Facing the fear of death," Rational Living, 2
      (1967), 20-1.
          "It is concluded 'that fear of mortality can be re-
      lieved with certain rational hopes based on scientific
      facts, in place of the irrational, unscientific faiths in
      reincarnation, the disembodied soul, and similar bro-
      mides....'"

2129 Longley, A. "Death full of wonder," Lamp, 62 (Nov. 1964),
      12-13.

2130 Lord, C. "The Moral and pastoral problems of the term'nal-
      ly ill patient," Linacre, 34 (Aug. 1967), 223-7.

2131 Louisell, D. "Euthanasia and biathanasia: on dying and kill-
      ing," Linacre, 40 (Nov. 1973), 234-50.

2131a Lovett, C. S. Death: graduation to glory--no funeral for
      me. Baldwin Park, Calif.: Personal Christianity,
      1975.
          Partial Contents: Only the body dies; Our unseen
      house; What's it like there? The resurrection process;
      Graduation ceremony. "The book shows the steps to
      take to make your 'graduation' painless for your sur-
      vivors. It even has a copy of the Graduation message."

2132 Lowery, D. "The Duty to live versus the right to die; dis-
      cussion of an agonizing family dilemma," Liguorian,
      52 (Jan. 1964), 39-45.
          Article discusses a family with an old member dy-
      ing of cancer. It is concerned with the right to die
      with dignity and offers a Christian position.

2133 Lueba, J. The Belief in God and immortality. Boston:
      Sherman French and Co., 1916.

2134 Luke, C. "Some observations on the theology of death,"
      National Liturgical Week, 23 (1962), 137-8.

2135 Lützeler, H. Trost im Sterben. Freiburg im Breisgau:
      Herder, 1942.

2136 Luyten, S., and K. Barth. Unsterblichkeit. Basel: Rein-
      hardt, 1957.

2137 MacAlpine, R. There is no death. N.Y.: Revel, 1884.
          Consists of a series of essays about life after death.

Presents religious points of view concerning questions asked by Christians.

2138 McCabe, H. "The Place of death and judgment, " Life Spirit, 18 (Feb. 1964), 308-21.

2139 McCormick, R. "Of sin and death, " Theological Studies, 29 (Dec. 1968), 679-85.
The relationship between sin and death is discussed, and the final-option theory of theologians who distinguish between mortal sin and sin-unto-death is presented.

2140 McCorry, V. P. "Face the facts: Holy week bids us face the fact of life which is death, " America, 120 (March 29, 1969), 372-3.
Presents two important Christian aspects concerning immortality.

2141 _____. "Finality; survival after death, " America, 188 (1971), 125.
A discussion about the parable of divers and Lazarus. The author offers five salient questions to consider.

2142 _____. "When Christ rose from the dead: earth died, " America, 110 (March 28, 1964), 466-7.
Discusses the death of Christ and points to the teachings of St. Paul. "Fear of death in the man of faith is senseless. "

2143 _____. "The Word: the Easter collect, " America, 100 (March 28, 1959), 756.
An interpretation of the Easter Mass, which assures the Christian of victory over death--through the resurrection of Jesus Christ.

2144 McCoy, M. C. To die with style. Nashville: Abingdon, 1974.
Description about feelings of death and their relationship to life.

2145 McGreachy, D. A Matter of life and death. Atlanta: John Knox Press, 1966.

2146 MacLean, N. Death cannot sever. N. Y.: Revell, 1933.
The author's "plea is for a fuller realization of the close fellowship between the living and the dead and a more sympathetic response by the Christian Churches to the work of psychical research in exploring the unseen world. "

2147 McMahon, J. "Catholic students look at death, " Common-

weal, 87 (Jan. 26, 1968), 491-4.
　　Analyzed are various responses of students writing
an essay on death. Points out the motivation for the
responses of rejectors of the traditional beliefs about
after-life.

2148 McNaspy, C. J. "Murder for mercy's sake," America, 107
　　　(Dec. 15, 1962), 1242-4.
　　　　Presents the Christian conception of man in relation
　　　to abortion and euthanasia.

2149 McWilliams, B. "Blessed are those who die slowly,"
　　　Liguorian, 52 (Dec. 1964), 38-41.

2150 Magni, K. "Reactions to death stimuli among theology stu-
　　　dents," Journal for the Scientific Study of Religion, 9
　　　(fall 1970), 247-8.

2151 Maguire, D. "The Catholic view of mercy killing," The
　　　Humanist, (July-Aug. 1974), 16-18.
　　　　Author states that "the Catholic position is quite
　　　sensitive to the human moral right to a good death.
　　　Considers this teaching to be ahead of the ethical posi-
　　　tion found in American legal structures."

2152 Maly, E. "A Man dies," Bible Today, 62 (Nov. 1972), 906-
　　　9.
　　　　Discusses the Christian attitudes about death and
　　　criticizes the Marxist and secular humanist attitudes
　　　about it.

2153 Manton, J. E. "Jewel in a casket: reflection on the funeral
　　　of a Carmelite nun," Ave Maria, 96 (Nov. 17, 1962),
　　　13-4.

2154 Marlé, R. "La Théologie dite de la mort de Dieu," Etudes,
　　　329 (Nov. 1968), 491-501.

2155 Martensen, L. H. An der Pforte des Todes. Hamburg:
　　　Furche Verlag, 1955.

2156 Martin, D. S., and L. Wrightsman. "Religion and fears
　　　about death: a critical review of research," Religious
　　　Education, 59 (1964), 174-6.

2157 _____, et al. "The Relationship between religious be-
　　　havior and concern about death," Journal of Social
　　　Psychology, 65 (April 1965), 317-23.
　　　　"Fifty-eight adults, members of three Protestant
　　　congregations, were surveyed regarding their religious
　　　attitudes, their religious participation, and their con-
　　　cern about death...."

2158   Martin, M. B.   "Death at sunset," National Review, 26
       (Nov. 22, 1974), 1356.
           History of death and dying; attempts to explain
       death in terms of latest trends including religions.

2159   Martin-Achard, R.   De la mort à la resurrection d'après
       l'Ancien Testament.   Neuchâtel, Switzerland: Delachaux
       and Niestle, 1956.

2160   Matz, M.   "Judaism and bereavement," Journal of Religion
       and Health, 3 (1964), 345-52.
           Discusses the bereavement observance of liberal
       Judaism and its practices.

2161   Mead, M.   "The Right to die," in Twentieth Century Faith;
       hope and survival.   N. Y.:   Harper, 1972.   pp. 150-2.
       (Religious Perspectives Series, no. 25.)

2162   Mercer, E.   Why do we die?   An essay in thanatology.
       London: K. Paul, Trench, Trubner and Co., 1919.
           A Bishop discusses the reason why we die.   In-
       cluded are causes of fear of death, and death as a
       revelation.   Written from a religious perspective.

2163   Micallef, P. J.   "Abortion and the principles of legislation,"
       Laval Théologique et Philosophique, 28 (Oct. 1972),
       267-303.

2164   Michalson, C.   Faith for personal crisis.   Nashville:
       Abingdon, 1958.
           A theology for crucial situations including death.
       The book is designed to provide guidance for situations
       that are inescapable and require significant decisions.

2165   Miguens, E.   "A Particular notion of sin," American Ec-
       clesiastical Review, 167 (Jan. 1973), 30-40.
           Presents Saint Paul's view of the relationship be-
       tween sin and death.   Points out "that death is universal
       reality: through one single man sin entered the world
       and, through sin, death."

2166   Miller, D. F.   "Death through the eyes of Christ," Liguorian,
       50 (Nov. 1962), 3-7.
           Article states that death has always been a means
       for spiritual growth.   It lists three important Christian
       approaches for meditating about death.

2167   Miller, R. C.   Live until you die.   Philadelphia: United
       Church Press, 1974.
           The author examines the case of preparing oneself
       for death.   He draws on Christian theology, psychology,
       sociology, medicine and the arts to reinforce the ac-
       ceptance of death.

2168 Minton, F. "Need for a theology of death," Christian Center, 87 (March 25, 1970), 352-5.

2169 Mondale, L. "Nothingness and death," Religious Humanism, 1 (winter 1967), 24-5.

2170 Montgomery, J. W. Is God dead? Grand Rapids, Mich.: Zondervan, 1966.

2171 Murchland, B. Death of God theology. N.Y.: Random, 1967.
      Some 18 authors survey the theme in a cultural and theological perspective.

2172 Murphy, R. Immortality and resurrection; four essays. N.Y.: Macmillan, 1965.

2173 "The Mystery of death," Catholic Digest, 31 (Oct. 1967), 84-6.
      States that "man rebels against death because he has within himself an eternal seed which cannot be reduced to matter. Christ conquered death and he freed man from death."

2174 Nelson, J. R. "Deicide, theothanasia, or what do you mean?" in The Meaning of the Death of God, edited by B. B. Murchland. N.Y.: Random House, 1967. pp. 192-202.

2175 Neophitos, A. "Euthanasia or death as a creative process-- the real question?" Homiletic and Pastoral Review, 73 (April 1973), 30-2.

2176 Nix, J. "She smiled and went away; eulogy," Linacre Quarterly, 31 (Feb. 1964), 18.
      Eulogy written by the author for his children as a memory of their mother which expresses how her Christian faith had sustained her in her suffering.

2176a Oakes, J. "Pastoral care of the dying and the bereaved," District Nursing, 11 (March 1969), 256-8.

2177 Ochs, R. The Death in every now. N.Y.: Sheed and Ward, 1969.
      The author "basing himself on Heidegger's philosophy and Karl Rahner's theology, reexamines death in a richly personal and profoundly fresh fashion...."

2178 Ogletree, T. Death of God controversy. Nashville: Abingdon, 1966.
      Includes Christian atheism, and deals with theological fragments, the problem of meaning, and provides a setting for radical theology.

2179 Oraison, M. Death--and then what? N.Y.: Newman Press, 1969.
      Discusses the Christian version of death and implores the reader to realize that the subject of death unites man because the question is personal and common. Offers insights from science and psychoanalysis about death.

2180 Ormea, F. Superamento della morte. Contributo al dialogo fra credenti e non credenti. Turin: Gribaldi, 1970.

2181 Ousley, J. D. "The Possibility of life after death," Religious Studies, 9 (June 1973), 157-69.

2182 Owst, G. Preaching in mediaeval England. Cambridge, 1926.

2183 Padovano, A. "American unbelief and the death of God," Catholic Theological Society of America Proceedings, 21 (1966), 113-48.

2184 Pahnke, W. N. "Psychedelic mystical experiences in human encounter with death," Harvard Theological Review, 62 (Jan. 1969), 1-32.
      Claims that psychedelic mystical experiences teach us that there is more to the range of human consciousness than we assume.

2185 Park, R. "Thanatology: a questionnaire and a plea for a neglected study," Journal of the American Medical Association, 58 (April 27, 1912), 1243-46.

2186 Parsons, T. "Religious symbolization and death," in Changing Perspectives in the Scientific Study of Religion, edited by A. W. Eister. N.Y.: Wiley, 1974. pp. 217-26.

2187 Paul VI, Pope. "Address to the faithful about death and time" (English trans.), L'Osservatore Romano, 46 (Nov. 15, 1973), 294.

2188 Pelikan, J. The Shape of death, life and immortality in the early Fathers. Nashville: Abingdon, 1961.

2189 Perkins, J. S. Through death to rebirth. Chicago: Theosophical Pub. House, 1974.
      Discussion of the method and the nature of reincarnation, and its implications for religion.

2190 Perske, R. "Death and ministry: episode and response," Pastoral Psychology, 15 (1964), 25-35.
      The efforts of a pastor are discussed who helps parishoners to accept their burden of pain due to a tragic episode.

2191 Petherbridge, J. "Darling--you're dying, " Pastoral Psy-
      chology, 8 (April 1957), 41-4.

2192 Porteus, B. "Poem on death, " in Summary of the Principal
      Evidences for the Truth and Divine Origin of the Chris-
      tian Revelation. Boston: Haverhill, 1819. pp. 137-49.

2193 "Preparation for death; a postulate to assist dying non-
      Catholics, " Liguorian, 52 (Nov. 1964), 53-4.

2194 Price, J. J. Rabbinic conceptions about death. LaSalle,
      Ill.: Open Court Press, 1920.

2195 Purdy, A. C. Reality of God--thoughts on the death of God
      controversy. Wallingford, Pa.: Pendle Hill, 1967.
      Pamphlet number 154 deals with the Death of God
      controversy and has implications for contemporary views.

2196 Rahner, K. "Death and humanism, " Herder Correspondence,
      4 (Feb. 1967), 63-4.
      States that "Christianity is the religion of the cross
      and death is the enigma for any humanism. "

2197 _____. On the theology of death. N. Y.: Herder and
      Herder, 1961.

2198 _____. "Zum Tode Verurteilt?" Wort und Wahrheit, 14
      (Nov. 1959), 653-7.

2199 Ratliff, L. C. "The Physician and minister caring for the
      terminal patient, " Journal of the Mississippi State Medi-
      cal Association, 13 (May 1972), 202-7.

2200 Reemtsma, K. "Ethical problems with artificial and trans-
      planted organs: an approach by experiential ethics, " in
      Ethical Issues in Medicine, edited by E. F. Torrey.
      Boston: Little, Brown, 1968. pp. 249-63.

2201 Reeves, R. B., Jr., comp. Pastoral care of the dying and
      the bereaved: selected readings. Edited by Robert B.
      Reeves, Jr., Robert E. Neale, and Austin H. Kutscher
      for the Foundation of Thanatology. N. Y.: Health Sci-
      ences Pub. Corp., 1973. (Journal Reprint Series.)

2202 Reich, W. T. "Death in modern theology, " Liturgy (Nov.
      1970), 20-1.

2203 Reik, T. Curiosities of the self: illusions we have about
      ourselves. N. Y.: Farrar, 1965.

2204 Ribes, B. "Les Chrétians face à l'avortement, " Etudes,
      (Nov. 1973), 571-83.

2205 Riemer, J., comp. Jewish reflections on death, foreword
      by Elizabeth Kübler-Ross. N.Y.: Schocken, 1974.

2206 Riski, B. "Death and resurrection," Homiletic and Pastoral
      Review, 73 (Nov. 1972), 54-7.

2207 Robinson, J. A. T. "Preaching death," Motive, 24 (Jan.-
      Feb.), 26-9.
      Discusses various ways of thinking about death found
      in the New Testament. Author takes issue with the
      three propositions as found in scripture.

2208 Rogers, W. F. "The Pastor's work with grief," Pastoral
      Psychology, 14 (Sept. 1963), 24.

2209 _____. Ye shall be comforted. Philadelphia: West-
      minster Press, 1950.

2210 Rose, M. D. The Joy of the Christian funeral. New Castle,
      Pa.: Westfield United Presbyterian Church, n.d.
      A sermon which provides discussion and examina-
      tion of "death and funeral practices in the light of
      Biblical teaching."

2211 Rush, A. C. Death and burial in Christian antiquity. Wash-
      ington, D.C.: Catholic University of America Press,
      1941.

2212 Russell, B. "Do we survive death?" in The Mysteries of
      Life and Death; great subjects discussed by great au-
      thorities. London: Hutchinson and Co., 1936.
      Bertrand Russell ponders the question of survival
      after death. He explores the concepts of mind, emo-
      tions, and habits.

2213 Saher, P. J. "Death, immortality, rebirth and salvation in
      the light of a new east-west synthesis, Part IV," in
      Eastern Wisdom and Western Thought; a comparative
      study in the modern philosophy of religion. London:
      George Allen and Unwin, 1969.
      Regarding philosophical thought, the author pleads
      for a new synthesis called world philosophy. "He
      traces the idea of the soul as the higher self in man
      through Zoroaster to western thought.... [I]n the east-
      west synthesis Aldous Huxley is described as pursuing
      wisdom as the goal of life, and describes experiments
      in spiritual consciousness."

2214 Scheff, T. "Towards a sociological model of consensus,"
      American Sociological Review, 32 (1967), 32-46.

2215 Scherzer, C. J. Ministering to the dying. N.J.: Prentice-
      Hall, 1963.

2216 Schideler, M. M. "Coup de Grace," Christian Century, 84
      (Jan. 4, 1967), 18.
            Presents arguments in favor of euthanasia on re-
      ligious grounds, and offers suggestions for legalization
      in extreme cases.

2217 Schurr, G. M. "Why bother about life beyond death?"
      Christian Century, 83 (April 1966), 424-6.
            States that the way man treats the idea of life be-
      yong death affects almost every other issue in religion
      and philosophy.

2218 Segerberg, O., Jr. The Immortality factor. N. Y.: Dutton,
      1974.
            Examines the physiological and psychological aspects
      of aging, death and immortality through life's stages.
      Presents theories of immortality and what effects these
      may have on man's life. The author is a journalist and
      presents his findings in a very instructive style.

2218a Sertillanges, A. De la mort pensees inedites de Jas du
      Revest-Saint-Martin, Haute Provence, 1963.

2219 Shepherd, J. B. "Ministering to the dying person," Pastoral
      Counselor, 4 (1966), 15-22.
            Down to earth and sensible suggestions for those who
      care for or are concerned about the dying patient.

2219a Sherlock, W. Practical discourse concerning death, from
      the 17th Glasgow ed. Albany, N. Y.: Pratt and Double-
      day, 1814.
            Contents: The several notions of death, and the
      improvement of them; Concerning the certainty of our
      death, and the time of our death, and the proper im-
      provement of it; Concerning the fear of death and the
      remedies against it.

2220 Simpson, M. "The 'Death of God' theology: some philo-
      sophical reflections," Heythrop Journal, 10 (Oct. 1969),
      371-89.
            Article is a criticism of the death of God theologi-
      ans because they have rejected transcendence.

2220a Sivananda, S. What becomes of the soul after death?
      Rikhikesh: Sivananda Pub. League, 1946.

2221 Sleeper, R. W. "The Resurrection of the body," Omega,
      3 (May 1972), 139-48.

2221a Sloyan, G. S. "The Last days of Jesus," Judaism, 20 (win-
      ter 1971), 56-68.

2222 Smith, D. "Why, O why, did he die?" Catholic Digest, 33
      (Dec. 1968), 137.

2222a Snyderwine, L. "Christian suffering and death," Homiletic
      and Pastoral Review, 73 (Oct. 1972), 68-71.

2223 Sockman, R. W. "Death," in The Meaning of Suffering.
      N.Y.: Woman's Division of Christian Service. Board
      of Missions. Methodist Church, 1961. pp. 93-113.
      Contents: How to face one's own death; How to
      accept the death of a loved one; How to help those who
      are bereaved; The art of leaving.

2223a Spiro, J. D. Time to mourn: Judaism and the psychology
      of bereavement. N.Y.: Bloch Pub. Co., 1968.

2224 Stahl, R. "Some reflections on the death of God," Religion
      in Life, 37 (winter 1968), 602-11.

2224a Starenko, R. C. God, grass, and grace: a theology of
      death. St. Louis: Concordia Pub. House, 1975.

2225 Stendahl, K., ed. Immortality and resurrection--death in the
      western world: two conflicting currents of thought.
      N.Y.: Macmillan, 1965.
      Deals with the distinction between immortality and
      resurrection. Included in this compilation is the famous
      Cullmann essay on the deaths of Socrates and Jesus.

2225a Stephens, S. Death comes home. N.Y.: Morehouse-Barlow,
      1972.
      Deals with the concept of consolation and various
      viewpoints on reflections of death and normal bereave-
      ment.

2226 Stowe, W. M. It all began with God. Nashville: Abingdon,
      1965.
      Bishop Stowe provides guidance with sermons--on
      the resurrection among others. He sums up his theme
      "that life begins and ends with God."

2226a Stuhlmueller, C. "Awaiting death with the Old Testament
      scriptures," Bible Today, 62 (Nov. 1972), 890-99.
      Provides information on "Old Testament history and
      points out that all the way to the second century before
      Christ, Israel had no explicit belief in personal immor-
      tality."

2227 Sullivan, J. "The Lord of death and dying," Listening, 6
      (fall 1971), 216-23.

2228 Taylor, J. The Rule and exercises of Holy dying. London:
      Bell, 1857.

2229 Taylor, M., ed. The Mystery of suffering and death. N.Y.:
      Alba House, 1973.

2230 Templer, D. I., et al. "Religious correlates of death an-
      xiety," Psychological Reports, 26 (June 1970), 895-7.

2231 The Theology of Altizer: critique and response, ed. by John
            B. Cobb, Jr. Philadelphia: Westminster Press, 1970.
            Includes a bibliography of the works of Thomas J.
            Altizer.

2232 Thielicke, H. Death and life. Philadelphia: Fortress
            Press, 1970.

2233 Throckmorton, B. H. "Do Christians believe in death?"
            Christian Century, 96 (July 23, 1969), 998.
                 States that Americans, for the most part, fail to
            come to terms with death and deny its reality.

2234 Tillich, P. "The Eternal now," in The Meaning of Death,
            edited by H. Feifel. N.Y.: McGraw-Hill, 1959. pp.
            30-8.
                 Theological discussion about death and the eternal.
            Remarks include the modes of time, death, and the
            human condition.

2235 Tobin, T. E. "Explaining death to a child," Liguorian, 47
            (June 1959), 22-4.
                 Article incorporates the many questions that children
            ask about the meaning of death. Includes a brief dis-
            cussion about the soul, heaven, and the meaning of death.

2236 Trese, L. J. "How a Christian dies," Ave Maria, 92 (Oct.
            29, 1960), 26-9.

2237 Troisfontaines, R. Je ne meurs pas. Paris: Editions Uni-
            versitaires, 1960.

2238 Ulanov, B. Death--a book of preparation and consolation.
            N.Y.: Sheed and Ward, 1959.

2239 Uzin, D. "The Final step," Cross and Crown, 19 (Dec.
            1967), 451-6.
                 Primary idea is that "one of the basic elements in
            death [is] the separation from this world. Authors say
            that this is the basic reason why the idea of death
            frightens people."

2240 Vahanian, G. The Death of God: the culture of our Post-
            Christian era. N.Y.: George Braziller, 1961.

2241 Van Antwerp, E. St. Augustine: the divination of demons
            and care for the dead. Washington, D.C.: Catholic
            University of America Press, 1955.

2242 Vass, G. "The Immortality of the soul and life ever last-

ing, " Heythrop Journal, 61 (July 1965), 270-88.
Discusses the theological and philosophical approach
to the immortality of the human soul. Presents historical counter-positions regarding immortality.

2243 Vetter, R. J. Beyond the exit door. Weston, Ont.: D. C.
Cook, 1974.
A true account of a father and the problems he encountered with the sudden death of his wife. His faith
and deep understanding makes for exciting reading.

2244 Vonier, D. A. Death and judgement. N. Y.: Macmillan,
1931.
The author presents a number of his essays on
theological (Catholic) and philosophical ideas concerning
death and immortality. Topics examined are cause of
death, death of Christ, temporal judgement, and others
including contacting the dead.

2245 Von Schoenborn, A. "The Cartesian cogito and the death of
God, " in God Knowable and Unknowable, edited by
Robert J. Roth. N. Y.: Fordham, 1973. pp. 73-84.
". . . [R]eflects on a particular transformation within
our tradition which is of crucial importance to the ques-
tion of the death of God. . . . "

2246 Wahl, C. W. "Games people play when they're dying, "
Medical Economics (Jan. 20, 1969), 106-20.

2247 Ward, J. "Christian ideas of faith and eternal life, " in
Essays in Philosophy. N. Y.: Macmillan, 1927. pp.
349-66.

2248 Weatherhead, L. Life begins at death. Nashville: Abingdon, 1969.
A series of thought provoking and often asked questions about death and answered by a minister. Touches
on reincarnation, immortality, last judgment, and others.

2249 Wentz-Evans, W. J. The Tibetan book of the dead. N. Y.:
Oxford University Press, 1972.

2250 Whitaker, O. Sister death. N. Y.: Morehouse-Barlow,
1974.
Treats death and dying in the Christian perspective.

2251 Wieser, T. "Evangelism and the death of God, " Ecumenical
Review, 20 (April 1968), 138-45.

2252 Wight, F. H. "Death in oriental lands, " in Manners and
Customs of Bible Lands. Chicago: Moody Press,
1953. pp. 142-6.

2253 Williams, D. D. <u>The Minister and the care of souls</u>. N. Y.: Harper, 1961.
Explanation of the Christian ministry to persons who need to be relieved of inner conflicts.

2254 Williams, W. V., et al. "Crisis intervention in acute grief," <u>Omega</u>, 3 (Feb. 1972), 67-70.

2255 Winckwarth, P. <u>Meditation on death</u>. London: Pax House, 1938.

2256 Winter, D. <u>Hereafter: what happens after death?</u> Wheaton, Ill.: Harold Shaw Publishers and The Christian Book Promotion Trust, 1972.
"The object of this book is to help bring back again the validity of immortality; to show that, properly understood there is nothing impossible, nothing even unlikely about 'life after death,' that many modern discoveries and insights make it even easier for us to accept immortality now, than it could have been for our grandparents...."

2257 Wood, G. "Sons of the resurrection: the Christian's victory over death," <u>National Liturgical Week</u>, 23 (1962), 29-38.

2258 Wood, W., and J. Wharton. <u>Death-bed scenes</u>. London: C. and J. Rivington, 1826. 3 vols.

2259 Zabkar, L. V. "Some observations on T. G. Allen's edition of the Book of the Dead," <u>Journal of Near Eastern Studies</u>, 24 (Jan.-April 1965), 75-87.

Part VI

SCIENCE

2260 Agnew, I. "Will freezing preserve life?" Science Digest,
71 (Dec. 1972), 84-5.
A discussion on the techniques used in cryogenics.
The article reports case-studies from the Soviet Union.

2261 Andree, R. A. "The Pros and cons of life prolongation by
extraordinary means," Science, 169 (1970), 717.
Proposes that there be a development of reliable
prognostic guidelines for the periodic evaluation of patients whose lives are being preserved artifically.

2262 _____. "When death is inexorable," Science, 169 (Aug.
1970), 21.

2263 Augenstein, L. "Cancel my reservation, St. Peter, I've de-
cided to stay on," in Come, Let Us Play God. N.Y.:
Harper and Row, 1969. pp. 37-54.
Presents ethical, moral, and value judgments involved because of revolutionary advances in science.

2264 Battista, O. "Science peeps into the face of death," Family
Digest, 19 (April 1964), 44-8.

2265 Beardsley, G. L. "The Fad of self-murder," Medical Practitioner, 20 (1904), 385-92.

2266 Biorck, G. "Thoughts of life and death," Perspectives in
Biology and Medicine, 11 (summer 1968), 527-43.

2267 Boyd, W. T. "The Deep deep freeze," in The World of
Cryogenics. N.Y.: Putnam, 1968. pp. 44-69.
Description of the "anti-death project--capsule for
frozen bodies" and the emerging roles of cryobiology,
cryosurgery, and cryogenics.

2268 Braun, H. Das Geheimnis vom Leben und Sterben. Eine
Darstellung der Abhanigigkeit der Lebensvergange von
den Umweltreinflussen. Tubingen: Mohr, 1949.

2269 Brodt, H. Uber den Tod; Eine naturwissenschaftliche Betrachtung. Berlin: Akademie-Verlag, 1958.

2270 Castleman, N. "Bioethics: research, action, and ethics," Science Teacher, 41 (Oct. 1974), 18-21.

2271 Clerc, A. "La Mort," Journal des Sciences Médicales de Lille, 73 (June 1953), 296-309.

2272 Cloud, W. "The Meaning of death," Popular Science, 183 (Sept. 1963), 2-21.

2273 Contiene, M. A. "Consideraciones sobre la muerte," en El Mundo de la Ciencia. Barcelona: Salvaf, 1965. Vol. 1. pp. 330-1.

2274 "Cryobiology," Time, 89 (Feb. 3, 1967), 57.

2275 Cutler, A., and R. C. W. Ettinger. "New hope for the dead," Esquire, 63 (May 1965), 63.

2276 Dastre, A. La Vie et la mort. Paris: E. Flammarion, 1918.
Life has always existed. Dastre's books state that death is a newcomer which has accompanied the evolution of animal life to higher levels.

2277 Deevey, E. S. "The Probability of death," Scientific American, 182 (April 1950), 58-60.
Article states that the increase in average life span in the U.S. is due to a decrease in infant and childhood mortality.

2278 "Definition of death," Science Digest, 65 (March 1969), 77.
Discusses the high percentages of people writing and thinking about death since the introduction of transplants.

2279 Dobzhansky, T. G. "Religion, death, and evolutionary adaptation," in Context and Meaning in Cultural Anthropology, edited by Melford E. Spiro. N.Y.: Free Press, 1965. pp. 61-73.

2280 _____. "Self-awareness and death-awareness," in The Biology of Ultimate Concern. N.Y.: New American Library, 1967. pp. 63-81.

2281 Doll, P. J. "The Rights of science after death," Diogenes, 70 (fall 1971), 122-41.

2282 Dorn, H. F. "Prospects of further decline in mortality rates," Human Biology, 4 (1952), 235-61.
Paper presents studies which indicate the prospects of further decline in mortality rates.

2283 Druss, R. G. , and D. S. Kornfeld. "The Survivors of cardiac arrest: a psychiatric study, " Journal of the American Medical Association, 201 (1967), 290-6.

2284 "Empirical proofs, " in Being and Death; an outline of integrationist philosophy, by J. F. Mora. Berkeley: University of California Press, 1965. pp. 232-37.

2285 Ettinger, R. C. W. Prospect of immortality. N. Y.: Doubleday, 1964.
Discusses the cryonics movement and its implications for the future of man.

2286 Evans, W. E. D. The Chemistry of death. Springfield, Ill.: C. C. Thomas, 1963.

2287 Ewing, L. S. "Fighting and death from stress in a cockroach, " Science, 155 (1967), 1035-6.
Provocative description of the violent behavior of two male cockroaches points out that death occurs independently of external damage.

2288 Ford, A. B. "Casualties of our time, " Science, 167 (Jan. 16, 1970), 256-63.
New sources and causes of death since World War II are discussed.

2289 Fortuyn, A. E. "Death; An Adaption, " Human Biology (1939), 408-9.
Presents the notion that only "those organisms deserve death which are replaced. Hence, propagation and death are inseparable parts of evolution. "

2290 Fox, R. C. "Training for uncertainty, " in The Student Physician, edited by R. K. Merton, et al. Cambridge: Harvard University Press, 1957. pp. 207-41.

2291 Fraser, G. R. "Population genetic studies in the Congo, " American Journal of Human Genetics, 18 (1966), 538-45.

2292 Gaylin, W. "Harvesting the dead: the potential for recycling human bodies, " Harper's Magazine, 249 (Sept. 1974), 23-30.
Contents: Redefining death; Precedents; Uses of the neomort; Cost-benefit analysis; Transplants.

2293 Gillon, H. "Defining death anew; brains oxygen use, " Science News, 95 (Jan. 11, 1969), 50.
Discusses various methods of determining death, and suggests the use of nitrous oxide gas to test the brain's use of oxygen as a better method.

2294 Giocco, A. "On the mortality in husbands and wives, " Human Biology (1940), 508-31.

2295 Goodman, J. M., et al. "Determination of brain death by isotope angiography," Journal of the American Medical Association, 209 (Sept. 22, 1969), 1869-72.

2296 Grahn, D., and J. Kratchman. "Variations in neonatal death rate and birth weight in the U. S. and possible relation to environmental radiation--geology and altitude," American Journal of Human Genetics, 15 (1963), 329-52.
Discusses neonatal deaths occurring within the first 28 days of life including birth weight to determine the effects of the environment on such deaths.

2297 Gregg, D. "Reassurance," American Journal of Nursing, 55 (Feb. 1955), 171-4.

2298 Hamilton, C. "Ecological and social factors in mortality variation," Eugenics Quarterly (1965), 212-23.

2299 Jonas, H. "Life, death and the body in the theory of being," Review of Metaphysics, 19 (1965), 212-23.

2300 Kahn, H. On thermonuclear war. Princeton, N. J.: Princeton University Press, 1960.

2301 Kass, L. R. "Death as an event," Science, 173 (Aug. 20, 1971), 694-702.

2302 _____. "Problems in the meaning of death," Science, 170 (Dec. 11, 1970), 1235-6.

2303 Kavaler, L. Freezing point: cold as a matter of life and death. N. Y.: John Day, 1970.
Discusses how cold will overcome death and that bodies will be thawed and restored to life in the near future. With the use of cryogenics man has the ability to possibly control his destiny.

2304 Kowet, D. "Never say die," Today's Health, 52 (July 1974), 20-3.
"At least 20 women and men have refused to accept death at the bottom line of life. So they have had themselves frozen for a future thaw and a new life. These are the pioneers of a controversial new science called cryonics ... the freezing of 'living' matter [which] has produced the science of cryo-preservation--the long-term storage of eyes, blood, and sperm for future use."

2305 Landsberg, W. H. Das Internationale Abkommen über die Todeserklarung Vermisster vom. 6 April 1950.... Cologne: Heymann, 1955.

2306   Langer, W. I.   "The Black death, " Scientific American, 210
       (1964), 112-22.

2307   LeShan, L.   "Human survival of biological death, " Main Cur-
       rents, 26 (Nov. -Dec. 1969), 35-45.

2308   Lipschutz, A.   Allgemeine Physiologie des Todes.   Braun-
       schweig: I. Vieweg und Sohn, 1915.

2309   Luria, S. M.   "Average age of death of scientists in various
       specialties, " Public Health Report, 84 (1969), 661-4.

2309a McClintock, M.   Cryogenics.   N. Y.: Reinhold, 1964.

2310   MacCluer, J. W.   "Monte Carlo methods in human popula-
       tion genetics, " American Journal of Human Genetics, 19
       (1967), 303-12.
             Discussion of a computer model that uses birth and
       death rates according to age.   Article states that most
       models assume that population is constant.   This model
       seeks to restrict that assumption.

2311   MacDonald, A.   "Systematic and scientific study of death in
       man, " American Journal of Psychology, 38 (1927), 153.

2312   Martin, D. , and L. Wrightsman.   "Religion and fears about
       death: a critical review of research, " Religious Educa-
       tion, 59 (1964), 174-6.
             Suggests new ways to scientifically investigate the
       subject of religion and the fear of death.

2313   Marty, M. E. , and D. G. Peerman, eds.   New theology
       number 10.   N. Y.: Macmillan, 1973.
             "The subject of this issue is Bios and Theology. "

2314   Mazur, P.   "Cryobiology: the freezing of biological sys-
       tems, " Science, 168 (May 22, 1970), 939-49.
             Discusses some general conclusions about responses
       of biological systems to sub-zero temperatures, and
       some unsolved questions concerning cryobiology.

2315   Miller, L. M.   "Neither life nor death, " Reader's Digest,
       (Dec. 1960), 55-9.
             Deals with the question of using "extraordinary"
       measures to prolong the lives of fatally old people, and
       gives pro and con views.

2316   Mohr, G. J.   When children face crises.   Chicago: Science
       Research Associates, 1952.

2317   Money-Kyrle, R. E.   "An Inconclusive contribution to the
       'Theory of the death instinct', " in New Directions in
       Psychoanalysis, N. Y.: Basic Books, 1955.

2318 Osler, W. Science and immortality. Boston: Houghton, 1904.

2319 Pearl, R. Biology of death. Philadelphia: Lippincott, 1922.
      Part of a series of monographs developed in a course
      of lectures delivered at the Lowell Institute in December
      1920. The author attributes much to the development of
      the science of biology, and describes the present state of
      knowledge regarding the subject of death.

2320 Prehoda, W. Suspended animation. Radnor, Pa.: Chilton,
      1969.
      Distinguishes first between hibernation and suspended
      animation. Then a description of the background and
      current research in cryobiology follows. Also examined
      are the theories of aging and possible ways to control it,
      and the major uses of suspended animation.

2321 Restrepo, A. Meditaciones biologicas sobre la muerte.
      Medellín, Colombia: Tip. Bedout, 1944.

2322 Rosenfeld, A. "New man; what will he be like?" Life, 59
      (Oct. 1, 1965), 94-6.
      An interesting look at the legal and practical prob-
      lems of freezing a dead man and bringing him back to
      life. Where the soul stops in the meantime and prob-
      lems of estates are discussed.

2323 Settig, M. Cryogenics; research and applications. Princeton,
      N.J.: D. Van Nostrand, 1963.
      Partial contents: Really new frontier; Great names
      in cold; Where cold is studied; How cold is used.

2324 Simko, A. "Death and the hereafter: the structuring of im-
      material reality," Omega, 1 (1970), 121-35.

2325 Simon, A., ed. The Physiology of death. Springfield, Ill.:
      C. C. Thomas, 1961.

2326 Strivastava, M. "The relationship between the birth rate and
      the death rate in stable populations with the same fer-
      tility but different mortality schedules," Eugenics Quar-
      terly, 13 (1966), 231-9.

2327 White, R. "The Scientific limitation of brain death," Hos-
      pital Progress, 53 (March 1972), 48-51.

2328 Wiley, J. P., Jr., and J. K. Sherman. "Immortality and
      the freezing of human bodies," Natural History, 80 (Dec.
      1971), 12-18.

2329 Wolfe, D. "Dying with dignity," Science, 168 (June 1970),
      1403.
      Deals with the analysis of death, prolongation of
      life, and the quality of life preserved.

Part VII

SOCIAL SCIENCES

2330 Abadi, M. "Psychoanalytic study of a basic fantasy on the fear of death," Revista de Psicoanálisis, 17 (1960), 431-48.

2331 Abderrahman, B. Le Suicide non-pathologique. Paris: Rodstein, 1933.

2332 Ablon, J. "Bereavement in a Samoan community," British Journal of Medical Psychology, 44 (Nov. 1971), 329-37.

2333 Abraham, C. "Thought and fear of death in aged with mental disorders," Schweitzer Archiv für Neurologie, Neurochirurgie und Psychiatrie, 90 (1962), 362-9.

2334 Abraham, H. S. "The Psychology of terminal illness, as portrayed in Solzhenitsyn's The Cancer Ward, " Archives of Internal Medicine, 124 (1969), 758-60.

2334a Abrahamsen, D. "A Study of Lee Harvey Oswald: psychological capability of murder," Bulletin of the New York Academy of Medicine, 43 (Oct. 1967), 861-88.
A psychological reconstruction of a mind and the events following the assassination to evaluate his capabilities of being an assassin.

2335 Abram, H. S. "Adaption to open heart surgery: a psychiatric study of response to the threat of death," American Journal of Psychiatry, 122 (1965), 659-67.
Various studies are cited regarding anxious and depressed patients who view the operation in terms of death and survival.

2336 _____ . "The Psychiatrist, the treatment of chronic renal failure and the prolongation of life," American Journal of Psychiatry, 124 (1968), 1351-7.

2337 _____ . "The Psychiatrist, the treatment of chronic renal failure and the prolongation of life: II," American Journal of Psychiatry, 126 (1969), 157-67.

2338 _____. Psychological aspects of stress. Springfield, Ill.:
           C. C. Thomas, 1970.

2339 Abrams, R. D. "The Patient with cancer--his changing pat-
           tern of communication," New England Journal of Com-
           munication, 274 (Feb. 10, 1960), 317-22.

2340 _____, et al. "Terminal care in cancer," New England
           Journal of Medicine, 232 (June 21, 1945), 719-24.
           Presents a study of an unselected sampling of 200
           patients known to tumor clinics of Boston hospitals who
           had died of cancer within one calendar year, 1941-1942.

2341 Abramson, F. D. "High fetal mortality and birth intervals,"
           Population Studies, 27 (July 1973), 235-42.

2342 Abramson, J. "Facing the other fact of life: death in recent
           children's fiction," Library Journal, 99 (Dec. 15, 1974),
           3257-9.

2343 Achille-Delmas, F. Psychologie Pathologique du suicide.
           Paris: Alcan, 1933.

2344 Achte, K. A. "Psychological factors and death," Nordisk
           Psykiatrisk Tidsskrift, 19 (1965), 268-73.

2345 Adams, B. N. The American family: a sociological inter-
           pretation. Chicago: Markham, 1971.
           The author contrasts death with divorce as it per-
           tains to the American family. The separatist subsociety
           of the Hutterites is described with their primary rela-
           tionships and their beliefs in living and dying. Disen-
           gagement theories are also presented with implications
           for the American family.

2346 Adler, A. "Das Todesproblem in der Neurose," Interna-
           tionale Zeitschrift, 14 (Jan.-March 1936), 1-6.

2347 _____, et al. Uber den Selbstmord, inbesonders den
           Schülerselbst mord. Diskussion des Wiener psycho-
           analytischen Vereins. Wiesbaden: J. F. Bergmann,
           1910.

2348 "Adolescent suicide," Time (Jan. 3, 1972), 57.

2349 Aginsky, B. W. "The Socio-psychological significance of
           death among the Pomo Indians," American Imago, 1
           (1940), 1-11.
           "Pomo Indians of Northern California cannot com-
           prehend suicide as we know it because they feel that
           every death is due to a result of indirect or direct re-
           taliation from the supernatural...."

2350 Agree, R. "Why children must mourn," Journal of Marriage
      and Living, 55 (Sept. 1973), 55-9.

2351 Aldenhoven, H. "Klinischer Beitrag zur Frage der Todesah-
      nungen," Psychotherapie, 2 (1957), 55-9.

2352 Aldrich, C. K., and E. Mendkoff. "Relocation of the aged
      and disabled: a mortality study," Journal of the Ameri-
      can Geriatrics Society, 11 (1963), 185-94.
      Paper discusses the factors that lead to a high
      mortality rate in the aged when they are moved into in-
      stitutions.

2353/4 Alexander, F. "The Need for punishment and the death
      instinct," International Journal of Psychoanalysis, 10
      (1929), 256-69.
      Author states that we should attempt "to understand
      the expressions of the self destructive or self injuring
      trends in a purely psychological way without any the-
      oretical assumptions."

2355 Alexander, I. E. "Studies in the psychology of death," in
      Perspectives in Personality Research, edited by H. P.
      David, and J. C. Brengelmann. N. Y.: Springer,
      1960. pp. 65-92.

2356 _____, and A. M. Alderstein. "Affective responses to
      the concept of death in a population of children and
      early adolescents," Journal of Genetic Psychology, 93
      (1958), 167-77.
      Describes the child's concept of death from ages
      5 to 16 and the effects it has upon him during the stages
      of development.

2357 _____; R. S. Colley; and A. M. Alderstein. "Is death
      a matter of indifference?" Journal of Psychology, 43
      (1957), 277-83.
      Article is concerned about the lack of psychological
      interest in death as a study. The author concludes by
      stating that the problem of death is an important source
      of man's motivation.

2358 Alexander, S. "They decide who lives, who dies: medical
      miracle and a moral burden of a small committee,"
      Life, 53 (Nov. 9, 1962), 102.

2359 Allard, R. C. Death house introduction. Salem, N. H.:
      Allard Publishers, 1970.

2360 Alleman, S. A. "The Structure of content of belief systems."
      Ph. D. dissertation, Purdue University, 1963.
      Explores the relationship between an individual's
      concept of death and the way in which he organizes his
      beliefs.

2361 Alpert, H. "Suicides and homicides," American Sociological
      Review, 15 (1950), 673.
      Compares homicide death rates to suicide rates
      among high and low socioeconomic groups.

2362 Altman, L. L. "West as a symbol of death," Psychiatry
      Quarterly, 28 (1959), 236-41.
      Author states that "the West has a host of metaphors
      and allusions in poetry, folklore, mythology, and anthro-
      pology that makes it a suitable representation of death."

2363 Alvarez, A. "The Art of suicide," Partisan, 3 (May 1970),
      339-58.
      Discusses the sharp rise of suicide among the
      artists of this century.

2364 _____. The Savage God: a study of suicide. N. Y.:
      Random House, 1970.
      Explores suicide from man's changing attitudes to-
      ward it, and the theories of Emile Durkheim and Freud.
      There is also a personal memoir of Sylvia Plath, the
      artist, and how she chose to die.

2365 American Academy of Pediatrics. Care of children in hospi-
      tals. Chicago: American Academy of Pediatrics, 1960.

2366 Anderson, B. G. "Bereavement as a subject of cross-cul-
      tural inquiry: an American sample," Anthropological
      Quarterly, 38 (1965), 181-200.

2367 Anderson, C. "Aspects of pathological grief and mourning,"
      International Journal of Psychoanalysis, 30 (1949), 38-
      55.

2368 André, R., and R. J. Pereira. "La Mortalité infantile au
      Portugal," Revue de l'Institut de Sociologie, 45 (1972),
      125-8.

2369 Anthony, S. The Child's discovery of death; a study in child
      psychology; with an introduction by J. C. Flugel. N. Y.:
      Harcourt, 1941.
      "This study is based on two sets of collected ob-
      servations. School children, including a small propor-
      tion from those in special schools, voiced their uncon-
      sidered thoughts and fancies through a method like that
      of the intelligence test, and through a/story-competition
      test; and a number of 'home records' of children's
      spontaneous talk were kept by a group of parents in-
      terested in this kind of research...."

2370 _____. The Discovery of death in childhood and after.
      London: Allen Lane, 1971.
      A psychological study of how children discover

death, and their resulting concepts of it.

2371 _____. "The Study of the development of the concept of
death," British Journal of Educational Psychology, 9
(1939), 276-7.
Discusses the problem of what death means to children at different stages of their development. Some 123
subjects were treated in the study.

2372 Archibald, H., et al. "Bereavement in childhood and adult
psychiatric disturbances," Psychosomatic Medicine, 24
(1962), 343-51.
The article limits itself to the definite factor of the
death of a parent and the problems that affect the survivors.

2373 Arehart, J. L. "Right to life: who is to decide?" Science
News, 100 (Oct. 1971), 293.

2374 Arendt, H. "The Concentration camps," Partisan Review,
15 (July 1948), 747.
Describes the inmate's experience of immediate suffering and recollections of the survivors of concentration
camps.

2375 Ariès, P. "La Mort et le mourant dans notre civilisation,"
Revue Française de Sociologie, 14 (Jan.-March, 1973),
125-8.

2376 Arnstein, H. S. What to tell your child about birth, illness,
death, divorce, and other family crises. Indianapolis:
Bobbs-Merrill, 1962.

2377 Aronson, M., et al. "The Impact of death of a leader on a
group process," American Journal of Psychotherapy, 16
(July 1962), 460-8.
Paper "describes and interprets certain processes
within a training research group before, during, and
after the death of its leader."

2378 Arthur, B., and M. L. Kemme. "Bereavement in childhood," Journal of Child Psychology and Psychiatry, 5
(1964), 37-49.
Deals with the loss of a parent and the extreme
emotional crisis that follows a child's reaction.

2379 Ashley-Montagu, M. Immortality. N.Y.: Grove Press,
1955.

2380 "Assassination inquiry; slow, careful," U.S. News, 56 (Jan.
27, 1964), 49.

2381 Atkinson, J. M. "On the sociology of suicide," Sociological

Review, 16 (March 1968), 83-92.

2382 Augustin, D. R. "Ceremonies in connection with the dead
      in Malolos, Bulacan," Philippine Sociological Review, 4
      (April-June 1956), 32-8.

2383 Baader, I. "Bedeutsame psychische und soziale Ursachen
      des Selbstmordes bei Kindern und Jungenslichen,"
      Monatsschrift für Kinderheilhunde, 103 (1955), 55-6.

2384 Bachofen, J. J. Versuch über die Gräbersymbolik der Alten,
      2d ed. Mit einen Vorwort von C. A. Bernoulli und
      einer Würdigung von Ludwig Klages. Basel: Helbing
      und Luchtenhahn, 1925.

2385 Bahle, J. Keine Angst vor dem Sterben; zur Psychologie
      des Angstfreien und schonen Sterbens. Hemmenhofen
      am Bodensee: Kulturpsychologischer Verlag, 1963.

2386 Bahnson, C. B. "Emotional reactions to internally and ex-
      ternally derived threat of annihilation." A symposium
      on human reactions to the threat of impending disaster
      at the 1962 meeting of the American Association for the
      Advancement of Science. Philadelphia, 1963.

2387 Bailey, R. M. "Economic and social costs of death," in
      The Dying Patient, edited by Orville C. Brim, Jr., et
      al. N. Y.: Russell Sage Foundation, 1970.

2388 Baker, D. C. The Assassination of President Kennedy: a
      study of the press coverage. Ann Arbor: University of
      Michigan, 1966.

2389 Bakwin, H. "Suicide in children and adolescents," Journal
      of Pediatrics, 50 (1957), 749-69.
            Discusses the alarming rate of suicide among chil-
      dren and adolescents. Statistics are compared in the
      following age groups: 10-14, 15-19, and college-age.

2390 Bälz, E. Uber die Todesverachtung der Japaner. Stuttgart:
      J. Engelhorns Nach F., 1936.

2391 Banay, R. S. "Study in murder," Annals of the American
      Academy of Political and Social Science, 284 (1952), 26-
      34.
            The public is conditioned to murder. The author
      states and describes levels for the motivation of such
      violent actions as subcultural, cultural, and supercul-
      tural.

2392 Banen, D. M. "Suicide by psychotics," Journal of Nervous
      Mental Disorders, 120 (1954), 349-57.
            Concerned with a detailed analysis of the records

of 23 patients who committed or attempted to commit
suicide while being treated for psychotic disorders.

2393 Banks, L. "Black suicide," Ebony (May 1970), 76-85.
Black suicides are twice as common as white in the
age bracket from 20-35.

2394 Barande, A. "L'Impulsion de mort comme non transgression, "
Revue Français de Psychanalyse, 32 (1968), 465-502.

2395 Barbé, A. "Suicide and homicide obsession impulse, "
Encéphale, 16 (1921), 304.

2396 Bard, B., and J. Fletcher. "Right to die, " Atlantic, 221
(April 1968), 59-64.
The father of a mongoloid child discusses his views,
and J. Fletcher examines the problems involved with the
right to die.

2397 Barnacle, C. H. "Grief reactions and their treatment, "
Diseases of the Nervous System, 10 (1949), 173-6.
Normal grief and morbid grief reactions are discussed which are pathological in that they can be prolonged or distorted states of depression. Includes case
studies.

2398 Barnes, M. J. "Reactions to the death of a mother, " in
The Psychoanalytic Study of the Child, XIX. N. Y. :
International Universities Press, 1964. pp. 334.

2399 Barnouw, V. "Chippewa social atomism: feast of the dead, "
American Anthropologist, LXIII (Oct. 1961), 1006-13.

2400 Barnum, M. C. "An Occupational therapist's observations
concerning President Kennedy's assassination; with
ramifications for understanding loss, " American Journal
of Occupational Therapy, 20 (Nov.-Dec. 1966), 280-5.

2401 Barrett, G. U., and R. H. Franke. "Psychogenic death, "
Science, 167 (Jan. 16, 1970), 304-6.
Hypothesizes that social, economic, and medical
variables account for differences in death rates, and
that psychological motives are unrelated.

2402 Barry, H. "Orphanhood as a factor in psychoses, " Journal
of Abnormal and Social Psychology, 30 (1936), 431-8.

2403 _____, and W. A. Bousfield. "Incidence of orphanhood
among fifteen hundred psychotic patients, " Journal of
Genetic Psychology, 50 (1937), 198-202.
Older patients have a smaller incidence of bereavement than those who develop a psychosis before the age
of twenty five.

2404 Bascue, L. O., and G. W. Krieger. "Death as a counseling concern," Personnel and Guidance Journal, 52 (May 1974), 587-92.

2405 Bataille, G. Death and sensuality: a study of eroticism and the taboo. N.Y.: Walker and Co., 1962.

2406 Beaver, M. W. "Population, infant mortality and milk," Population Studies, 27 (July 1973), 243-54.

2407 Beck, A. T.; B. B. Sethi; and R. W. Tuthill. "Childhood bereavement and adult depression," Archives of General Psychiatry, 9 (1963), 295-302.
      Some 297 patients are studied in a psychiatric ward to determine the relationship of orphans to depression.

2408 Beck, F. Diary of a widow: rebuilding a family after the funeral. Boston: Beacon, 1965.

2409 Becker, E. The Denial of death. N.Y.: Free Press, 1973.
      Man's innate fear of death is discussed, and how death becomes the source of human activity. The article also points out ways by which mankind transcends death.

2410 Becker, H. "The Sorrow of bereavement," Journal of Abnormal and Social Psychology, 27 (1933), 391-410.

2411 _____ and D. K. Bruner. "Attitudes toward death and the dead and some possible causes of ghost fear," Mental Hygiene, 15 (1931), 838-37.

2412 Bedau, H. A., ed. The Death penalty in America: an anthology. 2d ed. N.Y., Chicago: Aldine, 1968.
      Discusses the issue of capital punishment. Points out legal, criminological, penological, and psychological aspects.

2413 Bedell, J. W. "Role reorganization in the one-parent family: mother absent due to death," Sociological Focus, 5 (1971), 84.

2414 Bendann, E. Death customs: an analytic study of burial rites. N.Y.: Humanities Press, 1970.

2415 Bender, L., and P. Schilder. "Suicidal preoccupations and attempts in children," American Journal of Orthopsychiatry, 7 (1937), 225-34.

2416 Bendiksen, R. A. "Death and the child: an anterospective test of the childhood bereavement and later behavior disorder hypothesis." Ph.D. dissertation, University of Minnesota, 1974.

This study concludes that "the childhood bereavement and later behavior disorder hypothesis remain an open question, subject to further research, contrary to the psychological literature...."

2417 Benedek, T. "Todestrieb und Angst," Internationale Zeitschrift für Psychoanalyse, 17 (1931), 333-43.

2418 Benezra, E. E. "Duality of human nature," American Journal of Psychiatry, 125 (April 1969), 1456-7.
Describes the psychosocial conditions of hippies, and states their nonviolent philosophy in blocking out death and destruction.

2419 Bennett, A. E. "Recognizing the potential suicide," Geriatrics, 22 (1967), 175-81.
Impresses upon physicians, hospital personnel, and police the need to treat potential victims of suicide. Ways should be found to prevent its occurrence in communities.

2420 Benoleil, J. Q. "Assessments of loss and grief," Journal of Thanatology, 1 (May-June 1971), 182.

2420a Berardo, F. M. "Social adaptation to widowhood among a rural-urban aged population." Washington State University College of Agriculture, Washington Agricultural Experiment Station, December 1967 (Bulletin no. 689), pp. 1-31.

2421 _____. "Survivorship and social isolation: the case of the aged widower," Family Coordinator, 19 (1970), 11-25.

2421a _____. "Widowhood status in the United States: perspectives on a neglected aspect of the family life cycle," Family Coordinator, 17 (1968), 191-203.

2422 Berg, C. D. "Cognizance of the death taboo in counseling children," School Counselor, 21 (Sept. 1973), 28-33.
Examines the restrictions which prevail in our society regarding the subject of death. Understanding and guidance are given top priority when death becomes part of a child's personal experience.

2422a Bergler, E. "Psychopathology and duration of mourning in neurotics," Journal of Clinical Psychopathology, 3 (1948), 478-82.
Discusses various aspects of pathological mourning and the experiences which determine the duration of mourning in neurotics.

2423 Berkenau, F. "The Concept of death," Twentieth Century,

157 (April 1955), 313-29.

Examines the views of Freud, and the sense of immortality that cannot be eradicated by rational arguments or by the experience of the death of others.

2424 Berman, M. I. "The Todeserwartung syndrome," Geriatrics,
      21 (1966), 187-92.

      Describes experiences in an old age home where
      over 50 geriatric patients were interviewed for psychi-
      atric consultation or evaluation for short-term psycho-
      therapy.

2425 Bermann, E. Scapegoat; the impact of death-fear on an
      American family. Ann Arbor: University of Michigan
      Press, 1973.

2426 Bermann, G. "Der Selbstmord als Rache," Monatsschrift
      Psychiatrik Neurologie, 77 (1930), 297-309.

2427 "Bermuda; death of a governor," Economist, 246 (March
      17, 1973), 43.

2428 Bernada, M. "What do people think regarding death?"
      Vlaamisch Oprdedkundig Tijdschrift, 30 (1949), 32-40.

2429 Bernhart, K. K. "A Study of suicide in the U.S.," Social
      Forces, 2 (1933), 527-33.

2430 Bilz, F. E. Tote Leben und Umgeben uns, 3d ed. Dresden:
      Radebeul, 1922.

2431 Binford, S. R. "A Structural comparison of disposal of the
      dead in the Mousterian and the Upper Paleolithic,"
      Southwestern Journal of Anthropology, 24 (1968), 139-
      54.

      Compares the disposal of the dead as documented in
      the Mousterian and Upper Paleolithic with respect to age
      and sex.

2432 Biran, S. "Attempt at the psychological analysis of the fear
      of death," Confinia Psychiatrica, 11 (1968), 154-76.

2433 Birk, A. "The Bereaved child," Mental Health, 25 (1966),
      9-11.

      Presents ways to handle a bereaved child so that
      he won't feel rejected, especially if the surviving parent
      is too bereaved to help.

2434 Birtchnell, J. "Depression in relation to early and recent
      parent death," British Journal of Psychiatry, 116 (March
      1970), 299-306.

      Compares the incidence of early and recent parent
      death on a group of psychiatric patients.

2435 _____. "Early parent death and mental illness," British Journal of Psychiatry, 116 (1970), 281-8.

2436 _____. "Early parent death and psychiatric diagnosis," Social Psychiatry, 7 (1972), 202-10.

2437 _____. "The Possible consequences of early parent death," British Journal of Medical Psychology, 116 (1970), 572-3.

2438 _____. "Recent parent death and mental illness," British Journal of Psychiatry, 116 (March 1970), 284-97.
The "aim of the study is to determine whether more than the expected number of psychiatric patients have experienced parental bereavement during a period of years before admission."

2439 _____. "The Relationship between attempted suicide, depression and parent death," British Journal of Psychiatry, 116 (March 1970), 307-13.
Compares age and sex distribution of suicidal and non-suicidal patients.

2440 _____. "Some psychiatric sequalae of childhood bereavement," British Journal of Psychiatry, 116 (March 1970), 346-7.
"... [I]t is likely that early parent death contributes to some forms of mental illness...."

2441 _____; I. C. Wilson; O. Bratfos, et al. Effects of early parent death; papers. New York: Mss Information Corporation, 1973. (Mss series on attitudes toward death, no. 1.)

2442 Bishop, G. Executions--the legal ways of death. Los Angeles: Sherbourne, 1965.

2443 Bjerre, P. Death and renewal. London: Williams and Norgate, 1929.
A psychotherapist explains how life and death presuppose each other, and how existence is only a manifestation of this interdependence.

2444 Bjorksten, J. "For scientific breakthroughs we must go beyong restraints," The Chemist, 38 (May 1961).

2445 Blackman, M. B. "Totems to tombstones: culture change as viewed through the Haida mortuary complex, 1877-1971," Ethnology, 12 (Jan. 1973), 47-56.

2446 Blackwell, R. D. "Price levels in the funeral industry," Quarterly Review of Economics and Business, 7 (winter 1967), 75-84.

2446a Blake, H. J. "Is the black panther party suicidal?" Politics
      and Society, 2 (fall 1971), 287-92.
          Discusses the basic difference between white and
      black ideological concepts of death.

2447 Blauner, R. "Death and social structure," Psychiatry, 29
      (1966), 378-94.
          "... [A]nalyzes death orientation in a culture as a
      societal maintenance problem."

2448 Blazer, J. A. "The Relationship between meaning in life
      and fear of death," Psychology, 10 (May 1973), 33-4.
          Description of V. E. Frankl's theory of meaning
      and death and its relationship to life. It was hypothe-
      sized that a positive correlation exists between meaning
      in life and acceptance of death.

2449 Bloch, D. "Fantasy and the fear of infanticide," Psycho-
      analytic Review, 61 (spring 1974), 5-31.
          Discusses fantasy as a defense for survival, and
      that we must acknowledge its presence. Children's
      fear of being killed by their parents or of killing them
      is a dominant factor in fantasies.

2450 _____. "Feelings that kill: the effect of the wish for in-
      fanticide in neurotic depression," Psychoanalytic Review,
      52 (spring 1965), 51-66.

2451 Bloch, D. A., et al. "Some factors in emotional reactions
      of children to disaster," American Journal of Psychiatry,
      113 (1956), 416-22.

2452 Bluestone, H., and C. L. McGahee. "Reaction to extreme
      stress: impending death by execution," American Jour-
      nal of Psychiatry, 69 (1949), 393-6.
          Study is about 18 men and one woman at the Sing
      Sing death house who were convicted of murder in con-
      nection with a felony.

2453 Blum, G. S., and S. Rosenzweig. "The Incidence of sibling
      and parental death in the anamnesis of female schizo-
      phrenics," Journal of General Psychology, 31 (1944),
      3-13.
          States that schizophrenics have more sibling deaths
      in their anamnesis than do manic depressives.

2454 Boas, F. "The Idea of the future life among primitive
      tribes," in Race, Language and Culture, by F. Boas.
      N.Y.: Macmillan, 1940. pp. 596-607.

2455 Boase, T. S. Death in the middle ages; mortality, judg-
      ment and remembrance. N.Y.: McGraw-Hill, 1972.
          Library of Medieval Civilization Series.

2456 Bohannan, P. African homicide and suicide. Princeton,
     N.J.: Princeton University Press, 1960.

2457 Bordoni, M. Dimensioni anthropologiche della morte; saggio
     sulle ultime realte cristiane. Rome: Herder, 1960.

2458 Bornstein, J. The Politics of murder. N.Y.: William
     Sloan Associates, 1950.
     Opens the door on the mass assassinations that have
     become part of the policy of some governments, such as
     Nazi Germany and Stalin's Russia. The author suggests
     that historians must also become criminologists.

2459 Bowers, F. "Death in victory," South Atlantic Bulletin,
     30 (1965), 1-7.

2460 Bowlby, J. "Grief and mourning in infancy and early child-
     hood," Psychoanalytic Study of the Child, 15 (1960),
     9-52.

2461 _____. "Pathological mourning and childhood mourning,"
     Journal of the American Psychoanalytic Association, 11
     (1963), 500-41.

2462 _____. "Processes of mourning," International Journal of
     Psychoanalysis, 42 (1961), 317-40.
     Explores the mourning processes in young children,
     and the effects due to the loss of the mother that can
     lead to psychiatric illness.

2463 _____. "Separation anxiety," International Journal of
     Psychoanalysis, 41 (1960), 89-113.
     Postulates reasons for a child's tie to its mother
     and the anxiety which arises.

2464 Bowman, L. The American funeral: a study in guilt, ex-
     travagance and sublimity. Washington, D.C.: Public
     Affairs Press, 1959.

2465 Bradley, J. Lidice--sacrificial village. N.Y.: Ballantine
     Books, 1972.

2466 "Breaking funeral director's monopoly," Christian Century,
     81 (April 1964), 423.

2467 Breed, W. "Occupational mobility and suicide among white
     males," American Sociological Review, 28 (April 1963),
     179.
     Discusses the difficulty with crucial male role-work,
     as seen in a downward mobility, and proposes a struc-
     tural interaction theory of suicide.

2468 Brewster, H. H. "Grief: a disrupted human relationship,"

Human Organization, 9 (1950), 19-22.
Points out that excessive regret for lost interaction with the deceased can hinder the bereaved from accomplishing a job.

2469 Brill, A. A. "Necrophilia," Journal of Criminal Psychopathology, 2 (1941), 433-43.

2470 _____. "Thoughts on life and death or Vidonian All Soul's Eve," Psychiatric Quarterly, 21 (1947), 191-211.

2471 Brock, D. "Student suicides," America (March 13, 1965), 344-5.

2472 Brodsky, B. "The Self-representation, anality and the fear of dying," Journal of the American Psychoanalytic Association, 7 (1959), 95-108.
"Postulates that the fear of death is not exclusively derived from fear of castration, and the fear of desertion by the superego."

2473 Bromberg, W., and P. Schilder. "Death and dying: a comparative study of the attitudes and mental reactions toward death and dying," Psychoanalytic Review, 20 (1933), 133-85.

2474 Bronowski, J. "The Psychological wreckage of Hiroshima and Nagasaki," in Science, Conflict and Society, readings from "Scientific American," with introductions by Garrett Hardin. San Francisco: W. H. Freeman Co., 1969. pp. 23-5.
The author reviews the book Death in Life, by Robert Jay Lifton.

2475 Brown, F. "Depression and childhood bereavement," Journal of Mental Science, 107 (1961), 754-77.
Article discusses depression and childhood bereavement as factors in suicide and suicide attempts.

2476 Brown, L. B. "Attempted suicide: sleeping beauty phenomenon," New Zealand Nurses Journal, 63 (1970), 94.
Discusses female suicide and the indication that the female could most likely use a sleep method for its prevention. Cites various studies in New Zealand, Australia, and Great Britain.

2477 Brown, N. O. "Death," in Life Against Death: the psychoanalytical meaning of history. Connecticut: Wesleyan University Press, 1959.
The author attempts to derive from the writings of Freud an understanding of human history by examining fields of endeavor--e.g., eros, sublimation, anality, and resurrection of the body.

2478   Bucher, R. "Blame and hostility in disaster," American
        Journal of Sociology, LXII (1957), 467-75.

2479   Buckley, J. J. "Death without justice," Omega, 5 (fall
        1974), 193-7.
        In a guest editorial, the author surveys the death
        penalty and capital punishment and gives the viewpoints
        on life-related issues. He recommends the death
        penalty for some 30 crimes.

2480   Budge, E. A. The Mummy: chapters on Egyptian funeral
        archeology. Cambridge, 1893.
        A history of Egypt which examines and describes an
        Egyptian funeral, methods of mummifying, mummy cloth,
        canopic jars, the book of the dead, furniture, figures,
        and articles for the tomb, coffins, sarcophagi, and mum-
        mies of animals.

2481   Buhler, C. The Child and his family. N.Y.: Harper, 1959.

2482   Buhrmann, M. V. "Death--its psychological significance in
        the lives of children," South African Medical Journal,
        44 (May 1970), 586-9.
        Discusses the need to improve techniques of dealing
        with bereaved children and children facing serious ill-
        ness.

2483   Bui-Dang, H. U. D. "Vie et mort dans les populations,"
        Ethno-Psychologie, Revue de Psychologie des Peuples,
        27 (March 1972), 514.
        Statistical demographic study of natality and mor-
        tality and the effects of their fluctuation in various popu-
        lations.

2484   Bunch, J. "Recent bereavement in relation to suicide,"
        Journal of Psychosomatic Research, 16 (Aug. 1972),
        361-6.

2485   _____, et al. "Early parental bereavement and suicide,"
        Social Psychiatry, 6 (1971), 200.

2486   _____. "Suicide following bereavement of parents," Social
        Psychiatry, 6 (1971), 192-9.

2487   Bunston, A. "German idea of death," Living Age, 286 (Aug.
        28, 1915), 523-9.

2488   Burton, A. "Death as a countertransference," Psychoanalysis
        and the Psychoanalytic Review, 49 (1963), 3-20.
        Author states that it is not the intention of the Pope
        to make a case for or against the death instinct.

2489   _____. "Fear of death as countertransference," Omega,

2 (Nov. 1961), 287-98.

2490 Butler, R. N. "Attitudes toward death; an interview,"
Geriatrics, 19 (Feb. 1964), 58.
Dr. Butler answers questions concerning death atti-
tudes of elderly persons.

2491 Bynum, J. "Social status and rites of passage: the social
context of death," Omega, 4 (winter 1973), 323-32.

2492 Cain, A. C. "The Presuperego, 'turning inward,' of aggression," Psychoanalytic Quarterly, 30 (April 1961), 171-
208.
Concerned with the psychological effect of parent
suicide upon children. The article states that "case reports assume no relevance of the suicides...."

2493 _____. Survivors of suicide. Springfield, Ill.: C. C.
Thomas, 1972.
Sixteen contributors including E. S. Shneidman, discusses effects of suicide upon children, spouses and
parents of adolescents. Psychoanalytic case studies are
included.

2494 _____, and B. S. Cain. "On replacing a child," Journal
of the American Academy of Child Psychiatry, 3 (1964),
443-56.

2495 Calderone, M., ed. Abortion in the United States. N.Y.:
Harper, 1958.

2496 Calloway, N. D. "Patterns of senile death," Journal of the
American Geriatrics Society, 14 (1966), 156-66.
Concerned with the changes that occur in the patterns of death with time. A ten-year period during a
lifespan was selected for the study.

2497 Cameron, P. The Immanency of death," Journal of Consulting
Clinical Psychology, 32 (Aug. 1968), 479-81.

2498 Campbell, J. W. "Pointers from Hiroshima and Nagasaki,"
in The Atomic Story. N.Y.: Holt, 1947. pp. 231-42.

2499 Campbell, P. "Suicide among cancer patients," Connecticut
Health Bulletin, 80 (1966), 207-12.

2500 Canavan, F. "Freedom to die," America, 110 (Jan. 11,
1964), 33.

2501 Canning, R. R. "Mormon return from the dead stories:
fact or folklore," Utah Academy Proceedings, 42 (1965),
29-37.

2502 Cannon, W. P. "The Right to die," Houston Law Review, 7 (1970), 654-70.

2503 Cappon, D. "Attitudes of and toward the dying," Canadian Medical Association Journal, 87 (Sept. 1972), 693-700.
Primarily concerned with the desire to save the dying before the final exit. The following are some specific questions formulated: "What is the role of pain in dying? Is it to be avoided at all costs? Do people want to be told about their imminent death...? [H]ow early, and when would they want to learn about the details?"

2504 _____. "Attitudes on death," Omega, 1 (May 1970), 103-8.

2505 _____. "Attitudes toward death," Post Graduate Medical Journal, 47 (Feb. 1970), 257.

2506 _____. "The Dying," Psychiatric Quarterly, 33 (1959), 466-89.

2507 Caprio, F. S. "Ethnological attitudes toward death: a psychoanalytic evaluation," Journal of Clinical and Experimental Psychopathology, 7 (1946), 737-52.

2508 _____. "A Psycho-social study of primitive conceptions of death," Journal of Criminal Psychopathology, 5 (Oct. 1943), 303-17.
Discussion of legendary origin of death, mythological concepts among primitive peoples, death customs, and fear of death.

2509 Capstick, A. "Recognition of emotional disturbance and the prevention of suicide," British Medical Journal, 2 (1960), 1179-82.

2510 Caras, R. Death as a way of life. Boston: Little, Brown, 1971.
Examines "man as hunter from primitive times when hunting was a survival necessity to the present use of it for pleasure."

2511 Care of the child facing death, edited by Lindy Burton: foreword by I. J. Carré. London: Routledge and Kegan Paul, 1974.

2512 Carey, R. G. "Emotional adjustment in terminal patients: a quantitative approach," Journal of Counseling Psychology, 21 (Sept. 1974), 433-9.

2513 Cargnello, D. "Della morte et del morire, in psichiatria," Sistema Nervoso, 8 (March-April 1956), 113-25.

2514 Carmichael, B. "The Death wish in daily life," Psychoanalytic Review, 30 (1943), 59-66.
In everyday relationships, the average individual
finds it difficult to accept the concept of the death instinct, for in the unconscious we never die, and consciously we wish to die. Cites the case of a physician
who suffered acute depression.

2515 Carp, D. "Problème de la mort répresenté comme drame,"
Folia Psychiatrica, Neurologica et Neurochirurgica
Neerlandica, 51 (1948), 130-6.

2516 Carstairs, G. M. "Attitudes to death and suicide in an
Indian cultural setting," International Journal of Social
Psychiatry, 1 (1955), 33-41.
Discusses attitudes toward life and suicide in a vil-
lage of northwestern India. "For the villagers, death is
... but one incident in a long series of existences."

2517 Carter, R. M., and L. A. Smith. "The Death penalty in
California," Crime and Delinquency, 15 (Jan. 1969), 62-
76.
Examines case studies of all persons executed in
California, in the gas chamber at San Quentin, from
1938 to 1963.

2518 Cavan, R. S. Suicide. Chicago: University of Chicago
Press, 1928.
Study of the reasons behind suicide. The book begins "with a look at how members of a group organize
themselves, and how the suicide victim becomes dis-
organized...." The second part concerns the individual
side of the problem, and examples of case studies are
given.

2519 Chadwick, M. "Die Furcht vor dem Tode," International
Zeitschrift für Psychoanalyse, 15 (1929), 271-84.

2520 _____. "Notes upon the fear of death," International Journal of Psychoanalysis, 10 (1929), 321-34.
Article comments on the roots in the child's fear of
separation from the mother, and the originating and sus-
taining causes of fear of death.

2521 Chaloner, L. "How to answer questions children ask about
death," Parents Magazine, 37 (Nov. 1962), 48.
A study concerned with fundamental anxieties that
children have about death, and the need for discussing
these with the family.

2522 Chandler, K. A. "Three processes of dying and their behavioral effects," Journal of Consulting Psychology, 29
(1965), 296-301.

2523 Chandrasekhar, S. Infant mortality, population growth, and family planning in India. London: Allen and Unwin, 1972.

2524 Chapman, A. H. "Obsessions of infanticide," Archives of General Psychiatry (Chicago), 1 (1959), 12-16.

2525 Chase, H. C. A study of infant mortality from linked records: comparison of neonatal mortality from two cohort studies--United States. Washington, D. C.: U. S. Gov. Printing Office, 1950-1960.

2526 Chasin, B. "Neglected variables in the study of death attitudes," Sociological Quarterly, 12 (winter 1971), 107-113.
  Explores the effects of sex and income on the relationships between religious beliefs and death attitudes.

2527 _____. "Value-orientations and attitudes toward death." Ph. D. dissertation, University of Iowa, 1968.
  An attempt "to discover the ways in which value-orientations, secular and religious, were related to attitudes toward death...."

2528 Chethik, M. "The Impact of object loss on a six-year-old," Journal of the American Academy of Child Psychiatry, 9 (Oct. 1970), 624-43.
  A case study of a six-year-old boy who is emotionally disturbed and the impact of his mother's prolonged illness and death from cancer.

2529 Chevan, A., and J. B. Korson. "The Widowed who live alone; an examination of social and demographic factors " Social Forces, 51 (1972), 45-53.

2530 Chiassino, G., and L. Di Comite. "Sulla struttura della mortalità in Italia e il Belgio," Giornali degli Economisti e Annali di Economia, 31 (July-Aug. 1972), 446-68.

2531 "Child suicides: can these tragedies be prevented?" Good Housekeeping (Oct. 1969), 207-9.

2532 Childers, P., and M. Wimmer. "The Concept of death in early childhood," Child Development, 42 (Oct. 1971), 1293-1301.
  The authors indicate that the awareness of death in children is a function of age. Cognitive ability, concept formation, and early childhood experiences are all variable, and they are not demonstrated systematically in children until the age of ten.

2533 "Children view death in many ways," Science Digest, 73 (May 1973), 88.

A child's idea of death is revealed and shaped by his own experiences with death. Interviews were conducted by pediatricians at the University of Nebraska.

2534   Christ, A. E. "Attitudes toward death among a group of acute geriatric psychiatric patients," Journal of Gerontology, 16 (1961), 56-9.
        States that acute geriatric psychiatric patients could respond to questions about death and give meaningful answers.

2535   Ciocco, A., et al. "Four years mortality experience of a segment of the United States working population," American Journal of Public Health, 55 (1965), 587-95.
        Studies mortality experience of a group of males under the Old Age and Survivors Insurance system.

2536   Clayton, P. J. "The Depression of widowhood," Diseases of the Nervous System, 32 (Sept. 1971), 597-604.

2537   Cleghorn, S. "Changing thoughts of death," Atlantic Monthly, 132 (Dec. 1923), 808-12.

2538   "Clemency in Arkansas," Time, 97 (Jan. 11, 1971), 50.
        Discusses the commutation of death sentences of prisoners and focuses on the reasons behind Gov. Winthrop Rockefeller's commutation of all 15 death sentences of prisoners in Arkansas.

2539   "Closing death row," Time, 100 (July 10, 1972), 37.

2540   Cobb, B. "Psychological impact of long illness and death of a child on the family circle," Journal of Pediatrics, 39 (1956), 746-51.
        Attempts to set up a long-range investigation of the psychological impact of illness and death, from the response of families which experienced it.

2541   Cochrane, A. L. "Elie Metschnikoff and his theory of an 'instinct de la mort'," International Journal of Psychoanalysis, 15 (1934), 265-70.
        Discusses professor Metschnikoff's formulation of "Todestrieb" with Freud's death instinct.

2542   Cohen, B. Law without order: capital punishment and the liberals. N.Y.: Arlington House, 1970.

2543   Cohen, M., and L. M. Lipton. "Spontaneous remission of schizophrenic psychoses following maternal death," Psychiatric Quarterly, 24 (1950), 716-25.
        States that "the remission of acute schizophrenic psychosis shortly after maternal death is not an unusual or 'freak' occurrence."

2544 Cohen, R. J., and C. Parker. "Fear of failure and death, "
       Psychological Reports, 34 (Feb. 1974), 54.
       This study tested the hypothesis that male under-
       graduate students high in the fear of failure would also
       be high in the fear of death.

2545 "College suicides, " America (Oct. 29, 1966), 50-2.

2546 "Collegians threaten suicide most often, " Science News, 26
       (Oct. 30, 1965), 278.
       Article states that suicide is a greater threat to
       college students than any other population group in the
       U. S.

2547 Collett, L. J., and D. Lester. "The Fear of death and the
       fear of dying, " Journal of Psychology, 70 (1969), 179-
       81.
       Discusses the need for standardized measures of the
       fear of death.

2548 Collins, A. M., and W. E. Sedlacek. "Grief reactions
       among university students, " Journal of the National As-
       sociation of Women Deans and Counselors, 36 (summer
       1973), 178-83.
       Examines grief reactions of university students by
       student personnel and counseling staffs of the University
       of Maryland in an attempt to provide help with serious
       and pressing problems.

2549 Collins, V. Grief, how to live with sorrow. St. Meinrad,
       Ind.: Abbey Press, 1966.

2550 Comhaire-Sylvain, S. "Mort et funérailles dans la région
       de Kenscoff, " Revue de l'Institute de Sociologie (Haiti),
       2 (1959), 197-232.

2551 Conference on Identifying Suicide Potential. Teachers Col-
       lege, Columbia University, New York, 1969. Identifying
       suicide potential; conference proceedings. Edited and
       with commentary by Dorothy B. Anderson and Lenora J.
       McClean. New York: Behavioral Publications, 1971.
       (Social Problems series.)

2552 Connell, E. H. "The Significance of the idea of death in the
       neurotic mind, " British Journal of Medical Psychology,
       4 (1924), 115-24.

2553 "Consciousness of death, " Science Digest, 64 (Sept. 1968), 68.

2554 Cooke, R. E. "Is there a right to die--quickly?" Journal
       of Pediatrics, 80 (May 1972), 906-8.

2555 Coolidge, J. C. "Unexpected death in a patient who wished

to die, " Journal of the American Psychoanalytic Association, 17 (April 1969), 413-20.
Discusses the difficulty of medically explaining sudden death and points out that powerful emotions may be responsible for death. Cites the literature on the physiology and psychology of unexpected death.

2556   Cooper, D. S. Death of the family. N.Y.: Random, 1970.
Urges an abolishment of the present nuclear family system in favor of new forms of human relationships. The book also re-examines such things as homosexuality, mourning, instinct, love and greed.

2557   Cooperman, I. G.   "Second careers: war wives and widows, " Vocational Guidance Quarterly, 20 (1971), 103-11.

2558   "The Cop killers, " National Observer (Oct. 27, 1973), 1.

2559   Corey, L. G.   "An Analogue of resistance to death awareness, " Journal of Gerontology, 16 (1961), 59-60.
Study was to "determine empirically whether four operationally-defined modes of coping with death awareness differed in frequency between samples of young and old subjects. "

2560   Corfe, T. H.   "The Phoenix park murders, " History Today, 11 (1961), 828-35.
Discusses the double assassination in 1882 of the chief secretary of Ireland and the under-secretary and the resentment and anguish between the British and Irish.

2561   Cornils, S. Managing grief wisely. Grand Rapids, Mich.: Baker Books, 1967.

2562   Cosneck, B. J.   "Family patterns of older widowed Jewish people, " Family Coordinator, 19 (1970), 368-73.

2563   Cotter, Z. M.   "On not getting better, " Hospital Progress, 53 (March 1972), 60-3.

2564   Cottrell, J. Anatomy of an assassination. N.Y.: Funk and Wagnalls, 1966.

2565   Cousinet, R.   "L'Idée de la mort chez les enfants, " Journal de Psychologie Normale et Pathologique, 36 (1939), 65-75.

2566   Cowin, R.   "Problems of impending death. The role of the social worker, " Physical Therapy, 4 (July 1968), 743-8.
Effective presentation of guidelines which the social worker can use to help families face death.

2567   Craddick, R. A.   "Symbolism of death: archetypal and per-

sonal symbols, " International Journal of Symbology, 3 (Dec. 1972), 35-44.
Discusses the individual's subjective feelings about death and the physical process of death itself. Concepts cited are unconscious archetypes, personification, sleep, and symbolization. Some 18 references are appended.

2568 Creegan, R. F. "A Symbolic action during bereavement, " Journal of Abnormal and Social Psychology, 37 (1942), 403-5.

2569 Crotty, W. J. "Assassinations and their interpretation within the American context, " in Assassinations and the Political Order, edited by W. J. Crotty. N. Y.: Harper and Row, 1971. pp. 3-53.

2570 Crown, B. , et al. "Attitudes toward death, " Psychological Reports (supplement), 20 (June 1967), 1181-2.
Article points out that it is best to have a healthy sensitivity toward death; various attitudes are described.

2571 Cruvant, B. A. , and F. Waldrop. "The Murderer in the mental institution, " Annals of the American Academy of Political and Social Science, 284 (1922), 35-43.
"... [S]tatistical and descriptive study of the fate of all the individuals committed to Saint Elizabeth's Hospital while under charges or conviction of homicide" 1925-1951.

2572 Curl, J. S. The Victorian celebration of death. Detroit: Partridge Press, 1972.

2573 Curphey, T. J. "The Role of the forensic pathologist in the multidisciplinary approach to death. " Paper presented to the meeting of the American Psychological Association, Los Angeles, 1964.

2574 Cutter, F. "Robert Seymour; a psychohistorical autopsy, " Omega, 1 (Feb. 1970), 37-47.

2575 Dahlberg, G. "Suicide, alcohol, and war, " Acta Genetica, 1 (1948), 191-8.
Discusses the diminishing suicide rate during the war and the various ethical ideas about it.

2576 Dahlgren, K. G. On suicide and attempted suicide. Lindstedts: Lund, 1945.

2577 Dann, R. H. "Capital punishment in Oregon, " Annals of the American Academy of Political and Social Science, 28 (1952), 110-14.
Discusses the abolishment of the death penalty in 1914, and its restoration in 1920.

2578 D'annunzie, G. Contemplazione della morte. Milan: Fra-
      telli Treves, 1912.

2579 Das, S. S. "Grief and suffering, " Psychotherapy, 8 (spring
      1971), 8-9.

2580 _____. "Grief and the imminent threat of non-being, "
      British Journal of Psychiatry, 118 (April 1971), 467-8.

2581 David, H. P. "Abortion in psychological perspective, "
      American Journal of Orthopsychiatry, 42 (Jan. 1972),
      61-8.

2582 _____, and J. C. Brengelmann, eds. Perspectives in per-
      sonality research. N. Y.: Springer, 1960.

2583 Davis, C. "Feeling the negativity of death, " National
      Catholic Reporter, 8 (April 14, 1972), 8.

2584 Davis, F. B. The Death instinct: its meanings and implica-
      tions. (Harvard Honors Thesis.) Cambridge: Harvard
      University Press, 1959.

2585 Davis, J. A. "The Attitude of parents to the approaching
      death of their child, " Developmental Medicine and Child
      Neurology, 6 (June 1964), 286-88.

2586 Davis, J. C. "The Attitude of Florentines toward death,
      1375-1410. " M. A. thesis, Pennsylvania State Univer-
      sity, 1956.

2587 "Death and modern man, " Newsweek, 84 (Nov. 20, 1964),
      92-5.

2588 Death anxiety. Papers by H. W. Montefiore, Joseph R.
      Cautela, Robert N. Butler, et al. N. Y.: Mss Infor-
      mation Corp., 1973. (Mss attitudes toward death
      series.)
          Some articles included previously appeared in
      various journals.

2589 "Death in America, " Scientific American, 216 (Feb. 1967),
      56.
          Statistics describe the mortality rate 1954-1963.

2590 "Death in the palace, " Newsweek, 79 (Feb. 7, 1972), 35.

2591 "The Death industry--role conflicts of clergy and under-
      taker, " Time, 76 (Nov. 14, 1960), 63.

2592 "Death row: a new kind of suspense, " Newsweek, 77 (Jan.
      11, 1971), 23-7.

2593 "Delay on the death penalty: case of W. Maxwell, " Time,
      95 (June 15, 1970), 60.
         Article deals with the Supreme Court's inability to
      come to a decision regarding the death penalty.

2594 Dennehy, C. M. "Childhood bereavement and psychiatric ill-
      ness, " British Journal of Psychiatry, 112 (1966), 1049-
      69.

2595 DePolnay, P. Death and tomorrow. London: Secker and
      Warburg, 1942.
         Discusses the terror and events during the German
      occupation of France and other areas.

2596 Deshaires, G. La Psychologie de suicide. Paris: Presses
      Universitaires, 1947.

2597 Dessoir, M. Das Ich, der Traum den Tod. Stuttgart: Enke,
      1947.

2598 Dethlefsen, E., and J. Deetz. "Death's heads, cherubs, and
      willow trees: experimental archaeology in colonial ceme-
      teries, " American Antiquities, 31 (April 1966), 502-10.

2599 Deutsch, E. "Uber Kinderselbstmorde, " Archiv für Kinder-
      heitkunde, 38 (1903), 37-56.

2600 Deutsch, F. "Euthanasia: a clinical study, " Psychoanalytic
      Quarterly, 5 (1936), 347-68.
         Author expresses his fellings on euthanasia from
      personal experiences at the bedside of dying persons.

2601 Deutsch, H. "Absence of grief, " Psychoanalytic Quarterly,
      6 (1937), 12-22.
         Discusses the mourning process from Freud's point
      of view as a normal function of the bereaved individual.

2602 Deutsch, H. B. The Huey Long murder case. N. Y. :
      Doubleday, 1963.
         An investigation into the assassination with several
      theories as to how and why Long was shot.

2603 Devereux, G. "Funeral suicide and the Mohave social struc-
      ture: primitive psychiatry, " Bulletin of the History of
      Medicine, 11 (1942), 522-42.
         States that "the complete constitutionalization of
      funeral suicide among the Mohave Indians is functionally
      connected with certain basic aspects of Mohave society,
      culture, and social psychology. "

2604 _____. A Study of abortion in primitive societies. N. Y. :
      Julian Press, 1955.

2605 De Vos, G., and H. Wagatsuma. "Psycho-cultural signifi-
      cance of concern over death and illness among rural
      Japanese," International Journal of Social Psychiatry, 5
      (1959), 5-19.
          Discusses the relationship between concern over death
      and illness among rural Japanese. Authors used the
      Thematic Apperception Test material. The study revealed
      the mother-son relationship and supports the traditional
      family system and cultural sanctions.

2606 Dickstein, L. S., and S. J. Blatt. "Death concern, futurity,
      and anticipation," Journal of Consulting Psychology, 30
      (1966), 11-17.
          Explores the relationship between death concern and
      future time, and suggests characteristics of those with
      high and low concern.

2607 Diggory, J., and D. Rothman. "Values destroyed by death,"
      Journal of Abnormal and Social Psychology, 63 (1961),
      205-10.

2608 "Dilemma in dying," Time (July 19, 1971), 44.

2609 Di Salle, M. V. The Power of life or death. N. Y.: Ran-
      dom House, 1965.
          A book which presents two viewpoints. The one is
      a passionate polemic against capital punishment. The
      other is the anguished personal narrative of a former
      Ohio governor who, though opposed to capital punishment,
      felt compelled to enforce it.

2610 Diskin, M., and H. Guggenheim. "The Child and death as
      seen in different cultures," in Explaining Death to Chil-
      dren, edited by E. A. Grollman. Boston: Beacon,
      1967.
          (See also chapter four.)

2611 Dizmang, L. H. "Loss, bereavement and depression in
      childhood," International Psychiatry Clinics, 6 (1969),
      175-95.

2612 _____, et al. "Adolescent suicide at an Indian reserva-
      tion," American Journal of Orthopsychiatry, 44 (Jan.
      1974), 43-9.

2613 Dobzhansky, T. G. Mankind evolving. New Haven, Conn.:
      Yale University Press, 1962.

2614 Dockry, M. M. "Breaking the news to the children," Family
      Digest, 15 (March 1960), 58-61.

2615 Dombrowski, C. Les conditions psychologiques du suicide.
      Geneva: Imprimerie du Commerce, 1929.

2616 Donaldson, P. J. "Denying death: a note regarding some
      ambiguities in the current discussion," Omega, 3 (Nov.
      1972), 285-90.
      The author questions the notion of the denial of
      death and works toward a definition of how it can be
      measured.

2617 Donovan, R. J. The Assassins. N. Y.: Harper, 1955.
      Stories about seven men who killed or tried to kill
      U. S. Presidents. From Booth to Schrank to the would-
      be assassin of Teddy Roosevelt, the reader gets a com-
      plete case history of each. The author concludes that
      none was criminal, radical, nor mentally disturbed.

2618 Dorpat, T. L. "Psychiatric observations on assassinations,"
      Northwest Medicine, 67 (Oct. 1968), 976-79.

2619 _____, and H. S. Ripley. "A Study of suicide in the
      Seattle area," Comprehensive Psychiatry, 1 (1960), 349-
      59.

2620 Douglas, J. D. Social meaning of suicide. Princeton, N. J.:
      Princeton University Press, 1967.
      An attack on the way suicide statistics had previous-
      ly been analyzed. The claim is made that the statistics
      are biased, and must be approached in a new way,
      which the author presents, along with some analyses of
      his own.

2621 _____. "The Sociological analysis of social meanings of
      suicide," European Journal of Sociology, 7 (1966), 249-
      98.

2622 Dowd, D. W. Medical, moral and legal implications of
      recent medical advances. N. Y.: Da Capo Press,
      1971.

2623 Doyle, N. The Dying Person and the Family. Washington,
      D. C.: Public Affairs Committee, 1973. (Pamphlet no.
      485.)
      Studies indicate that people want to know when they
      are dying, and they also want to talk about it with im-
      plications for the family.

2624 Dublin, L. Suicide. N. Y.: Ronald Press, 1953.

2625 _____. Suicide: a sociological and statistical study.
      N. Y.: Ronald Press, 1963.
      Analysis of data on suicide rates by age, sex,
      marital status, ancestral nationality, race, cities and
      states. Includes a discussion on prevention.

2626 _____, and B. Bunzel. To be or not to be--a study of
     suicide. N.Y.: Harrison Smith and Robert Haas, 1933.

2627 Duffy, C. J. Eighty eight men and two women. N.Y.:
     Doubleday, 1962.
         An appeal to stop capital punishment by the former
     warden of San Quentin prison. During his stay as
     warden, 88 men and two women died in the gas cham-
     ber. He sketches each one and gives a reason they
     should not have died.

2628 Dumont, R. G., and D. C. Foss. The American view of
     death--acceptance or denial? Cambridge, Mass.:
     Schenkman, 1972.
         Analysis of the American attitudes toward death and
     the death wish and fear of death that pervades American
     culture.

2629 Durkheim, E. Suicide: a study in sociology. N.Y.: Free
     Press, 1960.
         A socio-psychological study of the interconnected-
     ness of suicide with different social and natural phe-
     nomena. The general nature of suicide is explained
     and some possible social causes and social types are
     developed by statistical evaluation.

2630 Durlak, J. A. "Measurement of the fear of death: an
     examination of some existing scales," Journal of Clinical
     Psychology, 28 (Oct. 1972), 545-7.

2631 _____. "Relationship between individual attitudes toward
     life and death," Journal of Consulting Clinical Psychology,
     38 (June 1972), 463.
         To find relationships between individual attitudes to-
     ward purpose in life and fear of death, a statistical re-
     port of test results from college and high school students
     was prepared.

2632 Dyck, A. J. "Questions of ethics," Harvard Theological Re-
     view, 65 (Oct. 1972), 453-81.

2633 Earle, A. M., and B. V. Earle. "Early maternal depriva-
     tion and later psychiatric illness," American Journal of
     Orthopsychiatry, 31 (1961), 181-6.

2634 Eaton, J. W. "The Art of aging and dying," Gerontologist,
     4 (1964), 94-100.
         Investigates the Hutterite religious sect and their at-
     titudes toward aging and death. Describes six universal
     problems of aging.

2635 Eck, M. "Thoughts about death and death instincts: apropos
     of some more or less recent books," Presse Médicale,

77 (Nov. 1969), 1829-32.

2636   Edelston, H.   "Separation anxiety in young children," Genetic
       Psychology, 28 (June 1942), 3-95.

2637   Ehrmann, H. B.   "The Death penalty and the administration
       of justice," Annals of the American Academy of Political
       and Social Science, 284 (1952), 73-84.
              Author states that the "death penalty does not pro-
       tect society from murderers."

2638   _____. The Untried case.   London: Martin Hopkinson,
       1934.
              This author believes that there is evidence which
       would gain for Sacco and Vanzetti a new trial.

2639   Eigen, M.   "Fear of death: a symptom with changing mean-
       ings," Journal of Humanistic Psychology, 14 (summer
       1974), 29-33.

2640   Eisenthal, S.   "Death ideation in suicidal patients," Journal
       of Abnormal Psychology, 73 (April 1968), 162-67.
              States that suicidal patients are not in fact psycho-
       logically closer to death than non-suicidal psychiatric
       patients.

2641   Eissler, K. R.   Psychiatrist and the dying patient.   N.Y.:
       International Universities Press, 1970.

2642   Eliot, T. D.   "Adjustment to bereavement," in Social Prob-
       lems in America, edited by A. M. Lee, and E. B. Lee.
       N.Y.: 1949.   pp. 286-7.

2643   _____.   "Attitudes toward euthanasia," Research Studies
       of the State College of Washington, 15 (1947), 131-4.

2644   _____.   "The Bereaved family," Annals of the American
       Academy of Political and Social Sciences, 160 (1932), 4.

2645   _____.   "Bereavement as a field of social research,"
       Bulletin of the Society for Social Research, 17 (1938), 4.

2646   _____.   "Bereavement as a problem for family research,
       and technique," The Family, 11 (1930), 114-5.

2647   _____.   "... Of the Shadow of Death," Annals of the
       American Academy of Political and Social Sciences, 27
       (1933), 380-90.

2648   _____.   "A Step toward the social psychology of bereave-
       ment," Journal of Abnormal and Social Psychology, 27
       (1933), 380-90.

2649 _____. "War bereavements and their recovery," Marriage and Family Living, 8 (winter 1946), 1-5.

2650 Elkinton, J. R. "Moral problems in the use of borrowed organs, artificial and transplanted," Annals of Internal Medicine, 60 (1964), 309-13.

2651 Epps, P. "Women in prison on attempted suicide charges," Lancet, 2 (1957), 182-4.
A study of 100 women in an English prison for attempting to commit suicide. States that depression, guilt, and lineliness are major factors.

2652 Escobal, P. Death row: Spain 1936. Indianapolis: Bobbs-Merrill, 1936.

2653 Eshelman, B. Death row chaplain. Englewood Cliffs, N.J.: Prentice Hall, 1962.
Written by a chaplain at San Quentin, this book given first hand information on how condemned men and women live in prison, face the knowledge of their fate, and finally die in the execution chamber.

2654 Etzioni, A. "Life, dying, death: ethics and open decisions," Science News, 106 (Aug. 17, 1974), 109-11.

2655 Euthanasia Educational Fund, Inc. The Right to die with dignity: a discussion of the medical, legal, social and ethical aspects of euthanasia. First Euthanasia Conference of the Educational Fund, November 23, 1968. N.Y.: Euthanasia Educational Fund, 1969.

2656 "Euthanasia in England: a growing storm," America, 122 (May 2, 1970), 463.
An editorial which discusses the euthanasia lobby in England and the opposition to it.

2657 "Evolution de la mortalité par suicide dans divers pays industrialisés," Population, 283 (March-April, 1973), 419-28.

2658 Fabian, J. "How others die--reflections on the anthropology of death," in Death in American Experience, edited by A. Mack. N.Y.: Schocken, 1973.
Describes "the use to which anthropological findings have been put in other contexts, notably in philosophical, psychological and sociological approaches to death in modern society."

2659 Fairbank, E. "Suicide," Journal of the American Medical Association, 98 (1932), 1711-15.
States that depression is most frequently associated with suicide in the mentally ill, but not all suicides are

due to mental illness.

2660 Farberow, N. L. "Training in suicide prevention for professional and community agents," American Journal of
Psychiatry, 25 (1969), 1702-5.
        Suicide prevention agencies and professionals have
a primary purpose in having a concerted effort in helping to diminish the taboo aspects of suicide.

2661 _____, and E. S. Shneidman. The Cry for help. N. Y.:
McGraw-Hill, 1961.

2662 _____. "A Study of attempted, threatened and completed
suicides," Journal of Abnormal and Social Psychology,
50 (1955), 230.
        Concludes that the suicidal patient is one with a his-
tory of serious suicidal attempts or threats.

2663 _____, and T. L. McEvoy. "Suicide among patients in
general medical and surgical hospitals with diagnosis of
anxiety reactions or depressive reaction," Journal of
Abnormal Psychology, 71 (1966), 287-99.
        Seeks to categorize suicide patients into various pat-
terns of behavior, and points out similar and dissimilar
characteristics of each.

2664 Farrar, C. B. "Euthanasia," American Journal of Psychiatry, 119 (May 1963), 1104.
        Comments on various aspects of euthanasia, and
questions the preserving of life without the personality.

2665 _____. "Suicide," Journal of Clinical and Experimental
Psychopathology, 12 (1951), 79-88.
        Discusses various religious and philosophical views
of suicide, including the Judeo-Christian view of sinful-
ness and suicide, and more liberal modern views.

2666 Fast, I., and A. C. Cain. "Fears of death in bereaved
children and adults," American Journal of Orthopsychiatry, 34 (1964), 278-9.
        Examines the meaning of death for children, and
presents data from clinical research. The significance
of bereavement for ego development is also discussed.

2667 _____, et al. "The Sense of being dead and of dying:
some perspectives," Journal of Projective Techniques
and Personality, 34 (June 1970), 190-3.
        Authors state that there is "no reason to expect
schizophrenic women to feel like dying women."

2668 Faulkner, J. E., and G. F. Dejong. "Religiosity in 5-D:
an empirical analysis," Social Forces, 45 (Dec. 1966),
246-54.

2669 "The Fear of death," Newsweek, 56 (Feb. 27, 1967), 56-7.
      Presents the views of hospital psychiatrists Drs.
      A. D. Weisman and T. P. Hackett, who favor telling
      patients that they are going to die.

2670 "Fear of death linked to career decision," United States Medi-
      cine (Oct. 1, 1967), 4.

2671 Federn, P. "The Reality of the death instinct," Psycho-
      analytic Review, 19 (1932), 129-50.

2672 Feifel, H. "Attitudes of mentally ill patients toward death,"
      Journal of Nervous and Mental Disease, 122 (1955), 375-
      80.

2673 _____. "Attitudes toward death: a psychological per-
      spective," Journal of Consulting and Clinical Psychology,
      33 (1969), 292-5.

2674 _____. "Death," in Taboo Topics, by N. L. Farberow.
      N.Y.: Atherton, 1963. pp. 8-21.
      The author contends that Americans should discuss
      openly and freely the process of dying.

2675 _____. "Death and dying: attitudes of patient and doctor,
      5; the function of attitudes toward death," Group for the
      Advancement of Psychiatry, (Symposium no. 11), 5 (Oct.
      1965), 633-41.

2676 _____. "Death--relevant variable in psychology," in
      Existential Psychology, edited by R. May. N.Y.: 1961.
      pp. 61-74.

2677 _____. "The Function of attitudes toward death," Group
      for the Advancement of Psychiatry, 5 (1965), 632-40.
      Investigates various death attitudes in hope of dis-
      covering the function of these attitudes as they relate
      to the way the person faces death.

2678 _____. "Scientific research in taboo areas--death,"
      American Behavioral Scientist, 5 (1962), 28-30.

2679 _____. "Some aspects of the meaning of death," in Clues
      to Suicide, edited by E. S. Shneidman, and N. L. Far-
      berow. N.Y.: McGraw-Hill, 1957. pp. 50-7.

2680 _____. "The Taboo on death," American Behavioral Sci-
      entist, 6 (May 1963), 66-7.
      Lists a number of prevailing attitudes toward death,
      and points out that Western culture hides from death in
      euphemistic language.

2681 _____, and R. Jones. "Perception of death as related to

nearness to death," Proceedings of the 76th Annual Convention of the American Psychological Association, 3
(1968), 545-6.

2682   Feinberg, D.   Preventive therapy with siblings of a dying
child.   N. Y.:   Center for Preventive Psychiatry, 1969.
This case study deals with the psychiatric intervention for two sisters whose brother is dying.   The emphasis is on reality orientation and the enhancement of
mourning through transference materials.

2683   Feldman, M. J., and M. Hersen.   "Attitudes toward death
in nightmare subjects," Journal of Abnormal Psychology,
72 (1967), 421-5.
Study investigated "whether subjects manifested
greater concern about death in proportion to nightmares."

2684   _____; P. J. Handal; and H. S. Barshal.   Fears related
to death and suicide.   N. Y.:   Mss Information Corp.,
1973.   (Attitudes toward death series, no. 5.)
"Attitudes toward death manifested in dreams and
nightmares, psychological theories on death, and attitudes toward death in suicidal subjects...."

2685   Ferenczi, S.   "The Unwelcome child and his death instinct,"
International Journal of Psychoanalysis, 10 (1929), 125.
Presents the view that the experience of being an
unwanted child is a factor in the development of the
death instinct in the individual.

2686   Ferrer, J. M.   "Death penalty: cruel and unusual," Time,
99 (Jan. 24, 1972), 54-5.

2687   Filler, L.   "Movements to abolish the death penalty in the
United States," Annals of the American Academy of Political and Social Science, 284 (1952), 124-36.

2688   Fisher, G.   "Death, identity and creativity," Omega, 2 (Nov.
1971), 303-6.

2689   Fitzgerald, R.   "The Natural and social phenomena of death,"
The Black Panther, 5 (1970), 8-10.

2690   Flath, D. W.   "Where the family of God is the family: the
role of the dead in Japanese households," American
Anthropologist, 66 (April 1964), 300-17.

2691   Fletcher, G. P.   "Legal aspects of the decision not to prolong life," Journal of the American Medical Association,
203 (Jan. 1, 1968), 65-8.

2692   _____.   "Prolonging life," Washington Law Review, 42
(June 1967), 999.

2693 Fliess, R. Symbol, dream and psychosis. New York:
      International Universities Press, 1972.
          The author explains two representations of
      death that could be called symbolic and contrasts
      his view with Freud's. See especially pages 8-
      12.

2694 Flornoy, B. The World of the Inca. N. Y.: Vanguard,
      n. d.
          History of the Inca people taken from Spanish ac-
      counts and archaeological evidence; Inca thoughts on im-
      mortality, among many other subjects.

2695 Fodor, N. "Jung's sermons to the dead," Psychoanalytic
      Review, 51 (1964), 74-8.
          Discusses "Jung's views on life and death and his
      communications through dreams, waking visions, with
      the dead. "

2696 Folta, J. R. "Nurses' perceptions of role requirements
      and role action in situations involving death in hospitals. "
      Ph. D. dissertation, University of Washington, 1963.

2697 Ford, R. E. , et al. "Fear of death of those in a high stress
      occupation, " Psychological Reports, 29 (Oct. 1971), 502.

2698 Forde, D. "Death and succession: an analysis of Yako
      mortuary ritual, " in Essays on the Ritual of Social Re-
      lations, edited by Max Gluckman. Manchester: Man-
      chester University Press, 1962. pp. 89-123.

2699 Foster, L. E.; E. Lindemann; and R. J. Fairbanks. "Grief, "
      Pastoral Psychology, 1 (June 1950), 28-30.
          Stresses the importance for the "clergy to distin-
      guish between healthy and morbid grief. "

2700 Foster, Z. P. "How social work can influence hospital
      management of fatal illness, " Social Work, 10 (Oct.
      1965), 30-5.
          Story of a social worker who helped to modify the
      ward culture for a group of hospital patients with fatal
      blood diseases.

2701 Fox, R. C. "A Sociological perspective on organ trans-
      plantation and hemodialysis, " Annals of the New York
      Academy of Sciences, 169 (Jan. 21, 1970), 406-28.

2701a _____, and J. P. Swazey. The Courage to fail: a social
      view of organ transplants and dialysis. Chicago: Uni-
      versity of Chicago Press, 1974.
          Contents: Patterns in therapeutic innovation:
      transplantations; The courage to fail ethos; Patterns in
      therapeutic innovation: dialysis.

2702 Fox, W. J. An Inquiry into the history of opinion concerning death, and the mental state induced by its approach.
London: C. Fox, 1838.

2703 Foxe, A. N. "Critique of Freud's concept of a death instinct, " Psychoanalytic Review, 30 (1943), 417-27.
The author finds "confusion and conflict in Freud's
lack of consistency and interpretation of the death instinct. "

2704 _____. "The Life and death instincts: criminological implications, " Journal of Criminal Psychopathology, 4
(1942), 67-91.

2705 Francaviglia, R. "The Cemetery as an evolving cultural
landscape, " Annals of the Association of American
Geographers, 61 (Sept. 1971), 501-9.

2706 Frankl, V. E. The Doctor and the soul: an introduction to
logotherapy, translated from the German by Richard and
Clara Winston. N. Y.: Knopf, 1955.
Frankl describes his Existenz-Analyse as an existential form of life as the goal of psychotherapy. He applies logotherapy to the meaning of life and the human
spirit.

2707 _____. "Existential escapism, " Omega, 2 (Nov. 1971),
307-12.

2708 _____. Man's search for meaning: an introduction to
logotherapy. N. Y.: Washington Square Press, 1963.
Presents logotherapy which is related to existentialism. Begins with a background of the author's experiences in a concentration camp, his reasons for developing logotherapy, and the use of it to help former
victims of concentration camps.

2709 _____. Psychotherapy and existentialism--selected papers
in logotherapy. N. Y.: Washington Square Press, 1967.

2710 Franz, A. "The Need for punishment and the death instinct, "
International Journal of Psychoanalysis, 10 (1929), 256-
69.

2711 Frazer, J. G. The Belief in immortality and the worship of
the dead. N. Y.: Macmillan, 1913.
Description of belief in immortality among primitive
races of Australia and Melanesia.

2712 _____. The Fear of the dead in primitive religion. N. Y.:
Macmillan, 1933. 3 vols.
A study of the place of ghosts or spirits of the
dead in primitive religions. Beliefs, ceremonies, and

practices of Indians, Chinese, and Africans are brought in to demonstrate the variety of treatment received by ghosts around the world.

2713 Freedman, R.; L. C. Coombs; and J. Friedman. "Social correlates of fetal mortality," Milbank Memorial Fund Quarterly, 44 (1966), 327-44.
Relates various factors that seem stable in determining the causes of fetal death.

2714 Freidman, P., and L. Lum. "Some psychiatric notes on the Andrea Doria disaster," American Journal of Psychiatry, 114 (1957), 426-32.

2715 Freud, S. Civilization, war and death, edited by John Rickman. London: Hogarth Press and the Institute of Psychoanalysis, 1953 (orig. pub. 1939).

2716 _____. "Dostoevsky and parricide," in Guilt: man and society, edited by R. W. Smith. N. Y.: Anchor Books, 1971. pp. 63-83.
Freud deals with four facets of the "personality of Dostoevsky: the creative artist, the neurotic, the moralist, and the sinner."

2717 _____. "Dreams and telepathy," in Collected Papers. New York: Basic Books, 1959. Vol. 4, pp. 408-35.

2718 _____. The Ego and the id; trans. by J. Riviere, rev. and newly ed. by J. Strachey. N. Y.: W. W. Norton, 1960.
"I believe that the fear of death is something that occurs between the ego and the superego.... [W]e know that the fear of death makes its appearance under two conditions ... namely as a reaction to an external danger and as an internal process, as for instance in melancholia."

2719 _____. "Mourning and melancholia" (1917), in Collected Papers. New York: Basic Books, 1959. Vol. 4.

2720 _____. "Our attitude towards death," in Collected Papers. New York: Basic Books, 1959. Vol. 4, pp. 304-17.

2721 _____. Reflections on war and death; trans. by A. A. Brill and A. B. Kuttner. N. Y.: Moffat, 1918.

2722 _____. "The Theme of three caskets," in Collected Papers. N. Y.: Basic Books, 1959. Vol. 4, pp. 244-56.

2723 _____. "Thoughts for the times on war and death," in Collected Papers. N. Y.: Basic Books, 1959. Vol. 4. pp. 288-317.

2724 _____. "Totem and taboo," in The Basic Writings of
Sigmund Freud, edited by A. A. Brill. N.Y.: Random
House, 1938.
Freud attempts to explain the origins of the taboos
on murder and incestuous relationships within the kin or
intimate group.

2725 Fried, C. "The Value of life," Harvard Law Review, 82
(1968), 1415.

2726 Friedman, D. B. "Death anxiety and the primal scene,"
Psychoanalysis and the Psychoanalytic Review, 48 (winter 1961-1962), 108-18.
Concerned with neurotic anxiety of death and "its
relationship to unconscious feelings about exclusion from
the primal scene.... [A] syndrome of death anxiety,
sleep disturbances, and a form of voyeurism referable
to a primal scene experience are (all) included."

2727 Friedman, J. "Paradoxical response to death of spouse,"
Diseases of the Nervous System, 25 (1964), 480-5.
Reports on cases in which the death of a spouse
brought about recovery from a depression state in the
remaining spouse, which is paradoxical.

2728 Friedman, P. "Sur le suicide," Revue Française de Psychanalyse, 8 (1935), 106-48.

2729 Friedman, S. B. "Childhood leukemia--a pamphlet for
parents," Washington, D.C.: U.S. Dept. of Health,
Education and Welfare, Public Health Service, 1965.

2730 _____. "Communication within the family of a fatally ill
child." Paper presented at the University of Rochester
School of Medicine, at a conference entitled "The Patient, Death, and the Family," held on April 30, 1971.

2731 _____; P. Chedoff; and J. W. Mason. "Behavioral observations of parents anticipating the death of a child,"
Pediatrics, 32 (1963), 610-25.
Article is the study of 46 parents of children with
neoplastic disease. Describes the early reactions of
parents, results, and the terminal phase.

2732 Friedsam, H. J. "The Coming years: social science perspectives on aging and death," Social Science Quarterly,
51 (June 1970), 120-8.

2733 Friendlander, K. "On the 'longing to die'," International
Journal of Psychoanalysis, 21 (1940), 416-26.
Examines whether the melancholic type of suicide is
the basis for every suicide committed, or whether other
mechanisms are involved.

2734   Fritz, M. A. "A Study of widowhood, " Sociology and Social
       Research, 14 (1929), 553-61.
              Studies fatherless families, and proposes guidelines
       for the successful adjustment of the widow.

2735   "From killers to priests, " Time, 97 (Jan. 18, 1971), 54-5.
              Discusses the prison life of several well-known men,
       such as Edgar Smith, George Jackson, James Earl Ray,
       and the Berrigans.

2736   Fuchs, W. Todesbilder in der modernen Gesellschaft.
       Frankfurt am Main: Suhrkamp, 1969.

2737   Fulton, R. L. "Attitudes toward death--a discussion, "
       Journal of Gerontology, 16 (1961), 63-5.

2738   _____. A Compilation of studies of attitudes toward
       death, funerals and funeral directors. Minneapolis:
       Center for Death Education and Research, University of
       Minnesota, 1971.

2739   _____. "Death and dying: some sociological aspects of
       terminal care, " Modern Medicine, 40 (May 29, 1972),
       74-7.

2740   _____. "Death and the self, " Journal of Religion and
       Health, 3 (1964), 359-68.
              Discusses previous studies on the relationship be-
       tween grief and death. Presents the current trends in
       coping with death in America.

2741   _____. "Death, grief and social recuperation, " Omega,
       1 (Feb. 1970), 23-8.

2742   _____. "On the dying of death, " in The Child and Death,
       edited by E. A. Grollman. Boston: Beacon, 1967. pp.
       1-18.

2743   _____. "Review of funeral customs the world over, "
       Sociological Quarterly, III, (1962), 251-3.

2744   _____. The Sacred and the secular: attitudes of the
       American public toward death. Milwaukee: Bulfin,
       1963.

2745   _____, and W. A. Faunce. "The Sociology of death: a
       neglected area of research, " Social Forces, 36 (1958),
       205-9.
              Presents a number of research suggestions and pos-
       sibilities for sociologists who have in the past neglected
       this area of death.

2746   _____, and J. Fulton. "A Psychosocial aspect of terminal

care: anticipatory grief, " Omega, 2 (May 1971), 91-
100.

2747   _____, and G. Geis. "Death and social values, " in
Death and Identity. N. Y.: Wiley, 1965. pp. 67-75.

2748   _____, and P. Langton. "Attitudes toward death: an
emerging mental health problem, " Nursing Forum, 3
(1964), 104-12.
Observes possible mental health problems related
to death because of our culture's conflicting attitudes toward it, and offers a solution to the problem.

2749   Furman, R. A. "A Child's capacity for mourning, " in
The Child in His Family, edited by E. J. Anthony, and
C. Koupernik. N. Y.: Wiley, 1973. Vol. 2, pp. 225-31.
Explores the factors that can interfere with the
utilization of the child's capacity to mourn, "and the
consequences for the child who fails to fulfill the requirements of the mourning task. "

2750   _____. "Death and the young child: some preliminary
considerations, " Psychoanalytic Study of the Child, 19
(1964), 321-33.
Studies from various perspectives, and the responses
of two children who had witnessed the tragic deaths of
their mothers.

2751   _____. "Death of a six year old's mother during his
analysis, " Psychoanalytic Study of the Child, 19 (1964),
377-97.
Study of the effects that the death of his mother had
on a boy who had just begun analysis at Hanna Perkins
School.

2752   Furtwängler, W. Die Idee des Todes in den Mythen und
Kunstdenkmalern der Griechen. Freiburg im Breisgau:
F. Wagner, 1860.

2753   Gabel, P. "Freud's death instinct and Sartre's fundamental
project, " Psychoanalytic Review, 61 (summer 1974),
217-27.

2754   Galdston, I. "Eros and thanatos: a critique and elaboration
of Freud's death wish, " American Journal of Psychoanalysis, 15 (1955), 123-34.

2755   Gans, H. J. "Why did Kennedy die?" Trans-Action, 5
(July-Aug. 1968), 5-6.
Describes murder as impeding the process of social
change in America, and points out the gravity of the
Kennedy assassination.

2756 Gardiner, A. H. The Attitude of ancient Egyptians to death
and the dead. Cambridge, England: Cambridge University Press, 1935.

2757 Gardner, M. J., and M. D. Crawford. "Patterns of mortality in middle and early old age in the country boroughs
of England and Wales," British Journal of Preventive Sociological Medicine, 23 (1969), 133-40.
Discusses "patterns of mortality in 61 county
boroughs having over 80,000 total population in 1961."

2758 Gardner, R., and K. G. Heider. Gardens of war: life and
death in the New Guinea stone age. N.Y.: Random
House, 1968.
A photographic study and record of a primitive tribe
in New Guinea. The pictures arranged in story fashion
describe the tribe's way of life, especially their practice of ritual warfare.

2759 Garma, A. "Within the realm of the death instinct," International Journal of Psychoanalysis, 52 (1971), 145-54.

2760 Gartley, W., and M. Bernasconi. "The Concept of death in
children," Journal of Psychology, 110 (1967), 71-83.
Children can accept death matter of factly. Their
fear of death is acquired by observing adult behavior.
Ages ranged from five to 14.

2761 Gay, M. J., et al. "The Late effects of loss of parents in
childhood," British Journal of Psychiatry, 113 (July
1967), 753-59.

2762 Geis, G., and R. Fulton. "Death and social values," International Journal of Social Research, 3 (1962), 7-14.
Comments on how the discussion of death has become an important subject for the social scientist in his
investigations.

2763 Gerard, M. C., and S. Hemery. "La Mortalité infantile en
France suivant le milieu social," Economie et Statistique,
48 (Sept. 1973), 38-41.

2764 Gerber, I. "Bereavement and the acceptance of professional
service," Community Mental Health Journal, 5 (1969),
487-96.

2765 Gertler, R.; E. Ferneau; and A. Raynes. "Attitudes toward
death and dying on a drug addiction unit," International
Journal of the Addictions, 8 (1973), 265-72.
"Administered a 'social concerns subscale' concerning attitudes toward death and dying to twenty-one 18-36
year old heroin addicts, 20 staff members on a drug
detoxification unit and 20 psychiatric patients matched

for age.... Interpretations of these attitudes and implications for treatment of drug addicts are discussed"
(Abstract).

2766 Gessain, R. "La Vie et la mort chez les Eskimos," Ethno-
Psychologie Revue de Psychologie des Peuples, 27
(March 1972), 125-36.

2767 Giardini, G. L., and R. G. Farrow. "The Paroling of
capital offenders," Annals of the American Academy of
Political and Social Science, 284 (1952), 85-94.

2768 Gibbs, J. P. "Marital status and suicide in the United
States," American Journal of Sociology, 74 (March 1969),
521-33.

2769 _____. Suicide. N. Y.: Harper and Row, 1968.

2770 _____. "Suicide," in Contemporary Social Problems,
edited by R. K. Merten and R. A. Nisbet. N. Y.:
Harcourt, Brace and World, 1961. pp. 260.

2771 _____, and W. T. Martin. Status integration and suicide.
Eugene: University of Oregon Press, 1964.
A good case from a sociological perspective which
indicates that the suicide rate varies inversely with the
degree of status integration in a society.

2772 Giddens, A. "Suicide, attempted suicide, and the suicidal
threat," Man, 64 (1964), 115-6.
Describes several neglected aspects of suicide.
Suggests that suicide sometimes functions to facilitate
social order.

2773 Gifford, S. "Death and forever: some fears of war and
peace," Atlantic Monthly, 209 (March 1962), 88-92.

2774 _____. "Freud's theories of unconscious immortality
and the death instinct: a reconsideration in the light of
recent history and modern biology," Journal of Thanatology, 1 (March-April 1971), 109.

2774a Gilder, G. "The Death of a single man," in Naked Nomads;
unmarried men in America. N. Y.: Quadrangle/New
York Times Book Co., 1974. pp. 22-28.
Story of P. J.'s death, and how "suicide is in-
creasingly the way young men die...."

2775 Gillibert, J. "Devil--mort," Revue Française de Psychanalyse, 31 (1967), 143-71.

2776 Gillin, J. L. "Murder as a sociological phenomenon,"
Annals of the American Academy of Political and Social

Science, 284 (1952), 20-5.

2777 Glaister, J. "Phantasies of the dying," Lancet, 2 (Aug. 1921), 315-7.

2778 Glaser, B. G. "Disclosure of terminal illness," Journal of Health and Human Behavior, 7 (1966), 83-9.
      Discusses various stages of terminal illness, the dying patient, and their relationships within the hospital. Offers insights about attitudes toward death.

2779 _____. "The Social loss of aged dying patients," Gerontologist, 6 (June 1966), 77-80.

2780 _____. "The Social loss of dying patients," American Journal of Nursing, 63 (1964), 119-21.
      Authors state that recognition of social loss may help a nurse avoid inequitable attention to different types of dying patients.

2781 _____. "Temporal aspects of dying as a non-scheduled status passage," American Journal of Sociology, 71 (1965), 48-59.

2782 _____. Time for dying. Chicago: Aldine, 1968.
      Traces all that surrounds a patient in a hospital once it is determined he is going to die. Included is an examination of the organizational structure, the way the staff reacts, and the way the patient is treated.

2783 _____, and A. L. Strauss. "Awareness contexts and social interaction," American Sociological Review, 29 (Oct. 1964), 669-79.

2784 Gluckman, M. "Mortuary customs and the belief in survival after death among the South-eastern Bantu," Bantu Studies, 11 (1937), 117-36.

2785 Goffman, E. Asylums. N.Y.: Doubleday, 1961.

2786 _____. Suicide motives and categorization of the living and the dead in the U.S. N.Y.: Mental Health Research Unit, n.d.

2787 Gold, M. "Suicide, homicide and the socialization of aggression," American Journal of Sociology, 63 (1958), 651-66.
      Discusses the "relationship between certain psychological and sociological theories ... [related] to homicide and suicide as an expression of aggression."

2788 Goldberg, S. B. "Family tasks and reactions in the crisis of death," Social Casework, 54 (July 1973), 398-405.

2789 Goldburgh, S.; C. Rotman; and J. Ondrach. "Attitudes of
       college students toward personal death," Adolescence, 2
       (1967), 212-29.

2790 Goldfarb, A. I. "Death and dying: attitudes of patients and
       doctor," Group for the Advancement of Psychiatry,
       (Symposium no. 11), 5 (1965), 591-606.

2791 Golding, M. P., and N. H. Golding. "Ethical and value is-
       sues in population limitation and distribution in the United
       States," Vanderbilt Law Review, 24 (April 1971), 495-
       523.

2792 Goldman, P. The Death and life of Malcolm X. N. Y.:
       Harper and Row, 1973.
         Centers mainly on Malcolm X's progressive estrange-
         ment from the Black Muslims, his attempts to start a
         new politics of blackness, his assassination and the re-
         sulting investigation and murder trial.

2793 Goldschmidt, W. "Freud, Durkheim and death among the
       Sebei," Omega, 3 (Aug. 1972), 227-31.
         Part of the Anthropological Studies of Death Series.

2794 Goody, J. "Death and social control among the Lo Dagaa,"
       Man, 59 (1959), 134-38.

2795 _____. "Death and the interpretation of culture: a biblio-
       graphic overview," American Quarterly, 26 (Dec. 1974),
       448-55.

2796 Gordon, D. C. Overcoming the fear of death. N. Y.: Mac-
       millan, 1970.
         Listed are many fears of death and the ways man
         has fought them over centuries. Fear of losing time,
         fear of decay, fear of losing self, and the fear of ces-
         sation of thought are all explored.

2797 Gordon, R. "The Death instinct and its relation to the self,"
       Journal of Analytical Psychology, 6 (July 1961), 119-35.
         Explores Freud's death instinct and presents case
         materials for evaluations.

2798 Gorer, G. Death, grief and mourning: a study of contem-
       porary society. N. Y.: Doubleday, 1965.
         A study of some 300 English adults which shows
         that those who do not accept man's mortality suffer sup-
         pressed guilt feelings and mental distress. Also dis-
         covered was the fact that those individuals who had a
         way of mourning were much better adjusted and able to
         go on than those who didn't. Appendices include related
         items.

2799 Gossage, H. L. "Tell me doctor, will I be active right up
      to the last?" Atlantic Monthly, 224 (Sept. 1969), 55-7.
      Discusses the denial of death as an attitude in young
      people and the elderly.

2800 Gough, E. K. "Cults of the dead among the Nayers, " Jour-
      nal of American Folklore, 71 (1958), 446-78.
      "A sociological and psychological analysis of the
      Nayar cults of the dead. Relates the role-structure and
      social functions of the cults to those of legal and eco-
      nomic institutions. "

2801 Goulait, R. Death cell. N. Y.: Beagle Books, 1971.

2801a _____. If dying was all. N. Y.: Ace Books, 1971.

2802 Gould, D. "Suicide scare, " New Statesman, 83 (Oct. 1971),
      430-40.

2803 Gould, R. E. "Suicide problems in children and adolescents, "
      American Journal of Psychotherapy, 19 (April 1965), 228-
      46.
      Presents observations regarding psychodynamic
      mechanisms and social influences as causes of suicide.

2804 Gove, W. R. "Sex, marital status and mortality, " American
      Journal of Sociology, 79 (1973), 45-67.

2805 Graber, G. H. Zeugung, Geburt und Tod: Werden und
      vergehen im Mythus und in der Vorstellung des Kindes.
      Zurich: Rasher, 1934.

2806 Green, J. C. "The Days of the dead in Oaxada, Mexico:
      an historical inquiry, " Omega, 3 (Aug. 1972), 245-61.
      Present-day customs in the city arise directly from
      the historical tradition.

2807 Green, J. S. "What constitutes legal death?" Journal of
      Indiana Medical Association, 61 (Aug. 1968), 1120-24.
      Attempts to draw from medical knowledge and actual
      legal cases a suitable guideline for legally declaring
      death.

2808 Green, M. , and A. J. Solnit. "Reactions to the threatened
      loss of a child: a vulnerable child syndrome, " Pedi-
      atrics, 34 (July 1964), 58-66.
      Presents the hypothesis that parental reactions to
      acute threatening illness in a child may have long-term
      psychological effects on both parent and child.

2809 Greenberg, B. S. , and E. B. Parker. The Kennedy assas-
      sination and the American public: social communication
      in crisis. Stanford, Calif.: Stanford University Press,

1965.
Deals with the American public's reaction to the assassination and how that reaction was shaped by information through society.

2810   Greenberg, I. M. "Death and dying: attitudes of patient and doctor, 4. Studies on attitudes toward death," Group for the Advancement of Psychiatry, (Symposium no. 11), 5 (1965), 623-31.
Presents the existentialist and psychoanalytic answer to the problems of death. Focuses on major concepts of each and their application to death and dying.

2811   Greenberg, J., and J. Himmelstein. "Varieties of attack on the death penalty," Crime and Delinquency, 15 (Jan. 1969), 112-20.
Examines the effects that capital punishment has had on the legal system and the arguments for and against it.

2812   Greenberger, E. "Fantasies of women confronting death," Journal of Consulting Psychology, 29 (1965), 252-60.
Investigates the significance of death for women who described stories and were then given the Thematic Apperception Test.

2813   _____. "Flirting with death: fantasies of a critically ill woman," Journal of Projective Technology, 30 (1966), 197-204.
"The TAT stories of a woman hospitalized for cancer are analyzed with particular attention to material which looks at death as a lover dating back to antiquity, and continues to live in the unconscious."

2814   Greene, W. A.; S. Goldstein; and A. J. Moss. "Psychosocial aspects of sudden death: a preliminary report," Archives of Internal Medicine, 129 (May 1972), 725-31.

2815   Greenhouse, H. B. "The Death-portents of ordinary people," in Premonitions: a leap into the future. N.Y.: Bernard Geis Associates, 1971. pp. 154-67.

2816   Greer, I. M. "Grief must be faced," Christian Century, 62 (1945), 269-71.
States "that grief can be denied, distorted, and even postponed. Quite often it is expressed through imaginary symptoms and physical disease."

2817   Gregory, I. "Studies of parental deprivation in psychiatric patients," American Journal of Psychiatry, 115 (1958), 432-42.
Studies psychological effects that the death of a parent or prolonged absence from home has on a child.

2818 Griessmair, E. Das Motiv der Mors Immatura in den
      griechischen metrischen Grabenschriften. Innsbruck:
      Wagner, 1966.

2819 Grinberg, L. "Two kinds of guilt--their relationship with
      normal and pathological aspects of mourning, " Interna-
      tional Journal of Psychoanalysis, 45 (April-July, 1964),
      366-71.

2820 Grinberg, R. "Aggression in the analysis of children, "
      Revista de Psicoanalisis, 29 (1972), 35-41.
          Aggression is discussed in relationship to the fear
      of one's own death, and how it is used as a defense.

2821 Grollman, E. A. The Child and death. Boston: Beacon,
      1967.

2822 Grosse, G., et al. The Threat of impending disaster. Cam-
      bridge, Mass.: MIT Press, 1964.

2823 Grossman, K. L. "Maternal age and parental loss, " British
      Journal of Psychiatry, 114 (Feb. 1968), 242-3.

2824 Grotjahn, M. "About the representation of death in the art
      of antiquity and in the unconscious of modern man, " in
      Psychoanalysis and Culture, rev. ed., edited by G. B.
      Wilbur, and W. Muensterberger. N.Y.: International
      Universities Press, 1965. pp. 410-25.

2825 _____. "Ego identity and the fear of death and dying, "
      Hillside Hospital Journal, 9 (July 1960), 147-55.

2826 Group for the Advancement of Psychiatry. "The Right to
      die: decision and decision makers, " GAP Report, 8
      (Nov. 1973), 667-751.
          The proceedings by GAP of a symposium concerned
      with the ethical, psychological, and legal aspects of dy-
      ing. Some clinical examples of the loneliness of pa-
      tients are reported.

2827 Gruhle, H. W. Selbstmord. Leipzig: Theime, 1940.

2828 Grünhut, M. "Murder and the death penalty in England, "
      Annals of the American Academy of Political and Social
      Science, 284 (1952), 158-66.
          Discusses the relationship of murder and the death
      penalty in England. Author states "there is no indica-
      tion of a logical connection between the two phenomena. "

2829 Guillot, E. E. "Abolition and restoration of the death penalty
      in Missouri, " Annals of the American Academy of Po-
      litical and Social Science, 284 (1952), 105-9.

2830 Gundolf, H. Totenkult und Jenseitsglaube. Mödding: St.
      Gabriel-Verlag, 1967.

2831 Gunther, M. "Why children commit suicide, " Saturday
      Evening Post, 240 (June 17, 1967), 86-9.

2832 Gutheil, T. G. "A Study of the image of death, " Harvard
      Medical Alumni Bulletin, 41 (winter 1967), 12-17.

2833 Gutmann, D. "The Premature gerontocracy: themes of
      aging and death in the youth culture, " in Death in
      American Experience, edited by A. Mack. N. Y.:
      Schocken Press, 1973. pp. 50-82.
          Partial contents: Youthful fixation on death; The
      normal psychology of aging; A developmental theory of
      adulthood and old age; Pre-senile youth: the counter-
      culture.

2834 Guttmacher, M. S. The Mind of the murderer. N. Y.:
      Farrar, Straus and Cudahy, 1960.
          Divided into three sections. The first looks, as
      would a clinician, at criminals in jail and in court soon
      after the crimes. The second takes a look at expert
      psychiatric testimony and its value. The final section
      deals with medical ethics regarding a doctor's right to
      keep files secret.

2835 Haas, M. "Toward the study of biopolitics: a cross-sec-
      tional analysis of mortality rates, " Behavioral Science,
      14 (1969), 257-80.
          Biopolitics is an important field of inquiry and can
      test the relationship between political and medical vari-
      ables in social systems. Examples of relationships be-
      tween domestic and foreign violence are discussed.

2836 Habenstein, R. W. "The Social organization of death, " in
      The International Encyclopedia of the Social Sciences,
      edited by David L. Sills. N. Y.: Macmillan--Free
      Press, 1968. Vol. 4. pp. 26-8.
          Describes how a social group or society must react
      to death. Considers death as a passage instead of an
      end.

2837 _____ . "Sociology of occupations: the case of the Ameri-
      can Funeral Director, " in Human Behavior and Social
      Processes, edited by R. A. Marshall. Boston: Hough-
      ton, Mifflin, 1962. pp. 225-46.

2838 Haberman, P. W. , and M. M. Baden. "Alcoholism and vi-
      olent death, " Quarterly Journal of Studies on Alcohol,
      35 (March 1974), 221-31.

2839 Hackett, T. P. , and A. D. Weisman. "Reactions to the imminence of death," in The Threat of Impending Disaster, edited by G. Grosse, H. Wechsler, and M. Greenblatt. Cambridge: MIT Press, 1964. pp. 300-11.

2840 _____. "The Treatment of the dying," Current Psychiatric Therapies, 2 (1962), 121-6.
Description of implications involved when telling a patient of his impending death.

2841 Hadwen, W. R. Premature burial. London: Swan Sonnenschein, 1905.

2842 Hahn, H. "Evolution in the graveyard," Midwest Quarterly, 10 (April 1969), 275-90.

2843 Haider, I. "Attitudes toward death of psychiatric patients," International Journal of Neuropsychiatry, 3 (1967), 10-14.
Reports on the results of a direct questionnaire given to 50 psychiatric patients over 50 years of age concerning their attitudes toward death.

2844 Hakim, A. "H U 133; how students feel about death," Sign, 52 (April 1973), 14-6.

2845 Halbwacks, M. Les Causes du suicide. Paris: Alcan, 1930.

2846 Hall, G. S. "Attitudes toward life and death in poetry," Psychoanalytic Review, 52 (spring 1965), 67-83.
Author states that "poetry is a mirror in which man sees himself reflected. How do poets regard death? What are their conceptions of it? What are their attitudes about life?"

2847 _____. "Thanatophobia and immortality," American Journal of Psychology, 26 (1915), 550-613.
Discusses the development of the fear of death in children and offers numerous examples about how the impressions of death take place.

2848 Hall, R. Abortion in a changing world. N.Y.: Columbia University Press, 1970.

2849 _____. A doctor's guide to having an abortion. N.Y.: New American Library, 1971.

2850 Hallowell, A. I. "Fear and anxiety as cultural and individual variables in a primitive society," Journal of Social Psychology, 9 (1938), 25-47.
Reports on the Berens River Indians' fear of cannibals and their communal efforts to kill those suspected of it.

2851 Halpern, S. "Thanatopsis: life's last stand," American

Imago, 21 (fall 1964), 23-36.
Discusses "Freud's theory of instincts, his view
that all life yearns to return to inorganic from which it
had sprung. " His approach to the question of immortality is also explored.

2852 Hamill, P. "The Mass murders, " Good Housekeeping (spring
1967), 162-3.

2853 Hamovitch, M. B. "Research interviewing in sensitive
areas I: research interviewing in terminal illness, "
Journal of Social Work, 8 (April 1963), 4-9.

2854 Handal, P. J. "The Relationship between subjective life expectancy, death anxiety, and general anxiety, " Journal of
Clinical Psychology, 25 (1969), 39-42.

2855 Harbison, J. "New patterns for American funerals, " Presbyterian Life (Aug. 1, 1964), 8.

2856 Harden-Hickey, J. A. Euthanasia; the aesthetics of suicide.
N. Y.: Truth Seeker Company, 1894.

2857 Harder, P. "Attitudes toward death of psychiatric patients, "
International Journal of Neuropsychiatry, 3 (Feb. 1967),
10-14.

2858 Hardgrove, C. , and L. H. Warrick. "How shall we tell the
children?" American Journal of Nursing, 74 (March
1974), 448-50.

2859 Hardt, D. V. "Development of an investigatory instrument to
measure attitudes toward death, " Journal of School
Health, 45 (Feb. 1975), 96-9.

2860 Hardwick, E. "Suicide and women, " Mademoiselle, 76 (Dec
1962), 158-9.

2861 Harmer, R. M. "Funerals, fantasy, and flight, " Omega, 2
(Aug. 1971), 127-35.
Describes in case studies examples of economic ex-
ploitation and the quality of modern funeral service. The
role and function of memorial societies is explored.

2862 _____. The High cost of dying. N. Y.: Crowell-Collier,
1963.

2863 Harmon, L. "Abortion, death and the sanctity of life, "
Social Science and Medicine, 5 (1971), 211-18.

2864 Harnik, J. "One component of the fear of death in early infancy, " International Journal of Psychoanalysis, 11 (1930),
485-91.

2865 Harrington, L. "Solemn undertaking," New Statesman, 84 (Dec. 22, 1972), 940-1.

2866 Harris, K. A. "The Political meaning of death: an existential overview," Omega, 2 (Nov. 1971), 227-40.

2867 Harrison, S. I., et al. "Children's reactions to bereavement --adult confusions and misperceptions," Archives of General Psychiatry, 17 (March 1967), 593-7.
Report which records the results of a study of the responses of children to the Kennedy assassination.

2868 Havens, M. C.; C. Leiden; and K. M. Schmitt. The Politics of assassination. N. J.: Prentice-Hall, 1970.
Ten case studies describe assassinations of important political leaders and the circumstances of each. Includes Patrice Lumumba, Martin Luther King, Huey Long, and others.

2869 Havighurst, R., Jr. "Extent and significance of suicide among American Indians today," Mental Hygiene (April 1971), 174-7.
Reports that the differences between Indian and white male suicide rates is only partly explained by their differences in socioeconomic status.

2870 Hayano, D. M. "Sorcery death, proximity, and the perception of out-groups: the Tawna Awa of New Guinea," Ethnology, 12 (April 1973), 173-91.

2871 Heckel, R. V. "The Day the President was assassinated: patient's reaction in one mental hospital," Mental Hospitals, 15 (1964), 48.
Records the reactions of patients in a mental hospital to the assassination of President Kennedy. Most patients manifested intensification of their defense reaction patterns.

2872 Heilbrunn, G. "The Basic fear," Journal of the American Psychoanalytic Association, 3 (1959), 447-66.

2873 Heinmann, P. "Notes on the theory of life and death instincts; development of psychoanalysis." N. Y.: International Universities Press, 1952.

2874 "Help for the family before and after a death," Patient Care Magazine, 4 (May 31, 1970).

2875 Hembright, T. Z. "Comparison of information on death certificates and matching 1960 census records: age, marital status, race, nativity and country of origin," Demography, 6 (1969), 413-23.

2876 Hendal, P. J. "The Relationship between subjective life expectancy, death anxiety and general anxiety," Journal of Clinical Psychology, 25 (1969), 39-42.

2877 Henderson, J. L. Wisdom of the serpent: the myths of death, rebirth and resurrection. N. Y.: George Braziller, 1963.
The first half of this book is devoted to a Jungian analysis of the meanings and variations of death as viewed as the essential conditions for growth and life in myth and contemporary experience. The second half consists of selected myths and illustrations.

2878 Hendin, H. Black suicide. N. Y.: Basic Books, 1965.
Investigates the serious problem of black suicide, why it occurs, and which blacks are most likely to be victims. Includes figures and graphs along with psychological test results and other illustrations.

2879 _____. "The Psychodynamics of suicide," Journal of Nervous Mental Disorders, 136 (1963), 236-44.
The discussion is based on different attitudes toward death and the afterlife.

2880 _____. "Suicide," Psychiatric Quarterly, 30 (1956), 267-82.
Deals with some of the dynamic constellations seen in suicide and with some of the emotional motivational factors involved. Study was done at the Bellevue Hospital, New York City, and included 100 cases.

2881 _____. Suicide and Scandinavia. N. Y.: Grune and Stratton, 1964.

2882 _____. "Suicide in Denmark," Psychiatric Quarterly, 34 (1960), 443-60.
States that suicide in Denmark is higher than in most European countries. "The Danish homicide rate is low while the homicide rate in the U. S. is 10 times higher than in Denmark."

2883 _____. "Suicide in Sweden," Psychiatric Quarterly, 35 (1962), 1-28.

2884 Henry, F., and J. F. Short. Suicide and homicide. N. Y.: Free Press, 1954.
Examines the relationships between suicide and homicide as dependent variables and other social phenomena as independent variables. Discusses points of agreement among the theories of sociologists, anthropologists, and psychologists concerning these relationships.

2885 "Her name will be remembered," Time, 64 (Nov. 1, 1954), 36.

Story of an Indian widow and how she killed herself
at her husband's funeral. Analysis of "suttee" and its
cultural implications.

2886 Herbert, B., Jr.   "Significance of maternal bereavement before age of eight in psychiatric patients," Archives of
Neurology and Psychiatry, 62 (1949), 630-37.

2887 Herbert, C.   The Roots of evil.   Boston: Little Brown,
1963.
The author has made an attempt to reduce all the
diverse material of criminology down to one book. The
main thesis is that cruel punishments make people
cruel. While presenting a history of crime and punishments, he also makes a case against capital (and cor-
poral) punishment.

2888 Hertz, R.   Mélanges de sociologie réligieuse et folklore,
avec une preface d'Alice Robert Hertz. Paris: F. Alcan,
1928.

2889 Herzog, A.   "A Clinical study of parental response to
adolescent death by suicide with recommendations for
approaching the survivors," in Proceedings of the Fourth
International Conference for Suicide Prevention, edited by
N. L. Farberow. Albany, N.Y.: Delmar, 1968.

2890 _____.   "Suicide can't be eliminated," New York Times
Magazine (March 20, 1966), 32-3.
Statistically shows that the typical suicide is committed by an older white male, probably from a lower
income group, suffering from depression.

2891 Herzog, E.   Psyche and death.   N.Y.: Putnam, 1967.

2892 Heuvelmans, B.   La Suppression de la mort.   Paris:
L'Arche, 1951.

2893 Heywood, R.   "Attitudes to death in the light of dreams and
other 'out-of-the body' experiences," in Man's Concern
with Death, edited by Arnold Toynbee. N.Y.: McGraw-
Hill, 1969. pp. 185-218.

2894 Hickerson, H.   "The Feast of the dead among the seventeenth
century Algonkians of the upper Great Lakes," American
Anthropologist, 62 (1960), 81-107.
"The Feast of the Dead" was mentioned by the
Jesuit missionary, Lalemant, in 1641. The French
called it tête des morts. It was employed as a means
to perpetuate alliances.

2895 High, D. M.   "Death: its conceptual elusiveness," Sound-
ings, 55 (winter 1972), 438-58.

2896 Hilgard, J., and M. F. Newman. "Strength of adult ego
following childhood bereavement," American Journal of
Orthopsychiatry, 30 (1960), 788-98.

2897 Hill, G. H. "Suicide and insanity," Proceedings of the
American Medical and Psychological Association (1904),
274-83.
"Determines to what extent persons who commit
suicide are sane or insane, and concludes that they are
neither sane nor insane."

2898 Hill, O. W. "The Association of childhood bereavement with
suicidal attempt in depressive illness," British Journal
of Psychiatry, 115 (1969), 301-4.
Discussion of the relationship of early parent death
and suicide. Brings out the attitudes of children toward
death.

2899 _____, and J. S. Price. "Childhood bereavement and
adult depression," British Journal of Psychiatry, 113
(1967), 743-51.
This study explores the incidence of childhood bereavement in 1483 depressed and 1059 non-depressed
psychiatric inpatients.

2900 Hill, R. "Bereavement: a crisis of family dismemberment,"
in The Family: a dynamic interpretation. Hinsdale,
Ill.: Dryden, 1951. pp. 470-99.

2901 Hillman, J. Suicide and the soul. N.Y.: Harper and Row,
1965.
Presents a theory of suicide with a Jungian point of
view.

2902 Hippler, A. E. "Fusion and frustration," American Anthropologist, 71 (1969), 1074-87.
States that sociological explanations of suicide are
not adequate in explaining various forms of suicide.

2903 Hitschmann, E. "Todesangst durch Tötungsdrang--ein
neurotischer Mechanismus," Zeitschrift für Kinderpsychiatrie, 3 (1936), 165-9.

2904 Hobart, C. W. "The Meaning of death," Journal of Existential Psychiatry, 4 (1964), 219-224.
Author discusses two primary sources about the
meaning of death. First, the arbitrary norms of culture; and second, the consequences of individual experience with death.

2905 Hocart, A. M. "Death customs," in Encyclopedia of the
Social Sciences. N.Y.: Macmillan, 1931. Vol. 5.
pp. 21-27.

2906 Hofer, G. "Death in the primitive works--on the question of
       death suggestion in Melanesia," Confina Psychiatrica,
       9 (1966), 93-114.

2907 Hoffman, F. H., and M. W. Brody. "The Symptom: fear
       of death," Psychoanalytic Review, 44 (1957), 433-38.

2908 Hoffman, F. L. Pauper burials and the interment of the
       dead in large cities. Newark, N. J.: Prudential Press,
       1919.

2909 Hogan, R. A. "Adolescent views of death," Adolescence, 5
       (spring 1970), 55-66.

2910 Holland, R. J. "Suicide as a social problem: some reflec-
       tions on Durkheim," Ratio, 12 (Dec. 1970), 116-24.

2911 Hollander, P. "Social values in education, religion, and
       death," in Soviet and American Society; a comparison.
       N. Y.: Oxford University Press, 1973. pp. 156-201.
       Death and value systems are compared in the U. S.
       and the Soviet Union.

2912 Holt, W. C. "Death by suggestion," Canadian Psychiatric
       Association Journal, 14 (1969), 81-2.

2913 Hooper, T., and B. Spilka. "Some meanings and correlates
       of future time and death among college students," Omega,
       1 (Feb. 1970), 49-56.
       This study was "based upon the assumption that one's
       present beliefs and behaviors are a function of perspec-
       tives on time and death...."

2914 Hooper, W. T. "Personal values and meanings of future time
       and death among college students." Ph. D. dissertation,
       University of Denver, 1962.

2915 Hopkins, E. "The Fountain of youth," Journal of American
       Oriental Society, 26 (1905), 1-67.

2916 Hopkinson, G., and G. Reed. "Bereavement in childhood and
       depressive psychosis," British Journal of Psychiatry,
       112 (1966), 459-63.
       Article discusses patients suffering from depressive
       psychosis and an unusually high incidence of parental
       loss.

2917 Horgan, J. J. "Death investigations," in Criminal Investiga-
       tion. N. Y.: McGraw-Hill, 1974. pp. 290-321.
       A history of and description of criminal investiga-
       tions of death. The chapter was originally designed as
       a text for law officers and illustrates various kinds of
       wounds made by weapons, the significance of bloodstains,

and the looks of death from asphyxia.

2918 Horn, Y. "The Children who want to die, " PTA Magazine,
       63 (Nov. 1973), 18-21.
       "Children who want to die easily want to live, but
       not in the way they have been living.... [C]hildren who
       want to die can be saved by those who are willing to
       look, listen, and love. "

2919 Howard, A., and R. A. Scott. "Cultural values and attitudes
       toward death, " Journal of Existentialism, 6 (1965-66),
       161-74.
       Discusses the various cultural values that affect
       American attitudes toward death. American patterns
       are contrasted with those of Polynesians.

2920 "How well prepared are you for death in the young?" Patient
       Care Magazine (May 31, 1970).

2921 Howard, J. D. The Detection of secret homicide. A study
       of sudden and unexplained deaths. N. Y.: Macmillan,
       1960. Vol. 15.

2922 Hsu, F. L. Under the ancestor's shadow. N. Y.: Colum-
       bia University Press, 1948.
       Presentation of a small town in southwest China.
       Details, symbols, and behavior are explained. The cul-
       ture and personality of the people is put forth in Western
       ideas.

2923 Huber, P. B. "Death and society among the Anggor of New
       Guinea, " Omega, 3 (Aug. 1972), 233-43.
       Deals with the "relationship between Anggor repre-
       sentations of the natural phenomenon of death and repre-
       sentations of the autonomous village..." (Abstract).

2924 Hunt, E. P. "Comparative infant mortality, " Children, 14
       (Jan. 1967), 39.

2925 Hunter, R. C. A. "On experience of nearly dying, " Ameri-
       can Journal of Psychiatry, 124 (1967-1968), 84-8.
       Concerned with the study of a patient with a hys-
       terical personality that encountered a painless threat to
       life.

2926 Hutschnecker, A. A. "Personality factors in dying patients, "
       in The Meaning of Death, edited by H. Feifel. N. Y.:
       McGraw-Hill, 1959. pp. 237-250.
       An investigation into the behavior of a dying person
       is compared with his earlier normal behavior. Dif-
       ferent kinds of behavior associated with different fatal
       illnesses are described.

2927 Iakovidis, E. "Mycenaean mourning customs," American
Journal of Archaeology, 70 (Jan. 1966), 43-50.

2928 Illich, I. "The Political uses of natural death," Hastings
Center Studies, 2 (Jan. 1974), 18-20.

2929 Inoguchi, H., et al. The Divine wind: Japan's Kamikaze
force in World War II. N. Y.: U. S. Naval Institute,
1958.
A history by two surviving pilots of the ten-month
life of the Japanese Kamikaze corps. Included are
strategic and tactical justifications for its use and the
arguments against it.

2930 International Order of the Golden Rule. How to explain death
to a child, by Dr. J. Rosenblum. International Order of
the Golden Rule, 1963. (On title page: "A Child Psychologist Talks to Parents on a Difficult Subject.")
This pamphlet "presents a practical and psychologically sound approach to the commonplace problem of
explaining the nature of death to children of all ages."

2931 Irion, P. E. The Funeral and the mourners. Nashville,
Tenn.: Abingdon Press, 1954.
A study designed to show how genuine strength and
readjustment can be gained by a funeral service.
Christian experience and pastoral psychology is drawn
upon to make a funeral a "helpful, therapeutic experience to the mourners."

2932 _____. The Funeral: vestige or value? Nashville, Tenn.:
Abingdon Press, 1966.
Attempts to find and describe those functions of a
funeral which are valuable and then offers a basis for
investigation, questioning, criticism, and reconstruction.
The study is based on the author's analysis of question-
naires he had sent to 160 clergymen who had conducted
funerals.

2933 _____. "In the midst of life ... death," Pastoral Psychology, 14 (June 1963), 7-14.
Author comments on the death-denying attitudes of
American society, and its heavy stress on the value of
youthful vigor.

2934 Irle, G. "Attitudes towards death in patients following suicide attempts," Nervenarzt, 39 (June 1968), 255-60.

2935 Isham, L. S. Survey of state laws governing the disposal
of the dead and regulating those who work with the
dead: a critical look at the laws. Hanover, N. H.:
Billings Lee, 1966.

2936 Israel, L. , and R. Cahn. "Un Suicide d'adolescent, "
        Cahiers Psychiatrie, 12 (1957), 84-95.

2937 Issacs, N. The Growth of understanding in the young child.
        London: Educational Supply Assoc. , 1961.

2938 Izikowitz, K. G. "The Gotr ceremony of the Boro Gadaba, "
        in Culture in History, edited by S. Diamond. N. Y.:
        Columbia University Press, 1960. pp. 509-30.

2939 Jachmann, F. Seelen--und Totenvorstellungen bei drei
        Bevolkerungruppen in Neuguinea. Weisbaden: F. Steiner,
        1969.

2940 Jackson, D. D. "Suicide, " Scientific American, 191 (1954),
        88-96.
        Outlines causes of suicide and suggests ways that it
        might be prevented.

2941 Jackson, E. N. "Grief and religion, " in The Meaning of
        Death, edited by H. Feifel. N. Y.: McGraw-Hill, 1959.
        pp. 218-33.
        Presents the elements necessary to create a co-
        herent psychology or philosophy of death and dying, in-
        cluding reality maintenance, healthful expression of feel-
        ings, and reinvestment of emotional capital.

2942 _____. "The Law and the right to grieve, " International
        Journal of Law and Science, 7 (Jan. -March, 1970), 1-10.

2943 _____. Telling a child about death. N. Y.: Channel
        Press, 1965.

2944 _____. Understanding grief. Nashville, Tenn.: Abingdon
        Press, 1957.

2945 _____. You and your grief. N. Y.: Channel Press, 1961.

2946 Jackson, N. A. A Child's preoccupation with death. Pitts-
        burgh: University of Pittsburgh, 1965.

2947 Jacobs, J. Adolescent suicide. N. Y.: Wiley-Interscience,
        1971.

2948 Jacobson, E. "Introjection in mourning, " International Jour-
        nal of Psychiatry, 3 (May 1967), 433-5.

2949 Jacobson, N. O. Life without death. N. Y.: Dell, 1973.
        Surveys the work of parapsychology, and describes
        its relationship to the question of life after death.

2950/1 Jacques, E. "Death and the mid-life crisis, " International
        Journal of Psychoanalysis, 46 (1965), 506-12.

Discusses the mid-life crisis in the mid-thirties, and describes the death rate in this period, especially among creative artists.

2952 Jaehner, D. "Uber Einstellung des Kleinkindes zum Tod, " Zeitschrift für Angewandte Psychologie, 45-46 (1933-1934), 262-88.

2953 Jaffa, B. "Attempt at the psychological analysis of the fear of death, " Confina Psychiatrica, 11 (1968), 154-76.

2954 Jarast, S. G. "El duelo en relación con el aprendizaje, " Revista de Psicoanalisis, 15 (Jan.-June, 1958), 31-5.

2955 Jaszi, O. "The Stream of political murder, " American Journal of Economics and Sociology, 3 (1943-1944), 335-55.
Discusses different types of political murder with that of tyrannicide.

2956 Jeffreys, M. D. W. "Samsonic suicides or suicides of revenge among Africans, " African Studies, 11 (1952), 118-22.

2957 Jelliffe, S. E. "The Death instinct in somatic and psycho-pathology, " Psychoanalytic Review, 20 (April 1933), 121-31.

2958 _____. "Review of the article 'Thanatophobia and Im-mortality' by G. Stanley Hall, " Journal of Nervous and Mental Disease, 45 (1917), 272-7.

2959 Jetter, L. E. "Some emotional aspects of prolonged illness in children, " Survey, 84 (May 1948), 165.

2960 Jeu, B. "Toute-puissance et immortalité ou les arrière-pensées du sport, " Ethno-Psychologie; Revue de Psy-chologie Peuples, 27 (Mars 1972), 15-37.

2961 Jha, M. "Death rites among Maithil Brahmans, " Man in India, 46 (1966), 241-7.

2962 Jokl, E. "Exercise and cardiac death, " Journal of the Ameri-can Medical Association, 218 (Dec. 1971), 1707.

2963 Jones, B. Design for death. Indianapolis: Bobbs-Merrill, 1967.
Deals with a cross-cultural approach to various facets of death.

2964 Jones, E. "On dying together, " in Essays in Applied Psycho-analysis. London: Hogarth, 1951. pp. 9-15.

2965 _____. "The Psychology of religion," British Journal of
Medical Psychology, 6 (1926), 264-69.
      Author lists several points concerning emotional
      problems surrounding death. The "dread of death is
      the expression of repressed death wishes against loved
      objects." He cites the themes of death and castration
      which are associated.

2966 _____. "An Unusual case of dying together," in Essays
in Applied Psychoanalysis. London: Hogarth Press,
1951.

2967 _____, and D. Laksowitz. "A Study of adolescent addicts
who die of an overdose: a sign approach," Psychiatric
Digest, 25 (1964), 21-30.

2968 Jordahl, E. K. Helping children understand death. Min-
      neapolis: University of Minnesota Agricultural Extension
      Service, 1968.

2968a _____. Planning and paying for funerals. Minneapolis:
University of Minnesota Agricultural Extension Service,
1969.

2969 Jores, A. "Der Tod des Menschen in psychologischer Sicht,"
      Medizinische Klinik, 54 (Feb. 13, 1959), 237-41.

2970 Joseph, S. M. Children in fear. N.Y.: Holt, Rinehart and
      Winston, 1974.

2971 Joyce, J. A. Capital punishment: a world view. N.Y.:
      Grove Press, 1971.

2972 Jung, C. G. "The Soul and death," in The Meaning of
      Death, edited by H. Feifel. N.Y.: McGraw-Hill, 1959.
      pp. 3-15.

2973 _____. Wirklichkeit der Seele. Zurich: Rascher, 1939.

2974 Kalish, R. A. "The Aged and the dying process: the in-
      evitable decisions," Journal of Social Issues, 21 (1965),
      87-96.

2975 _____. "An Approach to the study of death attitudes,"
      American Behavioral Scientist, 6 (1963), 68-70.
      Reports the results of the pretest of a research in-
      strument that attempts to find out attitudes toward death
      and dying.

2976 _____. "A Continuum of subjectively perceived death,"
      Gerontologist, 6 (1966), 73-6.
      Author states that "death can be understood as so-
      cial death, psychological death, and social immortality."

In his view, we are not just restricted to biological death.

2977   _____. "The Effects of death upon the family," in Death and Dying, edited by L. Pearson. Cleveland: Press of Case Western Reserve University, 1969. pp. 79-107. Looks at the significance of death in modern America. Reading and writing about death is beginning to make its impact on the kind of attention that is given to dying patients and their families.

2978   _____. "Life and death: dividing the indivisible," Social Science and Medicine, 2 (1968), 249-59. "Death may be defined physically, psychologically, socially, and sociologically. The implicit definitions of death may be important in determining reactions toward the dying person."

2979   _____. "Non-medical interventions in life and death," Social Science and Medicine, 4 (1970), 655-65.

2980   _____. "Of social values and the dying: a defense of disengagement," Family Coordinator, 21 (1972), 81-94.

2981   _____. "Social distance and the dying," Community Mental Health Journal, 2 (1966), 152-5. Attempts to determine the relative degree of avoidance elicited by the dying, and discusses the problems of mental health workers in their dealings with the dying.

2982   _____. "Some variables in death attitudes," Journal of Social Psychology, 59 (1963), 137-45.

2983   _____. "Widows view death: a brief research note," Omega, 5 (summer 1974), 187-92. This study compared death attitudes among widows and non-widows. "The interviews included such topics as expectations and preferences concerning funerals, fear of death, belief in immortality, and feelings as to appropriate behavior for widows and widowers."

2984   _____, and D. K. Reynolds. "The Meaning of death and dying in the Los Angeles Mexican-American community," Proceedings of the Sixth International Conference for Suicide Prevention, Mexico, December 5-8, 1972. Ann Arbor, Mich.: Edwards Bros., 1972. pp. 291-5.

2985   Kallmann, F. J., et al. "Suicide in twins and only children," American Journal of Human Genetics, 1 (1949), 113-26.

2986   Kane, F. "The Development of concepts of death," Proceedings of the Sixth International Conference for Suicide Prevention, Mexico, December 5-8, 1972. Ann Arbor,

Mich.: Edwards Bros., 1972. pp. 149-52.

2987 Kane, J. J. "The Irish wake: a sociological appraisal,"
Sociological Symposium, 1 (fall 1968), 11-16.
Describes the characteristics of the Irish wake both
abroad and among the immigrant Irish in the U.S.

2988 Karlin, A. Death thorn: magic superstitions and beliefs of
urban Indians in Panama and Peru. Detroit: Blaine-
Ethridge Books, 1971.

2989 Kastenbaum, R. "As the clock runs out," Mental Hygiene,
50 (July 1966), 332-6.
Discusses the research and testing being done with
the elderly and states the meaning of death is closely
related to the meaning of time.

2990 _____. "The Child's understanding of death; how does it
develop?" in Explaining Death to Children, edited by E.
A. Grollman. Boston: Beacon Press, 1967. pp. 89-
108.

2991 _____. "Death as a research problem in social gerontology: an overview," Gerontologist, 6 (1966), 67-9.
Several social scientists relate the results of their
personal experiences and death research in gerontology
for a symposium.

2992 _____. "The Mental health specialist and the American
death system," Psychiatric Opinion, 9 (Dec. 1973), 28-
37.
Examines the reasons for the lack of research by
mental health professionals in areas related to death and
death education. Other topics explored are terminal illness, suicide, and death from a mental health perspective.

2993 _____. "The Mental life of dying geriatric patients,"
Gerontologist, 7 (Part I, 1967), 100.
Positive verbal references to one's own death in
some 61 patients were heard more frequently than negative ones. The analysis of findings was observed by
hospital personnel.

2994 _____. "On death and dying. Should we have mixed feelings about our ambivalence toward the aged?" Journal
of Geriatric Psychiatry, 7 (1974), 94-107.

2995 _____. "On the future of death: some images and options," Omega, 3 (Nov. 1972), 307-18.

2996 _____. "On the meaning of time in later life," Journal of
Genetic Psychology, 109 (1966), 9-25.

Suggests that time frequently decreases in importance in the lives of aged persons. Comments about attitudes toward impending death.

2997 _____. "Psychological death," in Death and Dying, edited by L. Pearson. Cleveland: Press of Case Western Reserve University, 1969. pp. 1-27.
Describes the psychological aspects of death through a series of image phenomena: thanatomimesis, phenomenological death, social-death, and others.

2998 _____. "The Realm of death: an emerging area in psychological research," Journal of Human Relations, 13 (1965), 538-52.
Suggests that death is more amenable to scientific investigation than is sometimes thought.

2999 _____, and R. Aisenberg. Psychology and death. N.Y.: Springer, 1971.

3000 _____, and B. L. Mishara. "Premature death and self-injurious behavior in old age," Geriatrics, 26 (July 1971), 71-81.

3001 Katz, J. "On the death of the president: President Kennedy's assassination," Psychoanalytic Review, 5 (winter 1964), 661-4.

3002 _____. "The Right to treatment--an enchanting legal fiction?" University of Chicago Law Review, 36 (1969), 755-83.

3003 Keeler, W. R. "Children's reaction to the death of a parent," in Depression, edited by P. Hoch and J. Zubin. N.Y.: Grune and Stratton, 1954. pp. 109-20.

3004 Keen, E. "Suicide and self-deception," Psychoanalytic Review, 74 (winter 1973), 575-85.
Presents suicide as a possibility for ourselves, friends, and patients. Our culture views it as a disease, a crime, and an accident. "The issue of the article, whether and when to intervene in suicide, is to be a value issue, separate from scientific fact and theory."

3005 Kehoe, A. B., and T. F. Kehoe. "Cognitive models for archaeological interpretation," American Antiquity, 38 (April 1973), 150-4.

3006 Kelly, P. F. "Death in Mexican folk-culture," American Quarterly, 26 (Dec. 1974), 516-36.
Survey of the characteristic ways in which death has been treated in Mexican folk-culture. Many illus-

trations appear in the text.

3007 Kelly, W. H. "Cocopa attitudes and practices with respect
      to death and mourning, " Southwestern Journal of Anthro-
      pology, 5 (1949), 151-64.
      Informative paper is concerned with one of the
      tribe's reactions to death. The group is the Cocopa
      Indians. There is an excellent exposition of beliefs
      concerning the dead, the funeral ceremony, and the
      mourning ceremony.

3008 Kennard, E. A. "Hopi reactions to death, " American An-
      thropologist, 29 (1937), 491-4.

3009 Kephart, W. M. "Status after death, " American Sociological
      Review, 15 (Oct. 1950), 635-43.

3010 Kessner, D. M. "Assessing health quality--the case for
      tracers, " New England Journal of Medicine, 288 (Jan.
      25, 1973), 189-94.

3011 _____. Infant death: an analysis by maternal risk and
      health care. Washington, D. C.: National Academy of
      Sciences, 1973.

3012 Keyes, E. L. "The Fear of death, " Harper's Magazine, 99
      (1909), 208-212.

3012a Kidd, A. M. "Limits of the right of a person to consent to
      experimentation on himself, " Science, 117 (Feb. 27,
      1953), 211-12.

3013 Kidorf, I. W. "Jewish tradition and the Freudian theory of
      mourning, " Journal of Religion and Health, 2 (1963),
      248-52.

3014 Kihn, B. Der Tod als psychotherapeutisches Problem,
      Vorträge der Lindauer Psychotherapiewoche. Stuttgart:
      G. Thieme, 1952.

3015 Killian, E. C. "Effects of geriatric transfers on mortality
      rate, " Social Work, 15 (Jan. 1970), 19-26.
      Determines the effects of transferring 600 elderly
      geriatric psychiatric patients to other state hospitals,
      and examines the resulting mortality rate.

3016 Kindregan, C. P. The Quality of life; reflections on the
      moral values of American Law. Milwaukee: Bruce
      Pub. Co., 1969. (Impact Books.)

3017 Kirkham, J. F.; S. G. Levy; and W. J. Crotty. Assassina-
      tion and political violence. N. Y.: Praeger, 1970.

3018 Kirkland, W. M. New death. Boston: Houghton, 1918.
      An essay expressing the new attitudes toward death
      that the war had created. Also a complementary new
      attitude toward life. "The author speaks of the way the
      lads in the trenches meet the inevitable and as it were
      a joyous beginning."

3019 Kirkpatrick, J., et al. "Bereavement and school adjustment,"
      Journal of School Psychology, 3 (1965), 58-63.

3020 Kirschner, D. "The Death of a president: reactions of
      psychoanalytic patients," Behavioral Science, 10 (Jan.
      1965), 1-6.

3021 Kirtley, D. D., and J. M. Sacks. "Reactions of a psycho-
      therapy group to ambiguous circumstances surrounding
      the death of a group member," Journal of Consulting and
      Clinical Psychology, 33 (1969), 195-9.

3022 Kitagawa, E. M., and P. M. Hauser. Differential mortality
      in the United States: a study in socioeconomic epi-
      demiology. Cambridge, Mass.: Harvard University
      Press, 1973.

3023 Klaber, F. W. When children ask about death. N. Y.: So-
      ciety for Ethical Culture, 1950.

3024 Klausner, S. Psychiatry and religion. N. Y.: Free Press,
      1964.

3025 Klein, M. "Mourning and its relationship to manic depressive
      states," International Journal of Psychoanalysis, 21
      (April 1940), 125-53.

3026 Kliman, G. Preventive opportunities in childhood bereave-
      ment. (Death of a Parent Study.) N. Y.: Center for
      Preventive Psychiatry, 1964.
      Examines childhood bereavement and the psycho-
      logical effects of it. The effects of the loss of a parent
      and later-life mental illness is suggested in grieving in
      childhood. The clergymen and his role in helping be-
      reaved families is clearly emphasized.

3027 _____. Psychological emergencies of childhood. N. Y.:
      Grune and Stratton, 1971.
      Traumatic events of childhood including death and its
      resultant reactions are discussed.

3028 _____, et al. Facilitation of mourning during childhood.
      N. Y.: Center for Preventive Psychiatry, 1968.
      Discusses case studies of children psychologically
      disturbed because of the death of parents or siblings,
      and techniques used in helping them mourn.

3029 Klingberg, G. "The Distinction between living and not living
among 7-10 year-old children, with some remarks concerning the so-called animism controversy," Journal of
Genetic Psychology, 90 (1957), 227-38.
Deals with children's belief that objects that move
or make sounds, or both, are living objects.

3030 Klingensmith, S. W. "Child animism: what the child means
by 'alive'," Child Development, 24 (March 1953), 51-61.

3031 Kluckhohn, C. "Conceptions of death among the Southwestern
Indians," in Culture and Behavior. N. Y.: Free Press,
1962. pp. 134-49.

3032 Knapp, R. H. "A Study of the metaphor," Journal of Projective Technology, 24 (1960), 389-95.

3033 Knight, A. C. "Personality factors and mortality in the relocation of the aged," The Gerontologist, 4 (1964), 92-3.

3034 Knight, J. A. "Suicide: its meaning and prevention," in
A Psychiatrist Looks at Religion and Health, edited by
James A. Knight. Nashville, Tenn.: Abingdon Press,
1964. pp. 99-128.
Explores the motivations in suicide and the danger
signs in a potential suicide. Focuses on the phenomenon
of suicide as a problem in community mental health.

3035 Knower, E. "Death control," Humanist, 8 (1935-1936), 139-
42.

3036 Koening, R. "Dying vs. well-being," Omega, 4 (1973), 181-
94.
Focuses on those aspects which are more threatening
than death to the dying person. Fear, pain, and isolation may be more of a concern than the death concept itself.

3037 Kohl, M. "Beneficent euthanasia," The Humanist (July-Aug.
1974), 9-11.

3038 Koocher, G. P. "Childhood death, and cognitive development," Developmental Psychology, 9 (Nov. 1973), 367-
75.
"Employed Piaget's framework for conceptualizing
cognitive development to explore and analyze children's
attitudes toward death...." (Abstract.)

3039 _____. Talking about death with "normal" children: research strategies and issues. Boston: Children's Hospital Medical Center, 1973.
"... [D]iscusses some of the issues (beyond the
methodological considerations) involved in a study of

children's ideas about death and how these ideas relate to their cognitive development...." Available free from Dr. Koocher, Developmental Evaluation Clinic, Children's Hospital Medical Center, 300 Longwood Ave., Boston, Mass. 02115.

3040   _____. "Talking with children about death," American Journal of Orthopsychiatry, 44 (April 1974), 404-11.

3041   Kostrubala, T. "Therapy of the terminally ill patient," Illinois Medical Journal, 124 (1963), 545-7.

3042   Kotsovsky, D. "Alter und Todesfurcht," Schweizerische für Psychologie, 10 (1951), 42-53.

3043   _____. "Die Psychologie der Todesfurcht," Monatsberichte, 1 (1936), 21-40.

3044   Koupernik, C. "A Drama of our times: euthanasia," Concours Medical, 84 (1962), 4687-8.

3045   Kraft, W. F. "Dying, death, and nothingness," in A Psychology of Nothingness, by W. F. Kraft. Philadelphia: Westminster Press, 1974. pp. 145-58.
        "... [T]he author copes with the negative approaches toward nothingness that impede our growth ... [and] offers a new psychological approach to death and dying, which are the clearest articulations we know of nothingness."

3046   Krassnaliew, J. "Suicide, deontology, and law," Summaries of the Third International Congress of Social Psychiatry, 1 (Sept. 21, 1970), 65.

3047   Krige, E. J. "Loveda prayer--the light it throws on the ancestor cult," African Studies, 33 (1974), 91-7.

3048   Krippner, S. "The Twenty-year death cycle of the American presidency," Research Journal of Philosophy and Social Science, 2 (1965), 65-72.

3049   Kriss, R. P. "Murder in Munich," Saturday Review, 55 (Sept. 23, 1972), 27.
        Discusses the tragedy at the Olympic games and criticizes all concerned for so easily forgetting such acts of terrorism.

3050   Kroeber, A. L. "Disposal of the dead," American Anthropologist, 29 (1927), 308-15.

3051   Kron, J. "Learning to live with death," Omega, 5 (spring 1974), 5-24.
        Seminars and group therapy programs are described

regarding the experience of death.

3052 Krupp, G. R. "How children feel about death, " Parent's
      Magazine (April 1967), 54-5.
            Emphasizes the importance and value of giving chil-
      dren the opportunity to express themselves openly about
      death.

3053 Kübler-Ross, E. "Anger before death, " Nursing '71 (Dec.
      1971), 12-14.

3054 _____. "Death and the child. " A lecture given at a
      workshop, Caring for the Dying Child and His Family,
      at Babies Hospital, Columbia Presbyterian Medical Cen-
      ter, Jan. 21, 1972.

3055 _____. "Dying with dignity, " The Canadian Nurse, 67
      (Oct. 1971), 31-5.

3056 _____. "How the patient faces death, " Public Welfare,
      29 (Jan. 1971), 36-60.

3057 _____. "The Languages of the dying patients, " Humanitas,
      10 (Feb. 1974), 5-8.
            Description of a project conducted by the author
      which demonstrated that terminally-ill patients were will-
      ing to talk about their impending deaths.

3058 _____. "Psychology of dying. " Paper presented to the
      American Academy of Family Practice. Miami Beach,
      Fla. , Nov. 5, 1971.

3059 _____. "Psychotherapy for the dying patient, " Current
      Psychiatric Therapies, 10 (1970), 110-17.

3060 _____. "What is it like to be dying, " American Journal
      of Nursing, 71 (Jan. 1971), 54-61.
            Stresses that the dying person's need is to talk and
      have adequate dialogue with understanding people.

3061 Kutner, L. "Due process of euthanasia: the living will; a
      proposal, " Indiana Law Journal, 44 (1968), 539-54.

3062 Kutscher, A. H. "Anticipatory grief, death, and bereavement:
      a continuum, " in The Phenomenon of Death; faces of
      mortality, edited by E. Wyschograd. N.Y.: Harper and
      Row, 1973. pp. 40-53.
            The essay describes recent studies with emphasis on
      the dying patient and the implications presented for the
      survivors.   The roles of the attendent team are explained,
      and the author outlines 13 "effective tools for all who
      care for or surround the dying patient and his family. "

KUTSCHER   278   Social Sciences

3063 _____, ed. Death and bereavement. Springfield, Ill.:
     C. C. Thomas, 1969.
       Presents a clear explanation of how American so-
     ciety copes with grief and bereavement.

3064 _____. "The Foundation of thanatology," Mental Hygiene,
     53 (July 1969), 338-9.

3065 _____. "Practical aspects of bereavement," A paper
     presented at a seminar of the Thanatology Foundation
     at Columbia College of Physicians and Surgeons, Novem-
     ber 12, 1971.

3066 _____, and L. O. Kutscher, eds. For the bereaved.
     N. Y.: Frederick Fell, 1971.

3067 Langford, W. S. "Anxiety in children," American Journal
     of Orthopsychiatry, 7 (April 1937), 210-8.

3068 Langone, J. Death is a noun; a view of the end of life.
     Boston: Little, 1972.
       A factual examination of the changing medicolegal
     concept of death and dying. The author also considers
     euthanasia, capital punishment, and abortion. Argu-
     ments both pro and con are given as well as considera-
     tion to beliefs about the hereafter. Suitable for high
     school age groups.

3069 Langsley, D. G. "Psychology of a doomed family," Ameri-
     can Journal of Psychotherapy, 15 (1961), 531-8.
       Examines the "psychologic defenses with which a
     family and the individual members handled the threat of
     premature death."

3070 Larson, C. U. Communication during grief. A paper pre-
     sented at the annual meeting of the International Com-
     munication Association, Montreal, April 25-28, 1973.
       The physical and psychological difficulties which ac-
     company grief; and the intrapersonal and interpersonal
     communication behaviors exhibited by the bereaved are
     outlined. The therapeutic value of communication con-
     cepts for dealing with grief and bereavement is dis-
     cussed.

3071 Lasker, A. A. "Telling children the facts of death," Your
     Child (winter 1972), 1-6.

3072 Laura, G. L., and L. Pistola. "Structural analysis of sui-
     cidal behavior," Sociological Review, 37 (Aug. 1972),
     29-34.

3073 Laurence, J. A. A History of capital punishment. Secaucus,
     N. J.: Citadel Press, 1960.

3074   Lazarus, A. A. "A Case of pseudonecrophilia treated by be-
       havior therapy," Journal of Clinical Psychology, 24
       (1968), 113.
            Description of a 23-year-old male student with
       masturbatory fantasies focused on corpses. Behavior
       therapy was used for treatment.

3075   Le Braz, A. La Legende de la mort chez les Bretons
       armoricains, choix des textes. Introd. et notes par
       P. Helias. Paris: Editions Alpine, 1958.

3076   Leclaire, S. "La Mort dans la vue de l'obsédé," Psych-
       analyse, 2 (1956), 111-44.

3077   Leddon, S. C. "Sleep paralysis, psychosis and death,"
       American Journal of Psychiatry, 126 (Jan. 1970), 1027-
       31.
            Contrasts two case reports of patients who, in their
       psychotic productions, are preoccupied with death.
       Article is concerned with the relation of a psychosis and
       sleep paralysis.

3078   Ledoux, M. "Life, death, and creation," Revue Française de
       Psychanalyse, 36 (July 1972), 585-95.
            Discusses pertinent ideas in relationship to life,
       death, and creation. Some of the ideas are: sublima-
       tion, instinct of death, sexuality, and the ego.

3079   Lee, R. P. Burial customs, ancient and modern. Min-
       neapolis: Arya Co., 1929.

3080   Lehrman, S. R. "Reactions to untimely death," Psychiatric
       Quarterly, 30 (1956), 564-78.
            Article states that psychoanalytic investigations of
       pathological depressions have spurred scientific psychi-
       atric interest in reactions to loss due to death.

3081   LeShan, E. What makes you feel this way? N.Y.: Mac-
       millan, 1972.
            Deals with ways to better understand children in
       stressful situations. The author stresses that children
       should be encouraged to verbalize their feelings and
       emotions.

3082   LeShan, L. "Cancer mortality rate: some statistical evi-
       dence of the effect of psychological factors," Archives
       of General Psychiatry, 6 (1962), 333-5.
            Article discusses the number of studies of the
       psychological components of the etiology of neoplastic
       disease.

3083   _____. "Psychotherapy and the dying patient," in Death
       and Dying, edited by L. Pearson. Cleveland: Press

of Case Western Reserve University, 1969. pp. 28-48.
Interesting perspectives on life and death from the
psychotherapeutic point of view. The author uses some
masterpieces of literature to point out the important
work with patients.

3084 _____, and E. LeShan. "Psychotherapy and the patient
with a limited life span," in The Phenomenon of Death;
faces of mortality, edited by E. Wyschogrod. N.Y.:
Harper and Row, 1973.
From the therapeutic point of view it is important
for the therapist to help the patient at whatever point he
touches the patient's life. The emphasis is on the patient and his life regardless of the time limit. The
article records three letters written by patients during
and after psychotherapy.

3085 Leslie, R. C.; C. W. Wahl; and N. Kennedy. Helping the
dying patient and his family. N.Y.: National Assoc. of
Social Workers, 1960.

3086 Lester, D. "Antecedents of the fear of the dead: an analysis of cultural data," Psychological Reports, 19 (1966),
741.
States the societies which have love-oriented techniques of punishment should have a greater fear of the
dead than those endorsing physical techniques.

3087 _____. "Attitudes toward death and suicide in a non-
disturbed population," Psychological Reports, 29 (Oct.
1971), 368.

3088 _____. "Attitudes toward death held by a staff of a suicide prevention center," Psychological Reports, 28
(April 1971), 650.

3089 _____. "Attitudes toward death today and thirty-five years
ago," Omega, 2 (Aug. 1971), 168-73.

3090 _____. "Checking on the harlequin," Psychological Reports, 19 (1966), 984.
States that no association was found between the frequency of nightmare occurrences and the fear of dying.

3091 _____. "Ellen West's suicide as a case of psychic homicide," Psychoanalytic Review, 58 (1971-1972), 251-63.
The case of Ellen West and her therapist is told.
The case has been examined using psychoanalytic concepts of psychic homicide and masochism.

3092 _____. "Experimental and correlational studies of the
fear of death," Psychological Bulletin, 67 (1967), 27-36.
Presents demographic variables of the fear of death

and states that the concept needs new techniques.

3093 _____. "Fear of death and nightmare experiences, "
Psychological Reports, 25 (1969), 437-8.

3094 _____. "Fear of death of suicidal persons, " Psychological
Reports, 20 (1967), 1077-8.

3095 _____. "The Fear of death of those who have nightmares, " Journal of Psychology, 69 (1968), 245-7.
Discussion about students who are consciously concerned about death and have reported a greater number
of nightmares than students who manifest less concern.

3096 _____. "Fear of the dead in non-literate societies, "
Journal of Social Psychology, 77 (April 1969), 283-4.

3097 _____. "Inconsistency in the fear of death of individuals, "
Psychological Reports, 20 (1964), 1084.
Too often the fear of death in individuals has been
examined in relation to easily available factors such as
socioeconomic variables.

3098 _____. "The Need to achieve and the fear of death, "
Psychological Reports, 27 (Oct. 1970), 516.

3099 _____. "Relation of fear of death in subjects to fear of
death in their parents, " Psychological Record, 20 (fall
1970), 541-3.

3100 _____. "Schizophrenia and death concern, " Journal of
Projective Techniques and Personality Assessment, 33
(Oct. 1969), 403-5.

3101 _____. "Sex differences in attitudes toward death: a
replication, " Psychological Reports, 28 (June 1971), 754.

3102 _____. "Studies in death-attitude scales, " Psychological
Reports, 24 (Feb. 1969), 182.

3103 _____. "Studies in death attitudes, 2, " Psychological Reports, 30 (April 1972), 440.

3104 _____. "Voodoo death: some new thoughts on an old
phenomenon, " American Anthropologist, 74 (June 1972),
386-90.

3105 _____. Why people kill themselves. Springfield, Ill.:
C. C. Thomas, 1972.
A cross-disciplinary approach to the causes of why
people attempt to take their lives. Five sections present a summary of research findings.

3106 _____, and E. G. Kam. "Effect of a friend dying upon
      attitudes toward death," Journal of Social Psychology,
      33 (Feb. 1971), 149-50.

3107 Lester, G. Suicide. N. J.: Prentice-Hall, 1971.

3108 _____, and D. Lester. Suicide: the gamble with death.
      N. Y.: Spectrum, 1971.
           Contends that some cases of suicide can be pre-
      dicted. Individual case studies are examined, along
      with the reports and findings of psychologists.

3109 Levin, A. J. "The Fiction of the death instinct," Psychiatric
      Quarterly, 25 (1951), 257-81.
           Article takes issue with Freud's theory of the death
      instinct.

3110 Levin, T. "Leave it to George," in Invitation to a Dark
      Room. N. Y.: Macfadden Books, 1964.
           An analyst records his confrontation with a patient
      who eventually commits suicide.

3111 Levine, S. Deathrow: an affirmation of life. San Fran-
      cisco: Glide Urban Center Publ., 1971.

3112 _____. "Stress and behavior," Scientific American, 224
      (Jan. 1971), 26-31.

3113 Levisohn, A. A. "Voluntary mercy death; socio-legal as-
      pects of euthanasia," Journal of Forensic Medicine, 8
      (April-June, 1961), 57-9.

3113a Levi-Strauss, C. The Savage mind. Chicago: University
      of Chicago Press, 1966.
           Investigates the mind of primitive man and how it
      functions around experiences such as birth, life, and
      death.

3114 Leviton, D. "Death, bereavement, and suicide education,"
      in New Directions in Health Education, edited by D.
      Read. N. Y.: Macmillan, 1971.
           Clarifies goals and objectives of helping students to
      understand the relationship of life to death, and death to
      life.

3115 Levy-Bruhl, L. The Soul of the primitive. N. Y.: Praeger,
      1966.
           Contains Levy-Bruhl's contrast between primitive
      mentality and civilized mentality. There are chapters
      on the life and death of the individual, and the duality
      of the dead.

3116 Lewis, C. S. A Grief observed. N. Y.: Seabury, 1961.

3117 Lewis, O. A Death in the Sanchez family. N. Y.: Random
        House, 1969.
             A presentation of the impressions of the three
        Sanchez children on the death of their aunt.

3118 Li, W. L. "Comparative study of suicide," International
        Journal of Comparative Sociology, 12 (Dec. 1971), 281-6.
             Paper tests cross-culturally a number of interre-
        lated variables in order to account for differences in
        suicides, both within and between different societies.

3119 Lieberman, L., and A. Coplan. "Distance from death as a
        variable in the study of aging," Developmental Psychology,
        2 (1970), 71-84.
             Authors state that older people acknowledge their
        death and that studies of death and dying will contribute
        greatly to the psychology of aging.

3120 Lieberman, M. A. "Observations on death and dying,"
        Gerontologist, 6 (June 1966), 70-2.
             Describes "death as the end-point in a complex net-
        work of psycho-biological changes." Points out problems
        in researching death and the psychological variables in-
        volved.

3121 _____. "Psychological correlates of impending death:
        some preliminary observations," Journal of Gerontology,
        20 (1965), 181-90.

3122 Lifton, R. J. Boundaries: psychological man in revolution.
        N. Y.: Random House, 1969.
             Studies boundaries of destruction, death and life,
        the self or revolution and the New History. Attempts
        to show how the boundaries of our existence are con-
        tinually being broken down and restored.

3123 _____. Death in life--survivors of Hiroshima. N. Y.:
        Random House, 1967.
             Presents the various responses of people who sur-
        vived the atomic bombing of Hiroshima. The themes
        of death are outstanding.

3124 _____. History and human survival. N. Y.: Random
        House, 1961.
             "Essays on the young and old, survivors and the
        dead, peace and war, and on contemporary psycho-
        history" (subtitle). Contains the author's acceptance
        speech for the 1969 National Book Award in the sciences
        for Death in Life (see 3123).

3125 _____. Living and dying. N. Y.: Praeger, 1974.
             The book "responds to the problems with discussions
        of death and the life cycle, death in history, and sym-
        bolic immortality...."

3126   . "Mao Tse-Tung and the 'death of the revolution',"
       Trans-Action, 5 (1968), 6-13.
       States that changes taking place in China can be un-
       derstood as a quest for revolutionary immortality.

3127   . "On death and death symbolism: the Hiroshima
       disaster," in The Phenomenon of Death; faces of im-
       mortality, edited by E. Wyschogrod. N.Y.: Harper
       and Row, 1973. pp. 69-109.
       Lifton examines the psychological meaning of im-
       mersion in death, by interviewing survivors of Hiro-
       shima's encounter with the atomic bomb. His research
       is represented by an analytical approach to man's strug-
       gles to cope with those aspects of history which alter
       and threaten his existence.

3128   . "Psychological effects of the atomic bomb in
       Hiroshima: the theme of death," Daedalus, 92 (1963),
       462-97.

3129   Lindemann, E. "Psychological aspects of mourning," The
       Director, 31 (1961), 14-17.

3130   . "Symptomatology and management of acute grief,"
       American Journal of Psychiatry, 101 (1944), 141-8.
       "Acute grief is a definite syndrome with psycho-
       logical and somatic symptomatology." Observations are
       made of bereaved disaster victims of Cocoanut Grove
       Fire.

3131   , and I. M. Greer. "A Study of grief: emotional
       responses to suicide," Pastoral Psychology, 4 (1953),
       9-13.

3132   Lindner, R. M. "The Equivalents of matricide," Psycho-
       analytical Quarterly, 17 (1948), 453.

3133   Linn, L. "The Role of perception in the mechanism of
       denial," Journal of the American Psychoanalytical As-
       sociation, 1 (1953), 690-705.

3134   Lipschutz, L. S. "Some administrative aspects of suicide
       in mental hospitals," American Journal of Psychiatry,
       99 (1942), 181-7.
       Discusses death by suicide as a regular occurrence
       in mental hospitals. Offers historical data on suicides
       in public asylums in Wales, England, and the U.S.

3135   Lipson, C. T. "Denial and mourning," International Journal
       of Psychoanalysis, 44 (1963), 104-7.
       Uses the psychoanalytic method to explain various
       aspects of mourning and the struggle it creates within
       the individual.

3136   Litman, R. E. "Psychological-psychiatric aspects in certifying modes of death, " Journal of Forensic Science, 13 (Jan. 1968), 46-54.

3137   _____. "Sigmund Freud on suicide, " in Essays in Self-Destruction, edited by E. S. Shneidman. N. Y.: 1969.

3138   _____. "When patients commit suicide, " American Journal of Psychotherapy, 19 (Oct. 1965), 570-4.
"Most therapists regard suicidal potentiality as a disturbing element, complicating and sometimes restricting the therapeutic process, and requiring special care. "

3139   Little, J. C. "Psychiatrists' attitudes to abortion, " British Medical Journal, 1 (Jan. 8, 1972), 110.

3140   Locke, C. A., and V. Shelton. Let's face it now, 5th ed. N. Y.: Verity Publications, 1971.
A very practical pamphlet designed for the family survivors when the situation arises and when the father is taken by death.

3141   Lönnqvist, J., and K. A. Achte. "Witchcraft, religion and suicides in the light of the witch hammer and contemporary cases, " Omega, 5 (summer 1974), 115-25.
"A comparison is made between case histories described in The Witch Hammer (1487), and contemporary clinical cases ... similarities in attitudes toward accused witches and psychiatric patients are noted and discussed" (abstract).

3142   "Look at death feelings; helpers of grieving told, " National Catholic Reporter, 10 (Nov. 16, 1973), 2.

3143   Lopata, H. Z. "Living arrangements of American urban widows, " Sociological Focus, 5 (1971), 41-6.

3144   _____. "Loneliness: forms and components, " Social Problems, 17 (1969), 248-62.

3145   _____. "The Social involvement of American Widows, " American Behavioral Scientist, 14 (1970), 41-58.

3146   _____. "Social relations of widows in urbanizing societies, " Sociological Quarterly, 13 (1972), 259-71.

3147   _____. Widowhood in an American city. Morristown, N. J.: General Learning Corporation, 1972.

3148   _____. "Widows as a minority group, " Gerontologist (supplement), 11 (spring 1971), 67-77.

3149   Lovelace, B. M. "The Role of the recreation therapist with

the terminally ill child, " Therapeutic Recreation Journal,
8 (first Quarter, 1974), 25-9.
An objective is "to provide for each individual the
time and tools to use in re-creating and reinforcing his
ego identity so that he may continue his life as a total,
joyful and participating personality despite the illness
and its impact. " The recreation therapist is part of
and included in the professional team.

3150 Loveland, G. G. "The Effects of bereavement on certain
religious attitudes and behavior, " Sociological Symposium,
1 (fall 1968), 17-27.

3151 Lucas, R. A. "Social implications of the immediacy of
death, " Canadian Review of Sociology and Anthropology,
1 (Feb. 1968), 1-16.
Author states that individuals, groups, and societies
have developed patterns to cope with the social aftermath
of death.

3152 Lyons, E. The Life and death of Sacco and Vanzetti. London: Martin Lawrence, n. d.
Discusses the lives of Sacco and Vanzetti from their
childhood through their labor activities to their trial,
conviction, and execution.

3153 McCann, J. C. "Differential mortality and the formation of
political elites: the case of the U. S. House of Repre-
sentatives, " American Sociological Review, 37 (Dec.
1972), 689.

3154 McClelland, D. C. "The Harlequin complex, " in The Study
of Lives, edited by R. White. N. Y.: Atherton, 1963.
Explores the "Harlequin Complex" which causes individuals to be excited by their own deaths while still
fearing.

3155 McConnell, B. The History of assassination. Nashville,
Tenn.: Aurora Publishers, 1970.

3156 McConville, B. J., et al. "Mourning processes in children
of varying ages, " Canadian Psychiatric Association Journal, 15 (1970), 253-5.
Article discusses the underlying processes of
mourning in children to see if they are similar to adults.

3157 McCully, R. S. "Fantasy productions of children with a
progressively crippling and fatal illness, " Journal of
Genetic Psychology, 102 (1963), 203-16.

3158 MacDonald, A. "Death psychology of historical personages, "
American Journal of Psychology, 33 (1921), 552-6.
Discusses last words and statements of distinguished

people in history, and points out the importance of the dying hour.

3159   McDonald, M. "Farewell to a friend," American Journal of Nursing, 68 (April 1968), 773.

3160   _____. "A Study of the reactions of nursery school children to the death of a child's mother," in The Psychoanalytic Study of the Child, XIX. N. Y.: International Universities Press, 1964.

3161   McGee, R. K. "The Death investigation team," in Crisis Intervention in the Community. Baltimore: University Park Press, 1974. pp. 257-66.
        Models for crisis intervention programs are discussed. Describes the history, function, and interpretation of the psychological autopsy and death investigation service. Gives examples of the team's work.

3162   Mack, A., ed. Death in American experience. N. Y.: Schocken, 1973.
        Presents the sociological and anthropological aspects of the cultural dimensions of death. Examines the Judaeo-Christian tradition, existential philosophy, and medical technology to attitudes and practices regarding death.

3163   MacLurin, H. "In the hour of their going forth," Social Casework, 40 (March 1959), 136-41.
        The author states the necessity of the case worker's need to examine his feelings about death in order to be of maximum use in helping the client.

3164   Maddison, D. "The Factors affecting the outcome of conjugal bereavement," British Journal of Psychiatry, 113 (Oct. 1967), 1057-67.

3165   _____. "The Relevance of conjugal bereavement for preventive psychology," British Journal of Medical Psychology, 41 (Sept. 1968), 223-33.
        Study is about middle-aged widows who have several difficult tasks: the widow is required through the processes of mourning to detach herself from the loss object and to continue other relationships; the widow has to establish for herself a new role as an adult woman without a partner.

3166   _____, and A. Viola. "The Health of widows in the year following bereavement," Journal of Psychosomatic Research, 12 (Dec. 1968), 297-306.

3167   Maguire, D. C. Death by choice. N. Y.: Doubleday, 1974.
        The author examines the major issues involved in

the "right to death" controversy.

3168 _____. "Death, legal and illegal, " Atlantic Monthly,
(Feb. 1974), 72-85.
Discusses the problems of capital punishment, war,
and suicide, and points out the legal aspects concerning
them.

3169 Mahler, M. S. "Helping children to accept death, " Child
Study, 27 (1950), 98-9.
The difficulty of explaining and helping children to
accept death is discussed. Cites several cases where
parents deceived the child and how problems result because of deception.

3170 _____. "On sadness and grief in infancy and childhood:
loss and restoration of the symbiotic love object, " in
The Psychoanalytic Study of the Child, XVI. N.Y.:
International Universities Press, 1961. pp. 332-51.

3171 Malinowski, B. "Baloma: the spirits of the dead in the
Trobriand Islands, " Journal of the Royal Anthropological
Institute of Great Britain and Ireland, 46 (1916), 353-
430.
Discusses the various aspects of the views of death
held by the natives of the islands. Comments on the return of the spirits to the villages and beliefs in reincarnation.

3172 Malmquist, C. P. "Adolescents view death, " Minnesota
Journal of Education (Dec. 1970), 39.

3173 "Management of the dying patient and his family." Papers
by Nathan Schnaper, et al. N.Y.: Mss Information
Corp., 1974. (Mss series on attitudes toward death.)

3174 Manchester, W. The Death of a president: November 20...
November 25, 1963. N.Y.: Harper and Row, 1967.

3175 Mandelbaum, D. G. "Social uses of funeral rites, " in The
Meaning of Death, edited by H. Feifel. N.Y.: Mc-
Graw-Hill, 1959. pp. 189-217.
Discusses the value of funerals for the living in-
cluding social, political, and economic aspects for both
primitive and modern cultures.

3176 Mannes, M. Last rights. N.Y.: William Morrow, 1974.
The author has examined the taboo issues of euthanasia. She has talked with patients and doctors and
has enlightened us by bringing our ethical and spiritual
experience to bear upon the question of our last rights
as human beings.

3177 Marcovitz, E. "Man in search of meaning: hallucinogenic agents, " Delaware Medical Journal, 44 (March 1972), 72-4.

3178 _____. "What is the meaning of death to the dying person and his survivors?" Omega, 4 (spring 1973), 13-25.

3179 Marcus, J. T. "Death consciousness and civilization, " Social Research, 31 (autumn 1964), 265-79.

3180 Marek, Z., et al. "The Social and medico-legal aspects of sudden death in children under three years of age, " Przeglad Lekarsk, 22 (1966), 593-6.

3181 Maris, R. W. Social forces in urban suicide. Homewood, Ill.: Dorsey Press, 1969.
     Considers the effects of the social structure on individual behavior, the development of the sociology of suicide as a science, and finally how we might prevent it in the future.

3182 Markusen, E., and R. Fulton. "Childhood bereavement and behavioral disorders: a critical review, " Omega, 2 (May 1971), 107-17.

3183 Marris, P. Widows and their families. London: Routledge and Kegan Paul, 1958.

3184 Marshall, V. W. "Socialization for impending death in a retirement village, " American Journal of Sociology, 80 (March 1975), 1124-44.
     "Focuses on the last of these 'major adjustments' [in] preparation for ultimate death--and argues that congregate living facilities can provide optimal settings for this form of socialization...."

3185 Martin, D., and L. S. Wrightsman. "The Relationship between religious behavior and concern about death, " Journal of Social Psychology, 65 (April 1965), 317-23.

3186 Martin, E. Psychology of funeral service. N.Y.: Sentinel Printers, 1950.

3187 Masterson, J. F., Jr. "Suicide in adolescents, " American Journal of Psychiatry, 116 (Nov. 1959), 400-04.

3188 Mathews, J. N. "The Time my father died, " Motive (Jan.-Feb. 1964), 5-9.
     Story about the death of a father, the responses of the family to it, and the new and unusual experiences that followed.

3189 Mathis, J. L. "A Sophisticated version of voodoo death, "

Psychosomatic Medicine, 26 (1964), 104.

3190 Matse, J., et al. Bereavement. London: Butterworth, 1971.

3191 "Matter of life and death," Nation's Business, 58 (Nov. 1970), 27.
       Offers general and individual opinions concerning the abolishment or retention of the death penalty.

3192 Maurer, A. "Adolescent attitudes toward death," Journal of Genetic Psychology, 105 (1964), 75-90.
       "Essays on 'what comes to my mind when I think of death,' by 253 senior high school girls [who] were measured by idea and word analysis for degrees of maturity in attitudes toward death...."

3193 _____. "The Child's knowledge of non-existence," Journal of Existential Psychiatry, 2 (1961), 193-212.
       Author states that "there is considerable evidence that an understanding of death is a developmental feature of human intelligence and that its genesis is very early."

3194 _____. "The Game of peek-a-boo," Diseases of the Nervous System, 28 (1967), 118-21.
       "Proposes that 'peek-a-boo,' as one of the earliest interpersonal communications ... [not only establishes] a mode of responding to overtures and increasing sensory sensitivity ... [but also] establishes self confidence, an early sense of identity and helps to allay primordial anxiety because it addresses itself specifically to the problem of life and death...."

3195 _____. "Maturation of concepts of death," British Journal of Medicine and Psychology, 39 (1966), 35-41.
       Traces the origin of the preconceptual awareness of death in children from the prelogic of childhood to the idealism of adolescence.

3196 May, R. "The Daemonic: love and death," Psychology Today, 1 (Feb. 1968), 16-25.
       Examines the relationship between death and love, and states that every kind of mythology relates the sex act to dying.

3197 _____. "Love and death," in Love and Will. N.Y.: W. W. Norton, 1969. pp. 99-121.

3198 _____. The Meaning of anxiety. N.Y.: Ronald Press, 1950.
       Describes the common elements in modern theories of anxiety and formulates grounds for further study in relation to death.

3199 _____. "The Meaning of the oedipus myth," in Guilt:
man and society, edited by R. W. Smith. N. Y.:
Anchor Books, 1971. pp. 171-83.

3200 Meerloo, J. Suicide and mass suicide. N. Y.: Grune and
Stratton, 1962.

3201 Meissner, W. W. "Affective responses to psychoanalytic
death symbols," Journal of Abnormal and Social Psychology, 56 (1958), 295-99.
Attempts to account for anxiety reactions typical of
neurosis because of the fear of death.

3202 Melear, J. D. "Children's conceptions of death," Journal
of Genetic Psychology, 123 (Dec. 1973), 359-60.

3203 Menchen, A. By the neck; a book of hangings. N. Y.:
Hastings House, 1942.

3204 Menninger, K. The Crime of punishment. N. Y.: Viking
Press, 1968.

3205 _____. "Death from psychic causes," Bulletin of the
Menninger Clinic, 12 (1948), 31-6.
Suggests the possibility that some people can consciously will their own death and effect it without external devices.

3206 _____. "Hope," American Journal of Psychiatry, 116
(1959), 481.
Article concludes that the loss of hope seems to ac-
celerate the arrival of death in terminal patients.

3207 _____. Man against himself. N. Y.: Harcourt, Brace
and Co., 1938.
An examination of the axiom that everyone has an
urge to be constructive or destructive. These two desires are at war with each other. The destructive one
is seen by a desire either to kill, be killed, or die. A
very probing book, but only until the underlying factors
of these axioms have been scientifically proven, can any
of their implications be removed from the realm of
mere philosophical speculation.

3208 Menninger von Lerchenthal, E. "Death from psychic causes,"
Bulletin Menninger Clinic, 12 (1948), 31-6.

3209 Merkeley, D. K. The Investigation of death. Springfield,
Ill.: C. C. Thomas, 1957. (Police Science Series.)

3210 Meynard, L. Le Suicide. Paris: Presses Universitaires,
1958.

3211 Middleton, W. C. "Some reactions towards death among college students," Journal of Abnormal and Social Psychology, 31 (1936), 165-73.
Article deals with thoughts, attitudes, and behavior responses toward death found in two Midwestern Universities. Discusses data of male and female about dying, accidents, and after-life.

3212 Miller, P. W. "Provenience of the death symbolism in Van Gogh's cornscapes," Psychoanalytic Review, 52 (1965), 60-6.
Discusses cornscapes as representing the struggling world of man, and the mere stalks of grain without personality. The cornscapes also represent the longing for and horror of death.

3213 Milner, M. "A Suicidal symptom in a child of three," International Journal of Psychoanalysis, 25 (1944), 53-61.
Study of a three-year-old girl who expressed a suicidal symptom by refusing all food and drink for three days.

3214 Minot, C. S. The Problem of age, growth, and death. N. Y.: Putnam, 1908.

3215 Mirtley, D. D., and J. M. Sacks. "Reactions of a psychotherapy group to ambiguous circumstances surrounding the death of a group member," Journal of Consulting Clinical Psychology, 33 (April 1969), 195-9.

3216 Mitchell, M. E. "Bereaved children," in Stresses in Children, edited by V. P. Varma. London: University of London Press, 1973. pp. 57-71.
Deals with the role of the teacher in dealing with bereavement and the multiplicity of variables acting on the bereaved child. A section is devoted to how adults can help.

3217 _____. The Child's attitude toward death. N. Y.: Schocken Books, 1967.
Examines the religious, scientific, and sociological influences on British children and brings out the role of myth in the development of attitudes toward death.

3218 Mitchell, N. D. "The Significance of the loss of the father through death," American Journal of Orthopsychiatry, 34 (1964), 279-80.
Presents case-studies of fatherless families in which the father is absent due to death, and the implications this has for the surviving family.

3219 Mitford, J. The American way of death. N. Y.: Simon and Schuster, 1963.

Discusses the attitudes and economics of the funeral business. Author feels that funeral directors disguise the fact of death.

3220   Mitra, D. N.   "Mourning customs and modern life in Bengal, " American Journal of Sociology, 52 (1947), 309-11.
Describes the period of mourning in different communities and outlines the many restrictions imposed on the mourners.

3221   Monsour, K. J.   "Asthma and the fear of death, " Psychoanalytic Quarterly, 29 (1960), 56-71.
States that there could be a relationship between asthma attacks in children and the fear of death as a threat of separation from the mother.

3222   Montale, E.   "An Introduction to 'Billy Budd', " Sewanee Review, 68 (1960), 419-22.

3223   Moody, H. R.   "November 22, 1963, " Motive, 24 (Jan. -Feb. 1964), 38-9.

3224   Moore, J.   "The Death culture of Mexico and Mexican-Americans, " Omega, 1 (Nov. 1970), 271-91.

3225   Moore, V.   Ho for heaven!   Man's changing attitude toward dying; with designs by Horst V. Rhoden. N. Y.: Dutton, 1946.
A fascinating anthology of the ways men have met death from the days of ancient Hindus, Egyptians, and Greeks through the middle ages, the 18th century, etc., to soldiers and statesmen during World War II.

3226   Moore, W. E.   "Time--the ultimate scarcity, " American Behavioral Scientist, 6 (1963), 58-60.
Describes time and its relationship to fate.   Death is ultimate and inevitable and we have numerous attitudes about it.

3227   Moran, P. A. P. , and K. Abe.   "Parental loss in homosexuals, " British Journal of Psychiatry, 115 (1969), 319-30.

3228   Moreno, J. L.   "The Social atom and death, " Sociometry, 10 (1947), 80-4.
Social atoms change as we get older, and it is difficult to replace loss of membership.   "It is the phenomenon of social death, not from the point of view of the lively, not how we die from within, but how we die from without. "

3229   Morgan, E.   "A Humanist approach to the problems of death, " Humanist, 26 (1966), 52-4.

3230 Morgan, R. F. "Note on the psychopathology of senility:
      senescent defense against threat of death," Psycho-
      logical Reports, 16 (Feb. 1965), 305-6.

3231 Morgenson, D. F. "Death and interpersonal failure,"
      Canada's Mental Health, 21 (May 1973), 10-12.
          Suggests that human relations, interpersonal rela-
      tions, and interactions may slow the death process.
      Also discusses voodoo and contemporary attitudes to-
      wards the incurable.

3232 Morgenthau, H. J. "Death in the nuclear age," Commentary,
      32 (1961), 231-4.

3233 Moriarty, D., ed. Loss of loved ones: the effects of a
      death in the family on personality development. Spring-
      field, Ill.: C. C. Thomas, 1967.

3234 Morris, A. A. "Voluntary euthanasia," Washington Law Re-
      view, 45 (1970), 239-71.

3235 Morrissey, J. R. "A Note on interviews with children facing
      imminent death," Social Casework, 44 (1963), 343-5.
          Children of both sexes--ages 8 to 14--facing death,
      are interviewed at various intervals in the presence of
      the parents. Observations of the effects on all con-
      cerned are recorded.

3236 Morse, J. "The Goal of life enhancement for a fatally ill
      child," Children, 17 (March-April 1970), 63-8.

3237 Motto, J.; R. M. Brooks; C. Ross; and N. H. Allen.
      Standards for suicide prevention and crisis centers.
      N.Y.: Behavioral Publications and Human Sciences
      Press, 1974.
          "Provides specific operational guidelines for the
      application of standards and the identification of specific
      problems in crisis centers throughout the world....
      [T]he book focuses on program planning for particular
      local settings, standards for organizational structure,
      ethics, and program evaluation...."

3238 Muhsam, H. V. "Differential mortality in Israel by socio-
      economic status," Eugenics Quarterly, 12 (Dec. 1965),
      227-32.

3239 Munro, A. "Childhood parent-loss in a psychiatrically nor-
      mal population," British Journal of Preventive and Social
      Medicine, 19 (1965), 69-79.

3240 _____. "Parental deprivation in depressive patients,"
      British Journal of Psychiatry, 112 (1966), 443-57.

3241 _____, and A. Griffiths. "Some psychiatric non-sequelae of childhood bereavement," British Journal of Psychiatry, 115 (1969), 305-11.
    Discussion of parental bereavement in childhood. Information about 364 patients was used: 162 suffered from depression, 69 from schizophrenia, and 48 from an anxiety state. Eight psychiatrists in mental hospitals provided the data.

3242 Murgoci, A. "Customs connected with death and burial among the Roumanians," Folk-lore, 30 (1919), 89-102.

3243 Murphy, C., et al. "Who calls the suicide prevention center: a study of 55 persons calling on their own behalf," American Journal of Psychiatry, 126 (1969), 314-324.
    The author states that those calling on their own are psychiatrically ill; those who have attempted suicide before, those in depression, and those dissatisfied with life at this point need professional help.

3244 Nacht, S. "Instinct de mort ou instinct de vie?" Revue Française de Psychanalyse, 20 (1956), 405-16.

3245 Nagy, M. H. "The Child's theories concerning death," Journal of Genetic Psychology, 73 (1948), 3-27.
    Studies a child's concept of death at various age levels and reflects on his attitudes and feelings about death.

3246 _____. "The Child's view of death," in The Meaning of Death, edited by H. Feifel. N.Y.: McGraw-Hill. 1959. pp. 79-98.

3247 Nathan, T. S.; L. Eitinger; and H. Z. Winnick. "The Psychiatric pathology of survivors of the Nazi holocaust," The Israel Annals of Psychiatry and Related Disciplines, 1 (1963), 113.

3248 National Funeral Directors Association. "Should I go to the funeral? What do I say?" Milwaukee: NFDA, n.d.
    Points are made about the condolence or sympathy visit and the value of one's presence.

3249 _____. "Should the body be present at the funeral?" Milwaukee: NFDA, n.d.
    Pamphlet designed to help those who ask why the body should be present during the funeral.

3250 _____. "When a death occurs; needs... concerns... decisions." Milwaukee: NFDA, 1974.
    The funeral "permits facing openly, realistically and with dignity the crisis that death presents.... [I]t is well to consider the feelings of others who shared in

the life of the deceased and who wish to share in the
funeral as well. " (Blurb.)

3251 Natterson, J. M. "The Fear of death in fatally ill children
and their parents, " in The Child in his Family, edited
by E. J. Anthony, and C. Koupernik. Vol. 2. N.Y.:
Wiley, 1973. pp. 121-5.
A review of how children are informed about death,
the variety of reactions in the parents, and the role of
the clinician.

3252 _____, and A. G. Knudson. "Children and their mothers:
observations concerning the fear of death in mentally ill
children and their mothers, " Psychosomatic Medicine,
20 (1960), 456-65.
These children manifested behavioral changes in response to three factors: separation from the mother,
traumatic procedures, and deaths of other children.

3253 Neale, R. E. The Art of dying. N.Y.: Harper and Row,
1973.
Advice by a professor of psychiatry on experiencing
the fears of death and of life. Also included are the
dimensions of suicide, grief, and the images and concepts of death.

3254 _____. "Separating ourselves from death; excerpt from
art of dying, " New Catholic World, 216 (July-Aug. 1973),
178-82.

3255 Needleman, J. "The Perception of mortality, " in Care of
Patients with Fatal Illness, edited by L. P. White.
N.Y.: Annals of the New York Academy of Sciences,
1969. Vol. 164. Art. 3. pp. 733-38.

3256 Nelson, J. "As the patient sees it: public dying, " Medical
World, 80 (May 1954), 596-99.

3257 Nemtzow, J., and S. R. Lesser. "Reactions of children and
parents to the death of President Kennedy, " American
Journal of Orthopsychiatry, 34 (1964), 280-1.

3258 Nettler, G. "Review essay: on death and dying, " Social
Problems, 14 (1967), 335-44.
Suggests three types of problems which are posed
by writers on the subject of death and the means by
which these writings can be analyzed: problem of
aesthetics, problem of interpretation, problem of cor-
relation and sequence (of facts). The last includes the
situation of those dying in hospitals and mortuary literature of various backgrounds and positions.

3259 Neuringer, C. "Changes in attitude towards life and death

during recovery from a serious suicide attempt, " Omega,
1 (Nov. 1970), 301-9.

3260 _____. "Divergencies between attitudes towards life and
death among suicidal, psychosomatic and normal hospitalized patients, " Journal of Consulting Clinical Psychology, 32 (1968), 59-63.
"Attitudes toward life and death are gathered from
suicidal, psychosomatic and normal hospitalized patients
via semantic-differential ratings of the concept. "

3261 _____. Psychological assessment of suicidal risk.
Springfield, Ill.: C. C. Thomas, 1974.
Fifteen contributors attempt to assess suicidal risk
based upon evaluative and validity methods.

3262 "New debate on death penalty: major issue in California, "
U. S. News, 66 (May 5, 1969), 18.
Presents the problem that the Sirhan B. Sirhan
case poses to the advocates of the abolition of the death
penalty.

3263 Nichol, H. "The Death of a parent, " Canadian Psychiatric
Association Journal, 9 (1964), 262-71.
States that incidences of subsequent psychiatric illnesses following the death of a parent is low, but profound disturbances do occur in some cases.

3264 Niederland, W. "The Problem of the survivor, Part I:
some remarks on the psychiatric evaluation of emotional
disorders in survivors of Nazi persecution, " Journal of
Hillside Hospital, 10 (1961), 233-47.

3265 Niswander, G. D.; T. M. Casey; and J. A. Humphrey.
A Panorama of suicide. Springfield, Ill.: C. C.
Thomas, 1973.
Essentially a casebook of psychological autopsies of
18 New Hampshire suicide victims, with an eye for sui-
cide prevention and intervention.

3266 Nolfi, M. W. "Families in grief: the question of casework
intervention, " Social Work, 12 (1967), 40-6.

3267 Noon, J. A. "A Preliminary examination of the death concepts of the Ibo, " American Anthropologist, 44 (1942),
638-54.

3268 Norton, J. "Treatment of a dying patient, " Psychoanalytic
Studies of Children, 18 (1963), 541-60.
A depressed dying woman who had contemplated suicide received psychiatric treatment for the last few
months of her life and obtained protection against much
physical and emotional pain. Object loss, both actual

and threatened, is a major psychological problem of the dying patient.

3269   Obridik, A. J.   "Gallows humor--a sociological phenomenon, "
        American Journal of Sociology, 47 (1942), 709-16.
              Discusses the "positive effects of gallows humor as
        an index of strength and morale. "

3270   O'Connell, W. E.   "Humor and death, " Psychological Reports,
        22 (April 1968), 391-402.
              Study of the humor with which people approach their
        death.   The information was taken from a survey test
        given to college students.

3271/2 O'Dell, B. Y.   "Suicide in children, " Parent's Magazine,
        (Jan. 1969), 58-9.

3273   O'Hara, D. J.   Changes in mortality levels and family deci-
        sions regarding children.   Chicago: Rand, 1972.

3274/5 Olshaker, B.   What shall we tell the kids?   N. Y.:   Arbor
        House, 1971.

3276   Oltman, J., et al.   "Parent deprivation and the broken home
        in dementia praecox and other mental disorders, "
        American Journal of Psychiatry, 108 (1952), 685-93.
              Examines various studies which seem to indicate
        that the incidence of parental deprivation is significantly
        higher in schizophrenic patients than in normal ones.

3277   "On death as a constant companion, " Time (Nov. 12, 1965),
        52-5.

3278   "One every twenty minutes, " Medical World News, 8 (1967),
        73-8.
              An examination of the factors that cause people to
        use suicide as an escape mechanism.

3279   Opler, M. E.   "Further comparative anthropological data
        bearing on the solution of a psychological problem, "
        Journal of Social Psychology, 9 (1938), 477-84.

3280   _____.   "An Interpretation of ambivalence of two American
        Indian tribes, " Journal of Social Psychology, 7 (1936),
        82-115.
              An anthropological study of the Apaches concerning
        the strange contradictions between the mourning for the
        dead, the fear of them, and the taboos against them.

3281   _____.   "The Lipan Apache death complex and its exten-
        sions, " Southwestern Journal of Anthropology, 1 (1945),
        122-45.

3282 _____. "Reactions to death among the Mescalaro Apache, "
Southwestern Journal of Anthropology, 2 (1946), 454-67.
Discusses the grief, despair, and the concept of life
after death of this tribe.

3283 _____, and W. E. Bittle. "The Death practices and
eschatology of the Kiowa Apache, " Southwestern Journal
of Anthropology, 17 (1961), 383-94.
Discusses the fear and beliefs in ghosts among the
Apache and the traumatic experience death is to them.

3284 Orbach, C. E. "The Multiple meanings of the loss of a
child, " American Journal of Psychotherapy, 13 (1959),
906-15.
An attempt to "delineate the manifold associations
of a child's death to different aspects of his mother's
past and current experience. "

3285 Orenstein, H. "Death and kinship in Hinduism: structural
and functional interpretations, " American Anthropologist,
72 (Dec. 1970), 1357-77.

3286 Orlansky, H. "Reactions to the death of President Roosevelt, " Journal of Social Psychology, 26 (1947), 235-66.

3287 Osborne, E. When you lose a loved one. N. Y.: Public
Affairs Pamphlet no. 269, 1958.
The author covers such practical topics as bereavement, guilt, mourning, grief, funerals, helping children
cope with death, and family experiences.

3288 Ostow, M. "The Death instinct--a contribution to the study
of instincts, " International Journal of Psychoanalysis,
39 (1958), 5-16.

3289 Osuna, P., and D. K. Reynolds. "A Funeral in Mexico:
description and analysis, " Omega, 1 (Nov. 1970), 249-
69.

3290 Oulahan, R., Jr. "Euthanasia; should one kill a child in
mercy?" Life, 53 (Aug. 18, 1962), 34-5.
Story about a woman who killed her thalidomide de-
formed baby and the turmoil it created in pro and con
opinions on euthanasia.

3291 Pacyaya, A. G. "Changing customs of marriage, death and
burial among the Sagada, " Practical Anthropology, 8
(1961), 125-33.

3292 Page, I. H. "On death, " Modern Medicine, 39 (Sept. 20,
1971), 73-5.

3293 Pandey, C. "The Need for the psychological study of

clinical death," <u>Omega</u>, 2 (Feb. 1971), 1-9.

3294 Pandy, R. E., and D. I. Templer. "Use of the death an-
      xiety scale in an inter-racial setting," <u>Omega</u>, 3 (May
      1973), 127-30.

3295 Papageorgis, D. "On the ambivalence of death: the care of
      the nursing Harlequin," <u>Psychological Reports</u>, 19 (Aug.
      1966), 325-6.
          Takes issue with the McClelland hypothesis which
      suggests that attitudes about death are ambivalent in
      the case of women.

3296 Paris, J. "Responses to death and sex stimulus materials
      as a function of repression sensitization," <u>Psychological
      Reports</u>, 19 (Dec. 1966), 1283-91.
          Study is concerned with sensitizers that express an-
      xiety in literary materials dealing with both sex and
      death that would be repressive.

3297 Parker, E. B., and B. S. Greenberg, eds. <u>Communication
      in crisis: social research on the Kennedy assassination</u>.
      Stanford, Calif.: Stanford University Press, 1965.

3298 Parker, W. S. "Realities of responsibility: what are the
      real priorities in medical and nursing care?" <u>Nursing
      Times</u>, 67 (Aug. 26, 1971), 1053-54.

3299 Parkes, C. M. "The First year of bereavement: a longi-
      tudinal study of the reactions of London widows to the
      death of their husbands," <u>Psychiatry</u>, 33 (1970), 444-67.
          Examines the process of grief and change over time
      through interviews with 22 London widows under the
      age of 65.

3300 _____. "Recent bereavement as a cause of mental ill-
      ness," <u>British Journal of Psychiatry</u>, 110 (1964), 198-
      203.

3301 Parkin, M. "Suicide and culture in Fairbanks; a comparison
      of three cultural groups in a small city of interior
      Alaska," <u>Psychiatry</u>, 37 (Feb. 1974), 70-7.

3302 Parsons, T. "Death in American society--a brief working
      paper," <u>The American Behavioral Scientist</u>, 6 (1963),
      61-5.
          Primary purpose of the article is to "alienate cer-
      tain aspects of attitudes toward death in American soci-
      ety, and to analyze the cultural roots as they relate to
      social structure."

3303 _____, and V. Lidz. "Death in American society," in
      <u>Essays in Self Destruction</u>, edited by E. S. Shneidman.

N. Y.: Science House, 1967. pp. 133-70.

3304   ; R. C. Fox; and V. Lidz. "The 'Gift of Life' and its reciprocation, " in Death in American Experience, edited by A. Mack. N. Y.: Schocken, 1973. pp. 1-49.
Contents: The Judeo-Christian symbolization of life and death; Early christianity; Protestantism; The moral basis of modern medical ethics; The existential problem of death in medical perspective.

3305 Patry, F. L. "A Psychiatric evaluation of communicating with the dying, " Diseases of the Nervous System, 26 (Nov. 1965), 715-18.

3306 Pattison, E. M. "The Experience of dying, " American Journal of Psychotherapy, 21 (1967), 32-43.
Presents ways the clinician can help the dying patient to face death and ease the process of dying.

3307   . "Psychosocial predictors of death prognosis, " Omega, 5 (summer 1974), 145-160.

3308 Paul, N. L. "The Need to mourn, " in The Child in His Family, edited by E. J. Anthony, and C. Koupernik. N. Y.: Wiley, 1973. Vol. 2, pp. 219-24.

3309   . "Psychiatry: its role in the resolution of grief, " in Death and Bereavement, edited by A. H. Kutscher. Springfield, Ill.: C. C. Thomas, 1969.

3310   , and G. H. Grosser. "Operational mourning and its role in conjoint family therapy, " Community Mental Health Journal, 1 (1965), 339-45.
"The technique of operational mourning is designed to involve the family in a belated mourning experience with extensive grief reactions. "

3311 Pauw, B. A. "Ancestor beliefs and rituals among urban Africans, " African Studies, 33 (1974), 99-111.

3312 Pearson, J. "The Time of death: a legal, ethical and medical dilemma, " Catholic Lawyer, 18 (summer 1972), 243-57.

3313 Pearson, K. The Chances of death and other studies in evolution. London: Arnold Press, 1897.

3314 Peck, M. "Notes on identification in a case of depression reactive to the death of a love object, " Psychoanalytic Quarterly, 8 (1939), 1-17.

3315 Peck, R. "The Development of the concept of death in selected male children. " Ph.D. dissertation, New York University, 1966.

3316 Pederson, S. "Phallic fantasies, fear of death and ecstacy,"
      American Imago, 17 (1960), 21-46.

3317 Pescaru, A. "La Morbidité du personnel médical et sani-
      taire de Bucarest," Cahiers de Sociologie et de Démog-
      raphie Medicales, 13 (July-Sept. 1973), 71-6.

3318 Pescetto, G. "Representazione della morte nel Bambino,"
      Rassegna di Studi Psichiatrici, 46 (March-April 1957),
      165-80.

3319 Pessin, J. "Self destructive tendencies in adolescence,"
      Bulletin of the Menninger Clinic, 5 (1941), 13.

3320 Petriconi, H. Das Reich des Untergangs: Bermerkungen
      über ein mythologisches Thema. Hamburg: Hoffman,
      1958.

3321 Petrie, A. Individuality in pain and suffering. Chicago:
      University of Chicago Press, 1967.

3322 Pfister, O. "Schockdenken und Schockphantasien bei höchster
      Todesgefahr," Internationale Zeitschrift für Psycho-
      analyse, 16 (1930), 430-55.

3323 Phillips, D. P. "Birthdays and death." Paper presented to
      the American Sociological Assoc., San Francisco, Sept.
      1969.

3324 _____, and K. A. Feldman. "A Dip in deaths before
      ceremonial occasions: some new relationships between
      social integration and mortality," American Sociological
      Review, 38 (Dec. 1973), 618-96.
          "... [E]vidence suggests that the dip in deaths be-
      fore ceremonies (birthday, presidential elections, and
      Jewish Day of Atonement) results from some persons'
      postponement of death. Results are interpreted in terms
      of E. Durkheim's discussion of social integration and
      ceremonies" (Journal Abstract).

3325 Pichon, E. "Mort, angoisse, negation," Evolution Psychi-
      atrique, 1 (1947), 19-46.

3326 Pieroni, A. "Role of the social worker in a children's can-
      cer clinic," Pediatrics, 40 (Sept. 1967), 534-6.

3327 Pihlblad, C. T.; D. L. Adams; and H. A. Rosencranz.
      "Socio-economic adjustment of widowhood," Omega, 3
      (Nov. 1972), 295-305.

3328 Pincherle, G. "Mortality of members of Parliament,"
      British Journal of Preventive Sociological Medicine, 23
      (1969), 72-4.

3328a Pincus, L. Death and the family: the importance of mourning. N.Y.: Pantheon, 1974.

3329 Pine, V. R. "Comparative funeral practices," Practical Anthropology, 16 (March-April 1969), 49-62.

3330 _____. "Social organization and death," Omega, 3 (May 1972), 149-53.

3331 _____, and D. Phillips. "The Cost of dying: a sociological analysis of funeral expenditures," Social Problems, 17 (winter 1970), 405-17.

3332 Pitts, F., et al. "Adult psychiatric illness assessed for childhood parental loss," American Journal of Psychiatry, 121 (1965), Supplement I-X.
Discusses the loss of a parent in childhood as a kind of social event which could influence personality development and psychiatric illness in adulthood.

3333 Pokorny, A. D. "Moon phases, suicide, and homicide," American Journal of Psychiatry, 121 (July 1964), 66-7.
Suggests a positive relationship between suicides and murders the day before the perigee of the moon.

3334 Pollak, O. "The Errors of justice," Annals of the American Academy of Political and Social Science, 284 (1952), 115-23.
Discusses the errors of judgment that have led to the execution of innocent persons.

3335 Pollock, G. H. "On time, death and immortality," Psychoanalytic Quarterly, 40 (1971), 341-61.

3336 Polner, M., and A. Barron. The Questions children ask. N.Y.: Macmillan, 1964.

3337 Porter, W. H., Jr. "Some sociological notes on a century of change in the funeral business," Sociological Symposium, 1 (fall 1968), 36-46.

3338 Porterfield, A. L., and J. P. Gibbs. "Occupational prestige and social mobility of suicides in New Zealand," American Journal of Sociology, 66 (Sept. 1960), 147-52.

3339 Powell, E. H. "Occupations, status and suicide," American Sociological Review, 23 (April 1958), 131-9.
Discusses suicide and deals with anomie, the crucial factor in the etiology of suicide.

3340 "Power relations in three person groups," by T. M. Mills. American Sociological Review, 18 (1953), 351-7.

3341 Prattes, O. R. "Helping the family face an impending
      death, " Nursing '73 (Feb. 1973), 17-20.

3342 Preis, A. "Attitudes toward death and personality charac-
      teristics. " Thesis, University of Pittsburgh, 1971.

3343 Preston, S. H. "Demographic and social consequences of
      various causes of death in the United States, " Social
      Biology, 21 (summer 1974), 144-62.

3344 Prettyman, B. Death and the Supreme Court. N. Y.: Har-
      court, Brace and World, 1968.
            Study of the system of justice which is employed in
      convicting and sending men and women to their deaths.
      Includes the role of the Supreme Court in death sen-
      tences.

3345 Pretzel, P. W. Understanding and counseling the suicidal
      person. Foreword by H. J. Clinebell, Jr., and N.
      Farberow. Texas: Cokesbury, 1973.

3346 Pritchett, V. S. "Necrophobia, " New Statesman, 69 (April
      30, 1965), 684-5.

3347 "Pros and cons of an end to the death penalty, " U. S. News,
      72 (Jan. 31, 1972), 56.

3348 Pruden, W., Jr. Triple murder brings an echo of '60's
      strife, " National Observer (June 8, 1974), 4.

3349 Prudhomme, C. "The Problem of suicide in the American
      negro, " Psychoanalytic Review, 25 (1938), 187-204.

3350 Puckle, B. S. Funeral customs. N. Y.: Frederick A.
      Stokes, 1926.

3351 Purcell, C.; R. C. Leslie; and C. W. Wahl. Helping the
      dying patient and his family. N. Y.: National Assoc.
      of Social Workers, 1960.

3352 Purtilo, R. B. "Don't mention it: the physical therapist
      in a death denying society, " Physical Therapy, 52 (Oct.
      1972), 1031-35.

3353 Quinney, E. R. "Mortality differentials in a metropolitan
      area, " Social Forces, 43 (Dec. 1964), 222-30.

3354 "Race and education the most significant factors in attitudes
      of aged toward death, study shows, " Geriatric Focus,
      4 (Jan. 15, 1966), 2-3.

3355 Racy, J. "Death in an Arab culture, " Annals of the New
      York Academy of Sciences, 164 (Dec. 1969), 871-80.

States that the Arab culture has never had an opportunity to deny the reality of death. Lists factors that support this.

3356   Radin, P. The Story of the American Indian. N. Y. : Liverright, 1934.
An interpretive history of the American Indians presenting different aspects of their life, religion, war, art, and death.

3357   Rakoff, V. M. "Psychiatric aspects of death in America, " in Death in American Experience, edited by A. Mack. N. Y. : Schocken, 1973. pp. 149-62.
"America has its own death myths, its own way of coping with the terror; while the stereotype certainly lacks universal applicability, there is a dominant eschatology.... [W]hy is North America so particularly death-denying?"

3358   Ramos, S. "The Hardest lesson of all, " New York Times Magazine (Dec. 10, 1972), 94.
Description of the work of Gilbert Kliman and his staff in White Plains, N. Y. They handle methods of preventing and easing children's experiences with death.

3359   Ramzy, I. , and R. S. Wallerstein. "Pain, fear and anxiety, " Psychoanalytic Study of the Child, 13 (1958), 147-89.

3360   Rao, S. L. N. "On long-term mortality trends in the United States 1950-1968, " Demography, 10 (Aug. 1973), 405-19.

3361   Rapaport, H. N. "Funeral practices--U. S. model 1965, " The Torch, (spring 1965), 28-32.

3362   Rapoport, J. "A Case of necrophilia, " Journal of Criminal Psychopathology, 4 (1942), 277-89.

3363   Reckless, W. C. "The Use of the death penalty, " Crime and Delinquency, 15 (Jan. 1969), 43-56.

3364   Redl, F. When we deal with children. N. Y. : Free Press, 1966.
A selected group of writings which challenge techniques and concepts of child development. The "death wish" is also covered.

3365   Reed, A. W. "Problems of impending death. The concerns of the dying patient, " Physical Therapy, 48 (July 1968), 740-3.
A social worker and clergyman discuss the environmental aspect of the patient's life and the more interpersonal aspects of the concerns of dying patients.

3366 Remsberg, B., and C. Remsberg. "What four brave women told their children," Good Housekeeping, 164 (May 1967), 94-96.

3367 Resnik, H. L. P. "On the love of suicide," Commentary, 54 (Aug. 1972), 29-32.

3368 Rheingold, J. The Mother, anxiety and death: the catastrophic death complex. Boston: Little, 1967.
Considers three inseparable subjects: the mother-child relationship, the meaning of anxiety, and the psychology of death.

3369 Rhudick, P. J., and A. S. Dibner. "Attitudes toward death in older persons: a symposium," Journal of Gerontology, 16 (1961), 44-66.
Contains excerpts from papers delivered at a symposium on death attitudes of older people stating the findings of each contributing researcher.

3370 Richman, J., et al. "A Clinical study of the role of hostility and death wishes by the family and society in suicidal attempts," Israel Annals of Psychiatry and Related Disciplines, 8 (Dec. 1970), 213-31.

3371 Riegel, K. F.; R. H. Riegel; and G. Meyer. "A Study of the dropout rates in longitudinal research on aging and the prediction of death," Journal of Personality and Social Psychology, 5 (1967), 342-8.

3372 Riley, J. W., Jr. "Death and bereavement," International Encyclopedia of the Social Sciences, edited by D. L. Sills. N.Y.: Macmillan, 1968. Vol. 4, pp. 19-26.
An explanation of what death is. How it relates to man, culture, history, society, and individuals. Discusses the image of death and the current issues and attitudes about it.

3373 Ringel, E. Der Selbstmord. Vienna: Maudich, 1953.

3374 Rivers, W. H. R. "The Primitive conceptions of death," in Psychology and Ethnology, edited by H. Elliot Smith. N.Y.: Harcourt Brace, 1926. pp. 36.

3375 Roalfe, W. R. "The Psychology of suicide," Journal of Abnormal and Social Psychology, 23 (1928-1929), 59-67.

3376 Roberts, H. Euthanasia and other aspects of life and death. London: Constable and Co., 1936.

3377 Robertson, J. "Some responses of young children to loss of maternal care," Child-Family Digest, 15 (Sept.-Oct. 1956), 7-22.

3378 Robitscher, J. B. "The Right to die," Hastings Center Report, 2 (Sept. 1972), 11-14.

3379 Rochlin, G. Griefs and discontents: the focus of change. Boston: Little, 1965.

3380 _____. "The Loss complex," Journal of the American Psychoanalytic Association, 7 (1959), 299-316.

3381 Rogo, D. S. "Parapsychology--its contributions to the study of death," Omega, 5 (summer 1974), 99-113.
"... [P]sychical phenomena occur so often related to death that any psychological inquiry into the nature of death and dying should take into consideration the data parapsychology has amassed on the subject."

3382 Roose, L. J. "The Dying patient," International Journal of Psychoanalysis, 50 (1969), 385-95.
Discusses the problems which arise for the psychiatrists on hospital staffs when the depressed and dying cancer patient hasn't been told the truth.

3383 Rose, R. J. Maori European comparisons in mortality. Wellington, New Zealand: National Health Statistics Center, Department of Health, 1972.

3384 Rosenberg, B.; I. Gerver; and F. Howton. Mass society in crisis. N.Y.: Macmillan, 1964.

3385 Rosenblatt, B. "A Young boy's reaction to the death of his sister," Journal of the American Academy of Child Psychiatry, 8 (1969), 321-35.

3386 Rosenthal, H. "The Fear of death as an indispensable factor in psychotherapy," American Journal of Psychotherapy, 17 (1963), 619-30.
Discusses the "obligation of the psychotherapist to take cognizance of the universality, whether conscious or repressed, of anxiety regarding death."

3387 Ross, M. "Suicide among college students," American Journal of Psychiatry, 126 (1969), 220-25.
Discusses the high rate of suicide among college students. The author believes that among college students, suicide is both predictable and preventable.

3388 Roux, J. P. La Mort chez les peuples altaïques anciens et médievaux, d'après les documents écrits. Paris: Adrien-Mainsonneuve, 1963.

3389 Rubin, S. "The Supreme Court, cruel and unusual punishment, and the death penalty," Crime and Delinquency, 15 (Jan. 1969), 121-31.

3390   Rueda, T. "The Concept of death among French and Mexican suicidal persons, " Proceedings of the 6th International Conference for Suicide Prevention, Mexico, Dec. 5-8, 1972. N. Y.: Edwards Brothers, 1972.

3391   Ruff, W. "Das Sterben des Menschen und die Feststellung seines Todes, " Stimmen der Zeit, 182 (Oct. 1968), 251-61.

3392   Ruitenbeek, H. M., ed. The Interpretation of death. N. Y.: Aronson, 1973.
        A collection of essays of which the contributors react to the phenomenon of death with the focus on the psychotherapy of dying.

3393   Rushing, W. A. "Deviance, interpersonal relations and suicide, " Human Relations, 22 (Feb. 1969), 61-76.
        Deals with the relationship between suicide and forms of deviance, which generates frustration.

3394   Russell, O. R. "Moral and legal aspects of euthanasia, " The Humanist, (July-Aug. 1974), 22-7.

3394a   . Freedom to die; moral and legal aspects of euthanasia. N. Y. Human Sciences Press, 1975.

3395   Sainsbury, P. Suicide in London: an ecological study. N. Y.: Basic Books; London: Chapman and Hall, 1956.

3396   St. John-Stevas, N. Life, death, and the law. Cleveland: World, 1964.

3397   Salamone, J. "An Attitudinal study of funeral customs in Calcasieu Parish, Louisiana: a sociological analysis. " Ph. D. dissertation, Louisiana State University, 1966.

3398   . "An Empirical report on some controversial American funeral practices, " Sociological Symposium, 1 (fall 1968), 47-56.

3399   Sanderlin, O. "When someone dies: consoling the bereaved, " Catholic Layman, 77 (Nov. 1963), 37-41.

3400   Sanders, J. "Euthanasia: none dare call it murder, " Journal of Criminal Law, Criminology, and Police Science, 60 (1969), 351-9.
        Discusses barriers to legislation approving euthanasia and the various problems and opinions about it.

3401   Sarnoff, I., and S. M. Corwin. "Castration anxiety and the fear of death, " Journal of Personality, 27 (1959), 374-85.
        States the persons who have a high degree of castration anxiety show a greater fear of death after arousal of sexual feelings.

3402   Saucier, J. F.   "Anthropologie et psychodynamique de
       deuil, " Canadian Psychiatric Association Journal, 12
       (1967), 477-96.
              "Examined the behavior sequence of the child fol-
       lowing the mother's death.   The sequence is considered
       as the prototype of mourning behavior in adults in all
       human societies: protest, despair, and detachment. . . . "

3403   Saum, L. O.   "Death in the popular mind of pre-civil war
       America, " American Quarterly, 26 (Dec. 1974), 477-9.
       ". . . [A]ttempts to convey what ordinary people
       themselves said about death, and in part, it attempts to
       relate attitudes and beliefs to the depictions rendered by
       better minds both at the time and later. . . . "

3404   Schaeffer, S.   "Death fears and bereavement in a seven-
       year-old boy hospitalized eighteen months after the death
       of his father. "   Thesis M. N. Ed. , University of Pitts-
       burgh, 1967.

3405   Schilder, P.   "The Attitude of murderers toward death, "
       Journal of Abnormal and Social Psychology, 31 (1936),
       348-63.

3406   _____, and D. Wechsler.   "The Attitudes of children to-
       ward death, " Journal of Genetic Psychology, 45 (1934),
       406-51.
              Discusses children's views of death, and points out
       the child's fear of being murdered and dying in a disas-
       ter.

3407   Schlesinger, B.   "The Widowed as a one parent family unit, "
       Social Science, 46 (1971), 26-32.

3408   _____, and A. Macrae.   "The Widow and widower and
       remarriage: selected findings, " Omega, 2 (Feb. 1971),
       10-18.

3409   Schmale, A. H. , Jr.   "Normal grief is not a disease. "   A
       paper presented at a seminar of the Thanatology Founda-
       tion at Columbia College of Physicians and Surgeons,
       Nov. 12, 1971.

3410   _____.   "Psychic trauma during bereavement, " Interna-
       tional Psychiatry Clinics, 8 (1971), 147-68.

3411   Schmid, C. F.   Suicide in Seattle, 1914-1925: an ecological
       and behavioristic study.   Seattle: University of Washing-
       ton Press, 1928.

3412   Schmideberg, M.   "A Note on suicide, " International Journal
       of Psychoanalysis, 17 (1936), 1-5.
              Presents the psychoanalytic view of suicide and

states that aggression is a determining factor.

3413 Schmidt, B., and J. Schmidt. "Psychological death in head-
      shrinkers," American Journal of Psychiatry, 121 (1964),
      510-11.
          Discusses the Jibaro Indians of South East Ecuador
      and points out that the Jibaro is aware from childhood
      that somebody wishes he were dead.

3414 Schmiedeck, R. A. "Zur Psychodynamik von Tod und
      Trauer," Dynamische Psychiatrie, 1 (1968), 110-20.

3415 Schneck, J. M. "Hypoanalytic elucidation of the hypnosis--
      death concept," Psychiatric Quarterly (supplement), 24
      (1950), 286-89.

3416 _____. "Unconscious relationship between hypnosis and
      death," Psychoanalytic Review, 38 (1951), 271-75.
          States that for some individuals hypnosis is equated
      with death. Author states that "the so-called hypnotic
      state for animals has been the instinct to simulate death
      for protective purposes, the death-feint, and conscious
      simulation of death. Possibly, may be a defense reac-
      tion set up in a relation to conflict between the individual
      and his environment."

3417 Schneider, H. "Euthanasia: a comparative examination of
      its place within the scope of criminal law," Criminolog-
      ica, 7 (1969), 25-38.

3418 Schneiders, A. "Psychology of dying," Guild of Catholic
      Psychologists, 10 (Jan. 1963), 7-10.

3419 Schoenberg, B. B., et al. Anticipatory grief. N. Y.: Co-
      lumbia University Press, 1974.
          An anthology of articles written by professionals
      concerned with terminal illness, dynamics of grief, so-
      cietal response, childhood illness, and the clinical as-
      pects of death.

3420 _____, et al. Loss and grief: psychological management
      in medical practice. N. Y.: Columbia University Press,
      1970.
          "Deals with the effects of death and dying on both
      adults and children.... [It] is unique in its emphasis
      on psychological problems of the patient and of family
      members who have sustained or anticipate serious
      loss."

3421/2 _____, et al. Psychosocial aspects of terminal care.
      N. Y.: Columbia University Press, 1972.

3423 Schontz, F. C., and S. L. Fink. "A Psychobiological

Social Sciences   311   SCHORR

analysis of discomfort, pain and death, " Journal of
General Psychology, 60 (1959), 275-87.

3424 Schorr, A. L., ed. Children and decent people. N. Y.:
Basic Books, 1974.
Eleven experts examine "institutions that claim to
ensure the welfare of American children ... and their
findings reveal a dismal picture...."

3425 Schuessler, K. "The Deterrent influence of the death penalty, " Annals of the American Academy of Political and
Social Science, 284 (1952), 54-62.
Article analyzes statistical data as it bears on the
question of how much the death penalty deters people
from committing murder. The data was from the period
1925 to 1949.

3426 Schupper, F. X. "On love and the death drive, " American
Imago, 21 (fall 1964), 3-10.
Discusses passages from Freud's texts dealing with
eros and thanatos.

3427 Schur, M. "Discussion of Dr. John Bowlby's paper 'Grief
and Mourning in Infancy and Early Childhood', " The
Psychoanalytic Study of the Child, 15 (1960), 63-84.
Criticizes Dr. Bowlby's paper from the point where
it differs with psychoanalysis and developmental psychology with reference to grief and mourning in children.

3428 _____. "The Problem of death in Freud's writings and
life. " 14th Freud Anniversary Lecture, New York,
1964.

3429 Schur, T. J. "What man has told children about death, "
Omega, 2 (May 1971), 84-90.

3430 Schuyler, D. "When was the last time you took a suicidal
child to lunch?" Journal of School Health, 43 (Oct.
1973), 504-6.
Explains how one can be alerted to a possible suicide and the meaning of death to a child. The magni-
tude of the problem of the suicidal child is clearly
brought out.

3431 Scott, A. W., Jr. "The Pardoning power, " Annals of the
American Academy of Political and Social Science, 28
(1952), 95-100.
States that as long as "capital punishment continues,
the power to pardon in capital cases is bound to remain
an important element in the administration of criminal
justice. "

3432 Scott, W. C. "Deuil et Manie, " Revue Française de Psychanalyse, 29 (1965), 205-18.

3433 _____. "Mania and mourning," International Journal of
            Psychoanalysis, 45 (1964), 373-9.

3434 Searles, H. F.   "Schizophrenia and the inevitability of
            death," Psychiatric Quarterly, 35 (1961), 631-5.

3435 Segal, H.   "Fear of death: notes on the analysis of an old
            man," International Journal of Psychoanalysis, 39 (1958),
            178-81.
            Author concludes that the uncommon fears of death
            underlie many breakdowns in old age.

3436 Segers, M. C.   "Violence left and middle; use as a political
            tactic," Catholic World, 212 (March 1971), 307-8.
            Examines the behavior of the New Left factions and
            their rhetoric of violence and death.

3437 Seiden, R. H.   "The Problem of suicide on college cam-
            puses," Journal of School Health, XLI (May 1971), 243.

3438 _____, and B. Teitler.   Attitudes toward modes of death;
            Proceedings of the 6th International Conference for Sui-
            cide Prevention, Mexico, December 5-8, 1972.   N.Y.:
            Edwards Brothers, 1972.

3439 Sellin, J. T., ed.   Murder and the penalty of death.
            Philadelphia: Annals of the American Academy of Po-
            litical and Social Science, vol. 284, 1952.

3440 Sellin, T., ed.   Capital punishment.   N.Y.: Harper and
            Row, 1967.

3441 Sepulveda, B.   "Concept of death," Gaceta Medica de México,
            99 (July 1969), 631-33.

3442 Severud, F. N., and A. F. Merrill.   "The Nature of the
            Bomb, [and] The Hiroshima and Nagasaki Data," in The
            Bomb Survival and You.   N.Y.: Reinhold, 1954.   pp.
            29-87.
            These pages convey to the reader an understanding
            of the general characteristics and effects of the atomic
            bomb.   The discussion begins with August 6, 1945, and
            describes vividly the effects at Hiroshima and Nagasaki.
            The series of 21 photographs of Hiroshima and Nagasaki
            were taken by the U.S. Strategic Bomb Surveys.

3443 Shaffer, T. L.   "Approaches to death," Editorial Research
            Reports, 1 (April 21, 1971), 289-306.

3444 _____. Death, property, and lawyers: a behavioral ap-
            proach.   N.Y.: Dunellen, 1971.

3445 _____. "The Estate planning counsellor and values destroyed by death, " Iowa Law Review, 55 (1970), 376.

3446 Share, L. "Family communication in the crisis of a child's
fatal illness: a literature review and analysis, " Omega,
3 (Aug. 1972), 187-201.
Family communication is examined when the crisis
of a dying child exists. The two approaches--protective
and open--observe the child's reactions to his illness and
his conception of death.

3447 Sheatsley, P. B., and J. J. Feldman. "The Assassination
of President Kennedy: a preliminary report on public
reactions and behavior, " Public Opinion Quarterly, 28
(summer 1964), 189-215.

3448 Sher, B. D. "Funeral prearrangement: mitigating the undertaker's bargaining advantage, " Stanford Law Review,
15 (May 1963), 415.

3449 Sherrill, L. J., and H. H. Sherrill. "Interpreting death to
children, " International Journal of Religious Education,
28 (1951), 4-6.
Offers information to parents about children's mental
health regarding their knowledge of death.

3450 Shetrone, H. C. The Mound builders. N. Y.: Appleton,
1930.
Reconstruction of a prehistoric race in America
through exploration and interpretation of its mounds,
burials, and cultural remains.

3451 Shields, E. A. "Depression then suicide, " American Journal
of Nursing, 46 (1946), 677-9.

3452 Shneidman, E. S., ed. Death and the college student. N. Y.:
Behavioral Publications, 1972.
Discusses contemporary death, and written by college students themselves from a course at Harvard on
death and suicide.

3453 _____. "The Deaths of Herman Melville, " in Melville and
Hawthorne in the Berkshires, edited by H. Vincent.
Kent, Ohio: Kent State University Press, 1967.

3454 _____. Deaths of man. Foreword by Arnold Toynbee.
N. Y.: Quadrangle, 1973.
"... [W]ritten by a practitioner of clinical thanatology, modern and psychological in its approach, this
penetrating examination of death is infused with practical, literary, and philosophical understandings" (blurb).

3455 _____. "The Enemy, " Psychology Today, 3 (Aug. 1970),
37.

Outlines various aspects of death, and describes the death-seeker, the death-initiator, and the death-darer.

3456 _____. Essays in self-destruction. N. Y.: Science House, 1967.

3457 _____. On the nature of suicide. San Francisco: Jossey-Base, 1969.

3457a _____. "Orientation toward cessation: a re-examination of current modes of death," Journal of Forensic Science, 13 (Jan. 1968), 33-45.

3458 _____. "Orientations toward death: a vital aspect of the study of lives," in The Study of Lives. N. Y.: Atherton, 1963.
The essay attempts to stimulate new thinking on the conventional theories of suicide and death. The book as a whole tries psychologically to describe death phenomena and the role a person has in his own death.

3459 _____. "Precursors of suicide," Medical Insight, 1 (Nov. 1969), 404.
Deals with clues to potential suicide and syndromes of suicide.

3460 _____. "Prevention, intervention, and postvention of suicide," Annals of Internal Medicine, 75 (1971), 453-58.

3461 _____. "Suicide, sleep, and death: some possible inter-relations among cessation, interruption and continuation phenomena," Journal of Consulting Psychology, 28 (April 1964), 95-100.
Presents an "overview of some possibly productive parallels between sleep phenomena and death (particularly suicidal) phenomena."

3462 _____. "You and death," Psychology Today (June 1971), 43.
Records the results of a survey which indicated that people feel that death is more important than sex.

3463 _____, and N. L. Farberow, eds. Clues to suicide. N. Y.: McGraw-Hill, 1957.
"Considers the subject of suicide theoretically, experimentally, and clinically in terms of sociology, law, medicine, environmental and age factor, prevention and treatment."

3464 _____, and R. Litman. The Psychology of suicide. N. Y.: Science House, 1970.

3465 Shoben, E. J., Jr. "Culture, ego psychology, and an image of man," American Journal of Psychotherapy, 15 (July 1961), 395-408.

3466 Shoor, M. H., and M. H. Speed. "Death, delinquency and the mourning process," Psychiatric Quarterly, 37 (1963), 540-58.

3467 _____. "Delinquency as a manifestation of the mourning process," Psychiatric Quarterly, 37 (1963), 540-58.

3468 Shor, R. E. "A Survey of representative literature on Freud's death-instinct hypothesis," Journal of Humanistic Psychology, 1 (1961), 98-110.

3469 Shrut, S. D. "Attitudes toward old age and death," Mental Hygiene, 42 (1958), 259-66.

3470 Sichel, J. "Death fantasies in a child," Praxis der Kinderpsychologie und Kinderpsychiatrie (Göttingen), 16 (July 1967), 172-5.

3471 Siggins, L. D. "Mourning: a critical survey of the literature," International Journal of Psychoanalysis, 47 (1966), 14-25.
Examines the process of mourning, which ideally protects the open wound from raw and painful contact and leads at last to healing.

3472 "Signs of suicide: high rate among college students," Time, 91 (April 12, 1968), 60.
States that suicide is more common among college students than non-college goers, and describes the "signs of suicide."

3473 Silverman, P. R. "Services to the widowed: first steps in a program of preventive intervention," Community Mental Health Journal, 3 (1967), 37-44.
Widows under 60 are singled out in this study as having a high risk of developing mental illness. Mental health services and agencies who do preventive work are considered.

3474 _____. "The Widow as a caregiver in a program of preventive intervention with other widows," Mental Hygiene, 54 (Oct. 1970), 540-47.

3475 _____. "The Widow-to-widow program; an experiment in preventive intervention," Mental Hygiene, 53 (July 1969), 333-37.
Description of programs to help widows at the various stages of their grief.

3476 _____. "Widowhood and preventive intervention," Family

Coordinator, 21 (Jan. 1972), 95-102.

3477 Simmel, E. "Self preservation and the death instinct,"
      Psychoanalytic Quarterly, 13 (1944), 160-85.
          Discusses Freud's dualistic instinct theory of the
      libidinal constructive life instinct and of the non-libidinal
      self-destructive death instinct.

3478 Simmons, L. W. "Reactions to death," in The Role of the
      Aged in Primitive Society. New Haven, Conn.: Yale
      University Press, 1945.

3479 Simon, S. B.; L. W. Howe; and H. Kirschenbaum. Values
      clarification. N. Y.: Hart, 1972.
          The authors state that students can get a good grip
      on life through talking about death.

3480 Simon, W., and W. M. Hales. "Note on a suicide key in
      the Minnesota Multiphasic Personality Inventory," Ameri-
      can Journal of Psychiatry, 106 (1949), 222-23.
          Investigation suggests that "Psychoasthesia when
      coupled with depression, may determine the actual at-
      tempt at destruction in the schizophrenic."

3481 Sirken, M. G. "Design of household sample surveys to test
      death registration completeness," Demography, 10 (Aug.
      1973), 469-78.

3482 Sisk, G. "Funeral customs in the Alabama black belt, 1870-
      1910," Southern Folklore Quarterly, 23 (Sept. 1959),
      169-71.

3483 Sjövall, H. "Om diagnosen sjalvmord," Svenska Lakartidning,
      50 (1953), 1113-40.

3484 Skeels, D. R. "Eros and thanatos in Nez Percé river
      mythology," American Imago, 21 (fall 1964), 103-10.

3485 Slater, E. "Case for voluntary euthanasia," Contemporary
      Review, 219 (Aug. 1971), 84-8.

3486 Smart, M. "A Program on what death means to children for
      your discussion group," Parents Magazine and Better
      Homemaker (March 1965), 15-16.
          Examines the phases of grief and mourning in
      adults and children. Children under six years cannot
      conceive of the finality of death and they may mourn
      for many years over the deceased.

3487 Smith, A. L., and R. M. Carter. "Count down for death,"
      Crime and Delinquency, 15 (Jan. 1969), 77-93.
          Describes the day-to-day existence of an inmate
      in his final week on death row.

3488 Smith, E. H. Brief against death. N. Y.: Knopf, 1968.
Autobiography of a man on death row. He describes
his arrest and 4000-day battle to establish his innocence.

3489 _____. "Long wait: new trial for death house author, "
Time, 97 (May 24, 1971), 22.

3490 Smith, H. L. "Abortion, death and the sanctity of life, "
Social Science and Medicine, 5 (1971), 211-8.

3491 Snider, A. J. "Last rites, do they bring fear or reassurance?" Science Digest, 65 (June 1969), 60-1.
Deals with psychological effects of last rites on a
conscious and seriously ill patient.

3492 Solnit, A. J. "Who mourns when a child dies, " in The
Child in His Family, edited by E. J. Anthony, and C.
Koupernik. N. Y.: Wiley, 1973. pp. 245-64.
Takes up the interesting questions of secrecy,
privacy, peace, needs of the dying child, and the role
of the therapeutic team with the dying and surviving.

3493 Solomon, H. C. "Psychiatric implications of cancer, "
Rocky Mountain Medical Journal, 44 (Oct. 1947), 801.

3494 "Some thermodynamics and kinetics, " in To Live and to Die:
when, why, and how, edited by R. H. Williams. Chapter 4, "On the Origin of Life, " by E. H. Fischer.
N. Y.: Springer-Verlag, 1973. pp. 38-47.

3495 Spangler, J. A. "California's death penalty dilemma, "
Crime and Delinquency, 15 (Jan. 1969), 142-8.
Examines "California's legal machinery in capital
punishment cases, cites court decisions, and provides
tables showing number of persons on death row and how
long they have been awaiting execution. "

3496 Spiegelman, M. "The Broken family--widowhood and orphanhood, " Annals of the American Academy of Political and
Social Science, 188 (1936), 117-30.
Essentially a survey that is concerned with the
family broken by death. Outlines various problems that
present crises to a family.

3497 Spiers, P. S. "Father's age and infant mortality, " Social Biology, 19 (Sept. 1972), 275-84.

3498 Spilka, B. , et al. "Religion, American values and death
perspectives, " Sociological Symposium, 1 (fall 1968),
57-66.

3499 Spinetta, J. J. "The Dying child's awareness of death: a
review, " Psychological Bulletin, 8 (April 1974), 256-60.

Deals with the opinions of authors in the literature
which reveals the child's reactions of his illness. Future research in this area is also discussed.

3500 Spock, B. Problems of parents. Boston: Houghton, 1962.
Concentrates on a number of problems involving the
feelings of mothers and fathers concerning quarrels and
feelings of guilt.

3501 Stacey, C. L., and K. Marken. "The Attitudes of college
students and penitentiary inmates toward death and a future life," Psychiatric Quarterly (Supplement), 26 (1952),
27-32.

3502 _____. "Attitudes toward death and future life among normal and subnormal adolescent girls," Exceptional Children, 20 (1954), 259-62.

3503 Steen, J. W. "Hindrances to the pastoral care of the dying,"
Pastoral Psychology, 9 (March 1958), 27-32.

3504 Stein, S. B., et al. About others. N. Y.: Walker, 1974.
The book is designed for the family--for parents
and children dealing with the subject of death. Useful
for teachers as a resource in the classroom.

3505 Steiner, G. L. "Children's concepts of life and death: a
developmental study." Ph. D. dissertation, Columbia
University, 1965.
"... [S]tudy was concerned with distinguishing the
growing child's characteristic thinking about the concepts
of life and death, and with whether his ideas follow the
sequence of cognitive development hypothesized by Piaget...."

3506 Stengel, E. "Attitudes to death," Journal of Psychosomatic
Research, 10 (July 1966), 21.
Distinguishes between the doctor's attitude toward
death and his patient's attitudes. Stresses the importance of the doctor's knowing the difference and coping
with it.

3507 _____. "The Social effects of attempted suicide," Canadian Medical Association Journal, 74 (Jan. 15, 1956),
116-20.

3508 _____. Suicide: attempted suicide. Baltimore: Penguin
Books, 1964.
Close examination of suicide, its victims, statistics,
causes, methods, and prevention.

3509 Sterba, R. "Report on some emotional reactions to President Roosevelt's death," Psychoanalytic Review, 33 (Oct.
1946), 393-8.

3510 Stern, K.; G. M. Williams; and M. Prodos. "Grief reac-
      tions in later life," American Journal of Psychiatry,
      108 (1951), 289-94.
      Draws attention to certain features of grief reaction,
      particularly to older persons and contrasts these to those
      of younger persons.

3511 Stern, M. M. "Biotrauma: fear of death and aggression,"
      International Journal of Psychoanalysis, 53 (1972), 291-
      9.
      A "reformulation of the concepts of instinctual drive,
      trauma and aggression." This is related to man's view
      and fear of death.

3512 _____. "Fear of death and neurosis," Journal of the
      American Psychoanalytic Association, 16 (Jan. 1968),
      3-31.
      The author comments on the lack of psychoanalytic
      literature on the subject of the fear of death. He cites
      numerous authors dealing with dying patients, but points
      out that their contributions neglect the influence of the
      fear of death on mental development.

3513 _____. "Fear of death and trauma," Progress of Neurology
      and Psychiatry, 22 (1967), 457-63.

3514 Stewart, D. R. "Message of the kite," Reader's Digest, 95
      (July 1969), 122.
      A personal story of an elderly woman who traces
      her first experiences with death in her youth from bit-
      terness to acceptance.

3515 Still, J. W. "Are organismal aging and aging death neces-
      sarily the result of death of vital cells in the organ-
      ism?" Medical Annals of the District of Columbia, 25
      (1956), 77.

3516 _____. "We need to know not only when human life ends
      but even more important, when it begins," Archives of
      the Foundation of Thanatology, 2 (summer 1970), 66-74.
      Interprets life and death in levels: cellular, organ,
      psychic, and vegetative.

3517 Stokes, A. D. A Game that must be lost; collected papers.
      Chester Springs, Pa.: Dufour, 1973.

3518 _____. "On resignation," International Journal of Psycho-
      analysis, 43 (March-June, 1962), 75-181.
      Explains the mortality trends in Latin America,
      Asia, and Africa. They can be understood if we look
      at governments and their health agencies, rather than
      their fiscal systems.

3519   Storr, A. Human destructiveness. N. Y.: Basic Books,
       1972. (Columbus Centre Series--Studies in the Dy-
       namics of Persecution and Extermination.)
            A research monograph "designed to investigate, and
       to give some tentative explanation of, human destructive-
       ness, more particularly of that form which is directed
       towards the persecution and extermination of other hu-
       man beings."

3520   Stowe, L. "The Awesome challenge of Mount Aconcaqua,"
       Reader's Digest, 84 (March 1964), 106-11.
            Discusses why mountain climbers will continue to
       climb the most difficult mountain even though 25 persons
       have died trying.

3521   "Strange world of Lee Harvey Oswald: more light on the
       assassination," U. S. News, 55 (Dec. 16, 1963), 60-2.

3522   Strauss, A. L. "The Animism controversy: re-examination
       of Huang-Lee Data," Journal of Genetics and Psychology,
       78 (1951), 105-13.

3523   _____. "Awareness of dying," in Death and Dying, edited
       by L. Pearson. Cleveland: Press of Case Western Re-
       serve University, 1969. pp. 108-32.
            Traces historically the American perspectives on
       death, and implications for the future.

3524   _____. "Family and staff during last weeks and days of
       terminal illness," Annals of the New York Academy of
       Sciences, 164 (Dec. 1969), 687-95.
            Author states "the family must be prepared for the
       patient's death, the kinsmen need to be helped in their
       grieving, and that the kinsmen need to be coached in
       modes of behavior while at the hospital."

3525   _____. "Sociopsychologic studies of the aging process:
       problems of death and the dying patient," Psychiatric
       Research Reports of the American Psychiatric Associa-
       tion, 23 (Feb. 1968), 198-206.

3526   _____, and B. G. Glaser. Anguish: a case history of a
       dying trajectory. California: Sociology Press, 1970.

3527   Stub, H. R. "Family structure and the social consequences
       of death," in A Sociological Framework for Patient
       Care, edited by J. R. Folta, and E. S. Dech. N. Y.:
       Wiley, 1966.

3528   "Student suicides," Science News, 91 (Jan. 14, 1967), 45.
            Explores the myth that student suicides occur dur-
       ing finals. Rather, it shows them to happen during the
       first six weeks of a semester.

3529 "Student suicides mount," Science Digest, 64 (Aug. 1968),
      64-5.
      Author comments on how parental pressure to make
      good grades is helping to drive up the suicide rate
      among college students.

3530 Sturges, S. "Understanding grief," Menninger Perspectives,
      1 (April 1970), 9-12.

3531 Sudnow, D. "The Logistics of dying," Esquire (Aug. 1967),
      102.

3532 Sugar, M. "Normal adolescent mourning," American Journal
      of Psychotherapy, 22 (1968), 258-69.
      Study "considers the depressive symptoms to be a
      mourning process for lost infantile objects...."

3533 "Suicide in college," Trans-Action, 8 (Feb. 1971), 10.
      Studies student suicides and shows that almost all
      males and one female were from intact families where
      the parents have no history of mental illness.

3534 Sukenick, R. Sentence of death. N. Y.: Dial, 1968.

3535 Sullivan, H. S. The Meaning of anxiety in psychiatry and
      life. N. Y.: William Alanson White Institute of Psy-
      chiatry, 1948.

3536 Sullivan, J. M. "The Influence of cause specific mortality
      conditions on age pattern of mortality with special ref-
      erence to Taiwan," Population Studies, 27 (March 1973),
      135-42.

3537 Svenska, D. Tala om doden. Stockholm: Verbum, 1967.
      Deals with attitudes toward death and the problems
      encountered when talking about it.

3538 Swenson, W. M. "Attitudes toward death in an aged popula-
      tion," Journal of Gerontology, 16 (1961), 49-53.

3539 Symons, N. J. "Does masochism necessarily imply the
      existence of a death instinct?" International Journal of
      Psychoanalysis, 8 (1927), 38-46.

3540 Szasz, T. S. "On the psychoanalytic theory of instincts,"
      Psychoanalytic Quarterly, 21 (1952), 25-48.

3541 Szondi, L. "Thanatos and Cain," American Imago, 21 (fall
      1963), 52-63.

3542 Tarpley, F. A. "Southern cemeteries: neglected archives
      for the folklorist," Southern Folklore Quarterly, 27
      (Dec. 1963), 323-33.

3543 Tarter, R. E., et al. "Death anxiety and suicide attempters,"
      Psychological Reports, 34 (June 1974), 895-7.

3544 Tatie, T., and F. L. Hsu. "Varieties in ancestor wor-
      ship believs and their relation to kinship," Southwestern
      Journal of Anthropology, 25 (summer 1969), 153-72.

3545 Taves, I. Love must not be wasted; when sorrow comes,
      take it gently by the hand. N.Y.: Crowell, 1974.

3546 Temkin, O. "Medicine and the problem of moral responsibili-
      ty," Bulletin of the History of Medicine, 23 (1949), 1-20.

3547 Templer, D. I. "The Construction and validation of a death
      anxiety scale." Ph.D. dissertation, University of Ken-
      tucky, 1968.

3548 _____. "Death anxiety as related to depression and
      health of retired persons," Journal of Gerontology, 26
      (1971), 521-23.

3549 _____. "Death anxiety: extraversion, neuroticism and
      cigarette smoking," Omega, 3 (Feb. 1972), 53-6.

3550 _____. "Death anxiety in religiously very involved per-
      sons," Psychological Reports, 31 (Oct. 1972), 361-2.

3551 _____. "The Relationship between verbalized and non-
      verbalized death anxiety," Journal of Genetic Psychology,
      119 (Dec. 1971), 211-4.

3552 _____. "Religious correlates of death anxiety," Psy-
      chological Reports, 26 (June 1970), 895-7.

3553 _____; C. Ruff; and C. Frank. "Death anxiety: age, sex,
      and parental resemblance in diverse populations," De-
      velopmental Psychology, 4 (1971), 108.

3554 _____, et al. "Alleviation of high death anxiety with
      symptomatic treatment of depression," Psychological
      Reports, 35 (Aug. 1974), 216.

3555 _____, et al. "Fear of death and femininity," Psycho-
      logical Reports, 35 (Aug. 1974), 530.

3556 Terman, L. M. "Recent literature on juvenile suicides,"
      Journal of Abnormal Psychology, 9 (1914), 61-6.

3557 "Thanatology: death and modern man," Time, 84 (Nov. 20,
      1964), 92.
          Deals with the problems that dying imposes on al-
      most all who are associated with it.

3558 Thomas, L. V. "Vie et mort en Afrique: introduction a l'ethnothanatologie," Ethno Psychologie Revue de Psychologie des Peupples, 27 (Mars 1972), 103-23.

3559 Thompson, P. W. "Understanding the aged," Journal of the American Geriatric Society, 13 (1965), 893-99.
      Discusses identity and dependency as it relates to older people. Describes how to control our own feelings about death and serious illness.

3560 Thurmond, C. "Last thoughts before drowning," Journal of Abnormal Social Psychology, 38 (1943), 165-84.

3561 Tichauer, R. S. "Attitudes toward death and dying among the Aymara Indians of Bolivia," Journal of American Medical Women's Association, 19 (1964), 463-6.

3562 Tietz, W. "School phobia and the fear of death," Mental Hygiene, 54 (Oct. 1970), 565-68.

3563 Tolor, A., and M. Reznikoff. "Relation between insight, repression-sensitization, internal-external control and death anxiety," Journal of Abnormal Psychology, 72 (Oct. 1967), 426-30.

3564 Topping, C. W. "The Death penalty in Canada," Annals of the American Academy of Political and Social Science, 284 (1952), 147-57.
      Explores the effects of the death penalty in Canada and offers a factual study of it by using various capital crimes as a guide.

3565 Treaton, J. R. "Discussion of a symposium on attitudes toward death in older persons," Journal of Gerontology, 16 (1961), 44.

3566 Trubo, R. An Act of mercy: euthanasia today. N. Y.: Dutton, 1973.
      Concerned with the families of the suffering and dying. The author asks who has the right to determine whether an individual has the right to live or die?

3567 Tuckman, J.; R. J. Kleiner; and M. Lavell. "Emotional content of suicide notes," American Journal of Psychiatry, 59 (July 1959), 59.
      Study examined the content of suicide notes which involves three motivational components: the wish to kill; the will to be killed; and the wish to die.

3568 Tylor, E. B. Primitive culture. London: J. Murray, 1913.

3569 United Nations (Report). Capital punishment. N. Y.: United Nations Department of Economic and Social Affairs, 1968.

A report on capital punishment concerning the laws surrounding it and its deterrent effects in the member and some non-member nations.

3570 Updike, J. "Black suicide," Atlantic, 227 (Feb. 1971), 108-10.
      Deals with Dr. H. Hendin's cross-section study of 25 suicidal patients who were admitted to Harlem Hospital.

3571 Vallin, J. La Mortalité par génération en France depuis 1897. Paris: Presses Universitaires de France, 1973.

3572 Van Den Eynden, T. "Sociologen over doodsproblematiek een Literatuur-over-Zuht," Nens en Maatschappij, 48 (1973), 392-414.

3573 Veatch, R. Death and dying. Chicago: Claretian, 1967.
      Deals with death as a taboo topic, various views of this, and the management of the dying.

3574 _____, and E. Watkin. "Death and dying," U.S. Catholic and Jubilee, 37 (April 1972), 6-13.

3575 Vernick, J. J. "Meaningful communication with the fatally ill child," in The Child in His Family, edited by E. J. Anthony, and C. Koupernick. N.Y.: Wiley, 1973. pp. 105-19.
      The authors recommend that the child be offered the opportunity to talk about anything that will benefit him at any stage regardless of how difficult this might be for the concerned adult.

3576 Vernon, G. M. "Dying as a social-symbolic process," Humanitas, 10 (Feb. 1974), 21-32.
      "[B]oth living and dying behavior are in response to symbols, relative to the audience and relative to the situation."

3577 _____. Sociology of death: an analysis of death-related behavior. N.Y.: Ronald Press, 1970.

3578 _____. "Some questions about the inevitable-death orientation," Sociological Symposium, 1 (fall 1968), 82-4.

3579 _____, and C. W. Waddell. "Dying as social behavior: Mormon behavior through half a century," Omega, 5 (fall 1974), 199-206.
      "Distinction is made between biological, clinical, psychological and social death. In an analysis of death behavior of Mormons for 50 years, it was found that their rate is consistently lower than that of the U.S. and Utah" (Abstract).

Social Sciences 325 VERWOERDT

3580 Verwoerdt, A., and J. L. Elmore. "Psychological reactions in fatal illness. I. The prospect of impending death," Journal of the American Geriatrics Society, 15 (Jan. 1967), 9-19.

3581 Viderman, S. "De l'instinct de la mort," Revue Française de Psychanalyse, 21 (Jan. 1961), 89-131.

3582 Viorst, J. "Let us talk about death," Redbook, 141 (June 1973), 33.
The author informs the reader of the importance of discussing death openly, especially with children.

3583 Vold, G. B. "Extent and trend of capital crimes in the United States," Annals of the American Academy of Political and Social Science, 284 (1952), 1-7.

3584 Volkan, V. "Typical findings in pathological grief," Psychiatric Quarterly, 44 (1970), 231-50.
States the ways different psychoanalysts see the relationship between neurotic symptoms and bereavement.

3585 Volkart, E. H., and S. T. Michael. "Bereavement and mental health," in Explorations in Social Psychology, edited by A. H. Leighton, J. A. Clausen, and R. N. Wilson. N. Y.: Basic Books, 1957. pp. 281-307.

3586 Vollman, R. R., et al. "The Reactions of family systems to sudden and unexpected death," Omega, 2 (May 1971), 101-6.

3587 Von Ferber, C. "Death: an undigested problem for the medical man and the sociologist," Kölner Zeitschrift für Soziologie und Sozialpsychologie, 22 (June 1970), 237-50.

3588 _____. "Der Tod ein unbewältigtes Problem für Mediziner und Sozialogén," Kölner Zeitschrift für Soziologie und Sozial-Psychologie, 22 (1970), 237-50.

3589 Von Hug-Hellmuth, H. "The Child's concept of death," Psychoanalytic Quarterly, 34 (1965), 499-516.

3590 Von Witzleben, H. "On loneliness," Psychiatry, 2 (1958), 37-43.

3591 Wahl, C. W. "The Differential diagnosis of normal and neurotic grief following bereavement," Psychosomatics, 11 (March-April, 1970), 104-6.
Examines accumulated cases of grief reaction in order to determine if general characteristics of both normal and neurotic grief might be identified.

3592 _____. "The Fear of death," Bulletin of the Menninger

Clinic, 22 (9158), 214.

3593 _____ . "The Fear of death," in The Meaning of Death,
edited by H. Feifel. N.Y.: McGraw-Hill, 1959. pp.
16-29.
Discusses the various ways that contemporary man
uses to avoid death. Also points out rituals of the
death industry.

3594 _____ . "Suicide as a magical art," in Clues to Suicide,
edited by E. S. Shneidman, and N. L. Farberow. N.Y.:
McGraw-Hill, 1957. pp. 22-30.

3595/6 Wainwright, L. "Profound lesson for the living: seminar
at University of Chicago's Billings Hospital," Life, 67
(Nov. 31, 1969), 36-43.
A 22-year-old girl dying of leukemia describes her
experiences at a seminar. She tells of what she thinks
and how she feels about dying. An analysis of the terminally ill is provided by a psychologist.

3597 Wall, J. H. "The Psychiatric problem of suicide," American Journal of Psychiatry, 101 (1944), 404-6.
Discusses the problems of suicide. States that
certain warning signs are recognizable, and gives three
signs which suggest the possibility of suicide. Study
was made from 1933 to 1943.

3598 Wallis, W. D. Religion in primitive society. N.Y.: Appleton, 1939.
Takes an in-depth view of how primitive man
viewed his religions. Deals with such topics as the nature of the supernatural, religious ideas and practices,
and the religious treatment of the afterlife.

3599 Walters, M. J. "Psychic death; report of a possible case,"
Archives of Neurological Psychiatry, 52 (1944), 84-5.

3600 Warren, F. The Dance of death. London: Oxford, 1931.
Discusses American political life, communal ceremonies, holidays, myths, and rituals, "such as funerals ... and analyzes their meanings and the symbolism
involved...."

3601 Watson, L. The Romeo error; a matter of life and death.
N.Y.: Anchor Press, 1974.

3602 Waxberg, J. D. "Study of attempted suicides in psychotic
patients: a dynamic concept," Psychiatric Quarterly,
30 (1956), 464.
Paper deals with a study of 56 patients at Brooklyn
New York State Hospital who had attempted suicide.
The implications are described.

3603 "Way of suicide," Newsweek, 71 (April 1, 1968), 97.

3604 Weber, A. "Zum Erlebnis des Todes bei Kindern,"
      Monatsschrift für Psychiatrie und Neurologie, 107 (1943),
      9-16.

3605 Wechaler, H. "Community growth, depressive disorders and
      suicide," American Journal of Sociology, 67 (1961), 9-
      16.

3606 Weiner, A. "The Use of psychopharmacologic agents in the
      management of the bereaved." A paper presented at a
      seminar of the Thanatology Foundation at Columbia Col-
      lege of Physicians and Surgeons, Nov. 12, 1971.

3607 Weinmann, G. H. A Survey of the law concerning dead hu-
      man bodies, issued under the auspices of the Committee
      on medico-legal problems. Washington, D. C.: National
      Research Council of the National Academy of Sciences,
      1929.

3608 Weisman, A. D. "Death and responsibility: a psychiatrist's
      view," Psychiatric Opinion, 3 (1966), 22-6.
         States that psychiatrists can help patients who are
      dying by using the knowledge of psychodynamic princi-
      ples to help them achieve an acceptable death.

3609 _____. On dying and denying: a psychiatric study of
      terminality. N. Y.: Behavioral Publications, 1972.
      (Gerontology Series.)
         The main focus is to lay out the beginnings of a
      theory of death, defining the stages "terminal responses,
      significant questions, psychosocial death, and the like..."
      (Choice).

3610 _____. "Psychosocial death," Psychology Today, 6 (Nov.
      1972), 77-8.

3611 _____. The Realization of death: a guide for the psy-
      chological autopsy. N. Y.: Jason Aronson, 1974.
         The "psychological autopsy" deals with the investi-
      gation of pre-mortem testing of patients, and evaluation
      after their death. Case histories illustrate the pro-
      cesses the patient used in coping with death. The au-
      thor investigates the psychosocial processes involved in
      dying.

3612 _____, and R. Kastenbaum. The Psychological autopsy:
      a study of the terminal phase of life. N. Y.: Be-
      havioral Publications, 1968.
         The presentation of a type of autopsy which would
      study a person's life in its full complexity through col-

lection of observation, fact, and opinion, so that one is better able to understand the psychosocial components of death.

3613 _____, and T. P. Hackett. "Predilection to death," Psychosomatic Medicine, 23 (1961), 232-56.
Explains what it means when a patient is convinced of his imminent death, and distinguishes between it and fear of death. Several case studies with advice to physicians on how to handle the situation.

3614 Weiss, J. M. "The Gamble with death in attempted suicide," Psychiatry, 20 (1957), 17-25.

3615 Wenzl, A. Unsterblichkeit, ihre Metaphysische und Anthropologische Bedeutung. Berne: A. Franke, 1951.

3616 "When Kennedy died," Newsweek, 64 (Sept. 14, 1964), 61.
A report on how Americans reacted to the assassination of President Kennedy. His death caused symptoms among adults and children; 38 states were canvassed for information. Extensive interviews in depth.

3617 Wilbur, G. B. "Some problems presented by Freud's life-death instinct theory," American Imago, 2 (1941), 134-96.

3618 Wilkins, J. "Suicidal behaviors," American Sociological Review, 32 (1967), 286-98.
Discusses relationships among completed suicide, attempted suicide, suicidal warnings, and the value of knowing the way people are deterred from suicides.

3619 Williams, G. L. The Sanctity of life and the criminal law. N.Y.: Knopf, 1957.

3620 Williams, M. "The Fear of death--Part 1. The avoidance of the fear of death," Journal of Analytic Psychology, 3 (1958), 157-65.

3621 _____. "The Fear of death--Part II. The fear of death in consciousness," Journal of Analytic Psychology, 29 (1962), 29.

3622 Williams, R. H. "Our role in the generation, modification and termination of life," Archives of Internal Medicine, 124 (1969), 215.

3623 _____. "Propagation, modification, and termination of life: contraception, abortion, suicide, euthanasia," in To Live and To Die: when, why, and how. N.Y.: Springer-Verlag, 1973. pp. 80-97.

3624 _____. To live and to die: when, why and how. N.Y.:
Springer-Verlag, 1973.
Contains contributions to the literature of human
living, including such topics as: care of the dying, patients, and euthanasia.

3625 Williams, R. L., et al. "Religiosity, generalized anxiety
and apprehension concerning death," Journal of Social
Psychology, 75 (June 1968), 111-17.
Applies and tests Freud's view that religion is an
outgrowth of insecurity, and death impels man to fabri-
cate a divine person to protect him.

3626 Wind, E. "The Confrontation with death," International Journal of Psychoanalysis, 49 (1968), 302-5.
Discusses the macabre humor that prisoners used in
coping with impending death. Also discusses the survivor syndrome that can arise by the thought of aging.
The image of death is ever present.

3627 Winnicott, D. W. Playing and reality. N.Y.: Basic Books,
1971.
In discussing "Death and Murder in the Adolescent
Process," the author chronicles the contemporary concepts of adolescent development in relation to playing,
and adolescent and infant fantasy.

3628 Winograd, M. "Pathological mourning," in The Child in His
Family, edited by E. J. Anthony, and C. Koupernik.
N.Y.: Wiley, 1973. pp. 233-43.
Deals with the treatment of children with pathological
mourning through a case study approach.

3629 Winslow, F. Anatomy of suicide. London: Renshaw, 1840.

3630 "With sincere sympathy," Liguorian, 48 (Jan. 1969), 11-13.

3631 Wittgenstein, G. "Fear of dying and of death as a require-
ment of the maturation process in man," Hippokrates,
31 (July-Dec. 1960), 765-9.

3632 Wohlford, P. "Extension of personal time, affective states,
and expectation of personal death," Journal of Personality and Social Psychology, 3 (May 1966), 559-66.

3633 Wolfenstein, M. "Death of a parent and death of a president: children's reactions to two kinds of loss," in
Children and Death of a President, edited by M. Wolfenstein, and G. Kliman. N.Y.: Doubleday, 1965. pp.
62-79.

3634 _____. "How is mourning possible?" The Psychoanalytic
Study of the Child, 21 (1966), 92-123.

3635 _____. "The Image of the lost parent," Psychoanalytic
      Study of the Child, 28 (1963), 433-56.
              Explores the emotional problems created by the loss
      of a parent while the child is still in the growth stage.
      Dual aspects of images discussed are: near and far,
      present and absent, living and dead, etc. The time
      image is given emphasis by examples of A. E. Housman
      and the Belgian painter René Magritte.

3636 _____, and G. Kliman, eds. Children and the death of a
      president: multidisciplinary studies. N. Y.: Doubleday,
      1965.

3637 Wolff, K. H. "A Partial analysis of student reaction to
      President Roosevelt's death," Journal of Social Psy-
      chology, 26 (1947), 35-53.
              Analyzes two sets of documents having to do with
      written reactions of undergraduate students to the presi-
      dent's death.

3638/9 Wolff, S. "How children respond to death," New Society
      (March 27, 1969), 479-82.

3640 Wolfgang, M. E. "Suicide by means of victim precipitated
      homicide," Journal of Clinical Experimental Psycho-
      pathology, 20 (1959), 335-49.

3641 Wood, A. L. "The Alternatives to the death penalty,"
      Annals of the American Academy of Political and Social
      Science, 284 (1952), 63-72.
              Author states that an "alternative to the death
      penalty will be answered by individual morals and social
      values."

3642 Woodward, K. "Death in America," U.S. Catholic and Jubi-
      lee, 36 (Jan. 1971), 6-13.
              Explores the various aspects of death in America,
      and points out the social scientists' concern about the
      problem.

3643 Woolley, L. F., and A. R. Eichert. "Notes on the problem
      of suicide and escape," American Journal of Psychiatry,
      98 (1941), 110-18.

3644/5 Wylie, H. W.; P. Larzroff; and F. Lowry. "A Dying pa-
      tient in a psychotherapy group," International Journal of
      Group Psychotherapy, 14 (1964), 482-91.
              States the results of a group therapy session in
      which the therapists were forced to recognize their own
      fears of death.

3646 Wylie, M. "Living with grief," Family Health, 2 (March
      1970), 28.

3647 Yacoubian, J. H., and R. S. Lourie. "Suicide and attempted suicide in children and adolescents," in Behavior Pathology of Childhood and Adolescence, edited by S. L. Copel. N. Y.: Basic Books, 1973. pp. 149-65.
Partial Contents: Epidemiology of suicide; Historical view; Child's concept of death; Case studies; and Clinical implications.

3648 Yamamoto, J. "Cultural factors in loneliness, death and separation," Medical Times, 98 (July 1970), 177-83.

3649 _____, et al. "Mourning in Japan," American Journal of Psychiatry, 125 (1969), 1660-65.
Reports the results of 20 Japanese widows interviewed during the acute grief phase of mourning.

3650 Yamazaki, S. "The Physical attitudes of youths toward death," Japanese Journal of Psychology, 15 (1940), 469-75.

3651 Yarrow, H. C. "A Further contribution to the study of the mortuary customs of the North American Indians," First Annual Report, Bureau of American Ethnology, 1 (1879-1880), 87-203.

3652 Yarrow, L. "Maternal deprivation: toward an empirical and conceptual reevaluation," Psychological Bulletin, 58 (1901), 459-90.

3653 Yglesias, J. "Deaths I have known," Ramparts, 19 (May 1972), 42-7.

3654 Young, F. W. "Graveyards and social structure," Rural Sociology, 25 (Dec. 1960), 446-50.
Investigates the cemeteries of Repon and North Harbor, Canada. Author uses W. L. Warner's proposition that cemeteries express values and structure of a community.

3655 Young, W. H. "The Death of a patient during psychotherapy," Psychiatry, 23 (1960), 103-8.

3656 "Youthful suicides," Newsweek, 77 (Feb. 15, 1971), 70-1.
Explains the increase in the rate of youthful suicides, and gives the major causes of such deaths.

3657 Zeligs, R. "Children's attitudes toward death," Mental Hygiene, 51 (1967), 393-6.
Discusses the need for the survivors of a death in the family to discuss the subject of death and to acquaint the children with the facts of death.

3658 _____. "Children's experience with death," Medical In-

sight, 2 (March 1970), 92.
Presents a number of cases concerning parents explanations about death to their children. Author advises parents to discuss what happens truthfully and to express their feelings.

3659 _____. "Death casts its shadow on a child," Mental Hygiene, 51 (Jan. 1967), 9-20.
Story about the death of a one-year-old child and the responses of the parents and the other children. Also probes the causes of death of very young babies who die unexpectedly.

3660 Zilboorg, G. "Considerations on suicide with particular reference to that of the young," American Journal of Orthopsychiatry, 7 (1937), 15-31.
States that suicide "for many centuries has been considered a sin and a crime. This is one of the leftovers of a theological age."

3661 _____. "Fear of death," Psychoanalytic Quarterly, 12 (1943), 465-75.
The "fundamental psychological issue involved in the problem of morale is reduced to the problem of how one reacts to the fear of death."

3662 _____. "The Sense of immortality," Psychoanalytic Quarterly, 7 (1938), 171-99.

3663 Zim, H. S., and S. Bleeker. Life and death. N.Y.: Morrow, 1970.
Discusses the process of aging and what happens to the human body when it dies. Also covers burial customs of several North American Indian tribes, the Maoris, Hindus, and Pygmies.

3664 Zinker, J. C. Rosalee: motivation and the crisis of dying. Painesville, Ohio: Lake Erie College Press, 1966.

3665 _____, and S. L. Fink. "The Possibility for psychological growth in a dying person," Journal of General Psychology, 74 (1966), 185-99.
Investigates the possibility of positive aspects of human experience in an uneducated Southern woman.

3666 Zusman, J., and D. L. Davidson. Organizing the community to prevent suicide. Springfield, Ill.: C. C. Thomas, 1971.

Part VIII

AUDIOVISUAL MEDIA*

EXPLANATION OF SYMBOLS

F	film	P	photos and prints
FS	filmstrip	R	recording
K	kit	S	slides
MF	microfilm	T	tape
		TR	transparencies

3667 Adlerstein, A. M. "The Relationship between religious belief and death affect." Ann Arbor, Mich.: University Microfilms, 1963. (MF)

3668 "Adolescent Suicide--A Documentary." Produced by the Center for Death Education and Research. 54 min. 1973. (T)
"Dr. N. L. Farberow and his staff discuss the rising incidence of suicides among American youth, and speculate upon the reasons for the contemporary phenomenon...."

3669 "The Aged." Distributed by Carousel Films, Inc. 17 min. color. 1973. (F)
In his efforts to provide for his elderly parents, a Vietnam veteran is helped by "Geriatrics Project." The funding and activities of the project are shown. For high schools, colleges, and adults.

3670 "Ages of Man," Part 4, "Death." A CBS presentation released by McGraw-Hill Book Co. 23 min. sound (also in b and w). color. 16mm. with guide. 1966 (F) Produced by David Susskind.
"Sir John Gielgud reads from Shakespeare's tragedies, songs, and sonnets excerpts which treat the theme of death...."

---

*No prices have been included in the following list because of their rapid change. See AV Sources at the end of Part VIII for addresses of producers and distributors.

3671   "Aging." Produced by Communication Research Machines.
       21 min. color. 1973. (F)
            Presents psychological and biological patterns of
       aging and the place of old people in society. For col-
       leges and adults. Belongs to the "Psychology Today"
       series.

3672   "Aging." Available from Indiana University Audio-Visual Cen-
       ter. 30 min. 1967. (F)
            Two elderly men discuss life and loneliness. Dr.
       Maria Piers advocates reestablishing the role of grand-
       parents in family life. For colleges and adults. Be-
       longs to the "About People" series.

3673   "All the Way Home." Available from Films, Inc. 103 min.
       b and w. 1963. (F)
            Based on the story by James Agee, and produced by
       Alex Segal, this film explores attitudes toward death,
       illness, aging, and family relationships in the 1915 era.

3674   Alleman, S. A. "The Structure and Content of Belief Sys-
       tems." Ann Arbor, Mich.: University Microfilms,
       1964. Positive (Ph. D. thesis, Purdue, 1963). (MF)
            Discusses future life and the relationship to death.

3675   "The American Funeral." Distributed by Xerox--University
       Microfilms. 28 min. No. 6455. 1971. (Today's
       Mores.) (T)
            A "frank discussion involving a mortician, sociol-
       ogist and minister.... [I]n this discussion experts
       examine the funeral industry, its pros and cons, its
       etiology and its relevance in a transformed world."

3676   "Are Fears of Dying Fears of Living in Disguise?" Big Sur
       Recordings. Nov. 24, 1974 session. One-and one-half
       hours. No. 3940. (T)

3677   "The Art of Age." Produced by ACI Productions. 27 min.
       color. 1972. (F)
            Four senior citizens express reactions to inactivity and
       state that interests and activities should be pursued. For
       senior high schools, colleges, and adults.

3678   "The Art of Dying." Big Sur Recordings. Closing session.
       Nov. 24, 1974. One hour. No. 3990. (T)

3679   "Attitudes Toward Death." Big Sur Recordings. Nov. 24,
       1974 session. 1 1/2 hours. No. 3980. (T)

3680   "The Ballad of Alma Gerlayne." Produced by Association
       Films. (Insight Series.) INS--255--27 min. color
       (also in b and w). (F)
            Featuring Sheilah Wells, Lou Antonio, and Joseph

Campanella. "Getting the wealth, fame and men she always wanted, a beautiful young vocalist still can't find happiness. Lonely and guilt ridden, she turns to a man who hates life and preaches despair. She is seduced by him and commits suicide. "

3681 "Bereavement and the Process of Mourning. " (T) Produced by the Center for Death Education and Research.
"Dr. Paul Irion conceptualizes loss in terms of disrupted social relationships. He argues that the social adjustment of a bereaved individual is facilitated by the expression of his authentic feelings, funerary ritual and other outlets for the ventilation of strong feelings of grief. "

3682 "Between the Cup and the Lip. " Available from Mass Media Associates. 11 min. color. 1971. (F)
Animated film utilizing flashbacks to convey the pain and memories during bereavement. Symbols are used to convey both life and death.

3683 "Birth and Death. " Available from Filmakers Library, Inc. 16mm. "Birth, " 72 min. ("Birth, " 40 min. --educational version.) "Death, " 43 min. (F)
"A unique cinema vérité study of a young couple awaiting and finally having their first child, and a cancer patient's last days in a hospital for terminal illness. " The birth and death segments are available individually.

3684 "The Black Chicano and Oriental Americans and Death. "
Big Sur Recordings. 1 1/2 hours. No. 3840. (T)

3685 "Brian's Song. " Available from Learning Corp. of America. 75 min. color. 1972. (F)
Story of Brian Piccolo, a professional football player, who died of cancer at age 21.

3686 "Bye Bye Braverman. " Available from Audio Brandon Films. Directed and produced by Sidney Lumet. 94 min. color. 1968. (F)
Based on the novel "To an Early Grave, " by Wallace Markfield. Story about a promising author who dies unexpectedly and his four friends who attend the funeral.

3687 "Care of the Terminally Ill. " Available from Learning Arts. Includes recording, filmstrip, evaluation test, and training guide. 1971. (K)
The program examines the reactions of the patient and the patient's family as well as those of the nursing team.

3688 "Choosing Your Death; An Experiential Exercise. " Big Sur

Recordings. 3/4 hour. No. 3910. (T)

3689 Columbia Broadcasting System News (Producer). "The Sandpile series." Available from Carousel Films, Inc. Produced from "Look Up and Live" TV Series. b and w. 26 min. ea. (F)

The five films are keyed to the interest level of older youth. Topics discussed are sex, race relations, religion, meaning of life and death. The films are recommended by youth counselors for discussion groups, and each film is complete in itself, or can be used as part of the series. Part V--Death, "examines the meaning of life and death through dramatized vignettes. The cast discusses various concepts with Professor of Theology, Dr. William Hamilton."

3690 "Come and Take My Hand." Available from NBC Educational Enterprises. 30 min. color. (F)

A television public service by WKYC-TV in Cleveland. Shows the care of the dying by the staff of a religious home.

3691 "Confrontations of Death." Available from Oregon Center for Gerontology. 38 min. (F)

3692 "Confronting Death." Thomas More Mediatape. One cassette. No. M-46. 1972. (T)

A multi-voiced approach to a contemporary social problem. The cassette belongs to a series and can be used with both young people and adults.

3693 "Conversation with a Dying Friend." Produced by the Center for Death Education and Research. 30 min. (T)

An interview conducted by Connie Goldman with her friend who is dying of cancer.

3694 "Crib Death: A Sudden Infant Death Syndrome." Produced by the Center for Death Education and Research. 59 min. 1972. (T)

"... [E]ach year some ten thousand apparently healthy babies die suddenly and unexpectedly from crib death." Featured are Dr. John Coe and nurse Carolyn Szybist.

3695 "Cultural Aspects of Death and Dying." Big Sur Recordings. One hour. No. 3780. (T)

3696 "The Day God Died." Available from Association Films. INC-412. 27 min. color. INS-312. 27 min. b and w. (F)

Featuring Efrem Zimbalist, Jr., Beverly Garland, Mariette Hartley, Tim O'Connor, and Carol O'Connor. "God is officially declared dead. After a university

memorial service, faculty and regents meet for cock-
tails. Having rejected God, they have begun to live for
other things. When strange events occur, they are con-
fronted with the emptiness of their own lives. "

3697 "The Day Grandpa Died. " Available from King Screen Productions. " 12 min. color. 1970. (F)
A young boy remembers by-gone days with his
grandfather and gradually learns to accept death as part
of life.

3698 "Dead Is Dead. " Produced by Oxford Films, and narrated
by Godfrey Cambridge. 21 min. color. 1775.
Includes film guide. (F)
This film "seeks to fight drug addiction with shock-
ing truth. The truth about pill-taking in peaceful suburbs, about youth's flirtation with marijuana, glue and
other destructive chemicals; and the grisly truth about
the end of the road for junkies and pill poppers. "

3699 "Dead Man Coming. " Produced by Pyramid. 16mm. 24
min. 1971. (F)
A documentary filmed inside San Quentin. Describes what life is like inside a maximum security institution. For junior high, senior high, and adults.

3700 "Death. " BBC-TV. London, 1970. Released in the U. S.
by Time-Life Films. 45 min. sound. color. 16mm.
(Family of Man Series no. 7.) (F)
"Examines some of the customs associated with
death in different societies. "

3701 "Death. " Available from Carousel Films. 26 min. (Sandpile Series.) (F)

3702 "Death. " Available from Filmmakers Library, Inc. 16mm.
43 min. b and w. 1968. (F)
Focuses on a 52 year-old man who is single and
has a terminal illness. The documentary includes the
psychology of dying and how we communicate with patients.

3703 "Death. " Available from Indiana University Audio-Visual
Center. 29 min. b and w. (Eastern Wisdom and
Modern Life Series.) (F)
"Compares Eastern and Western concepts of death.
Examines the Buddhist idea of the value of death as the
great renovator. Shows and explains the concept of rein-
carnation. "

3704 "Death. " Available from Minnesota Manufacturing and
Mining, Medical Film Library. Prepared transparency
(8 x 10). (Health and Happiness of the Family Series.)
1967. (TR)

3705 "Death and Life." Center for Cassette Studies--Audio Text
     Cassette. 60 min. CBC305. (T)
          "A documentary illustrating what people from all
     walks of life think about death, what it means to them,
     how they visualize it, their fear of it...."

3706 "Death and the Child." Available from the Center for Death
     Education and Research. 45 min. (T)
          "Dr. Edgar Jackson directs his remarks to parents
     and to those in care-giving professions who will ul-
     timately share children's attitudes toward death...."

3707 "Death and the Family: From the Caring Professions Point
     of View." Available from the Center for Death Educa-
     tion and Research. 30 min. (Orig. an address at a
     symposium, April 1971.) (T)
          "Dr. D. Fredlund discusses children's attitudes to-
     ward death. She underscores the need for children to
     be made aware of death and for them to learn to accept
     loss in a realistic and healthy manner."

3708 "Death for Faith." Society for Visual Education. 31
     frames. color. 1957. (With utilization guide and
     reading script.) (FS)

3709 "Death in/on the Highway" (2 reels). NET--Indiana Univer-
     sity. 16mm. 60 min. 1965. (F)
          Investigation of driving skills and safety performances
     brought about by the high statistics in automobile acci-
     dents.

3710 "Death in the Chair" (photograph). "The Daily Tabloid," in
     This Fabulous Century; sixty years of American life.
     New York Time-Life Books, 1969. Vol. 3, 1920-1930,
     pp. 185. (P)
          In describing the Lucid Little Journals of the time,
     the picture shows the execution of Ruth Snyder, "who
     persuaded her lover to help kill her husband; both went
     to the electric chair in January 1928. To scoop its
     rival on the execution, the New York Daily News smug-
     gled an out-of-town (and therefore unfamiliar) photog-
     rapher into the death chamber. His camera was
     strapped to his leg; at the appropriate moment, he
     crossed his knee over the other, uncovering the lens,
     and squeezed a bulb in his pocket...."

3711 "Death: Its Psychology." Center for Cassette Studies--
     Audio-Text Cassette. 60 min. CBC316. (T)
          Documentary describing the stages of death by
     Kübler-Ross. A woman tells how she learned to accept
     her cancer, and her husband talks about his reactions
     and acceptance. For high schools, colleges, and gen-
     eral audiences.

3712 "Death of a Salesman. " Stanley Kramer Co. Released by
      Columbia Pictures Corp. , 1951. 115 min. b and w. (F)
      Based on the play by Arthur Miller.

3713 "The Death of a Smoker. " Produced-distributed by World
      Records, Inc. No. Oc3. (R)
      "A lecture by Dr. Alton Ochsner, president of the
      world famous Alton Ochsner Medical Foundation, New
      Orleans, and former Surgeon General. "

3714 "Death of Christ. " Released in the U. S. by Encyclopaedia
      Britannica Films, 1958. 25 frames. color. 35 min.
      (FS)
      Holy Bible in picture series--Catholic version.

3715 "The Death of God--1966--God, Man and Modern Thought. "
      Produced by Georgetown University Forum. 7 1/2 i. p. s.
      27 min. (T)
      The Rev. John L. Ryan begins by stating that "the
      two great prophets of the last century are Dostoevsky
      and Nietzsche, both having a relevance today in their at-
      titude toward God. ... " In the "latter part of the tape,
      the ideas of Dietrich Bonhoeffer, William Hamilton,
      Paul Van Buren, and Thomas Altizer are discussed. "

3716 "Death of God. " Produced by the Department of Religion and
      the School of Arts, Syracuse University, 1969. 16mm.
      21 min. color. (F)
      Narration "based on the books of Gabriel Vahani-
      an. ... " For colleges and adult groups.

3717 "Death of John. " Concordia Films. 21 frames. color.
      35mm. Includes phonodisc--2 sides, 12" 33 1/3 rpm.
      5 min. (Living Bible Series, with Leader's guide.)
      (FS, R)
      "An adaptation of the Biblical account of events lead-
      ing up to and including the death of John the Baptist. "

3718 "Death of Moses and Aaron. " Cathedral Films, Inc. 1958.
      32 frames. color. 35 min. plus disc. 33 1/3 rpm
      with study guide. (Life of Moses Series.) (FS, R)
      Events in the life of Moses including God's punish-
      ment.

3719 "Death of Our Biosphere. " Distributed by Xerox University
      Microfilms. 27 min. No. 24705. 1971. (Man Against
      His Environment Series.) (T)
      "Dr. Harry Commoner analyzes the cycle of life ...
      [and] points out that all of life runs in interconnecting
      cycles, a principle which modern technology does not
      seem to recognize. "

3720 "Death of Socrates. " BBC-TV. London. Released in the

U.S. by Time-Life Films. 1968. 45 min. sound.
b and w. 16mm. (Plato no. 2 Series.) (F)

3721 "Death of Superman." Produced by Association Films. INS--
431--27 min. color. INS--331--27 min. b and w. (F)
Featuring Britt Leach and Lane Bradbury. "A sim-
ple-minded young man searches for love ... talks to the
dolls he keeps in his room ... and [is] called the neigh-
borhood weirdo.... [A] tenant in the building where he
janitors shows him kindness. She promises love. But
emotionally upset by her impending abortion, she cruelly
rejects him. He is not able to comprehend this and
kills himself."

3722 "The Death of Tarzan." Produced by Barrandov Studios of
Prague, and released by Brandon Films. 72 min.
1968. (F)

3723 "Death of the Self." Available from the Center for Death
Education and Research. 28 min. (T)
Dr. John Brantner examines attitudes toward death.
"He discusses changes necessary in such attitudes that
could make possible more fully developed lives...."

3724 "Deathstyles." Released by Time-Life Films. 50 min.
sound. color. 16mm. 1972. (F)
"An experimental film about a nightmare automobile
journey to death and dehumanization through a monstrous
landscape..., Richard Nixon on the subject of death,
clips of the John Kennedy assassination and the killings
at Kent State."

3725 "Decisions: Life or Death." Produced by Association Films.
(Guidelines Series from National Catholic Office for
Radio and Television.) CO-218-30min. (F)
"Father Charles Curran, Dr. Kenneth Vaux, Dr.
Michael De Bakey, and the Methodist Hospital in Hous-
ton, discuss recent medical advances with ethics and
heart transplants."

3726 "Dialogue on Death." Produced by the Center for Death
Education and Research. 2 sides. 30 min. per side.
(T)
Discusses American attitudes towards death with
specific issues such as grief and mourning. The tape
features Dr. John Brantner, Robert Slater, and Robert
Fulton.

3727 "Diary of a Country Priest." Available from Audio Brandon.
Directed by Robert Bresson. (French dialogue with
English subtitles; narration in English.) 116 min.
1951. (F)
"... [T]he story of an ailing priest who believes

that he has failed to raise the moral level of his
parish.... [His] final words, uttered as he lies dying
of cancer, are 'all is Grace...'."

3728 "Do Funerals Help the Mourners?" Produced by Jeffrey
Norton Publishers, Inc. 28 min. No. 29070. Nar-
rated by L. Bowman, and E. N. Jackson. 1963.
(Psychologically Speaking Series.) (T)
"Discussion of the pomp and ceremony of death and
its relation to the dispersal of grief."

3729 "¿Dónde estan los muertos?" Mayse Studios. 55 frames.
b and w. 35mm. 1941. (FS)
"Uses Biblical text to explain what happens to the
dead and what Christ promised to those who believed in
Him. With Spanish captions."

3730 "The Dying Patient." Available from Office of Medical Education, University of California, Irvine, Calif. 60 min.
b and w. kinescope. 1971. (F)
A psychiatrist interviewer discusses with another
doctor the concerns of dying patients.

3731 "Erasmus, Disiderius." A Comfortable exhortacion agaynst
the chaunces of death, made by Erasmus... London:
1553. Colophon: Imprinted at London ... in the house
of Thomas Berthelet. Ann Arbor, Mich.: University
Microfilms. (MF)

3732 _____. Preparation to Deathe, a Boke as Devout as
Eloquent, compiled by Erasmus Roterodame... Londini,
in officina Thomae Berthe ... [1543]. Ann Arbor,
Mich.: University Microfilms. (MF)

3733 "Eric Hoffer: The Passionate State of Mind." Distributed by
Carousel Films. Produced by CBS-TV. 52 min. b
and w. 1967. (F)
Hoffer tells his views on politics and his experience
and knowledge of old age. For high schools, colleges,
and adults.

3734 "Ethical Issues and Dilemmas." Produced by Lansford Pub.
Co., SDE301C. (Contains six cassettes and two book-
lets.) (T)
"Five, 50-minute tapes consider the problem of
ethical norms and politics which are inevitably inter-
connected for citizens; how the issues of death and abortion are practical ethical concerns.... [I]ncludes a
booklet outline for the student and a teacher's manual
containing two alternate tests on each tape. A mini-
course" (Pub. cat.).

3735 "Experiences of Dying: A Matter of Style." Big Sur Recordings. 1 1/2 hours. No. 3830. (T)

3736 "Explorations." Produced--distributed by World Pacific
Records (a div. of Pacific Enterprises, Inc.). No.
H35e v. 2. (R)
In song and voice; includes survival, growth, and
rebirth. Read by Gerald Heard with music for voice
and organ.

3737 "Facing Death with the Patient--An On-Going Contract."
Produced by the Center for Death Education and Research. (T)
Dr. Vincent Hunt outlines general principles he has
found effective when dealing with dying patients. Originally delivered at the symposium in Minneapolis in 1971.

3738 "Fear of Death and Terminal Illness Counseling." Big Sur
Recordings. 1 1/4 hours. No. 3960. (T)

3739 "Free Fall and Death." Big Sur Recordings. 1 1/2 hours.
No. 3960. (T)

3740 "Freeze--Wait--Reanimate." Produced by Pacifica Tape Library. Pacifica Foundation. 58 min. BC1418. 1973.
(Mind and Body Series.) (T)
"Since the beginning of time, man has desperately
tried to avoid the one unavoidable fact of his life: death.
This program is a report on one such attempt to extend
life, through a visit to the Cryonics Plant in Long Island. It includes interviews with management of the
plant, and comments on cryonics by Isaac Asimov, noted
science fiction writer. Recorded in 1973" (Pub. cat.).

3741 "The Function of the Death Guide." Big Sur Recordings.
1 1/2 hours. No. 3740. (T)

3742 "Gift of Life/Right to Die." Available from Indiana University Audio-Visual Center. 15 min. b and w. 1968.
(F)

3743 "The Great American Funeral, Parts I and II." CBS News
TV. Released by McGraw-Hill Book Co. 54 min.
sound. b and w. 16mm. 1964. (F)
A documentary study of funeral practices in America, Denmark, and England. The film interviews ministers, morticians, and Jessica Mitford.

3744 "Grief." Available from Concord Films. 50 min. color.
1972. (F)
Personal accounts of reactions to loss. Includes
reactions to grief and bereavement.

3745 "A Grief Recovery Group." Produced by Abingdon. Part

II, tape II, side B, "Coping Constructively with Crises."
Part II includes four tapes. (T)
"A group acts as a caring community for each other
in handling bereavement constructively and becoming better able to help bereaved persons. "

3746 "Growing Old. " Produced and distributed by Creative Learning Center SC-486. (Cassette Library--Social Studies.)
(T)
"... [D]irectors of successful nursing homes relate
their views of entering such a facility...; the program
concludes with a statement by Roberta Brown, executive
secretary, Advisory Council for Aging, as she surveys
the priority needs of the elderly and supportive programs" (Pub. cat.).

3747 "Helping and Being Helped by the Dying. " Produced by
Abingdon. Part II, side A ("Coping Constructively with
Crises"). Part II. Four tapes. (T)
"An interview with a dying friend, and her reflec-
tions on the experience and what is helpful" (Religious
Book Review).

3748 "Home for Life. " Available from Films, Inc. 58 min. b
and w. 1967. (F)

3749 "How Could I Not be Among You: The Poetry of Ted Rosenthal, " Produced by Marshall Potamkin and directed by
Thomas Reichman. Distributed by Eccentric Circle
Cinema Workshop. 28 min. (F)
Portrait of a young man who has six months to live.
"Ted Rosenthal is a poet and the film deftly captures the
interplay between the reality of his growing awareness of
death and his attempts, as a poet to distill and synthe-
size these feelings into a personal and meaningful artistic
expression. " For ages 16 and up. Suitable for senior
high schools and church organizations.

3750 "How Death Came to Earth. " Contemporary Films/McGraw-
Hill. 14 min. color. No. 408641-3. 1972. (F)
An Indian folk tale explains why there is only one
sun and one moon. The film explains why they came to
earth and how the life and death cycle began. Includes
a teacher's guide and suitable for grades six and up.

3751 "Human Values and the Death Rite. " Big Sur Recordings.
1 1/2 hours. No. 3930. (T)

3752 "I Never Sang for My Father. " Available from Macmillan
Audio Brandon. 92 min. color. 1970. (F)
A feature film focuses on the search for identity
within family relationships at the time of death.

3753   "Ikiru" [To Live].   Available from Macmillan Audio Brandon.
       140 min.   b and w.   1952.   (F)
           Story of a middle-class, middle-aged Japanese man
       who is confronted with death.   "Perhaps because of our
       loss of religious faith we now treat death as the Vic-
       torians treated sex."   (One review is found in Time,
       cinema section, Feb. 15, 1960.)

3754   "In My Memory."   Available from National Instructional Tele-
       vision.   14 1/2 min.   color.   1973.   (F)
           Story of the death of a young girl's grandmother.
       Guilt feelings, memories, and doubts are demonstrated.

3755   "An Invitation to Explore the Arts of Dying and Edgar Jack-
       son."   Attitudes toward death.   Nov. 23, 1974 session.
       1 1/2 hours.   No. 3810.   Big Sur Recordings.   (T)

3756   "The Keymaker."   Available from University of Southern
       California, Cinema Division.   17 min.   color.   1970.
       (F)
           A student-produced film which conveys to the viewer
       how a widower has the motivation to keep living.

3757   L'Espine, Jean de.   A Treatise tending to take away the
       fears of death, and make the faithful man desire the
       same....   Newly translated out of the French... London:
       Printed by W. Iones, 1619.   "By M. D. S. A."   Ann
       Arbor, Mich.:   University Microfilms, 1973.   (MF)

3758   "A Life Span View of Death."   Big Sur Recordings.   1 1/2
       hours.   No. 3920.   (T)

3759   "Living and Death."   Available from Indiana University
       Audio-Visual Center.   29 min.   b and w.   (F)
           Krishnamurti lectures about fears of death which
       interfere with living.

3760   "Living with Dying."   Produced by Documentary Photo Aids.
       (Photo Aids Series.)   Complete set of 24, 11-x-14
       prints, teacher's guide and A Manual of Death Education
       and Simple Burial, by Ernest Morgan.   (P)
           "... [H]ow do our unenlightened attitudes about
       death diminish the 'quality' of our lives and our behavior
       toward each other?   Is denial of death a denial of life?
       This series explores these vital issues confronting a so-
       ciety oriented against death as a natural process" (Pub.
       cat.).

3761   "Living with Dying."   Produced by Sunburst Communications.
       1973.   Includes 2 sound filmstrips; part 1, 72 frames,
       14 min.; Part 2, 78 frames, 15 min.; each with phono-
       discs or tape cassettes and guide, for use with manual
       or automatic projector.   No. 110.   (FS)

Producer, Alison Weigel; editor, Arthur G. Warren Schloat, Jr. This set "examines the stages of life in all living things, peoples' concept of death, and their attempts to deny it. . . . [T]he presentation examines many of the psychological, social, and ethical aspects of death that have made death a difficult but inevitable subject for discussion and acceptance. . . . [S]uitable for ages eleven and up. The set can also be integrated with church and community groups as well as courses in sociology, social studies, psychology, and family living."

3762 "The Loved One." Available from Films, Inc. 116 min. color. 1965. (F)
A satirical film on the money-making aspects of the funeral business.

3763 "A Lover's Quarrel with the World." Distributed by Bailey Film Associates. 40 min. b and w. 1966. (F)
Robert Frost recites and interprets his work and enjoys his happy old age. For junior and senior high schools, colleges, and adults.

3764 "A Man Dies." Produced-distributed by E. M. I. Records, Middlesex, England. No. M368. (R)
Features children of St. James Church, LockLeaze, Bristol, England. The Bible Story is presented in a most pleasing style.

3765 Manchester, Henry Montagu. Manchester al mondo; Contemplatio mortis and immortalitatis, 3d impr. enl. London: Printed by J. Haviland for F. Constable, 1936. Ann Arbor: University Microfilms. (MF)

3766 "A Matter of Time." Available from Indiana University. Audio-Visual Center. 53 min. b and w. (F)

3767 "Meaning of Death in American Society." Produced by the Center for Death and Education and Research. 28 1/2 min. (F)
"Dr. Feifel offers the general proposition that our society has vulgarized death out of common experience. He discusses the implications of this modern development, both for the individual and society."

3768 Morray, William. A Short tratise of death in sixe chapters. Together with the aenigmatick description of old age and death written Ecclesiastes 12 chap exponed and paraphrased in English meetre. Edinburgh: Printed by I. Wrettoun, 1631. Ann Arbor, Mich. : University Microfilms. (MF)

3769 "The Mystery that Heals." Available from Time-Life Films. 30 min. color. (F)
Jung discusses his views of death.

3770   National Funeral Directors Association of the U.S., Inc.
       "The Florida Showcase." 30 min. 16mm. (Featuring
       William G. Hardy, Jr.) (F)

3771   _____. "The Funeral--From ancient Egypt to present-day
       America." Includes 12 slides and a descriptive manu-
       script. (S)

3772   _____. "The Funeral Gap." 23 min. color. (F)

3773   _____. "Funeral Service--a heritage, a challenge, a fu-
       ture." Includes 16 slides and a descriptive manuscript.
       (S)

3774   _____. "A Humanist Funeral Service." 21 min. color.
       16mm. (F)

3775   _____. "The Last Full Measure of Devotion." 27 1/2
       min. color. 16mm. (F)

3776   _____. "A Life Has Been Lived--A Contemporary Funeral
       Service." 16mm. color. (F)

3777   _____. "Of Life and Death," the new Catholic burial rite.
       27 1/2 min. color. 16mm. (F)

3778   _____. "Someone you Love has Died." 15 min. color.
       16mm. (F)

3779   _____. "Through Death to Life." (Tape cassette by
       Father Joseph M. Camplin.) (T)

3780   _____. "To Serve the Living." 27 1/2 min. color.
       16mm and 35mm. (F)

3781   _____. "Too Personal to be Private." 28 1/2 min.
       color. 16mm. (F)

3782   "Neglected Masterpieces of World Drama." Produced by
       Jeffrey Norton Pub., Inc. 73 min. No. 23129. Vol. 1,
       1969. (Recorded at the Poetry Center.) (T)
               "Analyzes Thomas Lovell Beddoes' masterpiece, the
       Gothic-romantic, poetic drama, Death's Jest Book.
       Sketches life of Beddoes and suggests possible source
       of his attitudes toward death and his ultimate suicide"
       (Pub. cat.).

3783   "Nell and Fred." Produced by the National Film Board of
       Canada, and distributed by McGraw-Hill Textfilms.
       28 min. b and w. 1972. (F)
               An elderly widow and her 90-year old boarder dis-
       cuss the advantages and disadvantages of moving into a
       senior citizens' home. Their decision is based upon

examining the home and discussions with friends. For
senior high school age groups and up.

3784 "New Deal. " Distributed by Carousel Films, Inc. 5 min.
b and w. 1973. (F)
A moving portrait of the aged and aging. Filmed in
cafeterias and coffee shops accompanied by dance music.
For senior high school age groups and up.

3785 "No Man is an Island. " Produced by Albert Saparoff, and
distributed by Dana Productions. 11 min. color. 16mm.
1973. (F)
The message "because I am involved in mankind" by
hand language of the deaf, coupled with the recitation of
John Donne's poem by Orson Welles, conveys to the
viewer the problems connected with intense suffering.
For ages 12 and up. Can be easily used in conjunction
with The Parting.

3786 "No Quarter. " Produced by Jimmy Page--Atlantic Recording
Corp. SD 7255. Stereo. 1963. Vocal by Robert
Plant. (R)
". . . [W]alking side by side with death the devil
mocks their every step. . . . "

3787 "Old Age: Out of Sight, Out of Mind. " Distributed by
Indiana University Audio-Visual Center. 60 min. 2
reels. b and w. 1967. (F)
Nursing homes and hospitals are examined for
medical and rehabilitation facilities for the aged.
Medical and government officials are concerned. For
colleges and adults.

3788 "Old Age--The Wasted Years. " Produced and distributed by
Indiana University Audio-Visual Center. 60 min. 2
reels. b and w. 1967. (F)
Interviews with elderly people with reduced in-
comes and those who are wealthy. Senior citizens,
government officials, and social workers are challenged
in providing for them. For colleges and adults.

3789 "One of the Missing. " Available from Audio Brandon. Directed, produced, and written by Julius D. Feigelson
and based on a story by Ambrose Bierce. 56 min.
color. 1971. (F)

3790 "Only Angels Have Wings. " Available from Audio Brandon.
Directed and produced by Howard Hawks. 121 min.
(F)
Deals with "the ways people cope with the knowledge
of imminent death . . . [and] portrays a small group of
people cut off almost entirely from the outside world
represented by darkness. . . . "

3791 "Optional Ways of Dying." Big Sur Recordings. 1 1/2 hours.
       No. 3750. (T)

3792 "Overcoming the Fear of Death. The Life Counseling Ap-
       proach." Big Sur Recordings. 1 1/4 hours. No.
       3760. (T)

3793 "Parents and the Dying Child." Big Sur Recordings. 1 1/2
       hours. No. 3820. Nov. 23, 1974 session. (T)

3794 "The Parting." Produced by Dunav Films and distributed by
       Wombat Productions. 11 min. color. 16mm. (In-
       cludes Teachers Guide.) (F)
           Examines and portrays the rites and ceremonies of
       a man's death and burial in a rural Yugoslavian village.
       The celebration of the resurrection of the soul to tolling
       bells and chanting is vividly portrayed by the whole
       community. For ages 16 and up.

3795 "Passing Quietly Through." Available from Grove Press--
       Film Division. 26 min. b and w. 1971. (F)
           Interesting dialogue between an aging man and a
       nurse. Topics include the life and death cycle and hu-
       man experiences.

3796 "The Patient as a Source of Information." Produced by
       Harper and Row, Publishers. 04-95366. (K)
           Parts one and two contain the effects of illness.
       Part of a "multimedia study program covering essential
       nursing concepts...." The kit contains audio cassettes
       and slides.

3797 "Peege." Distributed by Phoenix Films, Inc. 28 min.
       color. (F)
           A family visits their grandmother in a nursing
       home. Love and understanding transcend disease, ter-
       minal illness, and senility.

3798 "Personality Theory and Death." Produced by Jeffrey Norton
       Pub., Inc. 30 min. No. 29193. Recorded in 1962 by
       Herman Feifel. Complete series available. (T)
           "There has been an underemphasis in considering
       the role of attitudes toward death in influencing be-
       havior. We need to include sentiments concerning death
       in our personality studies and therapeutic horizons" (Pub.
       cat.).

3799 "Perspectives on Death: A Thematic Teaching Unit." Pro-
       duced by Perspectives on Death; Understanding Death
       series. Each component may be purchased separately.
       (K)
           The program consists of four components, given in
       entries 3800-3803.

3800 _____. _____. [1] Audio-visual package--containing
two color-sound filmstrips and two separate tape cassette presentations. See entry 3799.
(A)   "Funeral Customs Around the World."
"This 110-frame color filmstrip with cassette narration explores the funeral customs of various cultures
in many countries, including the U.S. It shows how all
civilizations share the common bonds of death, grief,
and the funeral process."
(B)   "Death Through the Eyes of the Artist."
"The 87-frame color filmstrip with cassette narration treats death as a universal phenomena that has in-
trigued artists for centuries. The artist has attempted
through style, color, subject matter and symbolism to
capture the face and mood of death, and thus make such
an illusive subject more real and more comprehensible."
(C)   "Death Themes in Literature."
"Authors, poets and dramatists have attempted to
come to grips with the most universal and least understood parts of life in a variety of ways. This 20-
minute cassette tape presentation illustrates these attempts, drawing from the writings of Shakespeare, Poe,
London, Wilder, Richard Armour, Dorothy Parker,
Ambrose Bierce, and others, each bringing a separate
insight into life's ultimate mystery."
(D)   "Death Themes in Music."
"In this 18-minute tape cassette presentation, selec-
tions from classical, jazz, folk and modern music are
used to illustrate how musicians have tried to express
their feelings and emotions about death through their
music. Death is expressed as a religious experience,
as a welcome release from an unpleasant life on earth,
as a threatening force and as a topic for a more light-
hearted treatment."

3801 _____. _____. [2] Anthology of Readings, The Individual, Society and Death.
"A 193-page softbound text designed to provide information on various aspects of death. The 24 selec-
tions include fiction, non-fiction and poetry discussing
the medical aspects of death, the grief process, funeral
practice and costs, death and children, the dying process and other facets of death and dying." See entry
3799.

3802 _____. _____. [3] Student Activity Book.
"Designed for classroom use in a course on death.
It provides a variety of activities to allow the student
to become involved with his learning and gain more
from the course." See entry 3799.

3803 _____. _____. [4] Teacher's Resource Book.
"Prepared to give guidance to the teacher for teach-

ing a six-week unit on death using the 'Perspectives on Death' unit. It includes daily lesson plans, suggestions, bibliography and vocabulary listing." See entry 3799.

3804 "Presentations and Discussion" (Saturday night). Big Sur Recordings. 1 1/2 hours. No. 3900. (T)

3805 "Professional/Personal Involvement with the Dying Patient." Big Sur Recordings. 1 1/2 hours. No. 3860. (T)

3806 "Professionals are Mortal Too." Big Sur Recordings. 1 hour. No. 3950. (T)

3807 "The Proud Years." Available from Center for Mass Communications. 28 min. b and w. 1956. (F)

3808 "A Psycho-Social Aspect of Terminal Care--Anticipatory Grief." Produced by the Center for Death Education and Research. 32 min. (Orig. a paper presented at a symposium in Nov. 1970.) (T)
       "Dr. Robert Fulton surveys present day social and medical practices in America as they affect the chronically ill or dying person...."

3809 "Psychosocial Aspects of Death." Available from Indiana University Audio-Visual Center. 29 min. b and w. 16mm. (F)
       Presents (for nurses) a terminally-ill patient, his actions, reactions, and interactions with the people around him.

3810 "Ready or Not, Here Comes Immortality." Produced by Pacifica Tape Library, Pacifica Foundation. 36 min. BC1233. 1973. (Mind and Body Series.) (T)
       "Jerry Tucille is the author of Here Comes Immortality, a book which details life-extension techniques. In this fast-paced interview, Tucille describes some of these techniques and goes on to discuss the moral, psychological, ecological and political consequences of immortality. Recorded in February, 1973" (Pub. cat.).

3811 "Reincarnation." Produced by the Theosophical Society and distributed by Modern Talking Pictures. 1973. (F)
       A cross-cultural film that explains the basis of reincarnation in all religious beliefs.

3812 "Religious Faith and Death: Implications in Work with the Dying Patients and Family." Produced by the Center for Death Education and Research. 31 1/2 min. (T)
       The Rev. Carl Nighswonger "discusses dying as the possible source of a rich, personal social experience particularly if one is allowed to participate in all of its appropriate emotions and feelings...."

3813 "Remembrance and Goodbye." Available from Film-makers
      Cooperative. 7 1/2 min. color. (F)

3814 "The Rest of Your Life." Distributed by Journal Films.
      28 min. color. 1968. (F)
      Examines a group of workers from all age groups
      who are considering retirement. For colleges and
      adults.

3815 "The Right to Die" (news closeup one-hour special). Written
      and produced by Marlene Sanders, narrated by Stephen
      Geer, and viewed over ABC on Saturday, Jan. 5, 1974.
      (F)
      "... I've come to terms with my condition, when
      it comes time to die, I'll be ready.... I wouldn't want
      to be kept alive to suffer more, or to live without my
      mental faculties...." The film indicates that society is
      making strides in facing death. Also available from
      Audio Brandon.

3816 "The Role of the Schools in Death Education." Produced by
      the Center for Death Education and Research. 27 min.
      (T)
      "Dr. Daniel Leviton expresses his views on the need
      for 'Formal Death Education' in the schools. He com-
      pares such education to sex education and stresses the
      value of an academic context ... and the prospect of
      crisis intervention facilities...."

3817 "Russell, Bertrand." Produced by Films, Inc. 30 min. 1958.
      (F) (Wisdom Series.)
      Russell talks about his 80 years--what he has
      learned and what he has not learned--the needs of the
      world, and his hopes for the future. For colleges and
      adults.

3818 "Searching for Values." Distributed by Learning Corp. of
      America. 15 films, ea. approx. 15 min. Complete
      series available. (F)
      Clarifies values concerning the decisions people
      make during their lives. Subjects include aging parents,
      right to die, unfair laws, and others.

3819 Shawe, G. The Doctrine of dying-vvell. Or the godly mans
      guide to glory. Wherein is briefly comprised a short
      view of the glorious estate of Gods saints in the kingdom
      of heaven.... London: Printed for F. Cowles, 1628.
      Ann Arbor, Mich.: University Microfilms. (MF)

3820 "Social Reconstruction After Death." Produced by the Center
      for Death Education and Research. 21 min. (T)
      "Dr. Jeanette Folta asks the question whether grief
      is due to the loss of the dead or the loss to the liv-

ing.... [Also she] discusses the consequences of the
fact that our society makes inadequate provisions for the
psychological replacement of a member of a group...."

3821 "Soon There Will Be No More Me." Produced by Churchill
      Films. 10 min. color. 16mm. 1972. (F)
          Records the reactions of a 19-year-old mother to
      her husband and daughter when she learns she is dying
      of cancer. Useful for program situations, and will
      stimulate discussion.

3822 Soto, Petrus de. The Maner to dye well. An introduction
      ... gathered out of manye good authors.... Imprinted
      at London by Richard Iohnes. 1579. "Written in Latin
      by Petrus de Soto." Ann Arbor, Mich.: University of
      Microfilms. (MF)

3823 "Stages of Dying." Produced by the Center for Death Educa-
      tion and Research. 32 min. (T)
          "Dr. Elizabeth Kübler-Ross tells of her first ex-
      perience of learning about death from the dying. She
      describes her theory of the five stages of dying and the
      symbolic verbal language that dying patients often use
      in an attempt to communicate their feelings...."

3824 "The Swan Song." Distributed by Carousel Films, Inc. 25
      min. color. 1972. (F)
          "An actor relives his personal and professional life.
      Adapted into play form in 1886 by Anton Chekhov. The
      film stars Richard Kileg and Michael Dunn." For senior
      high school and up.

3825 "Talking to Children about Death." Produced by the Center
      for Death Education and Research. 30 min. (T)
          "Dr. George Williams discusses ways to open the
      channels of communication between parent and child on
      the sensitive issue of death. He cautions us that
      thwarting children's efforts at greater understanding of
      death can result in serious emotional problems in later
      life...."

3826 "Ten Years Teaching on Death and Dying." Big Sur Record-
      ings. 1 1/2 hours. No. 3850. (T)

3827 "Terminal Illness Counseling Experience." Big Sur Record-
      ings. 15 min. No. 3772. (T)

3828 "They Need Not Die." Produced and distributed by Creative
      Learning Center. FS1017. 24 min. 16mm. color.
      (T)
          "Story of emergency rooms and the innovation of a
      shock-trauma unit."

3829 "Those Who Mourn. " Produced by Association Films. SP-
081. 5 min. color. (Films of Social Significance).
(F)
"Those Who Mourn explores the death of one man
and its meaning to his wife. But the film moves beyond
this particular experience, to encompass the spectrum of
mourning on both a personal and a universal level.
Particularly effective is the use of black and white pho-
tography contrasted against flashback scenes in color to
depict the harshness of death versus the warmth of
life... " (Pub. cat.).

3830 "Though I Walk Through the Valley.... " Produced and directed by Mel White. Distributed by Pyramid Films.
30 min. (F)
The production records Tony Brouwer's reactions to
his impending death by cancer. The film portrays his
fate and the ways he comes to terms with it. Suitable
for high schools, colleges, medical education workshops,
and in-training programs.

3831 "To Die Today. " Available from Film-makers Library, Inc.
50 min. b and w. 1971. (F)
Features Dr. Elizabeth Kübler-Ross and her lecture
about the fear of death and description of the five emotional stages prior to death.

3832 "Today's Funeral Director--His Responsibilities and Challenges. " Produced by the Center for Death Education
and Research. 25 min. (Originally an address presented at a symposium in May 1971.) (T)
"Mr. Glenn Griffin characterizes the contemporary
American funeral as an organized purposeful, group-
centered response to death. He examines the role of
the modern funeral director in terms of his actual and
potential service to survivors. "

3833 "The Transpersonal Experience of Death. " Big Sur Recordings. 1 1/2 hours. No. 3870. (T)

3834 "Ultimate Risk. " Available from Time-Life Films. 52
min. color. 1972. (F)
Records the death-defying experiences of five men
who put their lives on the line. Astronaut Borman discusses the motivation of each. Suitable for junior high
age group and up.

3835 "Understanding Changes in the Family. " Produced and distributed by Guidance Associates. color. 1973. (K)
Contents: Five sound filmstrips, each with phono-
disc, with teacher's guide, for use with manual or
automatic projector, no. 303246. With tape cassettes,
no. 303253.

3836   "Until I Die." Available from Video Nursing Inc.   30 min.
       color. 1970. (F)
              Attitudes toward death are explored based on the
       work of Elizabeth Kübler-Ross. Stages of death are dis-
       cussed, and there are interviews with patients with ter-
       minal illness.

3837   "Warrendale." Available from Grove Press Film Division.
       105 min. b and w. 1967. (F)
              A documentary by Alan King of a treatment center
       for emotionally disturbed children. Exhibited are re-
       pressions of normal grief.

3838   "What Can I Say?" Available from American Journal of
       Nursing Co. 31 min. b and w. kinescope. 1968.
       (F)
              Focuses on clinical aspects for nurses serving the
       dying.

3839   "What Man Shall Live and Not See Death?" Available from
       NBC Educational Enterprises. 57 min. color. 1971.
       (F)
              A documentary by Joan Konner who interviews a
       mother who is dying. Covered in the film are cryo-
       genics, euthanasia, medical training, and programs for
       the bereaved. A program to be used as an introduction
       to death education.

3840   "Where Are the Dead?" Available from Mayse Studio.   51
       frames. b and w. 35 min. 1943. (FS)
              One in a series of the Home Bible Course. Dis-
       cusses the destiny of man after death and the mortality
       of the Soul.

3841   "Who Should Survive?" Available from Medal of Greatness.
       26 min. color. 1972. (F)
              Down's Syndrome (mongoloid) infant is allowed to
       die; panel discussion on legal and ethical issues.

3842   "Why Do We Die?" Available from Eyegate House. (FS)
              Part of a set of filmstrips which discuss real rea-
       sons why we: work and play, feel, grow, have rules,
       have homes, and die. Grade level is designed for the
       educable mentally retarded and for primary use.

3843   "The Widow in America: a Study of the Older Widow."
       Produced by the Center for Death Education and Research.
       42 min. (T)
              "Dr. Helena Lopata explores the psychological and
       sociological problems created by widowhood in contem-
       porary society...."

3844   "Widows." Available from Mental Health Training Health

Program, Harvard Medical School. 43 min. b and w.
1970. (F)
    Deals with the problems of the bereaved. "Several
middle-aged mothers speak of their reactions to the
death of their husbands and the kings of help they found
useful.... "

3845 "With His Play Clothes On. " Available from the Order of
the Golden Rule Service Corporation. Produced by
Bill Goveia. 47 min. (Multiple screen film presentation.) (F)
    Available only to members of OGRSC and funeral
directors. A filmstrip is available to funeral directors
to use with care-giving teams in communities. Produced by a funeral director, and "portrays the suffering
and despair of survivors. It clearly demonstrates anger
and suspicions that are present ... with the death of a
child. " Aimed at the care-giving audience.

3846 "You See, I've Had a Life. " Available from Eccentric Circle
Cinema Workshop. 30 min. b and w. 1972. (F)
    Tells of Paul who developed leukemia and the ex-
periences the parents face together.

3847 "A Zen Approach to Dying. " Big Sur Recordings. 1 1/2
hours. No. 3890. (T)

3848 "Zen View of Dying. " Big Sur Recordings. 1 1/2 hours.
No. 3800. (T)

AV SOURCES

Abingdon Press
201 Eighth Ave. S.
Nashville, Tennessee   37202

ACI Productions
11th Floor 35 W. 45th St.
New York, N. Y.   10036

American Broadcasting Co.
1330 Ave. of Americas
New York, N. Y.   10036

American Journal of Nursing Co.
267 W 25th St.
New York, N. Y.   10001

Association Films
875 N Michigan Ave.
Chicago, Ill.   60611

Atlanta Recording Corp.
1841 Broadway
New York, N. Y.   10023

Audio Brandon Films
34 MacQuesten Pkwy. South
Mount Vernon, N. Y.   10550

Barley Films Associates
11559 Santa Monica Blvd.
Los Angeles, Calif.   90025

Big Sur Recordings
2015 Bridgeway
Sausalito, Calif.   94965

Brandon Films see
   Audio Brandon

Carousel Films, Inc.
1501 Broadway
New York, N. Y.   10036

Cathedral Films, Inc.
2921 West Alameda Ave.
Burbank, Calif.   91505

Center for Cassette Studies
   --Audio-Text Cassette
8110 Webb Ave.
North Hollywood, Calif.   91605

Center for Death Education
   and Research
University of Minnesota
1167 Social Science Building
Minneapolis, Minn.   55455

Center for Mass Communications
136 South Broadway
Irvington, N. Y.   10533

Churchill Films
662 N Robertson Blvd.
Los Angeles, Calif.   90069

Columbia Pictures Corp.
711 Fifth Ave.
New York, N. Y.   10035

Communication Research Machines
Del Mar, Calif.   90214

Concord Films
Nacton, Near Ipswich
Suffolk, England

Concordia Films
3558 S. Jefferson
St. Louis, Mo.   63118

Contemporary Films see
   McGraw-Hill

Creative Learning Center
105 Edgevale Road
Baltimore, Md. 21210

Dana Productions
6249 Babcock Ave.
N. Hollywood, Calif. 91606

Documentary Photo Aids
P. O. Box 956
Mt. Dora, Fa. 32757

Eccentric Circle Cinema
  Workshop
P. O. Box 1481
Evanston, Ill. 60204

E. M. I. Records
Middlesex, England

Encyclopaedia Britannica Films
425 N. Michigan Ave. Dept. 10A
Chicago, Ill. 60611

Eyegate House
146-01 Archer Ave.
Jamaica, N. Y. 11435

Film-makers Cooperative
175 Lexington Ave.
New York, N. Y. 10016

Films, Inc.
1144 Wilmette Ave.
Wilmette, Ill. 60091

Georgetown University Forum
37th & O Street, N. W.
Washington, D. C. 20007

Grove Press, Film Div.
53 E. 11th St.
New York, N. Y. 10003

Guidance Associates
41 Washington Ave.
Pleasantville, N. Y. 10570

Harper and Row Publishers
10 E. 53rd St.
New York, N. Y. 10022

Harvard Medical School
33 Fenwood Rd.
Boston, Mass. 02115

Indiana University
Audio-visual Center
Bloomington, Ind. 47401

Jeffrey Norton Publishers, Inc.
145 E. 49th St.
New York, N. Y. 10017

Journal Films
909 W. Diversey Pkwy.
Chicago, Ill. 60614

King Screen Productions
320 Aurora Ave.
N. Seattle, Wash. 98109

Lansford Pub. Co.
P. O. Box 8711
San Jose, Calif. 95155

Learning Arts
P. O. Box 917
Wichita, Kan. 67201

Learning Corp. of America
711 Fifth Ave.
New York, N. Y. 10022

McGraw-Hill Book Co.
1221 Ave. of Americas
New York, N. Y. 10020

McGraw-Hill Text Films
330 W. 42d St.
New York, N. Y. 10036

Macmillan Audio Brandon see
  Audio Brandon

Mass Media Associates, Inc.
2116 North Charles St.
Baltimore, Md. 21218

Mayse Studios
692 S. Arroyo Blvd.
Pasadena, Calif. 91105

Medal of Greatness
1032 33d St., N.W.
Washington, D.C.   20007

Minnesota Manufacturing and
  Mining Co.
Medical Film Library
2501 Hudson Rd.
St. Paul, Minn.   55119

Modern Talking Pictures
910 Penn Ave.
Pittsburgh, Pa.   15222

National Broadcasting Co.
Educational Enterprises
30 Rockefeller Plaza
New York, N.Y.   10020

National Funeral Directors Assoc.
135 West Wells St.
Milwaukee, Wis.   53203

National Institute of Mental Health
Drug Abuse Film Collection
National Audiovisual Denter (GSA)
Washington, D.C.   20409

National Instructional Television
  Center
1111 West 17th St.
Bloomington, Ind.   47401

Order of the Golden Rule
Services Corp.
P.O. Box 3586
Springfield, Ill.   62708

Oregon Center for Gerontology
133 Gill Coliseum
Corvallis, Ore.   97331

Oxford Films
1136 N. Las Palmas Ave.
Los Angeles, Calif.   90038

Pacifica Tape Library
Pacifica Foundation Dept. S 274
5316 Venice Blvd.
Los Angeles, Calif.   90019

Perspectives on Death
P.O. Box 213
De Kalb, Ill.   60115

Phoenix Films, Inc.
470 Park Ave. South
New York, N.Y.   10016

Pyramid Films
Box 1048
Santa Monica, Calif.   90406

Society for Visual Education
1345 Diversey Pkwy.
Chicago, Ill.   60614

Sunburst Communications
Hemlock Hill Road
Pound Ridge, N.Y.   10576

Syracuse University
1011 East Water St.
Syracuse, N.Y.   13210

Thomas More Assoc.
180 North Wabash Ave.
Chicago, Ill.   60601

Time-Life Books
Time, Inc., Rockefeller Center
New York, N.Y.   10020

Time-Life Films
43 W. 16th St.
New York, N.Y.   10011

University Microfilms see
  Xerox University Microfilms

University of California
Office of Medical Education
Irvine, Calif.   92664

Univ. of Southern Calif.
Cinema Division
Los Angeles, Calif.   90007

Video Nursing Inc.
2834 Central St.
Evanston, Ill.   60201

Wombat Productions
77 Tarrytown Rd.
White Plains, N. Y.   10607

World Pacific Records
8715 W. 3d St.
Los Angeles, Calif.   90048

World Records, Inc.
Waco, Texas   17610

Xerox University Microfilms
300 North Zeeb Rd.
Ann Arbor, Mich.   48106

AUTHOR INDEX*

*Symbols used in Part VIII are used herein, to wit: F (film), FS (filmstrip), K (kit), MF (microfilm), P (photos, prints), R recording), S (slide), T (tape), TR (transparencies).

Ayd, F. J. 1119
Ayers, R. H. 206
Ayuso Rivera, J. 299

B

Baader, I. 2383
Bach, J. S. 497
Bachmann, C. C. 1958
Bachofen, J. J. 2384
Backmann, E. L. 809
Bacon, A. 1959
Bacon, F. 300, 301, 341
Bacon, H. E. see Bacon, A.
Badawi, A. 302
Baden, M. M. 2838
Baeizner, E. 303
Baer, R. 1120
Bahle, J. 2385
Bahnson, C. B. 1121, 2386
Bahrmann, E. 1121
Bailey, R. M. 2387
Baker, D. C. 2388
Baker, J. M. 1122
Bakke, J. L. 1123
Bakker, C. B. 1124
Bakwin, H. 2389
Balduzzi, P. C. 1125
Baler, L. A. 1126
Ballinger, M. 1344
Balthasar, H. U. 304
Bälz, E. 2390
Balzac, H. 341
Banen, D. M. 2392
Banks, L. 2393
Banks, S. A. 1960
Barahal, H. S. 2684
Barande, A. 2394
Barash, M. 305
Barbé, A. 2395
Barber, T. X. 1127
Barckley, V. 1128, 1129
Barclay, D. 2395
Bard, B. 2396
Barey, P. 3836 (F)
Barker, J. C. 7
Barnacle, C. H. 2397
Barnard, M. 1130
Barnes, E. W. 1961
Barnes, H. E. 306
Barnes, M. J. 2398

Barnes, W. 341
Barnett, C. 1131
Barnhart, J. E. 307
Barnouw, V. 2399
Barnsteiner, J. H. 1132
Barnum, M. C. 2400
Barr, A. 1133
Barrett, G. U. 2401
Barron, A. 3336, 3683 (F), 3702 (F)
Barron, E. 3683 (F)
Barry, H. 1134, 1135, 2402, 2403
Barry, H., Jr. 1136
Barry, H., III 1136
Barshal, H. S. 2684
Barth, K. 341, 1057, 2136
Barton, B. A. 8
Barton, D. 207, 208
Barton, E. A. 1137
Bartsch, F. 1962
Basayne, H. 3688 (T), 3755 (T)
Bascue, L. O. 2404
Basdekis, D. 308
Basevi, W. H. F. 9
Bassett, S. D. 1138
Bataille, G. 2405
Battista, O. 2264
Baudelaire, C. P. 282
Bäuml, F. H. 309
Baxter, C. 1139
Bayly, J. 10
Beahan, L. T. 1140
Bean, W. B. 1963
Beardsley, G. L. 2265
Beasley-Murray, G. R. 1964
Beatty, D. 1141, 1964, 2201
Beaty, N. L. 310
Beau, W. B. 1142
Beaumont, J. 341
Beauvoir, S. de 11, 741, 909
Beaver, M. W. 2406
Beberman, A. 1965
Beck, A. T. 2407
Beck, F. 2408
Beck, I. 1226
Becker, D. 1143
Becker, E. 2409
Becker, H. 311, 2410, 2411, 3392
Beckett, S. 809, 1057
Beckwith, J. B. 1144

Brock, D. 2471
Broden, A. R. 3419
Brodsky, B. 2472
Brodt, H. 2269
Brody, B. A. 346/8, 349
Bromberg, W. 2473
Bronowski, J. 2474
Brontë, C. 341
Brontë, E. 341
Brooks, D. P. 1984
Brooks, R. M. 3237
Brooks, S. M. 1191
Brouwer, T. 3830 (F)
Brown, C. R. 341
Brown, F. 1192, 2475
Brown, J. 350
Brown, J. P. 1193
Brown, L. B. 2476
Brown, M. 213a
Brown, N. D. 1194
Brown, N. K. 1195
Brown, N. O. 2477
Brown, R. 3746 (T)
Brown, R. E. 1985
Brown, R. J. 1656
Brown, R. M. 1986
Brown, W. A. 341, 1987
Browne, T. 351
Browne-Olf, L. 595
Browning, E. B. 341
Browning, R. 341, 352,
    353, 854
Bruce, S. J. 1196
Brun, J. 354
Bruner, D. K. 2411
Bruner, E. 341
Brunner, S. 1988
Brunton, P. 1021
Bry, T. 1538
Bryant, W. C. 341
Bryson, K. A. 355
Buber, M. 475, 509
Bucher, R. 2478
Bucke, R. M. 341
Buckley, J. H. 352
Buckley, J. J. 2479
Bucove, A. D. 1197
Budge, E. A. W. 356,
    1989, 2480
Bugenthal, J. F. 357,
    752
Buhler, C. 2481

Buhrmann, M. V. 2482
Bui-Dang, H. U. D. 2483
Bulger, R. 1198
Bulka, R. P. 1990
Bullard, M. 341
Bullough, V. L. 31
Bultmann, R. 1993
Bunch, J. 2484, 2485, 2486
Bunston, A. 2487
Bunzel, B. 2626
Bunzel, R. 2487
Buonaiuti, E. 358
Buonarcoti, M. 341
Burchenal, J. 1549
Bürgel, B. H. 359
Burghardt, W. 360
Burhoe, R. W. 468
Burnand, R. 361
Burnett, W. M. 1199
Burns, R. 341
Burroughs, J. 341, 362
Burton, A. 2488, 2489
Burton, L. 2511
Burton, R. 341, 1021
Burtt, E. A. 1021
Bush, M. 1991
Busse, E. W. 1992, 1993
Butler, R. N. 2588, 2490
Butler, S. 341
Buxbaum, E. 33
Buxbaum, R. E. 1200
Bynum, J. 2491

C

Cabodevilla, J. 363
Cahn, R. 2936
Cain, A. C. 1201, 1202, 2492,
    2493, 2494, 2666
Cain, B. S. 2494
Calanes, A. 364
Calderone, M. 2495
Calderóne, P. 878
Caldwell, D. 1203
Caldwell, J. R. 1204
Calhoun, J. 3742 (T)
Callahan, D. 365, 826
Callahan, R. J. 1995
Callaway, E. 1205
Callaway, J. A. 1996
Calloway, N. D. 2496

Coplan, A. 3119
Corbin, A. 410
Corder, M. P. 1243
Corey, L. G. 2559
Corfe, T. H. 2560
Cornils, S. 2561
Cort, D. 51
Cortázar, J. 940
Corwin, S. M. 3401
Cory, W. 341
Cosacchi, S. 411
Cosgrave, J. O. 1021
Cosneck, B. J. 2562
Cotter, M. M. 1245
Cotter, Z. M. 1246, 2563
Cottrell, J. 2564
Countryman, F. W. 125
Cousinet, R. 2565
Cousins, N. 2019
Cowan, B. 3813 (F)
Cowin, R. 2566
Cowper, F. M. M. 1954a
Cox, I. W. 2020
Cox, P. R. 1247
Craddick, R. A. 2567
Crafoord, C. C. 1248
Crain, H. 412
Cramond, W. A. 1249
Crane, D. 1250, 1563
Crane, E. 2021
Cranfield, C. E. B. 2022
Crapsey, A. 413
Crase, D. 216
Crase, D. R. 216
Crashaw, R. 341
Crawford, M. D. 2757
Creegan, R. F. 2568, 3392
Cremation Assoc. of America
   117
Cremation Soc. of America
   68
Cremation Soc. of London 52,
   53
Crile, G. W. 1251
Croce, B. 341
Crocker, L. G. 414
Croly, G. 415
Cromp, G. 416
Crosby, T. 2022a
Crosson, F. J. 417
Crotty, W. J. 2569, 3017
Crow, W. B. 1021

Crown, B. 2570
Crumbaugh, J. C. 2448
Cruvant, B. A. 2571
Cullmann, O. 2023, 2225
Cumming, E. 2345
Cummins, G. 1021
Cumont, F. V. M. 418
Cumpston, J. H. L. 1252
Cunningham, M. F. 419
Curl, J. S. 2572
Curphey, T. J. 2573
Curran, C. 3725 (F)
Curran, W. J. 1253
Curtin, S. R. 420
Curtis, C. J. 2024
Cutler, A. 2275
Cutler, D. R. 1254
Cutter, F. 54, 2574

D

Dahlberg, G. 2575
Dahlgren, K. G. 2576
d'Albe, E. E. Fournier see
   Fournier, d'Albe, E. E.
Dallas, H. A. 421
Daniel, H. 422
Dann, R. H. 2577
D'Annunzie, G. 2578
Dante 341, 423, 481, 1039
D'arcy, M. C. 2025
Darcy-Bérubé, F. 2026
Darwin, C. 241
Das, S. S. 2579, 2580
Dastre, A. 2276
Daugherty, G. G. 210, 211
Davenport, W. 341
David, H. P. 2355, 2581,
   2582
Davidson, D. L. 3666
Davidson, G. W. 2027
Davidson, H. A. 1255
Davidson, R. P. 1256
Davidson, S. 1257
da Vinci see Leonardo da
   Vinci
Davis, C. 2583
Davis, D. R. 424
Davis, F. B. 2584
Davis, J. A. 2585
Davis, J. C. 2586

Epictetus 185, 341
Epicurus 185, 396, 832
Epps, P. 2651
Erasmus, D. 3731 (MF),
  3732 (MF)
Erichsen, H. 68
Erikson, E. H. 69
Ernst, C. 2046
Eron, L. 221
Escobal, P. 2652
Eshelman, B. 2653
Eskreis, N. 135, 2201
Ethel Percy Andrus Gerontology
  Center see Andrus Geron-
  tology Center
Ettinger, R. C. W. 809,
  2275, 2285, 2304
Etzioni, A. 2654
Euthanasia Educational Council
  3394, 3394a
Euthanasia Educational Fund
  2655, 3176
Euthanasia Soc. of America
  796, 1563, 3176
Evans, A. E. 1298
Evans, P. R. 1299
Evans, W. E. D. 2286
Evans-Wentz, W. Y. 1021,
  2048
Everett, M. S. 1563
Eversole, R. 473
Ewing, L. S. 2287
Exton-Smith, A. N. 1300
Eyck, P. N. V. 474

F

Fabian, J. 2658
Fairbank, E. 2659
Fairbanks, R. J. 2050, 2699
Falque, F. C. 2051
Fannon, P. 2052
Faraday, M. 341
Farber, L. H. 475, 509
Farberow, N. L. 1235, 1301,
  2660, 2661, 2662, 2663,
  2674, 3463, 3464, 3668 (T)
Fargues, M. 2053
Farmer, J. A., Jr. 222
Farnell, L. R. 476
Farrar, C. B. 2664, 2665

Farrow, R. G. 2767
Fast, I. 2666, 2667
Fast, C. J. 1202
Faulkner, J. E. 2668
Faulkner, W. 477, 478
Faunce, W. A. 2668, 2745
Fawerch, F. E. 479
Fechner, G. T. 341, 2054,
  2084
Federal Trade Commission 48a,
  84a
Federn, P. 2671
Fedin, K. 1025
Fehrman, C. A. D. 480
Feifel, H. 70, 71, 591, 1302,
  1303, 1304, 1305, 2672, 2673,
  2674, 2675, 2676, 2677, 2678,
  2679, 2680, 2681, 3062, 3392,
  3758 (F), 3767 (F), 3798 (T)
Feigelson, J. D. 3789 (F)
Feinberg, D. 2682
Fekete, I. F. 1460
Feldman, J. J. 2464, 3447
Feldman, K. A. 3324
Feldman, M. J. 2683, 2684
Felipe, R. P. 1875
Fellini, F. 809
Ferenczi, S. 2685
Fermaglich, J. L. 1306
Ferneau, E. 2765
Ferrante, J. M. 481
Ferrater-Mora, J. 482, 483,
  2284
Ferrer, J. M. 2686
Feuerbach, L. 396
Fiedler, L. 485
Filbey, E. E. 1307
Filler, L. 2687
Fink, E. 486
Fink, S. L. 3423, 3665
Finney, J. W. 167a
Finnis, J. 487
Fischer, E. H. 3494
Fischer, J. A. 488, 1308
Fishbein, M. 1309, 1310
Fisher, B. 489
Fisher, G. 1311, 2688
Fisher, J. R. 1312
Fitch, R. E. 2055
Fitts, W. T. 1313
Fitzgerald, E. J. 48a
Fitzgerald, F. S. 647

Harlan Lane Found. 2304
Harmer, R. M. 97, 98, 185,
  2861, 2862
Harmetz, A. 99
Harmon, L. 2863
Harnden, R. 565
Harnik, J. 2864
Haroutunian, J. 566
Harp, J. R. 1385
Harrington, A. 567
Harrington, L. 2865
Harris, E. E. 568
Harris, E. G. 2201
Harris, K. A. 2866
Harrison, J. 809
Harrison, S. I. 2867
Harrison, S. M. 569
Hartland, E. S. 2085
Hartley, M. 3696 (F)
Hartmann, F. 100
Harvard Medical School,
  Ad Hoc Committee of
  1240
Harvey, A. M. 1385a
Harvey, L. 25
Harvey, W. F. 1380
Hatt, H. E. 2086
Hattam, E. 570
Hauser, P. M. 3022
Havens, M. C. 2868
Havens, T. 246
Havighurst, R., Jr. 1386,
  2869
Hawes, S. 341
Hawks, H. 3790 (F)
Hawthorne, N. 276, 341,
  1016, 3453
Hay, W. H. 571
Hayano, D. M. 2870
Haynes, W. S. 1387
Hays, J. S. 1388
Hazlitt, W. 341, 572, 573
Heaney, J. J. 2087
Heard, G. 3736 (R)
Hearn, L. 101, 574
Heath-Stubbs, J. F. 575
Heckel, R. V. 2871
Hedenius, I. 576
Hedin, A. 102
Hedwig, K. 577
Heenan, C. 1409a
Hegel, G. W. 290, 341, 396,
  501

Heidegger, M. 151, 185, 306,
  396, 429, 501, 509, 547,
  578, 603, 623, 832, 956,
  1000, 1057, 2213
Heider, K. G. 2758
Heilbrunn, C. 2872
Heindel, A. F. 1021
Heinlich, H. J. 3419
Heinmann, P. 2873
Helburn, T. 341
Helderbrand, W. 712
Heller, J. J. 2088
Helmuth, N. 1819
Helson, G. A. 1389
Hembright, T. Z. 2875
Hemery, S. 2763
Hemingway, E. 409, 570, 579,
  592, 1075
Hendal, P. J. 2876
Henderson, D. K. 1390
Henderson, J. L. 2877
Hendin, D. 103
Hendin, H. 2878, 2879, 2880,
  2881, 2882, 2883
Hendrix, R. C. 1391
Henley, W. E. 341
Henry, F. 2884
Henry, W. 2345
Herbert, B., Jr. 2886
Herbert, C. 2887
Herbert, G. 341
Hermann, L. J. 1304
Herold, J. 580
Hersen, M. 2683
Hershey, N. 1392, 1393
Herter, F. 104
Hertz, R. 2888
Herzog, A. 2889, 2890
Herzog, E. 2891
Hesse, H. 581, 911, 3454
Heuscher, J. E. 582, 583
Heuvelmans, B. 2892
Heuyer, G. 1394
Heywood, R. 2893
Hickerson, H. 2894
Hicks, W. 1395
Hiers, J. T. 584
Higgins, A. 585
High, D. M. 2895
Hight, J. 2089
Hilgard, J. 2896
Hilgard, J. R. 1396, 1397
Hill, G. H. 2897

Ingersoll, R. G. 341
Ingham, M. B. 611
Inman, W. S. 1419
Innes, G. 1420
Inoguchi, H. 2929
International Order of the
  Golden Rule 108, 2930,
  3845 (F, FS)
Ionesco, E. 672
Irion, P. E. 109, 110, 111,
  112, 113, 114, 115, 191,
  2095, 2201, 2931, 2932
Irish, D. P. 227, 246
Irle, G. 2934
Irwin, I. H. 1021
Irwin, R. C. 1910
Isaacs, B. 1421
Isaacs, N. 2937
Isham, L. S. 2935
Isler, C. 1422
Israel, L. 2936
Izikowitz, K. G. 2938

J

Jablon, S. 1423
Jachmann, F. 2939
Jackson, D. D. 2940
Jackson, E. N. 27, 49, 2097,
  2098, 2201, 2941, 2942,
  2943, 2944, 2945, 3679 (T),
  3706 (T), 3728 (T), 3755 (T),
  3804 (T)
Jackson, N. A. 1424, 2946
Jacobi, J. 612
Jacobs, H. L. 2099
Jacobs, J. 2947
Jacobs, P. 116
Jacobson, E. 2948
Jacobson, N. O. 2949
Jacques, E. 2950/1, 3392
Jacques, J. 1425
Jaehner, D. 2952
Jaffa, B. 2953
Jaffe, L. 1426
Jaisrub, S. 1427
Jakobovits, I. 1428
James, E. O. 2100
James, H. 277, 341
James, T. N. 1428a
James, W. 590, 613

Jankelevitch, S. 614
Jankelevitch, V. 615
Jankofsky, K. 616
Jantz, H. 1429
Jarast, S. G. 2954
Jarecki, H. G. 1268a
Jarzynka, J. J. 1415
Jaspers, K. 396, 547, 617, 618
Jaszi, O. 2955
Jeans, J. 341
Jefferies, R. 341
Jeffers, F. C. 1430
Jeffreys, M. D. W. 2956
Jelliffe, S. E. 2957, 2958
Jennings, H. S. 1021
Jensen, G. D. 1431
Jerphagnon, L. 619
Jetter, L. E. 2959
Jeu, B. 2960
Jha, M. 2961
Jiménez, J. R. 1073
Joad, C. E. M. 1021
Johann, H. T. 620
John Crerar Library 117
John of Ruysbroeck 341
Johnson, A. 621
Johnson, A. B. 1432
Johnson, S. 341
Johnson, W. G. 622
Johnston, E. H. 1433
Johnston, T. 3756 (F)
Jokl, E. 2962
Jolivet, R. 623
Jonas, H. 624, 625, 2299
Jones, B. 2963
Jones, E. 2964, 2965, 2966,
  2967, 3392
Jones, F. 2967
Jones, J. C. 1434
Jones, K. S. 1435
Jones, L. 626
Jones, M. A. 2101
Jones, P. H. 118
Jones, R. 1305, 2681
Jones, T. T. 1436
Jones, W. T. 627
Jonkman, E. J. 1437
Jordahl, E. K. 2968, 2968a
Jores, A. 2969
Joseph, G. 628
Joseph, S. M. 2970
Joubert, J. 341

Sherrill, H. H. 3449
Sherrill, L. J. 3449
Sherwin, B. L. 928
Shestov, L. 260
Shetrone, H. C. 3450
Shibles, W. 185
Shields, E. A. 3451
Shirley, R. 1021
Shneidman, E. S. 396, 798,
  928a, 1235, 2661, 2662,
  3452, 3453, 3454, 3455,
  3456, 3457, 3457a, 3458,
  3459, 3460, 3461, 3462,
  3463, 3464
Shoben, E. J., Jr. 3465
Shontz, F. C. 3465
Shoor, M. H. 3466, 3467
Shor, R. E. 3468
Short, J. F. 2884
Shrut, S. D. 3469
Shute, N. 929
Sichel, J. 3470
Sidney, P. 341
Sieber, R. 1413
Siggins, L. D. 3471
Silverman, D. 1796, 1797,
  1798
Silverman, P. R. 189, 3473,
  3474, 3475, 3476
Simko, A. 2324
Simmel, E. 3477
Simmel, G. 930
Simmons, L. W. 3478
Simmons, S. 1799
Simon, A. 2325
Simon, S. B. 3479
Simon, W. 271, 3480
Simpson, K. 1800
Simpson, L. 1057
Simpson, M. 2220
Simpson, M. A. 1801
Sinclair, U. 1021
Singer, I. 186
Sirken, M. G. 3481
Sisk, G. 3482
Sisler, G. C. 1802
Sivananda, S. 2220a
Sjogren, C. O. 931
Skaddick, C. W. 1214
Skeels, D. R. 3484
Skipper, J. K. 1803
Skipper, J. K., Jr. 1804

Skottowe, I. 1659
Slater, E. 3485
Slater, P. E. 187
Slater, R. C. 161, 162, 3726
  (T)
Sleeper, R. W. 2221
Slochower, H. 932, 3392
Sloyan, G. S. 2221a
Smart, C. 854
Smart, M. 3486
Smith, A. G. 1805
Smith, A. J. K. 188
Smith, A. L. 3487
Smith, C. 1806
Smith, D. 2222
Smith, E. H. 3488, 3489
Smith, H. 1563
Smith, H. C. 261
Smith, H. L. 1807, 3490
Smith, L. A. 2517
Smith, R. W. 3199
Smith, S. L. 1808
Smith, S. M. 933
Smith, W. D. 934
Snell, D. 935
Snider, A. J. 3491
Snyder, R. 3710 (P)
Snyderwine, L. 2222a
Sobosan, J. G. 936
Society of Biosis (Calif.) 1563
Sockman, R. W. 2223
Socrates 396, 460, 848, 937,
  1069, 3720 (F)
Soddy, F. 1021
Soderblom, N. 938
Solitare, G. B. 1809
Solnit, A. J. 1810, 1811,
  1812, 2808, 3492
Solomon, H. C. 3493
Solow, V. D. 1813
Solzhenitsyn, A. 709, 2334,
  3176
Somerville, R. M. 262
Sontag, S. 939
Sophocles 341, 461, 854
Sorensen, K. C. 1122
Sosnowski, S. 940
Soto, P. 3822 (MF)
Spadafora, J. 263
Spangler, J. A. 3495
Spann, W. 1814
Spanos, W. V. 941

Abortion 60, 185, 332, 344, 348, 349, 365, 392, 403, 444, 487,
523, 649, 736, 737, 785, 892, 981, 988, 1026, 1041, 1195,
1310, 1374, 1469, 1503, 1731, 1752, 1807, 1833, 1834, 2109,
2148, 2163, 2204, 2495, 2581, 2604, 2848, 2849, 2863, 3016,
3068, 3139, 3490, 3619, 3623, 3721 (F), 3734 (T)
Acceptance of death (see also Stages of dying) 545, 632, 1359,
1533, 1741, 1768, 1890, 1927, 1973, 1982, 2005, 2026, 2080,
2164, 2167, 2395, 2448, 2815, 2891, 3012, 3062, 3454, 3608,
3697 (F), 3711 (T), 3740 (T), 3829 (F), 3830 (F), 3835 (K)
Accidents (see also Sports and risk of death; Threat of impending
death) 8, 95, 121, 145, 170, 1231, 1245, 1491, 1504, 1507,
1557, 1573, 1574, 1639, 1900, 2288, 2451, 2478, 2714, 3130,
3211, 3520, 3834 (F)
Accountability and the physician (see also Physicians, education
and training) 126a, 1736a
Advance declaration see Euthanasia
Agathanasia 1436
Aging and death (includes the process of aging and aspects of social loss) (see also Attitudes toward death in older persons;
Fear of death in the aged; Mortality in the aged; Nursing
Homes and aged views of death; Terminal care; Terminal illness) 48, 119, 187, 420, 630, 1094, 1096, 1137, 1335, 1533,
1580, 1591, 1679, 1827, 1842, 1899, 1909, 1928, 1929, 2099,
2496, 2732, 2737, 2779, 2833, 2974, 2993, 2999, 3042, 3214,
3371, 3469, 3478, 3525, 3539, 3559, 3663, 3671 (F), 3672 (F),
3673 (F), 3677 (F), 3679 (T), 3748 (F), 3768 (MF), 3784 (F),
3789 (F), 3824 (F)
Alienation and death see Separation and loss
American views of death (see also Concepts of death; Cultural
attitudes toward death; Funerals, American; Historical views
of death) 2027, 2619, 2628, 2740, 2744, 2833, 2920, 2933,
2977, 3162, 3219, 3249, 3302, 3303, 3304, 3357, 3403, 3498,
3523, 3600, 3642, 3675 (T), 3758 (T), 3808 (T)
Anger and death see Stages of dying
Animism controversy 3029, 3030, 3522
Anthropology and death 2279, 2382, 2457, 2658, 2711, 2712,
2752, 2758, 2766, 2784, 2794, 2800, 2807, 2818, 2830, 2870,

*Symbols used in Part VIII are used herein, to wit: F (film),
FS (filmstrip), K (kit), MF (microfilm), P (photos, prints), R
(recording), S (slides), T (tape), TR (transparencies).

2877, 2894, 2961, 3006, 3007, 3008, 3031, 3075, 3113a, 3115,
3171, 3224, 3267, 3279, 3280, 3281, 3282, 3283, 3285, 3291,
3320, 3356, 3388, 3450, 3542, 3544, 3615, 3651
Anxiety and awareness of impending death (see also Fear of death)
 1148, 1861, 1926, 2417, 2850, 2876, 3198, 3294, 3368, 3526,
 3535, 3543, 3547, 3553; castration anxiety 2965, 3401; childhood 2521, 2636, 3359; depressive 1276, 1759, 3548, 3554;
 neurosis and 1856, 2726, 3201, 3549; pain and 1511, 2503,
 3359; religious correlates of 2230, 3550; repressive resistance
 1353; suppressive 1759; verbalized and non-verbalized 3551
Art and death (includes representative drawings and illustrations
 from medieval, ecclesiastical, iconographic, and religious art)
 305, 326, 390, 398, 404, 406, 422, 467, 527, 542, 555, 559,
 586, 693, 698, 709, 730, 768, 806, 819, 842, 894, 963, 1027,
 1031, 1042, 1046, 1049, 2515, 2752, 3782 (T), 3800 (K)
Art counseling and death education 217
Assassination 172, 780, 924, 1191, 1464, 2380, 2388, 2400, 2458,
 2560, 2564, 2569, 2590, 2602, 2617, 2618, 2755, 2792, 2809,
 2867, 2868, 2871, 2955, 3001, 3017, 3155, 3174, 3257, 3258,
 3297, 3447, 3509, 3521, 3616, 3644, 3724 (F)
Attitudes toward death among pathologists 1105, 1263; among philosophers (see also Philosophy and death) 707; among poets (see
 also Literature and death--Poetry and death) 466; and sex differences 3101; as variables in research studies (see also Research on death) 2982, 3260, 3354; by nurses 296, 1186,
 1196, 1222, 1355, 1373a, 1388, 1410, 1517, 1552, 1634, 1667,
 1682, 1690, 1695, 1701, 1727, 1781, 1895, 1937, 3795 (F); by
 physicians 1175, 1194, 1203, 1221, 1727, 2720, 2790, 2810,
 3506, 3730 (F); in nightmare subjects 2683; in older persons
 (see also Aging and death) 33, 71, 81, 925, 965, 1094, 1302,
 1386, 1430, 1453, 1480, 1615, 1684, 1719, 1724, 1849, 1892,
 1928, 1929, 2534, 2634, 2799, 2994, 2996, 3354, 3369, 3469, 3538,
 3559, 3565, 3638, 3673 (F), 3763 (F); in patients following suicide attempts 2934; in western societies 291, 292; of children
 and the role of myth 179, 243, 272, 565, 2451, 2821, 2952,
 3038, 3039, 3040, 3052, 3217, 3245, 3251, 3406, 3449, 3657,
 3658, 3706 (T), 3707 (T); of mentally ill patients 2672, 2673;
 of murderers 3405; of parents to the death of their child
 2585; of physical therapists 1720, 3352; of psychiatric patients
 2843; of teachers 214; of therapists 1720; of young people
 120, 2789, 2799, 2844, 2859, 3192, 3211, 3501, 3502, 3650
Audiovisual media, use of (see also Part VIII--item numbers) 3667
 (MF) through 3848 (T); 183, 212a, 954
Autopsy, general 1550, 1844; psychohistorical 2574; psychological
 3161, 3265, 3611, 3612

Bargaining aspects of death see Stages of dying
Behavioral effects of death and personality theory (see also Psychology of death) 979, 2522, 2926, 2963, 3090, 3579, 3798 (T)
Bereavement (neutral status of recent loss) (see also Separation
 and loss) 104a, 155, 185, 281, 844, 1150, 1162, 1651, 1740,
 1780, 1967, 2160, 2332, 2410, 2642, 2647, 2764, 3063, 3065,

3066, 3190, 3372, 3399, 3682 (F); and mental health 3585; and mental illness (see also mental illness and death) 1134, 1135, 1136, 2403, 3300; and pastoral care (see also Counseling the dying, pastoral) 2176a; and recovery from war 2649; and school adjustment 3019, 3216; and social isolation 1923, 3681; and suicide education 3114; and the death of a pet (see also Children, reactions to the death of pets) 1523; and the nurses' role in (see also Nurses' role in the care of the dying) 1150; and the role of the teacher 3216; and the use of psychopharmacologic agents (see also Drugs, use of in managing the dying patient; Crisis intervention) 1496; as a field for family research (see also Research on death) 2646; as a field of social research (see also Research on death) 2645, 3216; as a subject of cross-cultural inquiry 2366; childhood 1192, 1257, 1329, 1398, 1523, 2378, 2433, 2475, 2594, 2611, 2666, 2896, 3026, 3182, 3216, 3241, 3404; and later behavior disorder hypothesis 2416; conjugal 1126, 1560, 3164, 3165; depressive 2434, 2440, 2459, 2475, 3241; determination of 1652; early parental and relation to suicide 2485; effects of on religious behavior 3150; effects on physical and mental health 1653, 1656, 3166; family responses to (see also Family and death) 17, 2644, 2900; maternal before age of eight 2886; normal 44, 122, 132, 1562, 2209; of parents following suicide 2486; outcomes following 1655, 1656, 3681; programs for 3216, 3839 (F), 3844 (F); reactions to 1654, 1655, 1656, 1713, 2568, 3066, 3166, 3419, 3830 (F), 3844 (F); relationship to separation and loss (see also Separation and loss) 1188, 1653, 2611, 3216, 3419, 3681; social psychology of 2648

Bibliographies (see also Research on death and dying) 16, 49, 60, 117, 122, 124a, 127, 132, 168a, 169, 183, 185, 188, 195, 201a, 310, 808/9, 880, 1590, 1868a, 1873, 2231, 2312, 2555, 2795, 3247a, 3446

Birth and death records, significance of (see also Certificates of death) 2, 1867, 3323, 3683 (F), 3734 (T), 3742 (F), 3829 (F)

Brain death 188, 1248, 1306, 1328, 1437, 1450, 1462, 1544, 1594, 1600, 1745, 1778, 1790, 1796, 1798, 1863, 1869, 1891, 2295, 2327, 3454

Burial customs (see also Burial rites; Funeral customs; Mourning) 9, 13, 46, 88, 92a, 124, 143, 246, 919, 978, 990, 1996, 2509, 3050, 3079, 3777 (F), 3783 (T)

Burial rites (see also Burial customs; Funeral customs; Mourning) 61, 87, 139, 661, 855, 1574, 2431, 2698, 2908, 2961, 3291, 3494, 3663, 3794 (T), 3801 (K)

Cadavers, use in medical schools 1709, 1737

Cancer (see also Terminal care; Terminal illness) 168, 1040, 1084, 1085, 1115, 1119, 1131, 1147, 1161, 1174, 1176, 1205, 1233, 1241, 1304, 1313, 1363, 1419, 1485, 1493, 1500, 1501, 1534, 1535, 1536, 1571, 1592, 1617, 1631, 1663, 1673, 1676, 1714, 1720, 1751, 1757, 1762, 1786, 1898, 1901, 1916, 1978, 2203, 2339, 2528, 3082, 3326, 3683 (F), 3685 (F), 3693 (T), 3711 (T), 3727 (F), 3821 (F), 3830 (F)

2372, 2492, 2751, 3003, 3028, 3239, 3633, 3635; reactions to
the death of pets (see also Bereavement and the death of a pet)
213, 1047; reactions toward death 5, 49, 163, 225, 236, 245,
1047, 1082, 1322, 2867, 3117, 3257, 3499

Christian views of death (see also Religious and theological views
of death; Theology of death) 10, 75, 232, 622, 730, 863, 902,
1960, 1963, 1966, 1972, 1983, 1984, 1987, 1994, 2000, 2002,
2021, 2025, 2028, 2033, 2038, 2039, 2041, 2044, 2067, 2069,
2073, 2079, 2091, 2093, 2101, 2118, 2123, 2141, 2142, 2143,
2152, 2153, 2165, 2166, 2173, 2176, 2179, 2187, 2192, 2196,
2207, 2210, 2211, 2219, 2220, 2222a, 2234, 2236, 2237, 2239,
2242, 2247, 2250, 2256, 2257, 3692 (T)

Clergy and dying patient relationships (see also Counseling the dying, pastoral; Terminal care) 141, 1141, 1954, 2003, 2112,
2253

Cognitive development and childhood death (see also Children and
their conceptualization of life and death) 3038, 3039, 3040,
3505

Communication (verbal) with the dying patient (see also Dialogue
about death as therapeutic experience; Terminal care; Terminal
illness) 252, 1274, 1404, 1408, 1451, 1819, 1820, 1849,
1878, 1882, 1885, 1965, 2339, 2340, 2654, 2674, 2783, 2981,
3054, 3057, 3060, 3169, 3305, 3365, 3382, 3551, 3575, 3702
(F), 3809 (F), 3823 (T)

Concepts of death (see also American views of death; Cultural attitudes toward death; Historical views of death; Right to die)
127a, 223, 244, 301, 335. 357, 427, 457, 462, 488, 601, 603,
735, 742, 750, 822, 859. 862, 1012, 1353, 1421, 1542, 1599,
1607, 1753, 1983, 2075, 2194, 2269, 2301, 2356, 2360, 2370,
2371, 2390, 2423, 2446a, 2509, 2532, 2533, 2552, 2605, 2760,
2805, 2946, 2986, 3172, 3195, 3202, 3245, 3246, 3267, 3315,
3339, 3374, 3390, 3441, 3443, 3505, 3589, 3703 (F), 3788 (K)

Consciousness of impending death (includes awareness of death and
aspects of searching for a personal identity) (see also Time,
significance of in impending death; Terminal care; Terminal
illness) 69, 581, 752, 758, 832, 1148, 1290a, 1347, 1383,
1402, 1695, 1956, 2031, 2070, 2072, 2092, 2233, 2280, 2503,
2559, 2688, 2740, 2797, 2825, 3749 (F), 3752 (F)

Consolation 311, 789, 2225a, 2238, 3248, 3399, 3623, 3624

Cot death see Crib death

Counseling the dying, by physicians 3738 (T), 3827 (T); by
psychologists 3792 (T); by psychotherapists 3083, 3084;
by social workers 3085, 3351; pastoral (see also Clergy and
dying patient relationships; Terminal care and pastoral opportunities) 1141, 1483, 1685, 1954, 1958, 1965, 1967, 1971,
1977, 1978, 1998, 2003, 2008, 2018, 2032, 2050, 2098, 2111,
2112, 2130, 2176a, 2190, 2191, 2208, 2209, 2214, 2219, 2653,
3503

Cremation 9, 28, 46, 47, 52, 53, 62, 68, 76, 84, 92a, 109, 115,
117, 118, 153, 160, 173, 246, 797, 1502, 1564

Crib death (see also Children, deaths of; Sudden infant death syndrome; Vulnerable child syndrome) 1157, 1159, 1214, 1242,
1244, 1295, 1348, 1381, 1613, 1872, 1875, 3659, 3694 (T)

Crisis intervention, forms of in death and dying (see also Bereavement and the use of psychopharmacologic agents; Counseling the
dying, pastoral; Drug abuse and death; Drugs, use of in
managing the dying patient; Grief reactions; Mental illness and
death; Nurses and patient relationships; Nurses' experiences
with the family of a dying patient; Nurses' role in the care of
the dying; Physicians and patient relationships; Physicians' experiences with the family; Physicians' role in the care of the
dying; Psychology of death; Psychotherapy and terminal illness; Suicide prevention; Terminal care, and professional team
approaches)   29, 151, 1104, 1226a, 1268a, 1269, 1289a, 1290,
1355a, 1385a, 1566, 1582a, 1736a, 1741a, 1759, 2377, 2424,
2682, 3004, 3161, 3163, 3235, 3243, 3265, 3266, 3454, 3618
(T)
Cryogenics (see also Research on death and dying)   185, 2260,
2267, 2274, 2275, 2285, 2302, 2304, 2309a, 2314, 2320, 2322,
2323, 2328, 3740 (T), 3839 (F)
Cryonics Societies   see   Cryogenics
Cultural attitudes toward death (cross-disciplinary approaches to)
(see also American views of death; Concepts of death; Historical
views of death)   87, 124, 291, 292, 399, 833, 834, 862, 949,
2349, 2375, 2390, 2445, 2447, 2454, 2586, 2603, 2605, 2610,
2612, 2619, 2628, 2658, 2690, 2694, 2698, 2705, 2711, 2715,
2743, 2794, 2800, 2824, 2830, 2877, 2885, 2919, 2922, 2923,
2929, 2938, 2939, 2963, 2987, 2988, 3006, 3007, 3008, 3018,
3031, 3047, 3075, 3079, 3113a, 3115, 3162, 3219, 3224, 3267,
3280, 3283, 3289, 3301, 3302, 3355, 3356, 3374, 3413, 3493,
3494, 3498, 3558, 3561, 3574, 3648, 3684 (T), 3695 (T)

Dead, fear of in primitive religions and societies   2063, 2508,
3086
Death education instruction (includes course outlines, curricula,
syllabi, study and teaching units, field trips, mini-courses,
etc.   For audiovisual media see item numbers 3667 (MF)
through 3848 (T); in adult and continuing education programs
222, 229, 237, 246, 253, 259, 264, 267, 3800 (K), 3830 (F);
in colleges and universities   185, 218, 219, 227, 232, 233,
234, 235, 242, 253, 259, 262, 269, 270, 2913, 2914, 3596,
3800 (K), 3830 (F); in elementary schools   204, 212, 212a,
213, 213a, 214, 215, 216, 217, 218, 225, 226, 228, 230,
239, 240, 243, 244, 245, 247, 248, 251, 266, 272, 273, 274,
773, 3800 (K), 3830 (F), 3842 (FS); in medical schools   207,
208, 210, 212b, 220a, 221, 227, 229, 231, 252, 259, 261,
1259, 1444, 1498, 1582, 1709, 1883, 1938, 3800 (K), 3830
(F); in middle schools and high schools   205, 211, 214, 216,
217, 218, 224, 235, 237, 241, 242, 259, 262, 264, 265, 269,
273, 274, 3172, 3800 (K), 3800 (F); in professional nursing
schools   220, 249, 252, 254, 255, 256, 257, 258, 261, 268,
1219, 1222, 1690, 1801, 2116, 2696, 2992, 3800 (K), 3830
(F), 3831 (F), 3838 (F), 3845 (F); in religious and theological
schools   206, 219, 236, 246, 250, 989, 1954, 1986, 2116,
3800 (K), 3830 (F); in schools of mortuary science   238, 271

Exercise and death   2962
Exhumation and re-interment   67, 1711
Existentialism and death (see also Philosophy and death)   296, 302,
   306, 357, 429, 460, 475, 547, 578, 582, 603, 617, 618, 623,
   634, 648, 652, 687, 696, 717, 719, 752, 803, 807, 822, 899,
   903, 941, 956, 1000, 1037, 2707, 2810, 2866, 3304

Faith for personal crisis, and the questions of life and death   42,
   1995, 2078, 2164, 2243, 3708 (FS), 3757 (MF), 3812 (T),
   3830 (F)
Family (entered here are items which deal with the effects of death
   on the family individually and collectively) and effects of death
   on personality development   3233; and role reorganization
   2413, 2556, 3218; and social consequences of death   3527; and
   terminal patients (see also Terminal care)   1908, 2623, 3026,
   3085, 3173, 3341, 3524, 3527, 3797 (F), 3812 (T); and the
   dying child   1508, 3793 (T), 3845 (F, FS); coping with impending death   1805, 1838, 3524; crisis (see also Separation and
   loss; Terminal care)   510, 1103, 1105, 1717, 2376, 2556,
   2788, 2900, 3069, 3117, 3188, 3496; death education   262; dialogue on death (see also Terminal care)   253, 2521, 2605,
   2614, 2623, 2730, 3328a, 3657, 3707 (T); disengagement theories   2345; grieving   3266, 3310, 3524; implications of parental
   death   741, 2378, 2398, 2435, 2436, 2437, 2438, 2439, 2440,
   2441, 2453, 2540, 2543, 2734, 2750, 2751, 2817, 2823, 2916,
   3003, 3028, 3140, 3160, 3218, 3227, 3239, 3240, 3263, 3276,
   3332, 3402, 3633, 3635, 3652, 3839 (F); observations of the
   implications of death and family centered care (see also
   Terminal care)   753, 1078, 1319, 1660, 1776, 1835, 1854,
   1918, 2408, 2562, 2690, 2874, 3183, 3273, 3752 (F), 3835 (K);
   reactions to sudden and unexpected death (see also Sudden infant death syndrome)   3586
Fear of death (here are entered items which deal with fear in the
   general population)   716, 722, 1090, 1266, 1570, 2051, 2128, 2239,
   2409, 2472, 2639, 3012, 3036, 3676 (T), 3705 (T), 3757 (MF),
   3759 (F), 3831 (F); and affective responses to psychoanalytic
   death symbols   3201; and aggression   3511; and asthma attacks
   in children   3221; and basic fantasy   2330; and castration
   2965; and ego identity   2824; and fear of failure (relationship)
   2544; and femininity   3555; and meaning in life   2448; and
   melancholia   2718; and mental distress in children and their
   mothers   3252; and mental distress in patients   1764, 2669;
   and neurosis   3512; and nightmare experiences   3093, 3095;
   and phallic fantasies   3316; and psychological analysis   2953;
   and psychological effects of last rites   3491; and relationship
   to aggression   2820; and relationship to career decisions   2670;
   and school phobia   3562; and the need to achieve   3098; as socioeconomic variables   3097; and suicidal persons   2684, 3094;
   and the frequency of nightmares   3090; as countertransference
   2489; as cultural variables in a primitive society   2850;
   causes of   7, 2162; experimental and correlational studies of
   3092; in children   179, 1678, 1942, 1948, 2156, 2520, 2820,

2847, 2970, 3117, 3251, 3406, 3592; in dying heart and cancer
patients 1304; in early infancy 2864; in ethnological studies
1611; in non-literate societies 3096; in parachute jumpers 1;
in persons and relationship to fear of death in their parents
3099; in phobic patients 1538; in primitive religions 2712;
in students 2631; in the aged (see also Aging and death) 1926,
2333, 2519, 3042, 3435; management of in patients with chronic
disease 1795; measurement of 2630; in wartime 1595, 2773;
of those in high stress occupations 2697; psychological analysis
of 2432, 2547; psychology of the 3043; significance of 144
Fetal death 1629, 1718, 2713
Forest Lawn Memorial Cemetery see Cemeteries, history and
development of
Freudian views of death 307, 1417, 1960, 2774, 2793, 3426,
3428, 3468, 3540, 3617
Funeral customs (entered here are items dealing with cross-cultural
and cross-disciplinary burial customs and rites) (see also
Burial customs; Burial rites; Historical views of death; Mourning rites and customs) 56, 77, 101, 135, 185, 386, 418, 467,
584, 841, 978, 1031, 1339, 1428, 1969, 2048, 2100, 2252,
2382, 2384, 2399, 2445, 2487, 2572, 2690, 2743, 2756, 2784,
2793, 2795, 2807, 2870, 2887, 2894, 2905, 2927, 2938, 2939,
2961, 2987, 3005, 3006, 3031, 3067, 3220, 3224, 3242, 3249,
3281, 3289, 3291, 3303, 3324, 3329, 3350, 3357, 3361, 3397,
3398, 3402, 3482, 3675 (T), 3700 (F), 3743 (F), 3760 (P),
3771 (S), 3794 (T), 3800 (K)
Funeral directing (includes education, training, functions and duties
of funeral directors) (see also Death education instruction, in
schools of mortuary science) 6, 10, 38, 51, 57, 62, 80, 82,
84a, 92, 92a, 114, 123, 158, 159, 161, 162, 174, 175, 176,
189, 246, 271, 292, 1339, 2466, 2738, 2837, 2861, 2865, 3337,
3448, 3728 (T), 3743 (F), 3773 (S), 3780 (F), 3832 (T)
Funeral directing and clergy relationships 111, 2064, 2591, 2699,
2941
Funerals, American (see also American views of death) 28, 31, 36,
64, 75, 85, 92, 92a, 93, 96, 108, 136, 147, 157, 2058, 2466,
2738, 2861, 3186, 3250, 3675 (T), 3728 (T), 3743 (F), 3770
(F), 3772 (F), 3776 (F), 3780 (F), 3799 (K)
Funerals (Church) 2095, 2097, 2106, 2210
Funerals, cost of 6, 18, 19, 24, 28, 31, 62, 74, 82, 83, 84a, 96,
97, 99, 102, 135, 157, 165, 193, 1897, 2446, 2861, 2862,
2968a, 3337, 3448, 3762 (F)
Funerals, therapeutic value of 32, 40, 64, 92a, 98, 108, 110,
112, 113, 136, 166, 191, 197, 246, 1502, 2058, 2210, 2861,
3175, 3248, 3249, 3250, 3774 (F), 3775 (F), 3780 (F), 3781
(F), 3799 (K)

Ghost fear and attitudes toward death 2411, 3283
Grief (psychological pain) 126, 1088, 1138, 1282, 1292, 1653,
2549, 2579, 2798, 3063; and social recuperation (see also
Separation and loss) 2468, 2741, 2798, 3419; and the law
2942; and therapeutic nursing care (see also Nurses' role in

the care of the dying) 1868; anticipatory 1569, 2746, 3063,
3420, 3799 (K), 3808 (T); empathy in the resolution of 1666;
infant and early childhood 1728, 2460, 3026, 3170, 3419, 3427,
3486, 3510, 3799 (K); intra/inter-communication concepts
3070; management of 1117, 1200, 1438, 1868, 1958, 2420,
2561, 2580, 3063, 3130, 3379, 3419, 3681 (T), 3745 (T), 3799
(K), 3820 (T); normal 112, 126, 132, 1736, 2190, 2208, 2397,
2549, 2699, 2941, 2944, 2945, 3063, 3116, 3530, 3591, 3799
(K), 3837 (F); pathological 1293, 1616, 1887, 2367, 2397,
3584, 3591; reaction depression 1587, 1664; relationship to
guilt 2098, 2798; psychoanalysis 1913; psychophysiological reactions of 1323, 3584; reactions (see also Crisis intervention)
1117, 1323, 1623, 1653, 1669, 1670, 2740, 2816, 3310, 3726
(T), 3735 (F), 3744 (F), 3799 (K), 3820 (T); in electric-
shock therapy 1587; in patients 1851, 2741; in university students 2548; role of in psychiatry 3309; role of the clergy
(see also Clergy and dying patient relationships; Counseling the
dying, pastoral) 2699, 2941

Harlequin complex and ambivalence of death 3154, 3295
Health care services for older persons (see also Terminal care)
    34, 1089, 3015, 3033, 3669 (F), 3690 (F), 3691 (F), 3746
    (T), 3788 (F)
Historical views of death (see also American views of death; Con-
    cepts of death; Cultural attitudes toward death; Funeral cus-
    toms; Funerals, American; Medieval aspects of death; Mourning
    rites and customs) 288, 291, 292, 338, 356, 364, 386, 399,
    402, 404, 414, 418, 440, 456, 462, 476, 517, 550, 555, 596,
    661, 692, 694, 712, 783, 784, 789, 791, 813, 818, 833, 858,
    870, 885, 887, 919, 943, 949, 950, 964, 971, 990, 992, 1027,
    1036, 1077, 1677, 1962, 1989, 2015, 2027, 2052, 2075, 2158,
    2480, 2694, 2715, 2752, 2756, 2758, 2807, 2824, 2906, 2927,
    3075, 3079, 3122, 3225, 3277, 3598
Homicide 386, 598, 1231, 2361, 2391, 2395, 2456, 2458, 2524, 2558,
    2571, 2602, 2724, 2735, 2776, 2787, 2828, 2834, 2838, 2882,
    2884, 2917, 2919, 2921, 3049, 3091, 3152, 3333, 3348, 3405,
    3439, 3640
Hope and death 1999, 3206, 3545
Humor and death 58, 526, 3269, 3270, 3762 (F)
Hypnosis and relationship to death 3415, 3416

Identity and death see Consciousness of impending death
Immortality and acceptance of non-being 1741, 2256; and chances
    of surviving death 774; and relationship to the existence of
    God (see also Religious and theological views of death; Philos-
    ophy and death) 534, 1970, 1972, 2056, 2133, 2140, 2188;
    and religious discourse (see also Religious and theological
    views of death) 633, 1961, 1972, 2054, 2137, 2140, 2181,
    2188, 2242, 2256, 3047, 3598, 3840 (FS); and science 2318,
    2328; and the dialectic of death 840; and the existence of a

demographic studies 1277, 1314, 1481, 1504, 1675, 1712, 1718,
    1818, 2291, 2296, 2326, 2406, 2483, 2523, 2530, 2589,
    2950/1, 3022, 3082, 3153, 3360; survival patterns 1354;
    trends 1100, 1466, 1609, 2282
Morticians see Funeral directing
Mourning rites and customs (see also Burial customs; Funeral
    customs; Historical views of death) and relationship to manic
    depression 3025, 3433; and relationship to guilt 112, 2798,
    2819; in infancy and early childhood (normal) 1459, 1728,
    2350, 2460, 2461, 2682, 2749, 2819, 3067, 3156, 3308, 3427,
    3532; pathological 2367, 2948, 3129; pathological in children
    2461, 2462, 2819, 3028, 3628; process of normal 65, 1405,
    1431, 1470, 1744, 1847, 2051, 2601, 2719, 2775, 3310, 3634,
    3466, 3467, 3681 (T), 3726 (T), 3829 (F)
Musical and choral themes of death 497, 759

Necrophilia 2469, 3074, 3346, 3362
Nurses and patient relationships (see also Nurses' role in the care
    of the dying; Physicians and patient relationships) 1084,
    1097, 1115, 1117, 1123, 1128, 1131, 1139, 1140, 1151, 1152,
    1172, 1174, 1189, 1241, 1271, 1278, 1350, 1356, 1373,
    1373a, 1399, 1440, 1442, 1471, 1552, 1626, 1649, 1698,
    1733, 1792, 1829, 1895, 3523, 3795 (F), 3796 (K), 3838 (F)
Nurses' education and training 220, 252, 254, 255, 257, 258,
    1132, 1479, 1792, 3298, 3796 (K), 3838 (F)
Nurses' experiences with the family of a dying patient 1331,
    1352, 1399, 1438, 1604, 1647, 1783, 1857
Nurses' reactions to the death of children 1388
Nurses' role in the care of the dying (see also Grief and thera-
    peutic nursing care; Physicians role in the care of the dying)
    256, 1150, 1152, 1193, 1256, 1271, 1278, 1312, 1319, 1321,
    1332, 1362, 1399, 1471, 1482, 1561, 1604, 1634, 1649, 1663,
    1697, 1698, 1699, 1700, 1703, 1704, 1733, 1760, 1763, 1768,
    1783, 1792, 1799, 1829, 1838, 1878, 1895, 1896, 1935, 1937,
    2696, 2780, 3838 (F)
Nursing homes and aged views of death (see also Aging and death)
    1089, 1528, 1735, 1759, 2352, 2424, 3746 (T), 3783 (F)

Organ transplants (see also Prolongation of life) 185, 404, 889,
    1112, 1162, 1248, 1249, 1341, 1382, 1457, 1513, 1537, 1551,
    1658, 1661, 1707, 1774, 1790, 1807, 1831, 1832, 1886, 1934,
    2086, 2263, 2278, 2292, 2701, 2701a, 3725 (F)
Orphanhood and relationship to depression 2407; as a factor in
    psychoses 2402

Parapsychological aspects of death (see also Premonitions of
    death) 67, 73, 401, 486, 561, 627, 930, 944, 2087, 2184,
    2949, 3381
Parricide 5, 2211, 2716
Pastoral counseling see Counseling the dying, pastoral

3000, 3023, 3042, 3043, 3045, 3058, 3119, 3120, 3121, 3123,
3125, 3127, 3128, 3189, 3205, 3261, 3293, 3368, 3375, 3381,
3413, 3418, 3517, 3590, 3596, 3599, 3601, 3610, 3702 (F),
3809 (F), 3810 (T)
Psychotherapy (see also Psychology of death)   group perspectives
     1538, 1743, 3014, 3021, 3051, 3215, 3644/5; reactions of pa-
     tients toward death   1464, 1742, 3059, 3083, 3084, 3215,
     3386; terminal illness and   1720, 1742, 3041, 3083, 3084,
     3392, 3655

Religious and theological views of death (see also Christian views
     of death; Eastern perspectives on death; Immortality and rela-
     tionship to the existence of God; Immortality and religious dis-
     course; Immortality and the existence of a Soul; Theology of
     death)   123a, 124a, 168a, 173a, 185, 201a, 206, 284, 488,
     585, 730, 938, 989, 1740, 1943, 1944, 1948, 1949, 1950,
     1954, 1955, 1960, 1966, 1970, 1972, 1979, 1981, 1983, 1986,
     1989, 1990, 1991, 1994, 1995, 1999, 2006, 2009, 2010, 2012,
     2015, 2016, 2017, 2023, 2024, 2026, 2028, 2029, 2031, 2033,
     2037, 2039, 2041, 2042, 2044, 2048, 2058, 2059, 2063, 2070,
     2073, 2074, 2082, 2090, 2091, 2092, 2093, 2094, 2096, 2097,
     2100, 2101, 2103, 2104, 2107, 2108, 2109, 2113, 2118, 2121,
     2122, 2131a, 2137, 2138, 2141, 2142, 2156, 2157, 2158, 2160,
     2162, 2164, 2165, 2166, 2171, 2173, 2186, 2188, 2194, 2204,
     2205, 2217, 2223a, 2224a, 2238, 2241, 2249, 2251, 2255, 2259,
     2312, 2501, 2712, 3141, 3185, 3285, 3311, 3491, 3498, 3544,
     3550, 3552, 3625, 3667 (MF), 3696 (F), 3715 (T), 3727 (F),
     3729 (FS), 3764 (R), 3768 (MF), 3811 (F)
Remorse   see   Consciousness of death
Research on death and dying (includes scientific methods, tech-
     niques, testing, etc., which utilizes death and dying as vari-
     ables in research designs) (see also Attitudes toward death as
     variables in research studies; Bereavement as a field for
     family research; Bereavement as a field of social research;
     Bibliographies; Cryogenics)   1250, 1304, 1439, 1782, 2263,
     2264, 2266, 2267, 2268, 2269, 2271, 2272, 2273, 2275, 2276,
     2278, 2279, 2280, 2281, 2282, 2285, 2286, 2287, 2289, 2291,
     2293, 2303, 2311, 2312, 2320, 2321, 2323, 2526, 2745, 2991,
     3119, 3120, 3302, 3369
Resurrection (includes items which deal with judgment of the dead)
     and purification after death   2082; and relationship to im-
     mortality   2172; beliefs in primitive religions   2043; Christian
     view of   1966, 1972, 2023, 2033, 2042, 2073, 2088, 2089,
     2102, 2159, 2206, 2257, 2877, 3794 (F); of Christ   938,
     1950, 1985, 1987, 2061, 2143, 3714 (FS); sermons on   2225
Right to die (conceptualizations of death with dignity and the in-
     dividuals rights in making decisions) (see also Concepts of
     death; Ethical problems; Euthanasia; Physicians role in the
     care of the dying; Terminal care)   104, 419, 493a, 544, 621,
     622, 708, 728, 753, 926, 982, 1083, 1101, 1106, 1111, 1120,
     1164, 1165, 1223, 1368, 1393, 1432, 1732, 1739, 1746, 1748,
     1765, 1794, 1808, 1852, 1860, 1917, 1925, 2132, 2161, 2358,

2373, 2396, 2500, 2502, 2554, 2654, 2725, 2826, 3167, 3176,
3378, 3523, 3742 (F), 3688 (T), 3815 (F), 3818 (F)

Separation and loss (implications of the effects on survivors and
    their adaptation to loss of loved-ones) (see also Bereavement;
    Family crisis; Grief and social recuperation) 428, 1143, 1176,
    1188, 1494, 1605, 1736, 1909, 2413, 2420, 2463, 2528, 2611,
    2636, 2808, 3080, 3284, 3314, 3377, 3380, 3421, 3648, 3652,
    3707 (T), 3744 (F), 3839 (F)
Sexuality and death   552, 1259, 1358, 2405, 2526, 2804, 3078,
    3101, 3196, 3462, 3477
Sleep and death   203, 1032, 2081, 3461
Society, social structure and death (includes death orientation and
    patterns of coping with the social aftermath of death) (see also
    Sociology of death) 229, 1846, 2447, 2491, 2607, 2617, 2627,
    2637, 2689, 2755, 2771, 2762, 2809, 2836, 2842, 2866, 2868,
    2887, 2908, 2910, 2923, 2928, 2955, 2983, 3009, 3151, 3184,
    3228, 3297, 3303, 3327, 3330, 3384, 3397, 3507, 3588, 3654,
    3684 (T), 3799 (K)
Sociology of death (see also Society, social structure and death)
    80, 1804, 2491, 2628, 2704, 2734, 2736, 2744, 2747, 2748,
    2762, 2769, 2770, 2771, 2772, 2782, 2798, 3009, 3181, 3184,
    3481, 3572, 3576, 3577, 3578, 3610, 3684 (T)
Solipsism (see also Consciousness of impending death; Philosophy
    and death) 387
Sports and risk of death (see also Accidents; Threat of impending
    death) 269, 1070, 1230, 1509, 2556, 2960, 3049
Stages of dying (see also Acceptance of death; Terminal care)
    42, 127, 128, 130, 218, 321, 583, 795, 1410, 1463, 1525,
    1756, 1768, 1782, 1890, 1927, 1982, 2167, 2233, 2409, 2418,
    2448, 2616, 2678, 2680, 2799, 2981, 3053, 3055, 3056, 3057,
    3062, 3133, 3352, 3355, 3573, 3609, 3711 (T), 3751 (S), 3823
    (T), 3831 (F), 3835 (K), 3836 (F)
Stillbirths 1133, 1196
Sudden infant death syndrome (see also Children, death of and re-
    actions of the family; Children, death of anticipated by parents;
    Children, death of during psychotherapy; Children, reactions to-
    ward death; Crib death; Vulnerable child syndrome) 1130,
    1144, 1199, 1207, 1215, 1229, 1315, 1320, 1327, 1334, 1351,
    1389, 1394, 1415, 1418, 1428a, 1459, 1460, 1556, 1583, 1633,
    1662, 1671, 1674, 1708, 1809, 1848, 1874, 3011, 3694 (T),
    3845 (F, FS); and guilt 1581; and relationship to infanticides
    1116; and socioeconomic factors 1876; and spinal injury 1865;
    causes 105, 1125, 1556, 1758, 1785, 1793, 1941; geographic
    distribution of 1675, 1815; impact on family and physician
    1682, 1754, 1880, 3586; social and medico-legal aspects 3180
Sudden unexpected death in the general population 1497, 1547,
    1606, 1624, 1705, 1749, 1843, 1844, 1877, 2243, 2555, 2814,
    2920
Suicide, and absurdity 367, 370; and aggression 2787, 3412; and
    depression 2659, 2733, 2890, 2898, 2899, 3451, 3480, 3543;
    and deviance 3393; and grief 3131; and insanity 2897; and

mental illness 1225, 1429, 2392, 2640, 2663, 2880, 2897,
2898, 3134, 3138, 3480, 3602, 3605; and occupational mobility
studies 2467; and relationship to bereavement 2484, 2486;
and relationship to guilt and despair 475; and sanity 2897;
and the Soul 2901; attempts at (successful) 2662, 3259, 3260,
3507, 3508, 3543, 3614, 3680 (F); attempts at (unsuccessful)
1468, 2419, 2440, 2476, 2576, 2662; attitudes (contemporary)
toward 2364, 2516, 2684, 2879, 3087, 3462; causes of 612,
1104, 1258, 1280, 1371, 1390, 1540, 1612, 2383, 2518, 2546,
2615, 2629, 2651, 2728, 2802, 2803, 2827, 2831, 2845, 2860,
2880, 2890, 2940, 3105, 3278, 3680 (F); childhood and adolescent 1209, 2383, 2389, 2415, 2531, 2612, 2831, 2947, 3213,
3271/2, 3430, 3660, 3668 (T); clues to potential 1644, 1659,
2551, 2679, 3034, 3108, 3459, 3472, 3597; comparative cross-
cultural studies of 3118, 3301, 3338, 3390; counseling 3345;
debates on 945; deterrents from 3618; emerging mental
health services 1140; ethical concepts of 966; historical aspects of 414, 2331, 2349, 2910, 3629; in literature 782; in
opera 1024; in patients following attempts at 2934, 3138; in
patients with cardio respiratory illnesses 1301; in prisons
2651; in psychiatric patients 1225, 1235, 1429, 2343, 2392,
2640, 3141, 3602; in the American Negro and psychological
test results 2878, 3349, 3570; in twins and only children
2985; morality of 597, 675, 676, 2575; notes--emotional contents of 3567, 3643; nurses' role in attempts at 1907; parental
1202, 2898; phenomenological studies of 612; philosophical aspects of 914, 2603, 2665, 3210; predictions of 3108; prevention (see also Crisis intervention) 233, 397, 1104, 1180, 1279,
1461, 1575, 1576, 1659, 2419, 2624, 2625, 2626, 2660, 2661,
2940, 2983, 3034, 3088, 3107, 3181, 3237, 3243, 3265, 3390,
3460, 3463, 3666; psychology of 2596, 2615, 2629, 3375, 3464;
reactions upon parents, children, and adolescents 945, 1202,
1575, 2343, 2493, 3131; religious views of 2665; sociology of
2381, 2621, 2629, 2769, 2770, 2771, 2902, 3072, 3181, 3463; statistics 2363, 2393, 2429, 2620, 2657, 2768, 2786, 2869, 2881,
2882, 2883, 2890, 3107, 3200; students (college) 2471, 2545,
2546, 3114, 3387, 3452, 3472, 3528, 3529, 3533; threat of
2772; treatment in the attempts at 1802
Suspended animation see Cryogenics
Symbolism of death in literary and religious perspectives 92a,
185, 285, 418, 718, 838, 886, 898, 1066, 1067, 1531, 2043,
2186, 2246, 2362, 2384, 2567, 2693, 3125, 3127, 3194, 3201,
3212, 3304, 3576, 3600, 3682 (F), 3800 (K)
Sympathy, forms of see Consolation

Terminal care, and implications for the family (see also Family ...)
1181, 1182, 1186, 1189, 1319, 1498, 1620, 1811, 1838, 1908,
2730, 2977, 3085, 3446, 3524; and pastoral opportunities (see
also Clergy and dying patient relationships; Counseling the dying, pastoral) 1685, 2008, 2032, 2050, 2083, 2112, 2176a,
3503; and professional team approaches (see also Consciousness
of impending death; Crisis intervention; Dialogue about death;